MW01200707

THE
WONDER
BOY

THE WONDER BOY

LUKA DONČIĆ AND THE CURSE OF GREATNESS

TIM MACMAHON

GRAND
CENTRAL

New York   Boston

Grand Central Publishing
Hachette Book Group
1290 Avenue of the Americas, New York, NY 10104
grandcentralpublishing.com
@grandcentralpub

First edition: March 2025

Grand Central Publishing is a division of Hachette Book Group, Inc. The Grand Central Publishing name and logo is a registered trademark of Hachette Book Group, Inc.

The publisher is not responsible for websites (or their content) that are not owned by the publisher.

The Hachette Speakers Bureau provides a wide range of authors for speaking events. To find out more, go to hachettespeakersbureau.com or email HachetteSpeakers@hbgusa.com.

Grand Central Publishing books may be purchased in bulk for business, educational, or promotional use. For information, please contact your local bookseller or the Hachette Book Group Special Markets Department at special.markets@hbgusa.com.

Library of Congress Cataloging-in-Publication Data
Names: MacMahon, Tim, author.
Title: The wonder boy : Luka Dončić and the curse of greatness / Tim MacMahon.
Description: First edition. | New York : GCP, [2025] | Includes bibliographical
    references.
Identifiers: LCCN 2024044021 | ISBN 9781538740712 (hardcover) |
    ISBN 9781538740736 (ebook)
Subjects: LCSH: Dončić, Luka. | Basketball players—United
    States—Biography. | Dallas Mavericks (Basketball team)—History. | Basketball
    players—Slovenia—Biography. | Real Madrid de Baloncesto—History.
Classification: LCC GV884.D645 M33 2025 | DDC 796.223092 [B]—dc23/
    eng/20241018
LC record available at https://lccn.loc.gov/2024044021

ISBNs: 9781538740712 (hardcover), 9781538740736 (ebook)

Printed in the Canada

MRQ

10 9 8 7 6 5 4 3 2 1

To my wife, Maria; kids, Baylee, Finlee, Lukah, and Liam;
and Pops MacMahon
—TM

CONTENTS

CHAPTER 1

"LET'S MAKE SURE THIS ONE STAYS IN A MAVERICKS UNIFORM"

LUKA DONČIĆ DIDN'T KNOW MUCH ABOUT THIS STRANGE CITY that would be his new home other than it was hot, and he had heard there were a bunch of cowboys. He was half the globe away from Slovenia, the small European country he was from, and had just stepped foot in Texas for the first time a few hours ago. The teenager whose chinstrap beard couldn't quite connect with his thin mustache had yet to explore Dallas, much less get comfortable.

Dončić certainly wasn't in his comfort zone while sitting on a dais in front of a large room in a corner of the American Airlines Center, a space that usually serves as a Tex-Mex restaurant. It was the day after the 2018 NBA draft, when the Dallas Mavericks traded up a couple of spots to land Dončić with the third overall pick, and the team had flown him in along with second-round pick Jalen Brunson for a press conference. Of the four languages he spoke fluently,

Dončić was least comfortable with English, although he didn't enjoy speaking to the media much in any of them. He didn't have to do it often as a kid sensation with Real Madrid, the powerhouse club that Dončić had just led to EuroLeague and Spanish-league titles, and that was how he preferred it.

Donnie Nelson, on the other hand, definitely didn't mind having a microphone that afternoon. He was the Mavericks' president of basketball operations, a big personality who was born in Iowa and grew up in Massachusetts but had taken on a Texan persona (down to the Lucchese boots on his feet) in the two decades since he'd followed his father, Don, to Dallas. The Mavs hadn't had many drafts worth celebrating since the Nelsons landed a goofy German kid named Dirk Nowitzki in 1998, but Nelson was confident that Dallas had just found its next franchise player, and he was happy to take a victory lap.

After welcoming the Brunson and Dončić families to the "Friendship State," using an obscure nickname for Texas, Nelson made a point to thank several members of his scouting staff, particularly those stationed in Europe or who traveled extensively overseas. He left out Dallas's analytics department, whose ranking of Dončić as the best player in the class by a wide margin was key to convincing owner Mark Cuban to trade up for him—but Nelson had never been much of a numbers guy. Then Nelson made a show of praising the players' agents, who were seated in the front row, saying he wanted to "publicly extend the family relationship" and reminding everyone of how long they'd known each other.

Nelson started with Brunson's agent Leon Rose, who had built Creative Artists Agency's basketball division, which included several stars among its long list of NBA clients. As Nelson mentioned, when they first met 25 years before, Rose's only client was Brunson's father, Rick, a journeyman who played for eight teams during his nine-year career. Nelson gushed about Rose building his career "the good old-fashioned way, through toughness and perseverance," and jokingly thanked him for blocking teams from drafting Jalen Brunson, starting with the 20th overall pick until the Mavs went on the clock at No. 33. Nelson chuckled, reaching to his left and patting the leg of Brunson, who wore a black suit with a white shirt and black tie, looking like an MBA graduate reporting for his first day of work on Wall Street. Nelson's punch line generated a toothless grin from the undersized point guard who'd won two national titles and was the NCAA player of the year for Villanova.

Nelson then moved on to Dončić's lead agent, Bill Duffy, a familiar name to Mavericks fans primarily because he represented Steve Nash, who Nelson made sure to mention. "You had another international player, a young Canadian," Nelson said as Dončić unscrewed the lid on a water bottle and took a swig. Nelson reminisced about the night 20 years before, when the Mavs not only got Nowitzki in the draft but also scored Nash in a trade with the Phoenix Suns, a brilliant move Nelson had lobbied his coach/general manager/dad to make.

This was pretty awkward. Nash will always be remembered in Dallas as the legend who the Mavs let leave. When Nash returned to Phoenix in free agency in 2004, the Mavs' decision not to match the Suns' offer for the 30-year-old star (who happened to be Nowitzki's best friend) was so controversial that Cuban published a 4,411-word post on his site, BlogMaverick.com. He felt the need to explain "all the logical, illogical, emotional and financial scenarios" in a process that led to such a painful result for the franchise and its fans. Cuban's strained relationship with Duffy fell in the emotional category: "I'm not a big fan of his and he knows it," Cuban wrote then.

Nash, of course, made the Mavs look like fools, winning MVP the next two seasons and instantly turning the Suns into a contender while running an offense that revolutionized the league. Bickering between Don Nelson and Cuban about who was to blame for losing Nash was a factor in the bitter divorce between owner and coach/GM, who stepped down the next season and ended up suing to collect deferred salary. Somehow, Donnie Nelson not only survived the split but was also promoted to become the Mavs' top basketball executive. Cuban, years after the fact, admitted that letting Nash go was the biggest basketball mistake he ever made.

But that bizarre bit of Mavericks history didn't matter to Dončić, who was a toddler at the time. Duffy has the sort of thick skin required to thrive in such a cutthroat business, so as far as he was concerned, bygones from a generation ago were bygones. However, just in case anyone somehow forgot about the Mavs botching Nash's free agency during his prime, Nelson used it as fodder for another joke.

"Welcome back, and, um, let's just make sure this one stays in a Mavericks uniform," Nelson said, reaching over Brunson to squeeze Dončić's right leg. "What do you say, Bill?"

Some courtesy laughter broke out. Dončić, wearing a blue polo shirt buttoned to the top underneath an unzipped khaki jacket, cracked a smile. Mavs coach Rick Carlisle, sitting to Dončić's left and not exactly known for his sense of humor, remained stone-faced.

Nelson had spoken an uncomfortable lump of truth in jest. There is pressure that comes along with drafting an NBA prodigy, a billing the Mavs believed Dončić fit even though three teams had passed on the chance to select him. With superstars, it boils down to this: keep them happy—which typically requires building a contender around them, at the minimum—or they might eventually leave. The clock starts ticking as soon as a prized lottery pick is selected.

FRANCHISES GO TO GREAT LENGTHS TO POSITION THEMSELVES TO poach superstars from other teams. Case in point: The Mavs traded for the 60th and final pick in this 2018 draft to select Kostas Antetokounmpo—"A nice developmental player for us in the G League," Nelson said with a straight face. He was a skinny, 6-foot-10 forward who had averaged 5.2 points and 2.9 rebounds per game during his lone season at Dayton, a mid-major program that finished a few games under .500 that year, and just so happened to be the younger brother of Giannis Antetokounmpo.

Giannis had developed into a dominant force in the five years since the 2013 draft, when Nelson unsuccessfully lobbied Cuban to select the mysterious teenage prospect out of Greece's second division league. He had just finished the first season of a four-year, $100 million extension of his rookie contract, but his potential to become an unrestricted free agent in the summer of 2021 had already become a focal point for front offices around the league. For the Mavericks, the opportunity to establish ties with the Antetokounmpo family justified taking a second-round flyer on a marginal prospect. He spent a season on a two-way deal with the Mavs, and when he was released, the Los Angeles Lakers pounced on the opportunity to claim Giannis's little brother off waivers. (All of the posturing proved irrelevant when Giannis signed a maximum extension in 2020, a year before he would have become an unrestricted free agent—a deal he agreed to immediately after Milwaukee made a trade for Jrue Holiday that eliminated Antetokounmpo's doubts that the Bucks could win a title.)

That provides a glimpse of the sort of posturing that happens in the NBA to give even the slightest percentage boost to the odds of landing a franchise-changing player. The roots of this phenomenon date back more than five decades to when Oscar Robertson, a Hall of Fame guard who was president of the NBA Players Association, filed a class-action antitrust lawsuit against the league in April 1970, fighting for free agency. At the time, the NBA had a "reserve" clause, bounding a player to one team for the duration of his career at the team's option.

Robertson v. National Basketball Association dragged on in the court system for six years before being settled in 1976, two years after Robertson had retired, granting players free agency after their contracts expired, although teams were allowed the right to match offers to keep players. The looming threat of that lawsuit being settled had emboldened Kareem Abdul-Jabbar to push for a trade to one of his preferred destinations: New York, Washington, or Los Angeles. He was following in the footsteps of another legendary big man, Wilt Chamberlain, who managed to force a 1968 trade from Philadelphia to Los Angeles after a contract dispute with 76ers ownership. Bucks management was first informed of Abdul-Jabbar's intentions during an October 1974 meeting with the star center and his advisor, Sam Cooke, at a Sheraton hotel in Milwaukee. The Bucks had won the 1971 title in Abdul-Jabbar's second season, when Robertson arrived in Milwaukee via trade after years of haggling over his salary with Cincinnati Royals ownership, but he wasn't happy in Milwaukee. Cooke, a prominent UCLA basketball booster, did most of the talking on behalf of Abdul-Jabbar, who was entering the final season of his contract.

"Milwaukee just wasn't where a big-city boy could be comfortable, he said," former Bucks team president William Alverson recalled years later. "In essence, it was a foreign culture to Kareem. He wanted out, he *would* be out, one way or another. The implication was that if he had to sit out a year, he would. We believed him."

As discreetly as possible, the Bucks spent the next season exploring their options in the trade market for Abdul-Jabbar. His trade request became public in March 1975, when Marv Albert reported it on a broadcast out of New York, focusing on the potential of the Harlem native going to the Knicks. A few months later, the Bucks finalized a deal to send Abdul-Jabbar to the Lakers. The package that Milwaukee received in return: Dave Meyers and Junior Bridgeman, the recent first-round picks the Lakers had selected at the Bucks' urging; young starters Brian Winters and Elmore Smith; and $800,000, which was more than twice Abdul-Jabbar's salary the previous season. It proved to be a bargain for the Lakers, who won five titles during the 14-year tenure of Abdul-Jabbar, who finished his career as the league's all-time leading scorer.

"Milwaukee had been great, and I'd hoped I had paid back the fans for their support with a championship and a lot of exciting games," Abdul-Jabbar wrote 46 years after the trade in the wake of the Bucks finally winning another NBA title, thanks in large part to Antetokounmpo. "But I wanted to live in a larger city that was more culturally and ethnically diverse. And I wanted to expand my own game, see what I was capable of with other players. I was well aware how short the lifespan is of an NBA player and wanted to be as active as possible in forging my own career."

For a generation, Abdul-Jabbar stood as an exception: a superstar who changed teams on his own terms while in his prime. It was a rarity for years, even after the beginning of unrestricted free agency with the collective bargaining agreement signed in 1988. That was surely the preference of longtime NBA commissioner David Stern, who was the league's lead attorney on the lawsuit brought by Robertson.

The league has been different since "The Decision," the infamous ESPN event in July 2010 during which LeBron James announced his free agency choice to a national television audience of more than 13 million people, plus a live audience of children who packed the Boys & Girls Club in Greenwich, Connecticut. It was eight days into his free agency, following highly publicized meetings with six teams. After 19 mostly innocuous questions from his hand-picked interviewer, Jim Gray, on the TV special that drew intense criticism—"ill-conceived, badly produced and poorly executed," Stern called it days later—James finally uttered the one sentence that changed the fabric of the NBA forever.

"In this fall, I'm going to take my talents to South Beach and join the Miami Heat," James said.

Cleveland was crushed. The Cavaliers landing the No. 1 overall pick to draft James—the kid from nearby Akron who had been labeled "The Chosen One" on a *Sports Illustrated* cover as a high school junior and still more than lived up to the hype—was storybook stuff. With the 18-year-old rookie's arrival, a moribund franchise had immediately become relevant.

For the next seven years, the Cavaliers catered to James—and for good reason, as he earned Rookie of the Year, six All-NBA selections, and a pair of MVP awards in that span. Owner Dan Gilbert built a $25 million practice facility between Cleveland and Akron so it'd be easier for James to commute from his hometown, where he owned a palatial estate. Gilbert gave James significant input on staffing decisions, including hiring one of the star's friends at a salary that was more than some assistant coaches made. The Cavaliers dipped into the luxury tax deeper and deeper every time they made a trade for a veteran—Ben Wallace and Mo Williams and Shaquille O'Neal and Antawn Jamison—that James believed could help him deliver a title to Cleveland. The Cavaliers had become perennial contenders—making a run to the 2007 NBA Finals, where they were swept by the San Antonio Spurs, and finishing the regular season with the league's best record in 2008–09 and 2009–10—but hadn't been able to get over the hump.

So it stung when James determined it all wasn't enough to earn his unconditional loyalty, just as he was approaching his prime. As some fans burned his No. 23 jersey, Gilbert addressed them by penning a scathing public letter, written in Comic Sans font, that read like a message board rant. He referred to James as "our former hero" but never by name and told fans that they "simply don't deserve this kind of cowardly betrayal." Gilbert concluded the letter with a ridiculous, all-caps statement: "I PERSONALLY GUARANTEE THAT THE CLEVELAND CAVALIERS WILL WIN AN NBA CHAMPION-SHIP BEFORE THE SELF-TITLED FORMER 'KING' WINS ONE." The Heat, of course, soared to the top of Las Vegas's NBA championship odds the second that James said the words "South Beach." His declaration came days after All-Star power forward Chris Bosh, who spent the first seven seasons of his career with the Toronto Raptors, had committed to sign with the Heat in free agency. They were joining Dwyane Wade, the 2006 NBA Finals MVP, in Miami. So began the NBA's so-called superteam era.

"I feel like it's going to give me the best opportunity to win and to win for multiple years, and not only just to win in the regular season or just to win five games in a row or three games in a row. I want to be able to win championships," James said moments after announcing his decision. "And I feel like I can compete down there."

There were cries of collusion around the NBA after three stars from the loaded 2003 draft class—all of whom had been cornerstones of their own franchises—plotted over years to form an instant championship favorite. The three stars had discussed the possibility on plenty of flights and bus rides and in hotels around the world while playing together on Team USA. The Heat, acting on intel from Wade, carefully planned to create enough salary-cap flexibility to add a pair of stars in free agency. The three stars met before free agency began and kept in touch throughout the process, even as James took meetings with the Nets, Knicks, Clippers, and Bulls, as well as the Cavaliers (but not the Mavericks, despite Cuban's best efforts). The balance of power had shifted in the NBA because of some recruiting and scheming, similar to what routinely occurs on the grassroots AAU circuit.

It was difficult enough, if not impossible, for the league office to deal with the tampering. A franchise that actually waited for the official opening of free agency, which at the time occurred at midnight ET on July 1, would be left watching helplessly as deals got finalized in the first few minutes. Mutual interest between free agents and teams is frequently reported days—or weeks, even months—in advance. It isn't reasonable to expect the NBA to police conversations between players, many of whom have relationships that date back to their adolescence or even earlier.

"The three players are totally within their rights to talk to each other," said Stern—who fined Gilbert $100,000 for the letter and further inflammatory comments made in a follow-up interview—after the league's annual Board of Governors meeting the next week. "That is not tampering."

Welcome to the NBA's player-empowerment era. To a lot of the league's owners and executives, this was akin to cracking open Pandora's box. The player-driven formations of several star clusters and how those teams have fared—some raised banners, others went bust—have been the dramatic focal points in the league for a decade and a half.

LeBron provided the road map and used it to move on multiple occasions, adding to his legacy at each stop. The Heat fell a bit short of James's "not two, not three, not four, not five, not six, not seven" predicted championship count—and the parade plans were put on hold for a year by Dallas's title run, with Dirk Nowitzki as the Mavericks' lone star. But Miami won a pair of championships in James's four-season run before he went back to Cleveland, where he delivered the city's first professional sports title in half a century. He won another ring with the Lakers after moving to Los Angeles, where James could maximize his business interests in the entertainment world.

The Cavaliers had bottomed out during James's absence, winning a total of only 97 games over the four seasons. That ultimately helped Cleveland become an intriguing option again for James, as the Cavaliers were positioned for an unprecedented run of lottery luck, drafting No. 1 overall in three of four years. Anthony Bennett was a bust, but Kyrie Irving was a two-time All-Star already at age 22, and with some significant influence from James, Cleveland flipped freshly drafted rookie Andrew Wiggins to Minnesota for perennial All-Star power forward Kevin Love. It wasn't as splashy as the star trio James joined in South Beach, but the Cavaliers had constructed an instant contender.

The Cavaliers' breakthrough—after losing the Finals twice to the Golden State Warriors, a title team built primarily through the draft—probably played a major role in the formation of the NBA's next superteam. If Cleveland hadn't come back from a 3–1 deficit to defeat the Warriors in the 2016 Finals, would Kevin Durant have gone to Golden State to join Stephen Curry, Klay Thompson, and Draymond Green? Not that Durant's decision to leave Oklahoma City, which blew its own 3–1 lead in the conference finals to the Warriors, to join a team that had just set the NBA's record for regular-season wins was generally viewed favorably. But he left OKC after nine years to boost Golden State back to the top of the league, not to hop on a three-peat bandwagon.

Durant's move was made possible by a historic spike in the salary cap that summer, due to a massive influx of money from the league's new television deal. The possibility hung over the Thunder's heads for the entire 2015–16 season, intensifying the spotlight on the dynamic between Durant and his fellow homegrown co-star Russell Westbrook, every interaction analyzed for evidence of Durant's frustration. (The Warriors endured a similar experience a few seasons later, before Durant, not content with two championships and three Finals appearances, bolted to the Brooklyn Nets in free agency to form a star partnership with his friend Irving.) The Durant-Westbrook duo seemed destined to be the cornerstone of a dynasty when they led the Thunder to the 2012 Finals as 23-year-olds, but Oklahoma City never got back to that stage. Green, in particular, pounced on that doubt by intensely recruiting Durant. The rest of Golden State's core joined during the free agency window, as Curry, Thompson, Green, and Andre Iguodala traveled to the Hamptons with the Warriors' contingent to meet with Durant.

"It really pains me to know that I will disappoint so many people with this choice, but I believe I am doing what I feel is the right thing at this point in my life and my playing career," Durant wrote in a *Players' Tribune* post announcing his decision to go to Golden State on July 4. Soon thereafter, Westbrook posted pictures of cupcakes from his Fourth of July cookout, knowing Durant would recognize the sweet treats as the Thunder's oft-used euphemism for being soft.

This was a crisis for the NBA. A team that had won two of the three most recent titles—and a record 73 games in the season it fell short—had just added an MVP in his prime. A small-market franchise that had drafted and developed a superstar suddenly had nothing to show for him, losing Durant as soon as he became an unrestricted free agent at the expiration of his second contract. The league attempted to address the issue by adding the "super-max" clause to the collective bargaining agreement—essentially, stars who qualify can be paid significantly more if they stick with their original teams—but that didn't slow the trend. Kawhi Leonard, Anthony Davis, James Harden, Paul George, Damian Lillard, Irving, and Westbrook are among the stars who have changed teams in recent years, most of them multiple times, and several getting their way at the end of contentious situations.

For better or worse, the transaction game (real and potential) has driven interest and media coverage in the league at least as much as the actual games. Clicks and views soar most during the days leading up to the trade deadline and to open free agency, even more than the playoffs. Commissioner Adam Silver has delicately embraced the player-empowerment trend, saying that while the league wants players to honor their contracts, "a certain amount of player movement is good." Silver can either take that stance or be at odds with the league's most marketable attractions.

"I don't think it's bad for the league," Durant said during the 2023 All-Star Weekend, days after he got his wish granted by being traded from Brooklyn to Phoenix. "It's bringing more eyes to the league, more people are more excited. The tweets that I get; the news hits that we got from me being traded, Kyrie being traded; it just brings more attention to the league—and that's really what rakes the money in, when you get more attention. So, I think it's great for the league, to be honest."

That's the reality of the modern NBA, which revolves around its superstars and caters to them more than any other professional sports league. The Mavericks enjoyed immunity from that with Nowitzki, who was fiercely loyal throughout his career while setting a record for the longest tenure with one team, but that's once-in-a-lifetime kind of luck. They certainly weren't naive enough to believe they'd be similarly blessed with such blind trust from his successor.

Dallas was fortunate enough to find a worthy successor as Nowitzki's career was winding down. Dončić hasn't only proven the Mavericks right and the skeptics wrong; he far exceeded even the loftiest expectations, establishing himself as a perennial first-team All-NBA pick before signing his second contract. He's one of the league's most entertaining stars, a trash-talking magician with the ball who makes historic statistics seem routine. That puts him on the short list of players other franchises plot to acquire years before he might become available, hoping to land on his preferred list if Dončić eventually requests a trade, and accumulating assets necessary to make such a deal if the Mavs don't have much of a choice.

Preying on another franchise's downfall, Dallas's in this instance, is practical NBA strategy. There's no greater gift in the game than getting one of the precious few players great enough to be the centerpiece of a championship team. However, the work is only beginning for those fortunate franchises. The hard part is keeping those superstars happy. The curse that comes with the gift is the fallout if it fails.

CHAPTER 2

EL NIÑO MARAVILLA

"THIS IS SO BORING!" LUKA DONČIĆ MOANED.

The Lido di Roma Tournament featured a day off for each of the age-13-and-under teams competing at the event, an opportunity for some education and to experience Italian culture. The Union Olimpija team packed into a van to make the short trip to Ostia Antica, a massive archaeological site and popular tourist destination at the location of ancient Rome's harbor city, where remains have been discovered that date back to the fourth century BC.

"Bad idea," remembered Matteo Picardi, the tournament director and organizer of the field trip. Every five minutes or so, the tall kid with dirty blond hair who was clearly the leader of the Ljubljana, Slovenia, squad approached Picardi to complain.

"Let's go to a basketball court!" Dončić pleaded.

A basketball court, without question, was where Dončić felt most comfortable. A lot of players call the court their sanctuary. For Dončić, a phenom with a flair for entertaining, it was a stage.

Dončić grew up in Slovenia—a small country in the basketball-mad Balkans that gained its independence from the former Yugoslavia in 1991—as Saša Dončić's son. His dad was a six-time All-Star in the Adriatic League with a guard's game, a big frame, and a giant personality, a man with whom everyone in the country wanted to sip some wine or chug a beer, and a great many succeeded. Saša's playing career spanned almost two decades, and for the last several years, little Luka was essentially part of his teams. He hung out in the locker room before and after games and usually sat under the basket during the action, sweeping the gym floor when called upon. The boy always had a ball within reach, jacking up jump shots or putting on impromptu dribbling exhibitions in time-outs and at halftimes.

When Saša jumped from the Slovenia club Domžale to Union Olimpija, his 8-year-old son went with him, joining the longtime powerhouse's youth program. He practiced with his age group for a grand total of 16 minutes before the coaches realized that Dončić belonged with much better competition, putting him with the 1996-born group, kids three years older than he was. After one practice with the older group, Dončić was promoted to the Olimpija selection team—a feeder system for the pro club—where he routinely dominated his age group and more than held his own when playing in age groups three or four years older.

The game isn't just easy for Dončić; it's natural. "I don't even think he sees. I think he feels," said Lojze Šiško, who was the director of Union Olimpija's youth program. "You can learn to see, but you can't learn to feel what is on the court. There's a big difference."

As much as is possible for a 13-year-old son of a pro, Dončić had carved out his own name in Slovenian basketball circles and beyond before the Italian trip. Months earlier, he'd even received an invitation from Real Madrid, one of Europe's most prestigious clubs and arguably the world's best basketball team outside of the NBA, to play for its squad in the Minicopa Endesa, the junior version of a high-profile Spanish tournament. Dončić starred, scoring 20 points in a championship game loss to Barcelona, capping the performance by banking in a half-court shot at the buzzer—a meaningless bucket but quite memorable, nonetheless.

Nobody who witnessed Dončić's performance on the afternoon of April 9, 2012, will ever forget it. The boy played with a flair in that small Roman gym—where wooden beams crisscross the ceiling and much of the light comes from windows in the dull, sea-green walls behind the baskets—that foreshadowed his future performances in front of packed crowds filling the world's most famous arenas.

Dončić, wearing his father's No. 4, put the finishing touches on Union Olimpija's run to the Lido di Roma Tournament title with a 54-point triple-double in the championship game rout against the Italian club SS Lazio. Dončić scored at will, putting up 39 points by halftime, shooting three-pointers with effortless form, and displaying a polished, innovative off-dribble game—attacking at ease with either hand, freezing defenders by changing directions and speeds, creating space in crowds with pivots and power, finishing with an array of floaters and scoop shots.

With the score lopsided in the second half, Dončić sought the spectacular, passing the ball like a young artist playing with his paints and enjoying the experimental process. No-look feeds, behind-the-back passes, driving full speed, and blindly flipping the ball behind his head to an open teammate. He nutmegged a kid while bringing the ball up the floor, crossing over by dribbling between the helpless Italian boy's legs.

"In this moment I told someone that he reminded me of a young Dražen Petrović," longtime Olimpija basketball chief Srečko Bester said, invoking the name of arguably the greatest guard ever to come out of Europe. "He was a killer with a baby face. It was so easy for him."

Was all that showmanship necessary? Maybe not, but it sure was fun. Dončić has always had an intense competitive drive and a tendency to get bored when he isn't challenged. It's why his coaches, from age 8 up to the NBA, orchestrate practice drills to have winners and losers as often as possible. During games, Dončić sometimes challenges himself to see what magic tricks he can pull off, stretching his imagination while testing the limits of his skill set. Overmatched opponents become extras in his theater acts.

There were only an estimated 600 spectators in the crowd that afternoon, but word of Dončić's sensational performance spread quickly. He wasn't just one of the best basketball prospects ever seen in Slovenia, a nation of just more than 2 million people that had produced a handful of NBA players. He was an elite talent by European standards, which is why Real Madrid soon offered Dončić a five-year contract to leave home for Spain and train in its renowned youth academy, which would put him on track to eventually play for a perennial EuroLeague contender. Dončić had also already landed on the radar of at least one NBA franchise's scouting department.

Roberto Carmenati, a scout stationed in his native Italy, called one of his bosses soon after the Lido di Roma Tournament. "Tony, there's an amazing kid that you must go see!" former Mavs director of player personnel Tony Ronzone recalls Carmenati saying.

"At that age, you hear that all the time," Ronzone said. "You're like, right, okay. But he's just a special kid."

Whether to accept Real Madrid's offer was an emotional decision for Dončić. At 13, was he ready to leave the comforts of home in Slovenia for the unfamiliar land and language of Spain? His mom, Mirjam Poterbin, suggested that he could wait a little bit to make such a life-changing commitment. Dončić replied that he wanted to go, deciding that he was willing to sacrifice his adolescence in pursuit of his potential as an international basketball star, prompting mixed reactions in his hometown.

"Maybe some other staff at Olimpija, the GM, maybe they were angry because he was leaving," said Šiško, the director of Union Olimpija's youth program. "But the coaches working with him in the last three years with Olimpija, we knew that it was a great opportunity, and he must leave Ljubljana to become such a big player."

It was agonizing for Poterbin, a former model and beauty salon owner who had divorced Luka's father in 2008, raising their son in a Ljubljana apartment that overlooked the outdoor basketball courts where he spent much of his free time. After leaving Luka at Ciudad Real Madrid, the club's expansive campus about fourteen miles north of the city, Poterbin bawled on the flight back to Slovenia. The cultural transition was tough on Dončić, too, who lived in a small dorm room with roommates from Spain and Bosnia, attending school around a demanding basketball schedule. He had to rely on hand gestures to communicate with his first Real Madrid coaches as he learned to speak Spanish.

The basketball transition, however, wasn't hard at all. As he had done in Slovenia, Dončić dominated while playing against older boys, drawing comparisons to Ricky Rubio and Nikola Mirotić, prospects recruited by Spanish clubs in their early teens who blossomed into EuroLeague stars before becoming first-round NBA draft picks. Months after Dončić had moved to Madrid, the Spanish newspaper *ABC* proclaimed that he had emerged as the best basketball prospect in all of Europe.

Another clear sign that Dončić was destined for the NBA: he signed with BDA Sports, the agency run by Bill Duffy, one of the league's most powerful agents. Duffy's client list is headlined by Hall of Famers Yao Ming and Steve Nash and includes a pair of prominent Slovenians: Rasho Nesterović, Dončić's godfather, who played 12 years in the NBA; and Goran Dragić, Saša's former teammate who was starring for the Phoenix Suns at the time.

"When we recruited him when he was 13 years old, we already knew we had something special in our hands, which was going to be very different from other players we'd had before in Spain," said Quique Villalobos, a former Real Madrid player who was BDA's representative in Spain. "We weren't 100 percent sure, but we had the feeling we had some kind of gold in our hands."

Dončić collected MVP awards while leading Real Madrid's teams to championships at top junior tournaments throughout Europe's elite club circuit. Real Madrid's established pros followed Dončić's exploits in the same manner in which Americans keep up with a generational college prospect projected for NBA stardom, such as Zion Williamson during his lone season at Duke. "When he played guys his age, he was killing them! We always checked his numbers," said Salah Mejri, a center on that Real Madrid squad. Dončić started practicing with Real Madrid's top team at age 15 and even appeared in a preseason game.

By then, the Spanish sports newspaper *Marca* had dubbed him "El Niño Maravilla." Translation: The Wonder Boy.

Dončić rarely returned home during those years, as Real Madrid required an around-the-calendar commitment. He only made one appearance in the junior levels of the Slovenian national team's system, playing for the under-16 team in a December 2014 friendly tournament in Székesfehérvár, Hungary. A series of events in the opening minutes of that tournament—a relatively low-intensity atmosphere, with nothing at stake—provided a glimpse of Dončić's blend of remarkable talent and ruthless competitiveness.

Romania's starting lineup included a guard who was a Patrick Beverley type—undersized, overaggressive, not extraordinarily talented, but a contributor because he took great pride in being a pesky pain in the ass. Soon after the opening tip, the kid caught Dončić with an elbow above the eye, causing blood to spill.

Dončić had to sub out, and after getting some treatment from the team's athletic trainer, he seethed on the bench while pressing a towel to his face to stop the bleeding. About four minutes later, Dončić threw down the towel and barked that he was ready to check back in to the game. He demanded that the coach put him back in at the next dead ball—not that there would have been any debate.

"Luka was like, 'I want to play! I want to play!'" Andraž Marolt, a reserve guard on that Slovenian squad, excitedly recalled. "The rest was history."

On the next possession, Dončić strategically called for a pick and roll. The kid who opened the cut above Dončić's eye wasn't his primary defender, but Dončić wanted instant revenge, so he ordered his teammate who was being guarded by the Romanian Pat Bev to set the screen.

Dončić attacked off the dribble and got exactly what he wanted: his assailant switching onto him, and a split second too late. Dončić drove into the paint and took off toward the rim, throwing down a tomahawk dunk despite midair contact from his target. As Dončić rattled the rim—a notable event in and of itself for a 15-year-old who wasn't exactly known as a high flyer—the Romanian guard crashed to the court with a thud.

But Dončić wasn't done humiliating this opponent. Upon landing, Dončić grabbed the ball and delivered a hard, two-handed pass into the chest of his foe, who lay flat on his back. Dončić then shouted a vile insult at the kid, disparaging his masculinity. Dončić earned a technical foul and made his point.

Dončić proceeded to destroy the Romanian squad, finishing with 34 points and nine rebounds in only 15 minutes to lead Slovenia to a rout. He dominated the rest of the tournament, too, averaging 35.3 points in wins over Romania, Czech Republic, and Poland. His 45 points in the final carried his team to a blowout win over a Polish squad that had recently defeated the Slovenians by 25—when Dončić didn't play.

"He was like a myth," Marolt said.

The legend of Luka, sometimes referred to as the Slovenian pearl by Spanish media, kept building over the ensuing months as he continued lighting up the highest levels of European junior basketball. He looked like a man playing against boys despite usually being the youngest on the floor by a few years. And he looked in place while practicing with a Real Madrid senior team that featured a handful of former NBA players and was led by Spanish legend Sergio Llull.

By the time Dončić celebrated his 16th birthday on February 28, anticipation had built for his official debut with Los Blancos, as he'd often sat on the bench in uniform awaiting the opportunity. It finally came on April 30, 2015, in garbage time after Real Madrid had sealed its 15th win in 16 games. Head coach Pablo Laso, a fiery former Real Madrid point guard, had been ejected earlier in the game. Assistant Jesús "Chus" Mateo summoned Dončić late in the game, stopping him in front of the bench for a discussion as the kid nodded. At the next dead ball, with 1:28 remaining and Real Madrid up by 18, Dončić checked in, eliciting a standing ovation from a sizable chunk of the crowd at the 15,000-seat Palacio de Deportes.

If Dončić felt nervous, it didn't show. Seventeen seconds later, the first time he'd touched the ball in a pro game, Dončić swished a catch-and-shoot three-pointer from the right wing. A big smile broke out on his face as he jogged back on defense, high-fived a teammate, and listened as the fans erupted in applause.

"Todo el porvenir en sus manos," a game story in the Spanish newspaper *El Mundo* concluded. Translation: all the future is in your hands.

That three ended up being Dončić's lone bucket for Los Blancos that season, as he logged only eight minutes over three games. Real Madrid won the Liga ACB and EuroLeague titles, so finding minutes for a 16-year-old phenom wasn't exactly a top priority. But it felt like a matter of when, not if, Dončić would emerge as a superstar in Europe, and eventually the NBA.

BY THAT POINT, DONČIĆ WAS DONE DOMINATING THE JUNIOR levels, having earned a roster spot on Real Madrid's top team. But he played sparingly in that 2015–16 season, when savvy NBA scouts would attend games against lower-level competition on Los Blancos' schedule, knowing Dončić would likely get more minutes in those contests. The defending champions' depth chart, particularly in the backcourt, featured veterans with impressive pedigrees: Sergio Rodríguez and Rudy Fernández, first-round picks who returned to Real Madrid after serving as NBA rotation players; and Llull, the longtime star for Los Blancos who had rebuffed lucrative offers from the Houston Rockets to remain in Spain.

"I have to make the most of every opportunity. Laso tells me to play as I know how to," Dončić said in Spanish during one of the few times Real Madrid made him available to reporters that season. His role was a frequent topic of discussion for the local media, which often mentioned that Dončić's father had a long pro-basketball career, and his mother was a world champion dancer, as if to explain how the teen had such a natural feel for the game and beautiful footwork. The press wanted to see more of the prodigy—and there was no doubt among Real Madrid's players that Dončić was ready.

"He was dominating practice," recalled Willy Hernangómez, a center on that Real Madrid team who started his NBA career the next season. "He was just pure talent. We were around talented players as well, but even there, he was unique. He was just having fun playing basketball."

Fernández underwent back surgery in December, sidelining the veteran for a few months and opening up some minutes for the 16-year-old sensation. Dončić was never intimidated, no matter the level of competition or his coach's intensity. Case in point: During a December game against CSKA Moscow, which won that season's EuroLeague title, Laso called a time-out with a few minutes left in the second quarter specifically to cuss out his team. He stared directly at Dončić while spewing Spanish expletives and demanding that Real Madrid run a play, any play. Dončić didn't blink, nodding calmly as Laso cursed up a storm, veins popping out of the coach's temples. Dončić responded by swishing a three on the next possession, then draining two more over the next couple of minutes. This kid's confidence couldn't be rattled.

Dončić made his first trip to America that summer. Upon his

agent Duffy's recommendation, Dončić spent a few weeks training at the Santa Barbara, California, facility of Peak Performance Project, aka P3. It was a chance for Dončić to work with P3's renowned sports science and training staff, and to play pickup games against NBA players who also trained at the facility. Once again, with barely a whisker on his face, Dončić more than held his own. Other players were stunned that the broad-shouldered dude—who controlled the pace of the pickup games with ingenuity and poise—was only 17.

"Yo, I just met this kid," guard Josh Richardson, who was preparing for his second season with the Miami Heat, recalled telling his friends. "He's going to be the first pick in the draft."

Back in Europe the following season, now wearing No. 7 as a tribute to EuroLeague legend Vassilis Spanoulis, Dončić was a regular in the rotation when Rodríguez returned to the NBA. Rotations in Europe tend to run much deeper than the NBA, and the games are eight minutes shorter, played at a significantly slower pace, with less space to operate in the half-court due to different defensive rules and court measurements, so statistics typically don't quite translate. But it was incredibly impressive for a 17-year-old to average 7.8 points, 4.4 rebounds, and 3.7 assists in 20 minutes per game against Liga ACB and EuroLeague competition. This was a high school kid helping his team win in the world's second-best league.

"It's a special case, but I've always tried not to let this be Dončić's team," Laso said that season in an interview with the Spanish publication *Cinco Días*. "This is Real Madrid. If I treated Dončić in a special way, he would make the rest of the players ugly. He has earned what he is doing. I always tell him that he is going to have to prove more because I am not going to give him anything."

Dončić seized the opportunities he was given, and there were occasions when he dominated. He became the youngest player in Liga ACB history to post a double-double—and youngest to dish out double-digit assists—when he had 23 points and 11 assists in an early December win over Fuenlabrada. Days later, with Llull resting due to right-knee soreness, Dončić put on a clutch shotmaking show in a 96–91 win over Lithuanian power Žalgiris Kaunas.

With the score tied and 1:40 remaining, Dončić caught the ball with the shot clock ticking down and his left foot touching the crown on Real Madrid's half-court logo. He dribbled to his right, between his legs to the left, and once more to the left before launching from a few feet behind the three-point arc with a smaller guard's hands in his face. Swish.

On the next possession, with Los Blancos up three, Dončić was near the half-court logo again and went to work. He dribbled between his legs and crossed back over once, twice, as he worked his way near the top of the arc. He accelerated right, snatched the ball back between his legs, and launched another contested step-back three from close to the same spot. Dagger.

"I've never seen him nervous," Laso said in Spanish during a postgame interview.

Dončić still wasn't old enough to get his driver's license in Spain—his 18th birthday came at the end of that February—but he was already generating hype as potentially the best prospect ever produced in Europe and likely a high NBA lottery pick. His brilliance at such a young age in the Liga ACB continued to draw comparisons to Rubio and Mirotić, but Dončić was on another level, perhaps even better than the Balkan-raised legends before him, Dražen Petrović and Toni Kukoč.

Petrović and Kukoč were foundational pieces of the great Yugoslavian program that threatened USA's reign in men's basketball. Petrović starred as a teen, when Yugoslavia earned a bronze medal in the 1984 Olympics, and again for the silver-medal squad in 1988, when the Soviet Union defeated the USA in the semifinal round. Yugoslavia won the FIBA World Cup in 1990, when 21-year-old Kukoč earned the MVP, defeating a USA team full of college stars.

That was one of the final straws that forced Team USA to reconsider its policy against using NBA players, resulting in the formation of the famous "Dream Team" for the 1992 Olympics. By that point, however, Yugoslavia was no more, a civil war having split the nation into six federations. Vlade Divac, the 7-footer who was the Los Angeles Lakers' starting center, played for his native Serbia. Petrović, Kukoč, and bruising power forward Dino Radja played for Croatia, losing to Team USA in the gold-medal game.

Petrović is discussed in especially reverential tones across Europe, particularly in Balkan territory. He was the first European to establish himself as a bona fide NBA star, biding his time while buried on the Portland Trail Blazers' loaded depth chart for a season and a half before being unleashed after a trade to the New Jersey Nets. He averaged 21.4 points per game during his two full seasons with the Nets, earning third-team All-NBA honors in 1992–93, before tragedy struck that summer. Petrović died in an automobile accident on the German Autobahn, a legend passing away just as he was entering his prime.

Dončić wasn't the pure shooter that Petrović was—not many were, no matter where they were from—but his showmanship and fearlessness were certainly reminiscent of the Croatian frequently referred to as "Mozart." People saw shades of "Petro" when Dončić wrapped the ball behind his back and between the legs on a drive through traffic for a layup, fired a no-look laser to a teammate who didn't even know he was open, or swished a clutch jumper. You couldn't pay a bigger compliment to a Balkan kid.

There were also elements of Dončić's game that reminded the European basketball community of Kukoč, whose long NBA career was highlighted by winning three championship rings and a Sixth Man of the Year award with the Chicago Bulls. Dončić wasn't as tall, but like the 6-foot-11 Kukoč, he possessed a point guard's game in a power forward's frame. They dominated with feel for the game as much as skill, like saxophone players who didn't need to read sheet music.

Dončić would be considered a disappointment if he didn't surpass the feats of those legends, but he didn't consider the weight of those expectations to be a burden. It's why he sacrificed his adolescence to leave Slovenia for Spain. He believed he would be great and embraced the pressure to fulfill that potential—and accepted accountability when the road to greatness got bumpy.

For example, Dončić started and stunk it up when Real Madrid faced the Turkish power Fenerbahçe in the 2017 EuroLeague Final Four. Dončić played seventeen scoreless minutes in the loss in Istanbul. Dončić didn't speak to the media much all season, but he told the Spanish radio station Onda Cero after the loss that he played a "fatal game" and apologized to his teammates.

This was by far the biggest stage of Dončić's young life to that point, and he failed. He didn't have to wait long, however, for another opportunity to prove himself. He made his first official appearance for the Slovenian national team that summer and seized the opportunity to emerge as a co-star alongside Dragić, the veteran NBA guard whose pro career began years before as a teammate of Dončić's dad in the Balkan-based Adriatic League.

Since the program's inception in 1991 up to that time, Slovenia had produced some solid teams but only once advanced past the EuroBasket quarterfinals—not surprising, considering it's such a small country competing against nations with populations 20 or 30 times larger. That put Dončić and his teammates in position to make history after getting through group play unscathed and blowing out Ukraine in the round of 16, the first batch of elimination games. Latvia, featuring New York Knicks rising star Kristaps Porziņģis, stood in the way of Slovenia making its deepest EuroBasket run ever.

Dragić had established himself as the best Slovenian player ever by that point. He was 31, still in his prime, having just averaged 20.3 points and 5.8 assists per game for the Miami Heat. He was months away from being named an NBA All-Star, an honor never before bestowed on a Slovenian. Dragić was the lone active NBA player on the Slovenian squad and clearly the team's leader, but his teenage teammate didn't take a back seat.

"You could see he's starting to take over in the sense of, OK, he knows he's really good," Slovenian forward Vlatko Čančar, who also had an NBA future, said of Dončić. "He was not afraid of nobody."

Porziņģis and Dragić dueled for much of that quarterfinal, a pair of high-level NBA talents living up to that billing. But it was Dončić who dominated down the stretch, taking over the game after Latvia slashed a 13-point Slovenian lead to 2, scoring 12 of his 27 points in the final six minutes. Dončić halted Latvia's momentum by going right at the 7-foot-3 Porziņģis, putting him in a pick and roll and attacking after a switch with a between-the-legs crossover before accelerating for a finger roll. He banked in a 30-footer with the shot clock running down, a bit of good fortune mixed in with his fearlessness. He burned Porziņģis on another switch, taking advantage of the big man's concerns about getting blown by again by drilling a step-back three. And Dončić sealed the 103–97 win—the biggest victory in the Slovenian program's history to that point—by calmly making four free throws in the final 21 seconds. Dončić displayed a combination of *cojones* and skill to send Porziņģis and the Latvians home—and prompted the New York tabloids to hype up the possibility of the Knicks landing the Slovenian teen at the top of the next draft.

"The bigger the challenge, the more difficult the situation is—he feels the sparks and he's willing to compete," said Igor Kokoškov, the longtime NBA assistant who was Slovenia's head coach. "He's just never afraid of the moment. After the first couple of days, he felt like, 'This is where I belong. Regardless of my age, I can lead this group.'"

Dončić finished two assists short of a triple-double in Slovenia's surprisingly easy semifinals win over Spain, which had won gold at three of the previous four EuroBasket tournaments. That set up a meeting with Serbia, a Balkan rival with a much richer basketball history, for the championship. The weight of the opportunity kept Dragić awake deep into the night before the championship game.

He couldn't believe how soundly the kid he was rooming with was sleeping, as Dončić was snoring away without a care in the world. "He doesn't feel pressure," Dragić said.

Dončić isn't immune to injury, however, and his left ankle rolled over violently after blocking a Serbian's shot midway through the third quarter. He had to be helped to the bench and covered his face with a towel as he realized that he wouldn't be able to return to the title game. Slovenia still won, 93–85, as Dragić scored 35 to claim the EuroBasket MVP award and cement his status as the greatest basketball player in his country's history—at least temporarily. Dragić knew then that Dončić was destined for greatness.

"He's going to be the best player in Europe in a couple of years, trust me on that. In the NBA, too," Dragić proclaimed during an on-court interview moments after the championship game win. "Mark my words, he's going to be one of the best in the whole world!"

Dončić returned to Real Madrid with the EuroBasket trophy tattooed below the ribs on his right side and significantly more responsibility. Llull, Los Blancos' longtime superstar guard, would be sidelined for several months due to a serious knee injury that prevented him from playing that summer for Spain. Dončić, 18, who'd earned the Rising Star honor as EuroLeague's best young player the previous season, needed to fill the legend's large shoes if Real Madrid had any real hope of contending.

"I have no pressure. Everyone asks me that," Dončić told Spanish reporters before the season, when he was noncommittal on the possibility of declaring for the next NBA draft. "But this is basketball. And I love it. You can't feel pressure doing something you like."

If there was any doubt that Dončić was up to the challenge, it was eliminated almost instantly. He took the EuroLeague's MVP honor for October, becoming the youngest player ever to win the monthly award. There were bumps in the road that season—an ejection and temper tantrum, some missed time due to minor injuries—but there were a heck of a lot more highlights than hard times.

Dončić, living up to his mentor Dragić's declaration that he'd be the best player in Europe, authored a series of signature moments during Real Madrid's regular season. Most memorable: a last-second, game-winning three Dončić drilled to hush Red Star Belgrade's notoriously hostile home crowd. The shot was preceded with a step-back move so sudden that the defender had to put his hand on the floor to prevent himself from falling.

Dončić repeated as the Rising Star winner, but he claimed much more significant awards, too. He was named the Liga ACB and Euro-League MVP, becoming the youngest player to receive both honors. "Much deserved. Congratulations, young king," his idol Spanoulis said in Spanish while presenting the EuroLeague MVP trophy to Dončić during the Final Four, which was held in Belgrade. The next day, Dončić claimed one more major honor—EuroLeague Final Four MVP—after Real Madrid defeated Fenerbahçe in the championship game.

All along, Dončić had put off discussing his future, declining to say whether he'd play in the NBA the next season, although there wasn't much doubt. NBA TV sent a crew to the Final Four to capture Dončić content. More than half of the NBA's teams sent scouts, including the owner of the No. 1 overall pick, the Phoenix Suns, whose owner, Robert Sarver, sat courtside, with VP of basketball operations James Jones behind him in the second row. Despite winning Final Four MVP, Dončić didn't do anything to overwhelm the scouts in the wins over CSKA Moscow and Fenerbahçe, averaging 15.5 points, five rebounds, and three assists in the pair of victories.

"I'm just focused right now on how we're going to celebrate this right now, the EuroLeague trophy," Dončić told reporters after swigging champagne in the victors' locker room. "I'm not thinking about anything else."

Dončić still wasn't done with Real Madrid. The Liga ACB playoffs started that weekend, so he couldn't celebrate *too much*, the teen mentioned with a coy smile. Real Madrid rolled through those playoffs—losing only one game in three series, finishing off the best-of-five finals against Baskonia in four games. Dončić exited with one last unforgettable shot, a three that served as a fitting bookend to his Real Madrid tenure, a dagger late in the fourth quarter that he flipped in off one foot in the final second of the shot clock.

During the postgame medal ceremony, Dončić sat down on the stage and shed a few tears. He had achieved all of the goals within his reach while in a Real Madrid uniform, racking up titles and MVPs, establishing himself as the most accomplished European teen prospect ever. For the rest of that day into the night, it was time for Dončić to reflect and celebrate.

Dončić skipped the festivities planned in Madrid the next day. He hopped on a flight to New York to attend the NBA draft at the Barclays Center in Brooklyn to learn where the next challenge would take him.

CHAPTER 3

A TANK AND A TRADE

THE MAVERICKS HAD 15 MINUTES TO CHANGE THE COURSE OF the franchise. The 2018 NBA Draft had officially started with the Phoenix Suns on the clock to make the first overall pick. Dallas owned the No. 5 pick, the result of blatant tanking and bad lottery luck, and desperately wanted to make a deal to move up.

The Mavs' front office felt assured that the first two picks would pass without their target being taken, knowing that the Suns and Sacramento Kings had prioritized other prospects. Nelson had been on the phone with Hawks general manager Travis Schlenk, trying to work a trade that would allow them to take Dončić with the No. 3 pick.

Finally, as the draft began with teams allotted five minutes per pick, Cuban stepped outside of Dallas's draft room and called the Hawks' majority owner Tony Ressler on his cell phone.

"We're like, 'The general managers have too much on their mind. We've got to figure this out,'" Cuban said. "That's what ended up happening."

The deal got done: a swap of the third and fifth picks in that draft, with Dallas giving up their first rounder the next year, as long as it wasn't in the top five, which would have delayed that payment another year. Dončić wore a Hawks cap when he shook Adam Silver's hand on the stage, while Oklahoma guard Trae Young sported a Mavs cap minutes later, as the trade hadn't yet been made official, an awkward but common routine during NBA drafts. But the Mavs had their man, the phenom they planned to make the next face of the franchise.

"The logic is, if you think he's a game-changing player for you, a franchise-changing player, you don't care about your next pick," Cuban said. "You just want that player."

Dallas's decision-makers had had this player in mind for months as they searched for ways to be as dreadful as possible most of the previous season. They lived in the bizzarro world where wins created pained expressions for everyone in the organization except the players.

One case in point occurred on February 10, when Dirk Nowitzki, wearing his warm-ups and a towel around his neck since subbing out of the game with 7:09 remaining, strutted up and down the sideline in front of the Mavericks' bench in celebration. He cocked his hands above his left shoulder and mimicked the two-hand dunk that 26-year-old undrafted rookie Maxi Kleber had just thrown down over Lakers forward Julius Randle, much to the delight of maximum-salaried starters Harrison Barnes and Wesley Matthews, who joined Nowitzki, the longtime face of the franchise, as spectators down the stretch.

This wasn't garbage time, however, as Kleber's highlight dunk bumped the Mavs' lead to 4 with 79 seconds remaining at the American Airlines Center. Carlisle had recently pledged a commitment to "player development," a phrase commonly used as cover for playing lineups that increase the likelihood of losing—or tanking, to put it simply. And the Mavs had done a lot of that lately, dropping seven of their previous eight games to enter the night with a 17–38 record, which was tied for the worst in the NBA.

The Mavs had recently begun relying on an extremely unproven four-man core to close games, playing a few undrafted players on minimum contracts (Kleber, Salah Mejri, and Yogi Ferrell) along with raw rookie point guard Dennis Smith Jr. That quartet, which played a total of 12 minutes together in the first three and a half months of the season, had been on the floor while the Mavs blew a 10-point lead in the final 4:42 of a loss to the Clippers earlier in the week. They had played together for 24 minutes already in February, the equivalent of one half in which the Mavs were outscored by a whopping 38 points before mustering a closing kick against the Lakers, when Doug McDermott rounded out Dallas's anti-clutch lineup in his first game after arriving in a trade.

After the 130–123 victory, a reporter asked Carlisle an innocuous question about how much fun the final few minutes must have been. Carlisle crinkled his nose and pursed his lips, looking like he just smelled a fart, a frequent facial expression of his. He then made his best attempt at feigning enthusiasm.

"Listen, I love winning," Carlisle said. "I love winning. You know that."

Any pretense that the Mavs actually wanted to win disappeared days later, when Cuban inexplicably admitted the obvious. Cuban got starstruck as a guest on *House Call with Dr. J*, an obscure podcast hosted by NBA legend Julius Erving, and blurted out details of a blunt conversation he had recently had with 39-year-old Nowitzki and some of Dallas's other veterans.

"I'm probably not supposed to say this, but, like, I just had dinner with a bunch of our guys the other night, and here we are, you know, we weren't competing for the playoffs. I was like, 'Look, losing is our best option,'" Cuban said on the podcast. "Adam [Silver] would hate hearing that, but I at least sat down and I explained it to them. And I explained what our plans were going to be this summer, that we're not going to tank again. This was, like, a year and a half tanking, and that was too brutal for me. But being transparent, I think that's the key to being kind of a players' owner and having stability."

Silver had let it slide the previous spring when Cuban mentioned during an appearance on *The Dan Patrick Show* that the Mavs "did everything possible to lose games" after being eliminated from play-off contention in the 2016–17 season. At least the crime had already been committed in that case, putting the Mavs in position to get the No. 9 overall pick, the highest Dallas's selection landed in the lottery since Nowitzki's draft class in 1998. Silver couldn't ignore Cuban's confession while in the act of tanking, fining him $600,000 for "public statements detrimental to the NBA."

The tanking strategy, not to mention the public admission, was an embarrassment for a proud franchise that hadn't won a playoff series since the Mavericks' storybook title run in 2011. Nowitzki especially hated the topic, calling tanking talk "aggressive," which the big German used as a synonym for offensive. "I'm obviously not a fan," Nowitzki said, vowing to always play his minutes hard. Carlisle hated it, too.

"We don't like each other, but I will tell you this: He's the most competitive coach I've ever been around," said Mike Procopio, a player development coach on that staff. "He understood it. Of course, he would do it, but he's just too competitive. He called us in; 'Hey, I just want to let you guys know, this is what we're doing.' It fucking ripped him apart. You could tell he was doing it because the lineups he would throw out there were just ridiculous."

It was difficult to argue against the logic of bottoming out and boosting the odds of winning the lottery after the Mavs had steadily drifted into irrelevancy, wasting the twilight of Nowitzki's Hall of Fame career with one front-office failure after another. It was a basketball embarrassment, and the Mavs' business operations were shamed by a *Sports Illustrated* exposé published in mid-February 2018 regarding "a corporate culture rife with misogyny and

predatory sexual behavior," focusing on former team CEO Ter-
dema Ussery, among others. "It's not something we tolerate," Cuban
replied to *Sports Illustrated*, months before making a $10 million
donation to women's organizations upon the conclusion of an NBA
investigation. "I don't want it. It's not something that's acceptable.
I'm embarrassed, to be honest with you, that it happened under my
ownership, and it needs to be fixed. Period. End of story." The Mavs
were a franchise desperate for positive developments.

DALLAS'S GRADUAL DESCENT INTO NBA PURGATORY BEGAN WHEN
Cuban got greedy in the wake of the Mavs' championship run and
the lockout that followed. Cuban, who always considered himself
to be smarter than the competition, studied the new collective bargaining agreement closely and decided that Dallas's best path to
another championship would be via creating salary-cap space and
chasing superstars in free agency. That meant making the unpop-
ular decision to allow core players to leave following an aging roster's surprising title run. Center Tyson Chandler, the final piece to
the Mavs' championship puzzle, whose athleticism and intensity
complemented Nowitzki so well, signed a four-year, $55 million
deal with the New York Knicks after Cuban extended only one-year
offers. The Mavs also made minimal effort to keep feisty guard J. J.
Barea, an undrafted success story whose surprise entrance into the
starting lineup shifted momentum in the Finals against the Miami
Heat, before he agreed to a four-year, $16 million deal with the Min-
nesota Timberwolves. Sixth man Jason Terry, Nowitzki's sidekick
since Nash's departure, awkwardly spent the next season knowing
that the Mavs had no intention to re-sign him after his contract
expired that summer.

"Did you read the CBA?" Cuban would snap at any media member
who dared to question the wisdom of his plan. The Mavs opted to go
all-in on pursuing "big fish," to borrow an oft-used Donnie Nelson

term, and Cuban firmly believed that his popularity among players would be a major factor in making Dallas a free agency destination. At that point, although he couldn't say it on the record, Cuban had confidence that the Mavs could poach Dwight Howard and Chris Paul from the small-market franchises that had drafted them. Imagine surrounding Nowitzki, who was in his thirties but still one of the league's best offensive weapons, with an All-NBA center and an All-NBA point guard, both just entering their prime. Dallas might have had a dynasty, but it didn't quite work out that way.

That ambitious plan fizzled well before the 2012 free agency period. Paul was traded to the LA Clippers—after the league office vetoed a deal that would have sent him to the Lakers—before the start of the lockout-delayed season and exercised the option in his contract for the 2012–13 season. He signed another long-term deal with the Clippers after that contract expired. Howard waffled on whether to exercise a similar option in his contract with the Orlando Magic, changing his mind in multiple conversations with team management leading up to the 2012 trade deadline, before finally committing to stay. Then he changed his mind again, forcing a trade that summer to the Lakers.

The Mavs pursued All-Star point guard Deron Williams in free agency that summer, but it was a half-hearted pitch. Cuban skipped the meeting with Williams in New York to film *Shark Tank* in Los Angeles, which Williams perceived as disrespectful and Cuban later claimed was intentional self-sabotage, as he'd had second thoughts on whether Williams was worth a maximum contract. (Cuban's assessment was proven to be accurate, as Williams and the Nets agreed to a buyout a few frustrating years later, at which point Williams signed with Dallas on a one-year, $5.5 million deal.)

Dallas loaded up on one-year deals in the 2012 offseason to preserve future salary-cap space, essentially punting on the next season, when the Mavs finished .500 to snap a dozen-year streak of winning campaigns and playoff appearances. They still had hope of landing a big fish, specifically Howard, who'd endured a disappointing season in LA. The Mavs went all-in on their pitch to Howard during a three-hour meeting, which featured an animated comic book–style video starring the center as a superhero. The two-minute video concluded with a message as the cartoon version of Howard shredded his Lakers jersey to reveal a Mavericks logo on his chest: "BEING A MAVERICK ENDS WITH…GLOBAL DOMINATION!"

Howard decided instead to sign with the Houston Rockets, pairing with a superstar in his prime, James Harden. The Rockets' recruiting efforts were fronted by charismatic forward Chandler Parsons. He was also represented by agent Dan Fegan and had the team option for the final season of his rookie contract declined as a bit of under-the-table quid pro quo, allowing Parsons to make a salary leap from six figures to eight figures the following offseason.

The desperate pursuit of Howard came at a drastic cost for the Mavs, albeit uncertain at the time, as Dallas twice traded down in the draft to squeeze a bit less than the $400,000 in cap space necessary to make a full-max offer to Howard. Nelson lobbied hard to select a raw European teenager named Giannis Antetokounmpo with the 13th overall pick, comparing him to Dr. J and declaring that he could be the best player in the draft. Instead, the Mavs ended up with the No. 18 overall pick, which they used on Shane Larkin, a diminutive point guard who scored a grand total of 132 points during his lone season in Dallas and was out of the NBA three more teams and three years later.

"He's making us look bad for sticking to our plan," Cuban admitted during one of his pregame chats with the media while sweating on his StairMaster before a meeting with Antetokounmpo's Bucks in December 2014, by which time the "Greek Freak" had just begun blossoming into one of the NBA's most intriguing young prospects. "That was Donnie. [Drafting Antetokounmpo] is what Donnie wanted to do and I said we should stick to the plan. The whole point is that I wanted to stick to the plan and Donnie was like,

'This guy's going to be good. I'll risk everything that he's going to be good.' I said, 'I believe you, Donnie.'

"But still, what if all of the sudden we find out that so-and-so is dying to come to the Mavs and now you don't have the cap room? That's why we put together a plan, and our consolation wasn't too bad."

The Mavs' consolation prizes—Monta Ellis at that point, then Parsons, and eventually an ill-advised trade for Rajon Rondo—never produced a single playoff series win. As Nowitzki neared the end of his career, the Mavs were stuck on the mediocrity treadmill, a phrase coined by Cuban to describe the NBA's version of purgatory—not good enough to make a playoff run, not bad enough to land a high enough pick to draft an elite prospect. The simplest path out of that muck of the middle, and hopefully into title contention eventually, is to sink to the bottom. That's why teams tank, a tactic the Mavs employed down the stretch in 2016–17, a season doomed by Dallas opening 6–20 as Nowitzki missed most of the first two months due to Achilles tendon soreness. The Mavs faded toward the finish, losing nine of their last 11 games, to claim the ninth-best odds in the lottery. They ended up with the No. 9 overall pick—their highest since 1998, when they traded down from No. 6 to get Nowitzki with the ninth pick—and selected Smith, despite Carlisle preferring Donovan Mitchell. (In fairness, Carlisle voiced that opinion more loudly after Mitchell emerged as a star for the Utah Jazz than in the days leading up to the draft.)

Dallas still desperately needed a franchise-type of talent to take the torch from Nowitzki. A 2–14 start to the 2017–18 season eliminated any doubt about that and made it an obvious decision to place lottery positioning atop the Mavs' priority list. Dallas limped to the finish line, losing 12 of its last 14 games, while giving heavy minutes to players who can be politely described as fringe prospects, to secure the third-best lottery odds. Nelson had one particular prospect in mind: Dončić, the European kid he'd been personally scouting since he was called up to Real Madrid's top team at age 16.

"Donnie Nelson was the one who thought he was going to be exceptionally good, and exceptionally good early," Carlisle said.

"Donnie Nelson was spot on this the whole time," said Duffy, Dončić's lead agent. "I had this feeling and thought that [Dončić] could play point guard, that he was like a cross between Magic and Bird. That's the first thing I saw. He's a triple-double machine. I saw that, and then Donnie saw that. I just remember him saying, 'He's a point guard. He's like Magic.' You're damn right he is."

Fortunately for the Mavericks, Nelson's opinion was far from the consensus among NBA executives, scouts, and talent evaluators, despite Dončić's unprecedented dominance of the highest levels of European competition by a player so young. Doubts persisted about his athleticism and explosiveness. Few projected him as a point guard in the NBA, as the most frequent comparisons were to playmaking forwards who happened to have pale complexions, such as Gordon Hayward or Hedo Türkoğlu. One GM grumbled that if Dončić struggled to get past Nick Calathes, an elite EuroLeague guard whose NBA career lasted two unremarkable seasons, how could he possibly be expected to beat anyone in the league off the dribble? How could he defend NBA guards and wings? "The biggest concern is his lack of athleticism, which could really be a problem defensively as there are questions regarding which position, if any, he can guard in the NBA," Nelson said before the draft, a pretty transparent attempt to add to the doubts about Dončić.

"I don't think it's fair to put on him this moniker the best young European to ever come over here. Because I think that's going to be terribly unfair to him," ESPN's Fran Fraschilla said before the draft, stating an opinion shared by many in the NBA. "I think he's going to be a very good NBA player. If I were to rate him the way teams rate guys—which is All-Star, starter, rotation player, fringe player, etc.— I would say he's going to be a very successful starter in the NBA.

With a chance, at times, to be an All-Star. But I do not see him as a transcendent talent."

There was a perception that Dončić was so polished after five years in Real Madrid's system that he didn't have much room to improve. Some scouts also came away from trips to Spain with a sense that Dončić would be too satisfied once he got NBA riches. And there were rampant concerns about Dončić's commitment to diet and conditioning. Those were reinforced by scenes in an *ESPN the Magazine* profile by Mina Kimes of Dončić stopping his electric-blue Porsche Panamera at a convenience store to purchase an armload of Snickers bars before driving to the Hard Rock Cafe, where he ordered the Famous Fajitas and a plate of nachos. "Con doble queso," he told the waiter.

Those perceived flaws—as well as perhaps the history of high-lottery Euro busts such as Andrea Bargnani, Darko Miličić, Nikoloz Tskitishvili, Jan Veselý, Mario Hezonja, and Dragan Bender—prevented Dončić from ranking atop many draft boards. However, he was still widely projected as a top-three pick. So it felt like a disaster when bad lottery luck struck again for Dallas, a franchise that has never moved up but has been bumped down in the lottery on multiple occasions. The Mavs held the fifth overall pick after the Ping-Pong balls popped out, behind the Atlanta Hawks and Memphis Grizzlies. "Of course...," Nowitzki tweeted at the moment.

"I was honestly devastated," Nelson said later. Making matters worse, the teams holding the top two picks featured men in prominent positions who had close ties to Dončić. The Suns, who won the lottery after having the league's worst record, had recently hired Kokoškov as head coach. The longtime NBA assistant's candidacy was boosted by coaching the Slovenian national team, starring Dončić alongside Goran Dragić, to a EuroBasket title. The Kings, seventh in the odds, jumped to No. 2 in the draft. Sacramento's general manager was Vlade Divac, the former Yugoslavia/Serbia star whose roots in European basketball, especially the Balkans, ran as deep as anyone's. Divac had known Saša Dončić for decades, dating to when they were both part of Yugoslavia's national program.

Days after the lottery, Nelson approached the Suns' contingent at the scouting combine in Chicago to make his interest in moving up in the draft known. "He would say, 'Hey, let me know what we can do,'" Kokoškov said. "He made it clear they wanted Luka. Donnie Nelson didn't have any doubts. Donnie was focused. He was so determined to get it done, whatever it takes. They wanted Luka only and nobody else."

Soon thereafter, members of each franchise's front offices traveled to Belgrade to scout Dončić at the EuroLeague Final Four. Suns owner Robert Sarver and VP of basketball operations James Jones sat in courtside seats, as Phoenix general manager Ryan McDonough was conspicuously absent, a hint at his diminishing power within the organization months before he was fired and replaced by Jones. Divac, a legend in his native Serbia, attended the semifinals but raised eyebrows by flying back to Sacramento before the championship game. Nelson and his right-hand scout Ronzone represented the Mavs.

"I was glad every time he lost a foot race or didn't look very athletic, to be honest with you," Nelson said, cracking up with laughter. "I was cheering for him to screw up in the European championships. I just wanted him to drop!"

Word soon circulated that the Suns had fixated on Arizona center Deandre Ayton as their first choice despite hiring Kokoškov. Ayton was not considered a controversial pick—he sat atop most draft boards as a 6-foot-11 physical specimen with a soft touch—but the fact that he attended Sarver's alma mater less than two hours away from Phoenix made him even more attractive to a franchise desperate to create buzz in their market. The opinion of Kokoškov, a first-time NBA head coach, was not sought within the organization.

"Getting that job, I was overwhelmed with a lot of stuff," Kokoškov said. "Honestly, we didn't spend any time talking about it. It gave me a clear sign that the decision was already made. I wasn't even asked. Which may be [because of] the fact that I had a relationship with Luka."

So he could sleep well, Kokoškov made a point to pitch Sarver on his vision of an offseason plan, approaching the owner on draft day. He lobbied to use the No. 1 overall pick on Dončić and to put a four-year offer sheet in the $100 million range on the table for Rockets center Clint Capela, a 24-year-old restricted free agent who was the sort of switchable rim protector, rebounder, and lob threat Kokoškov saw as an ideal complement for a dynamic offensive backcourt featuring Dončić and Devin Booker.

It was a brief conversation that Sarver blew off. The Suns took Ayton with the top pick. After a long, drawn out negotiation, Capela settled for a five-year deal from the Rockets worth $85 million plus incentives. Phoenix poached another Houston starter at a significantly lower price, signing 33-year-old forward Trevor Ariza to a one-year, $15 million deal. Ariza, who was miserable with a rebuilding team, was traded the week before Christmas. Kokoškov didn't last too much longer with the Suns, getting fired at the end of a 19–63 season.

The Mavs knew well before the Kings went on the clock that Sacramento was not a real threat to select Dončić, either. "Vlade knew too much," one scout who worked for the Kings at the time said, noting that Divac had deep intel on Dončić's work habits and penchant for enjoying nightlife. It reminded him of Luka's father, Saša, who is beloved in Slovenian basketball circles despite the widespread belief that he didn't achieve his full potential, due in large part to his love of food and wine. Some joke that Saša spent as much time in the pub he owned near Ljubljana's train station as at the gym.

But Divac's decision came down to his evaluation of Dončić's talent and fit on Sacramento's roster. The Kings were confident they had drafted a franchise cornerstone with the fifth overall pick the previous year, taking point guard De'Aaron Fox, who was Sacramento's representative at the lottery. There were concerns about pairing Fox with another playmaker who was most comfortable operating as a primary offensive initiator, but such fit issues are typically overlooked if a potential superstar talent is available. Divac did not consider Dončić to be of that caliber. The 7-foot Serbian favored going big, and it was no secret that he was enamored with Duke power forward/center Marvin Bagley III, even though Divac was part of a Kings contingent, along with owner Vivek Ranadivé, that had traveled to Madrid in early June for a dinner meeting with Dončić.

"Marvin is for us a better fit. A better player. A great talent," Divac said after drafting Bagley at No. 2. "It was an easy decision." He was fired two years later.

So the Mavs honed in on the No. 3 pick, their original slot in the lottery that was now property of the Hawks, as the spot they needed to target. Atlanta, whose front office and ownership group were split on preferring Dončić or Young, was willing to discuss a deal that allowed Dallas to move up two spots—but at a premium price.

"If we would have stayed at three, we would have taken Luka," then–Hawks general manager Travis Schlenk said. "We had worked with his agent. He did a physical with us that morning in New York. I was on the phone with Bill Duffy, his agent, and telling him that our press conference was going to be Monday…. But then Dallas came in an hour or so before the draft. I told them all along that it would take another lottery pick for us to slide back. That's when the conversations got started."

This kind of deal required Cuban to be fully on board. He had ignored Nelson's advice many times over the previous two decades, including the draft five years earlier when Cuban passed on Antetokounmpo despite Nelson's pleas. But there was a drastic difference with this European teen prospect, who had proven himself against that continent's best competition. "He was the top player on our board," Cuban said. "It wasn't even close."

Years later, Cuban claimed that there wasn't a consensus among the Mavs' scouts that Dončić was the best player in the draft, which runs contrary to the credit he gave the scouting department after the draft. ("That's bullshit!" one of the scouts shouted when informed of Cuban's recent assertion.) There is no dispute, however, that Dallas's analytics army ranked Dončić "ten miles ahead of everybody else," as Cuban said, by far the premier prospect in the class.

That included a consultant who had quietly become the voice that Cuban valued most regarding personnel decisions, unbeknownst to almost everybody—including Nelson. Haralabos "Bob" Voulgaris had amassed a fortune as a professional gambler, using his in-depth NBA statistical data to consistently beat the sports books, so frequently that he couldn't find a casino in Las Vegas that would continue to take his bets. He had also built a large Twitter following due to his insightful, biting NBA commentary that was often critical of coaches and front offices. Cuban had been privately paying Voulgaris $2 million per year to share his data and opinions and wanted to officially hire him to a prominent front-office position. Voulgaris agreed, if the Mavs could meet one condition.

"The deal I made with Mark is that if they drafted [Dončić], I would come work for the team full time," Voulgaris said. "I told Mark that he was very, very similar to James Harden, that he'd be a top-five MVP candidate at some point within his first five years. I don't think Mark would have done the deal just on Donnie. I'm actually positive he wouldn't have done the deal just on Donnie."

Nelson had the green light to make a deal with the Hawks, but talks started slowly. Schlenk proposed including a swap of veteran wings who weren't in either franchise's long-term plans: Kent Bazemore and Wesley Matthews, which would have been a major financial win for the Hawks. Bazemore was owed $18.1 million in the upcoming season and $19.3 million the following year. Matthews would make $18.6 million that season in the final year of his deal, an expiring contract that could be valuable in the trade market.

That part of the discussion eventually got dropped, but the conversation between the GMs continued, much of it focused on the protection the Mavs would put on the next year's draft pick they'd be sending the Hawks. Atlanta's analytics group projected that the Mavs would finish with the NBA's eighth-worst record, meaning the pick would be in the middle of the lottery. Nelson needed to prevent the worst-case scenario of giving away a high lottery pick. Dallas had a backup plan—taking Duke center Wendell Carter Jr. at No. 5— but that would have been a massive disappointment.

The deal got done with minutes to spare. It was, in the words of Carlisle, "a defining moment in this rebuild." The two players the Mavs predicted to be franchise pillars—Smith, the lottery pick who'd just wrapped up a second-team All-Rookie year, and Barnes, who'd led Dallas in scoring the previous two seasons after signing a maximum contract in free agency—showed up to the day-after-draft press conference to publicly welcome their new teammates. Nelson compared Dončić and that pair to Nowitzki, Nash, and Michael Finley, the trio that led the Mavs back to relevancy after a decade of being an NBA laughingstock.

The Mavs could pat themselves on the back for winning the draft. But that created pressure to win on the court again. There was a natural urgency to succeed as soon as possible, but patience was necessary to build a sustainable contender with Dončić as the centerpiece.

"We're going to propel forward with the idea that we've got to start winning games," Carlisle said, emphasizing that he expected Dončić and Smith to complement each other extremely well. "We've got to do everything possible to create an amazing chemistry with these young men, and everybody's got to be tied together."

Carlisle mentioned that he saw shades of the late, great Drazen Petrović, whom he had coached as a New Jersey Nets assistant, in Dončić's game, as well as glimpses of Manu Ginóbili and Toni

Kukoč. Then the coach caught himself: "I really feel it's important that we shouldn't try to compare this guy to anybody. Let him be himself. Let his game take its own form."

Dončić didn't seem fazed by any of the pressure to succeed Nowitzki as the face of the franchise. The Mavs' belief in him was nice, but Dončić appeared to appreciate the doubts about him even more.

"I like challenges," Dončić said. "When they say you're going to be good, I like to be challenged. When they say you're not going to be good, I say, 'Let's see.'"

CHAPTER 4

THE RANT AT THE RITZ

THICK TENSION HUNG IN THE AIR OF THE TORONTO RITZ-Carlton ballroom as the Mavericks shuffled in for a team meeting nine days into Dončić's rookie year. They had arrived at the hotel in the early morning hours after a two-plus-hour flight from Atlanta, followed by going through Canadian customs—a trip that felt a lot longer on the heels of a humiliating, nationally televised performance against the Hawks that dropped Dallas's record to 2–2.

Unlike Dončić's dud of an NBA debut—a blowout loss to Ayton and the Suns, also broadcast on ESPN—the Slovenian teen got off to a sizzling start in this made-for-TV, early season matchup of high-profile rookies. Dončić had scored a dozen points midway through the first quarter, highlighted by a step-back three and a pair of pretty floaters off drives. He was making it look easy, much as Dončić did during a pair of wins in the previous two games that bumped the Mavs above .500 for the first time since the end of the 2015–16 season

Dallas was up 42–22 at the end of the first quarter in Atlanta—as Trae Young, the player swapped for Dončić on draft night, struggled—and led by 26 four minutes into the second quarter, more than doubling the Hawks' score. Then Dončić faded into the background and Dallas fell apart. By the time Dončić and Young exchanged smiling hugs and handshakes after the final buzzer, the Mavericks had managed to blow the third-biggest lead in franchise history.

The film session the next day, run by an irate Carlisle, wasn't going to be fun. He was embarrassed by how disjointed Dallas appeared during its collapse and felt the need to fix everything four games into a new era. It didn't matter that Nowitzki (ankle surgery) and Barnes (hamstring strain) didn't play due to medical issues. Carlisle made it clear, clip after clip, that the kind of effort he saw in Atlanta was completely unacceptable.

Suddenly, Carlisle paused the video and declared that he needed to address "the elephant in the room." He called out Smith, in front of the entire team and basketball staff, for being "jealous" of Dončić. Smith snapped back at the coach.

"What?! We real cool!" Smith said, genuinely surprised by Carlisle's assertion. With a confused look toward Dončić, Smith asked if there were any issues he wasn't aware of. A shocked Dončić shook his head, appalled that his coach seemed determined to drive a wedge between himself and his teammate.

There were obvious questions about the fit on the floor between the Mavs' two young lottery picks, both of whom were best with the ball in their hands, but it was preposterous to portray Smith as anything but welcoming to Dončić. Smith texted his new teammate on draft night to welcome him to Dallas, showed up to Dončić's introductory press conference the next day to greet him in person, and made a point to serve as the new kid's guide around town. They were neighbors at 1900 McKinney, an upscale high-rise apartment building less than a mile from the American Airlines Center, and often hung out together, whether they went out to dinner and/or a club, or stayed in and played video games. "I don't even like *Fortnite!*" Smith said with a laugh years later, but he played it because it was Dončić's favorite game.

Smith felt like Carlisle picked on him relentlessly during his rookie year. Within the first few months of that season, Carlisle had indeed lost faith that Smith could develop into a worthy franchise cornerstone, seeing the No. 9 overall pick as a point guard with an inconsistent jumper whose acrobatic highlights were outweighed by his poor decisions and feel for the game. Those flaws made Carlisle comfortable closing games with Smith when the Mavs were tanking, although it annoyed him that Smith piled up meaningless stats and was a focal point for the franchise's marketing efforts. Carlisle definitely didn't trust Smith when the Mavs were trying to win.

That became apparent in Atlanta, when Smith turned his right ankle with a little more than four minutes remaining. Carlisle used that as cover for benching him down the stretch, even though Smith told reporters after the 111–104 loss that he was fine to finish the game. Carlisle called for 13-year veteran J. J. Barea to come off the bench, signaling for the spark plug from the Mavs' 2011 title team immediately after Smith committed his fifth turnover of the night with 2:49 remaining, this one on a leaping pass to Dončić off a drive into traffic. During a time-out a minute later, Smith sat on the bench next to Dončić, hoping to be subbed back in for the finish. After realizing that wasn't happening, Smith muttered a few words to Dončić before getting up and walking to the fringe of the huddle.

Smith bore the brunt of Carlisle's wrath the next day and sat out the road loss to the Raptors—the lone game he missed, purportedly due to that ankle sprain—but he was hardly alone to blame for the debacle in Atlanta. Dončić fizzled after his scorching start, missing nine of eleven shots before a meaningless layup with twelve seconds left, and was a defensive liability down the stretch. So was center

DeAndre Jordan, which was particularly concerning considering that the two-time first-team All-Defensive selection was being paid almost $23 million, in large part to serve as an anchor on that end of the floor. Dončić looked like a matador as the help defender on Kent Bazemore's drive for the dagger dunk, stepping aside to avoid being posterized after briefly considering an attempt to challenge the Hawks' wing at the rim. But the appropriately colored paint parted like the Red Sea because Jordan nonchalantly turned and spectated instead of handling his responsibilities as the screen defender in a basic pick and roll. It's the kind of poor-effort play that would drive any coach crazy (and one that became all too common during Jordan's brief stint in Dallas).

"I gave you guys my trust, but now that's over," Carlisle ranted at his team in the Ritz-Carlton ballroom. Veins were popping out of the temples on his shaved head as he hurled expletives at his players. Carlisle ran hot on a regular basis, and he was really steamed now—extraordinarily so, given how early it was in the season.

What a welcome to the NBA for Dončić. After only four games, a fissure had opened between him and his coach—a major issue with a stubborn, young star whose trust is tough to earn, easy to lose, and extremely difficult to regain.

Dončić, like almost everyone else in the room including players who had been coached by Carlisle for years, sat in stunned silence. Several jaws dropped toward the floor. The 6-foot-11, 265-pound Jordan hopped out of his chair and onto his feet.

"Coach, you can't talk to us like that!" Jordan said, his deep voice booming. He had been part of some harsh film sessions and team meetings during his decade-long tenure with the Clippers, particularly while being coached by Doc Rivers in the final five seasons, but Jordan had never heard or seen anything like this from an NBA coach. He made it clear that Carlisle went too far, a message that resonated among the rest of the Mavericks.

It was, however, rather awkward for Jordan to serve as a team spokesman. After all, he was only a few years removed from embarrassing the franchise by reneging on his commitment to come to Dallas on a max deal in free agency following a high-profile, hard-partying recruiting campaign fronted by Chandler Parsons and Mark Cuban. Days after the trio toasted the decision with the big man's friends, family, and agents at his Pacific Palisades home—tequila for the millionaires, vodka for the billionaire because "it was still morning," as Cuban explained—Jordan ghosted the Mavericks. He holed up in his Houston home with a Clippers contingent on the final day before free agency deals could become official and signed to stay in LA. That reversal resulted in the NBA shortening the moratorium period and the Mavs rapidly descending into the tanking strategy during Nowitzki's twilight. So Jordan's delayed arrival in Dallas on a one-year deal was pretty bizarre, especially him emerging as the temporary voice of the team. But somebody had to speak up. Cooler heads prevailed before the meeting ended, but Carlisle had effectively lost his voice with the team, with more than 95 percent of the season to play.

CARLISLE QUICKLY REALIZED THAT HE HAD MADE A MONUMENTAL mistake, the kind of error that can put a coach's job in jeopardy, even one whose tactical brilliance had played a key role in delivering the lone NBA championship to Dallas. He sensed something drastic had to be done, so four days after his tirade in Toronto, Carlisle apologized to the team during another meeting in their San Antonio hotel. Carlisle's voice quivered, and he appeared to be on the verge of tears at times during his speech.

"Guys didn't necessarily think it was real," an assistant coach on that staff said in retrospect. Carlisle, though, didn't only offer hollow words. He proposed a solution to the problems that he had connecting to the players on a personal level. Carlisle appointed Jamahl Mosley, who was in his fifth season as an assistant coach with the

Mavs and had just been promoted to defensive coordinator, as the point man in managing relationships between the coaching staff and the locker room. Mosley was immensely popular among the players, as had been the case during his previous coaching stops with the Nuggets and Cavaliers. He was 40 at the time, still had the wiry physique he did during his overseas playing career, and possessed a natural charisma that made it easy for him to bond with players.

It's not as if Mosley waved a magic wand to cure all that ailed the Mavs. Dallas lost to the Spurs in overtime that night, despite 31 points from Dončić, and dropped the next two games as well. Signs of selfishness were especially apparent during and after a November 2 loss to the Knicks that extended the Mavs' skid to six straight losses, dating to the Atlanta abomination.

"It starts with me. I take responsibility for this game and the way our team's struggling," Carlisle said after the loss to the Knicks. "I'm the leader of this thing and I've got to do a better job of getting these guys playing harder, playing more together. What we did tonight was very disappointing."

Jordan had blatantly stolen an otherwise uncontested defensive rebound from Dončić in the third quarter, bumping the airborne rookie out of the way with his left forearm while tipping the ball to himself. Dončić, who had been dealing with a sore back, reacted by slumping his shoulders and shooting a frustrated look toward Cuban in the owner's usual baseline seat by the Mavs' bench. "A microcosm of our season so far," one of the team's leaders mumbled about that moment in the locker room after the loss. The Mavs' veterans had already grown weary of Jordan chasing stats but not doing much dirty work, frustrated that he'd only roll hard to the rim if a dunk seemed available and that he obviously prioritized putting up big rebounding numbers over playing defense. Then Wesley Matthews, a vet on a large expiring contract, loudly complained to Donnie Nelson outside the locker room and within earshot of some media after getting only six shots against the Knicks. That discussion continued in Nelson's office with Carlisle joining, and the coach did a little damage control after the next practice, denying to the media that the postgame conversations with Matthews had been contentious. But the Mavs soon snapped out of their funk, going on a 12–3 run that, along with Nowitzki's continued rehab from ankle surgery, fueled hope that maybe the Mavericks really could be competitive during Dončić's rookie year.

"Jamahl saved our season," said Procopio, who served as a sounding board for Dončić and several other players. "Rick read the room, because Rick didn't give a lot of leeway to assistants, but he figured it out after the first few games—when our players were calling it a day and it was going to be bad for everybody—that Jamahl was the one guy who could rally the troops. That saved Rick and it saved our season. It would have been, like, Sacramento Kings bad. He knew that [Mosley] had the players' ear. That was the one assistant that could do that. Players were fed up with [Carlisle]. They quit on him for sure."

The concerns about whether Dončić and Smith fit as a pair persisted even as the Mavericks started putting wins together. Dallas's offensive efficiency with that duo on the floor actually went from bad during the 3–8 start to worse as the Mavs' wins started coming. Carlisle began staggering their minutes more to allow Dončić to operate with a well-spaced floor and the ball in his hands. And Dončić was producing the sort of scoring, rebounding, and assist numbers that had only been seen before from one NBA teen: LeBron James.

Carlisle had requested that Voulgaris and his analytics department run reports to determine whether the Dallas offense was better with Dončić or Smith bringing the ball up the floor. The results confirmed that Dončić, whose position Carlisle considered "unclear" when studying his game before the draft, needed to play point guard, not the small forward spot where he began his NBA career.

"Rick thought he was a three. He didn't know he was a point guard," Voulgaris scoffed years later. "You can't see that? But again, that was so he could tell the player, 'This is why he's the point guard. We've got numbers that show it.'"

Carlisle, however, insisted that he'd realized Dončić was best suited to run the offense on a regular basis after his first couple of days playing pickup ball at the Mavs' facility. He was a bit puffy, several pounds heavier than his Real Madrid weight but still dominating against NBA veterans. "He was playing the point and he was seeing everything, he was making amazing passes look so simple," said Carlisle, who told members of the coaching staff at the time that he saw a lot of his old Celtics teammate Larry Bird in Dončić's game. "He was impacting every part of the game. He was getting a lot of rebounds. He was finding people on time, on target. It was clear that he could play point guard, let's put it that way."

That meant that Smith was essentially in the way. As quietly as possible, Dallas attempted to engage teams around the league in trade discussions involving Smith. At one point early in the season, Voulgaris was optimistic that the Mavs could make a deal with the Suns that would have swapped Smith for rookie forward Mikal Bridges. In hindsight, that deal would have been a steal for Dallas, as Bridges blossomed into a phenomenal two-way forward who was a major contributor as Phoenix eventually emerged as a contender, and ended up being the centerpiece of the package the Suns sent the Nets in the 2023 Kevin Durant trade. At the time, Bridges was a 10th overall pick who was struggling mightily for a bad Phoenix squad that had a glaring hole at point guard.

"That was the deal that I was pushing for, and there were people that thought they were not willing to give up on Dennis Smith Jr. for just a drafted player who hadn't even played much yet," Voulgaris said. "This is like the first month of the season. A) Trades don't ever get done the first month of the season, is what I was told. B) One of the people had mentioned something like, 'I don't want a Chauncey

Billups–type situation with Dennis Smith Jr.' where he turns into something and we gave up on him. I think my comment was, 'Look, I can be fairly certain that he's not going to be a Chauncey Billups–type player.' That was more of a Mark thing."

Smith, to his credit, adapted to a lesser offensive role and focused his energy on impacting games defensively even as his relationship with Carlisle continued to sour. He attempted to remain professional despite feeling like Carlisle made a point to pick on him, often ripping Smith in meetings when he was the lone player in a room with several coaches, and delivered conflicting messages on how much he wanted Smith to push the pace. Rajon Rondo, the former All-Star point guard who felt his career was damaged by the feud with Carlisle during his half-season Dallas tenure, privately reached out to Smith to counsel the 21-year-old on how to handle what they perceived to be unfair treatment from the coach.

Perhaps the high point of Smith's stint with the Mavericks occurred in an early December home win over the LA Clippers, despite him scoring only 9 points. A chunk of one of his front teeth went flying onto the court with 3:10 remaining in the third quarter when Smith caught a Patrick Beverley elbow to the mouth while diving for a loose ball. He returned for the final 10:45 and sealed the win with a blocked shot on Clippers star forward Tobias Harris, who'd attempted to use his six-inch height advantage to bully Smith on a post-up only to get stuffed. Carlisle called it "one of the best competitive things I've seen in a long time." The Mavs' spontaneous celebration resulted in some meme material from Dončić, who'd sat out the game to nurse a minor hip strain and responded to Smith's heroics by springing off the bench and flexing in his black sport coat over a white graphic T-shirt with his eyes opened wide and his mouth opened comedically wider.

"I got my tooth knocked out, but I came back in looking pretty as a girl," Smith said with a big smile of his own, showing off the tooth he had temporarily repaired before returning, with more dental work required the next day. "It was just a freak accident. It happens. I came back in the game, finished the game, and we got the win. That's all that matters."

Smith's clutch stop was even more impressive because he was playing with a painful sprained right wrist. The injury soon caused Smith to miss all but one game over a three-week stretch, which didn't exactly come as a disappointment to Carlisle, as it removed the complications from putting Dončić at point guard. The Mavs got a glimpse of that when Smith missed a November 24 home game against the Celtics, an Eastern Conference contender. Dončić appeared perfectly comfortable during a 15-point, eight-assist performance in a win. He also snapped back at Carlisle during a time-out the coach called in response to the rookie's turnover on a daring pass in an otherwise phenomenal first quarter. If you tug at Dončić's leash, be ready for him to bark.

The friction between coach and phenom about creative freedom was a consistent subplot during Dončić's rookie season. Carlisle had earned a reputation as a control freak, having clashed with accomplished veteran point guards Jason Kidd and Rondo about play calling, ultimately relinquishing the reins to Kidd and running Rondo out of town. Some of that type of tension developed between Carlisle and Dončić as well, but their on-court issues were more stylistic disagreements. Dončić, playfully nicknamed "The Matador" by Procopio as a nod to his natural showmanship and Spanish roots (although it also fit his defensive tendencies), enjoyed experimenting with the spectacular, particularly as a passer. It would drive Carlisle crazy if Dončić tried to bank a pass off the backboard in traffic. Carlisle was concerned that Dončić—whose combination of production, panache, and playful joy, at least when things were going well, had created the kind of hype that's rare for a rookie—hunted highlights to please his rapidly expanding base of Instagram followers. Carlisle also hated how often Dončić launched step-back threes, a shot the rookie took more often than anyone other than reigning MVP and scoring leader James Harden.

"He told him right to his face, 'You can stick that step-back up your ass. It only works in 'Muh-laga' and Venice,'" said Procopio, a Boston-bred wiseass whose sense of humor didn't exactly endear him to Carlisle. "He actually pronounced Málaga wrong. I actually thought that was one of Rick's best lines and I used it on Luka no less than 75 times the rest of that season. But he was adamant about it."

Dallas's veterans, who were accustomed to Carlisle's controlling approach, considered Dončić's defiance a source of great comedy. "He may shoot a 30-foot step-back and it may not go in; Coach: 'I don't want to see it anymore!'" Devin Harris said early that season, cracking up. "And he may shoot six more.... And he'll make 'em."

It was fitting that a step-back three—capping a ridiculous, one-man rally to beat Harden's Rockets—served as the signature moment that cranked the Luka hype machine into overdrive. The sense that Dončić was an emerging sensation had already been humming along by that Saturday afternoon on the second December weekend, as evidenced by the Mavericks flying in the Ringer's Isaac Lee and Jason Gallagher to perform their viral tribute song, a hilarious spoof of Leonard Cohen's classic "Hallelujah." During a second-quarter time-out, standing in front of the full-figured male dance squad known as the Mavs ManiAACs, Gallagher played the guitar while Lee crooned.

> *Well I heard there was a wonder boy*
> *That many teams would not employ*
> *But you don't really care for Euros, do ya?*
> *So where would he go? The fourth? The fifth?*
> *Or would he fall and be a Knick?*
> *The baffling Kings took Bagley over Luka*
> *Halleluka, halleluka, halleluka, haleluuuuuuuuuuuuka*

The sellout crowd cracked up throughout the three verses and roared its approval at the song's conclusion. Nowitzki, who was still days away from making his season debut, which was delayed months by a setback suffered playing pickup ball in September, and other Mavs smirked on the bench and gave Dončić some teasing glances. But the timing was a bit awkward, considering that Dončić had been dreadful so far that day, missing seven of his eight shots from the floor.

It didn't get much better for Dončić until he suddenly dominated crunch time. It started with a catch-and-shoot three from the left corner to cut Dallas's deficit to 5 points with 2:50 remaining. He followed that the next possession with a step-back three over Houston center Clint Capela from a few feet beyond the top of the arc. Then Dončić tied the score, driving with P. J. Tucker riding his right hip before bumping the Rockets' burly defensive stopper several feet and putting up a soft floater over Capela, an awe-inducing sequence of strength and skill. The grand finale to Dončić's fireworks display was a spectacular step-back three after Capela switched onto him again.

As coolly as he did in Madrid against Žalgiris Kaunas a couple of years earlier, Dončić dribbled between his legs once, twice, three times while sizing up the big man and then accelerated toward the basket. *Screeeeech!* Dončić slammed on the brakes and reversed direction—displaying the same type of stop-and-start athleticism that made the similarly skilled Harden special—going back between his legs again and gathering the ball. Capela still had a foot in the paint as Dončić rose for a shot that swished through the net, giving the Mavs the lead for good. Dončić, having just gone from off day to orchestrating an 11–0 run in just 111 seconds, pantomimed strumming a guitar while he took a circuitous jog toward the bench during the ensuing time-out. The crowd erupted.

"We were looking at each other like, 'Oh shit!'" Barea said. "Like, 'Wow. Special.'"

"It's pretty clear he's got a flair for the moment," Carlisle said. "He's unafraid. You don't see that every day."

Dončić didn't come across as too impressed with himself afterward, but then again, he rarely gave the media much to work with. He treated his media obligations like most kids his age treated math homework: he'd do the bare minimum, nothing more, not enjoying it one bit. He mentioned that he "wasn't good at all" for most of the game, which was accurate, given that he had more buckets in that 111-second explosion than the rest of the outing combined. "I get confident in the end of games," Dončić said, and he might have shrugged if it didn't require some effort. "I would say that I feel comfortable.... I'm just glad my team believes in me."

That was a massive understatement. The Mavericks didn't just believe in Dončić; they hoped to build around him for a couple of decades to come. It had become clear that he'd be taking the torch from Nowitzki as the (baby) face of the franchise, but that description just scratched the surface of Dončić's potential. He could be a face of the league.

"Perhaps there was an idea that there was a ceiling on him. I don't see it, unfortunately for us," Sacramento coach Dave Joerger said when the Kings came to town the next weekend, comments that were perceived as a pretty transparent jab at his GM Divac. "But he's great for them and he's great for our league."

EVERY MAVERICKS MOVE GOING FORWARD WOULD BE MADE WITH Dončić in mind. Every decision, from play calls to personnel moves, must be viewed through the Dončić prism—a perspective that made a critical call by Carlisle in a late December road loss to the New Orleans Pelicans particularly puzzling.

That was the night that Smith returned after missing 10 of the previous 11 games, an absence that some members of the staff believed was longer than necessary while Nelson shopped Smith around the league. The Mavs had just snapped a six-game losing streak, a skid that coincided with a creaky Nowitzki coming back to play a bit role off the bench, but the buzz about Dončić kept building. Carlisle made a point during his pregame media availability to downplay any issues that might arise with Smith returning to play alongside Dončić.

"In my view, it's a very overanalyzed aspect of our team," Carlisle said, keeping a straight face outside the visitors' locker room at New Orleans's Smoothie King Center. "And people need to get off of it and let these guys play and grow together. That's the right way to approach this."

Dončić proceeded to light up the Pelicans despite being guarded primarily by Jrue Holiday, arguably the best perimeter defender in the game. Crunch time turned into a scoring duel between Dončić and perennial All-Star power forward Anthony Davis, who was a month away from making his trade request. Dončić gave the Mavs the lead with a corner three with 4:33 remaining, created by Smith's drive and dish, and turned to talk a little trash to a chirping fan as the ball splashed through the net. (He loved to listen to the crowd on the road to find a little extra motivational fuel.) Dončić hit a running floater off a pick and roll a couple of minutes later, only for Davis to immediately respond with his sixth bucket of the quarter. Then Dončić, isolated against Holiday on the right wing, dribbled behind his back and launched a deep step-back three to give the Mavs the lead again with 68 seconds to go.

Then things got funky for the Mavs in the final minute. After E'Twaun Moore stripped Dončić from behind near half-court, Davis made an and-one baseline jumper over Jordan to put the Pelicans up two. Dončić drove to the basket, but Holiday got him this time, swatting the ball off the glass. The Mavs got one more chance, still trailing by 2, with four seconds on the clock. The stage was set for Dončić to deliver.

But Dončić barely stepped into the frontcourt and didn't touch the ball on the inbounds play after Carlisle's time-out. He was a decoy. Smith passed the ball in to Jordan and immediately got it back on a dribble handoff that the Pelicans switched. Smith took three dribbles to the right wing and tried to shake Davis with a crossover before driving down the lane. He didn't get his runner off in time, and it bounced off the back rim anyway.

Standing on the Pelicans' half-court logo as the play unfolded, Dončić shot a frustrated look toward Carlisle. When the buzzer sounded, he turned and glared at the bench, his right fist clenched. As the Pelicans celebrated ending a five-game losing streak of their own, Dončić looked away and then glared toward the bench again, shouting an expletive or two. He clearly wanted the ball with the game on the line.

"Yeah, I did," Dončić said after cooling off postgame. "But we had a great look. We have so much talent on this team, anybody can take that shot." Dončić might not have been media savvy, but he knew the ramifications of complaining publicly about a coaching decision and didn't have any interest in going that route. The Mavs had enough messiness without Dončić adding to it with his mouth.

Smith was sidelined again a week and a half later due to an injury, this one of the mythical variety. The official injury report designated Smith with "mid-back tightness," but the truth was that the Mavs put him on the shelf because they were intensifying efforts to trade him, having discussed potential deals with the Knicks, Magic, and Lakers, among other teams. After ESPN reported Dallas's intention to trade Smith, the Mavs removed him from the injury report, but Smith suspiciously called in sick to the next day's practice. "A stomach bug," Carlisle called it.

"We all get into this business knowing that it's dynamic, knowing that trades are possible, knowing that everything's possible," Carlisle said after that practice. "Coaching changes, you name it. It's already a boiling pot of water, and a couple of degrees here or there, big deal. We've all got to come in and be professionals and play and coach, regardless. That's how I view it."

Smith seemed to flaunt his defiance the following day, when he ate lunch out at the vegan restaurant Spiral Diner in the Bishop Arts section of Dallas. He made sure that was known by replying "Nice to meet u my guy!" on Twitter to a fan with the handle @Snackmaster35, who had tweeted about eating lunch next to Smith: "Super nice guy. You Dallas folk, quit trying to run him out of town."

"Dennis is still sick. He will not be here," Carlisle said before that night's home game against the Spurs. He claimed ignorance about Smith's lunch out. Carlisle refused to say whether he had any recent discussions with the point guard, and he cussed out a reporter in his office after the loss for inquiring in the locker room about the coach's strained relationship with Smith.

"Dennis does a lot of great things for us," Dončić said. "He's a great player. I miss him."

Smith didn't join the team on a road trip to Indiana and Milwaukee that weekend, either. However, trade talks stalled, and the sides came to the awkward agreement that Smith would come back when the Mavs returned home. Carlisle informed the team about Smith's looming return and encouraged them to embrace their teammate, as if that had been an issue.

"I get along with my teammates," Smith said after contributing 17 points, eight rebounds, and four assists to help beat the Clippers in his comeback. "The bad-teammate card has never been a thing for me. I love everybody in the locker room, and I feel like it's a mutual feeling."

Dončić described the entire saga as "bad for the team, bad for the player, bad for everybody." But the Mavs managed to come out of it playing well, winning three of four games in a stretch that started with the victory over the Clippers. Smith started and played well, averaging 15.5 points, 6.0 rebounds, and 7.5 assists per game in that span.

The fourth of those games was quite a memorable evening in Madison Square Garden, "The Mecca" of basketball. Nowitzki hadn't announced that he'd be retiring at the end of the season, but fans in road cities where he'd likely be appearing for the final time gave him goodbyes befitting his legendary status. At the Garden, always one of his favorite arenas, Nowitzki responded with his best performance of what had been an extremely difficult season. He had a vintage stretch in the second quarter, scoring 9 points in a span of 2:28 that featured a pair of his famous one-legged fadeaways. He sat out most of the second half, but Nowitzki subbed back in late to satisfy the "We want Dirk!" chants and bid adieu with a couple more buckets. Kristaps Porziņģis, sporting a tailored gray suit with purple stripes while nursing the surgically repaired knee that had sidelined him all season, was among the several Knicks to pay their postgame respects, dapping and chatting up both of the Mavs' star European imports, the teenage sensation and the 40-year-old legend.

Smith's triple-double was a mere footnote, but Carlisle made sure to praise the 13-point, 10-rebound, 15-assist performance. "It means that they can play together, if you ask me," Carlisle said, referring to Smith and Dončić. "I thought Smith's game was fairly exceptional."

Nowitzki signed autographs and posed for pictures with the locker room attendants and other MSG employees, so the Mavs took a bit longer than usual to get to the airport for their flight to Detroit, where they'd play the Pistons in the second game of the back-to-back. Smith awoke from his usual game-day nap in his hotel room the next afternoon and noticed that he had just missed a call from Dorian Finney-Smith, his best friend on the team.

"What's good, bro?" Smith said after calling Finney-Smith back.

"That shit real?" Finney-Smith asked.

"What you talking about?" Smith asked. Finney-Smith replied that there were reports he'd been traded. A notification popped up on Smith's phone at that moment, detailing the deal that would send him to New York as part of a package for Porziņģis and other players.

"Damn," Smith said to his buddy. "I guess it is."

CHAPTER 5

THE ARRIVAL OF THE "UNICORN"

KRISTAPS PORZIŅĢIS AND HIS OLDER BROTHER/AGENT, JĀNIS, HAD a simple message to deliver when they marched into a meeting they requested with Knicks management a week before the 2019 trade deadline. He did not want to be in New York anymore, at least not on that side of the East River, and the Knicks were informed that Porziņģis would not sign a long-term deal with them as a restricted free agent that summer. The Porziņģis brothers requested a trade and provided a list of four preferred destinations that included Brooklyn, Miami, Toronto, and the LA Clippers.

The meeting lasted less than five minutes, and it didn't take much longer than that for the news to leak. The Knicks' relationship with the former fourth overall pick had become increasingly strained during his three-and-a-half-year tenure, so Porziņģis's firm stance didn't come as a surprise. Nor was it much of a disappointment to Knicks management. New York was prepared after general manager Scott Perry and team president Steve Mills spent much of the previous night's game against the Mavericks discussing a deal with Donnie Nelson behind closed doors.

Nelson and Cuban, who watched the game from his regular road seat in the second row of the Mavs' bench, tried to seal the deal with a handshake that night. Perry and Mills asked for more time, and after Porziņģis provided the cover to blame the breakup on him, the proposed New York-Dallas deal got done soon thereafter.

THE "UNICORN," THE NICKNAME BESTOWED ON PORZIŅĠIS BY Kevin Durant due to the 7-foot-3 Latvian's unique blend of size and skill, was headed to Dallas. With Nowitzki soon to exit stage left, the Mavericks had acquired a pair of European phenoms within months of each other. Cuban and Nelson envisioned the Dončić-Porziņģis partnership—or Porziņģis-Dončić, if you preferred—as the foundation of a contender sooner rather than later and for years to come.

"We obviously think Porziņģis is a great young talent, similar in many ways to Dirk," Carlisle said during his regular pregame interview on the team's radio broadcast that night. "This is kind of a Dirk-and-Nash type of situation, only these guys are taller."

The full trade included seven players and a pair of draft picks: Porziņģis, Tim Hardaway Jr., Courtney Lee, and Trey Burke to Dallas for Jordan, Matthews, Smith, and first rounders in 2021 and 2023. The latter pick would be top-10 protected for two years. That detail didn't seem important, though, considering that Dallas anticipated making deep playoff runs by that point. Nelson and Cuban felt like they'd pulled off a coup, swooping in to land a 23-year-old All-Star in a deal that dominated the NBA discussion for several days.

"The trade was less about trying to build a winner versus creating a big splash," Voulgaris said years later. "It made Donnie like the guy around the team. Like, 'Oh, this is what Donnie does!' Nobody even knew about it. Nobody knew about this deal at all. It was a Mark and Donnie thing, and that was it."

The only time Voulgaris was involved in internal discussions about Porziņģis prior to the trade, he recalled, was when he'd submitted a list of potential restricted free agent targets to Cuban weeks beforehand. (Voulgaris reported directly to the owner and rarely communicated with Nelson.) Voulgaris put Porziņģis at the top of the list, due to his talent and the buzz that the Knicks wouldn't match a significant offer for him. Porziņģis and the Knicks had been publicly at odds since his second season, and it was no secret that the Knicks planned to aggressively target big names in free agency.

The Knicks' original trade talks with the Mavericks started on a much smaller scale: a Matthews-for-Hardaway swap. Matthews, 32, didn't fit into Dallas's future plans but had value in the trade market as an $18.6 million expiring salary. The Mavs became especially motivated to move him after he bristled about his role early in the season and Dallas became determined to give Finney-Smith an opportunity as the defensive stopper in the starting lineup. The Knicks needed to dump the contract of Hardaway, who was owed more than $37 million over the next two seasons, to create salary-cap space. Dallas was intrigued by the potential of Hardaway, a gunner who had been an inefficient scorer, playing with an elite passer. This sort of financially motivated deal typically includes a first-round pick going to the team taking on the longer contract.

Dallas had another large expiring salary it was willing to move in Jordan's $22.9 million, as it had become apparent early in the season that the big man's tenure with the Mavs would be temporary. The Knicks were also looking to dump Lee, who was on the books for $12.8 million the next season. The Mavs might have been able to squeeze a pick or two out of the Knicks, who'd be paying to position themselves to pursue two max-salary free agents in a summer when the whispers were that Durant and Irving would be a package deal. "And then it quickly morphed into the KP thing," Voulgaris said.

A couple of days before the Mavs made their annual visit to Madison Square Garden, the Knicks put Porziņģis on the table. Nelson, with Cuban's support, pounced on the opportunity to acquire a star to pair with Dončić, all while keeping the scenario as secretive as possible.

"Mark sent me a message: 'We might have something. I think you'll like it, but I'm stupidstitious. I don't want to tell you about it,'" Voulgaris recalled. "I thought it was just going to be like a small move around the edges, whatever. I didn't think it was going to be a massive deal. And I thought we were getting picks back when we first did the deal, because Mark said there might be a pick or two involved. I was like, 'Oh, great.' I didn't realize we were giving.

"So that was tough. But it's tricky, man. It's tough. This job's not easy. I definitely empathize with someone who is the GM of the team and who's got a very involved owner who is very opinionated, and then he's got other people nipping at his heels for the job."

Voulgaris insists he would have argued against taking such a big swing during Dončić's rookie year: "Why are you mortgaging the future when you don't even know what type of player he is [or] what type of player would fit around him?" he asked rhetorically. However, that opinion would have been in the distinct minority within the organization, where the excitement of pairing two young stars was palpable, even though it wasn't immediately clear when Porziņģis would return from the torn ACL he'd suffered almost 12 months before.

"We're building a championship team here," Carlisle said. "That's obviously a lot of what this deal is all about."

The deal also got an enthusiastic seal of approval from Nowitzki: "I think if you have a chance to add a franchise-caliber player like Porziņģis, you've just got to go for it.... He's got a franchise-type player game. He's a perfect fit for the new NBA. He's mobile enough to play the four, he can be a spread-five, he can roll, block shots, post. Before he got hurt, he played a great all-around game—and he's got the work ethic to be great."

Dončić's public response to the deal didn't exactly drip with exuberance, but that was the norm for his interactions with reporters. "Obviously, it caught me a little by surprise. But he is an amazing player, so we're happy to have him," said Dončić, who tended to use the word "amazing" to describe a lot of people. "And my relationship with Dennis, Wes and DeAndre is going to keep on. They're such amazing guys."

The trade was widely praised by the media and celebrated by fans in Dallas. A sweet-shooting 7-footer (with a few extra inches) wasn't exactly a tough sell in a town that had enjoyed Nowitzki's legendary two-decade tenure. It felt fortuitous that the Mavs had a pair of potential Euro superstars in place as Nowitzki, the greatest NBA player that continent had produced, was in the midst of his probable swan-song season. T-shirts depicting three goats—a large one with Nowitzki's 41 and two babies with Dončić's 77 and Porziņģis's 6— became popular among Mavs fans.

Meanwhile, Knicks management—usually as media averse as any front office in the league—went to great lengths to spin the blockbuster deal that was being panned by the city's tabloids and sports radio shows. The second paragraph in the team's press release announcing the deal was a quote from Perry, the GM, that mentioned "the uncertainty regarding Kristaps' free agent status and his request today to be traded" as a factor in the "trade that we are confident improves the franchise." In a conference call with the media that evening, they continued to point the finger at Porziņģis for forcing their hand.

"Over time it became clear to us Kristaps wasn't completely on board with the plan we had laid out," Mills said. "He's a great player. But this morning in a meeting he confirmed he no longer wanted to be a Knick. It was time to pull the trigger."

Porziņģis responded with a cryptic post on his Instagram stories that night that read: "The truth will come out :)". He took a few more passive-aggressive jabs at the Knicks on social media over the weekend.

The perception was that the Knicks gave up Porziŋġis—a player with the potential to be worthy of the Madison Square Garden marquee—for an underwhelming return. New York's front office felt fortunate to be able to dump so much salary while getting a pair of first-round picks and a 21-year-old recent lottery pick, but they didn't get any benefit of the doubt due to two decades of incompetency under owner James Dolan, especially as the Knicks had bottomed out with the NBA's worst record at the time. That at least was projected to provide 14 percent odds of winning the lottery, where the prize would be Duke's Zion Williamson, a freakish athletic specimen who was the most hyped prospect since LeBron. Dolan had more hope to sell now after the Knicks created about $75 million in cap space, and made a rare radio appearance on ESPN New York's *The Michael Kay Show* to do so.

"New York is the mecca of basketball and we hear from people all the time, from players, from representatives about who wants to come," Dolan said, months before Durant and Irving signed with the crosstown Nets instead. "I can tell you from what we've heard, we're going to have a very successful offseason when it comes to free agents."

Not that Dallas didn't assume some significant risk in the deal. Durability issues were part of the package with Porziŋġis, as the Knicks' in-house MSG Network reminded fans during Smith's New York debut. "Tore ACL Feb. 6, 2018 vs. MIL," and "Played in 186 of possible 296 career games with NY," read a graphic detailing Porziŋġis's tenure with the franchise, along with a mention of the skipped exit meeting with the front office. The Mavs made the deal without knowing when Porziŋġis would return from the ACL injury. The day after the trade, Cuban and the Porziŋġis brothers agreed for him to rehab the remainder of the season, focusing on working on his body and biomechanics while easing back into basketball activity.

"That was the plan from the beginning, and we're sticking to the plan," Porziņģis said during his introductory press conference in Dallas four days after the trade. The Mavs fully committed to the plan by hiring Porziņģis's physiotherapist Manolo Valdivieso, whom he'd been working with since his late teen years playing pro ball in Spain. Valdivieso moved to New York in the fall of 2017 to work full time with Porziņģis, who paid his salary and travel expenses out of his own pocket, which became yet another source of contention between Porziņģis and the Knicks. Cuban and the Mavs, on the other hand, welcomed Valdivieso with open arms, full salary and benefits and a seat on the team plane.

That started a trend of Porziņģis's wishes being granted, part of the recruiting process to persuade him to stay with a team that wasn't included on his list of preferred destinations. Not that Porziņģis really had much leverage, as he was on the last year of his rookie contract before entering restricted free agency, meaning the Mavericks would have the right to match any offer he received. The only route around that would have been to refuse to sign anything in the summer other than a one-year qualifying offer worth $4.5 million, which would have made Porziņģis an unrestricted free agent the following offseason. The Porziņģis camp leaked that possibility as a plausible scenario hours after the trade, but it was a hollow threat considering he'd be sacrificing almost $23 million from his maximum salary in the 2019–20 season, not to mention the security of a long-term deal worth up to $158 million over five years.

The Mavs prioritized making Porziņģis and the people important to him as comfortable and content as possible. Carlisle and Cuban both made a point of publicly acknowledging Jānis, who had feuded with the Knicks' front office, as well as Valdivieso early in the post-trade press conference, when Hardaway, Lee, and Burke politely sat on the dais while reporters peppered Porziņģis with questions. The most pressing question, of course, was whether Porziņģis planned to make a long-term commitment to the Mavs that summer.

Porziņģis stammered for a second when first asked that question, so Cuban stepped in. "I can answer that for you. Yeah, he does," Cuban said.

"There you go," Porziņģis said with a smile. NBC 5's Newy Scruggs, not satisfied with Cuban putting words in Porziņģis's mouth, pressed: "Kristaps, is that true?"

"I can answer that one, too," Cuban said, butting in once again.

"Listen, we're on the same page," Porziņģis said with a laugh. "Don't even ask."

PORZIŅĢIS HAD QUICKLY WARMED UP TO THE IDEA OF A LONG-TERM partnership with Dončić. The two young stars certainly seemed like a fit, on and off the floor. They had similar backgrounds, hailing from Eastern European countries and then going pro as teens in Spain before entering the NBA. They didn't know each other well but were friendly and had mutual respect, dating to their EuroBasket meeting. They also had a close mutual friend in Willy Hernangómez, who was like a big brother to Dončić during his Real Madrid days and Porziņģis's best buddy on the Knicks during the season and a half they spent together. And it was easy to imagine how they might mesh on the court, the pick-and-roll magic an elite young playmaker could make with a remarkably skilled big man who was still approaching his prime.

"I get excited every time I think about it," Porziņģis said. "I really think we can be something special. I think about basketball 24/7, and I really see us being very special on the court and fun to watch, so I'm excited about it."

Carlisle had already compared the duo to a supersized version of the Dirk-Nash combination. But this time, Cuban noted, he wouldn't make the mistake of breaking up this star tandem prematurely.

"Our goal is to keep these two together for the next 20 years," Cuban said. It was a bit of hyperbole, but Cuban made his point:

with Dončić and Porziņģis, the Mavericks had their franchise pillars in place for the foreseeable future.

There ended up being no drama with Porziņģis's restricted free agency, as he agreed to a deal minutes after the Mavericks could officially offer it the evening of June 30. Once again, Cuban gave Porziņģis everything he could possibly ask for. He didn't just get the $158 million maximum contract before playing a single second for the Mavericks. That was the assumed offer when the trade was made, but people around the league wondered whether the Mavericks would fight for injury protection in the contract language. There was precedent set with a superstar who had durability concerns a couple of years earlier, when Joel Embiid's max extension with the Philadelphia 76ers included outs for the team in case of contractually specific catastrophic injuries. Other deals include clauses attached to minutes or games played. Porziņģis's contract was fully guaranteed—and even had a player option for the fifth season.

"That was just like Mark trying to show or Donnie trying to show, 'Oh, we're a class organization. We're going to keep this guy, blah, blah, blah,'" Voulgaris said later. "But he wasn't going to refuse his restricted free agency. He wasn't going to refuse that, not with his injury concerns."

The Mavs made another significant—and surprising—trade before the February 7 trade deadline. Harrison Barnes, who'd led the team in scoring the previous two seasons and was just entering his prime at 26, got shipped to the Sacramento Kings. It was a straight salary dump, with essentially retired Zach Randolph's expiring contract (but not the former All-Star himself) coming to Dallas. The Mavs also got Justin Jackson, taking a flyer on a mid–first round pick still on his rookie deal, but the trade was made to clear the books of Barnes's $25.1 million player option for the next season.

As if that weren't insulting enough, the deal was agreed to midway through the third quarter of the Mavs' home game against the Charlotte Hornets the night before the deadline. After subbing out and taking a seat on the bench, Barnes was informed about the trade by fans who saw the news on Twitter. It was an unfortunate way for Barnes, a model citizen and consummate pro, to have his Dallas tenure end.

"It's crazy," Dončić said that night of the flurry of departures. "I don't like it at all. I don't like it."

He was particularly dismayed that the Mavs, who needed to create a roster spot to complete the deal, waived reserve center Salah Mejri. It was a logical move considering that the big man rarely played, but Mejri was Dončić's best friend on the roster, having looked out for him as a Real Madrid veteran when Dončić was promoted to the Spanish club's top team. They were close enough that on the rare occasions Dončić agreed to do sit-down interviews for TV stations, it was always on the condition that Mejri would also be part of it. "Probably I wouldn't be the player I am now if he wouldn't [have been] here to get me through my first days," Dončić bemoaned. After the formality of waiving Randolph, the Mavs re-signed Mejri days later, primarily to please their young star.

The Barnes deal put Dallas in position to pursue another star in free agency that summer, even after taking on the contracts of Hardaway and Lee. At the time, the Mavs believed they could land Kemba Walker, a high-scoring Charlotte guard who had just been selected as an All-Star for the third straight year but was unlikely to get the major raise he had earned from Michael Jordan's Hornets.

"We like stars and lots of them," Nelson crowed. "Mark is a gunslinger, man. Some things never change. That's why it's really fun to be a part of his posse."

The Mavs paid lip service to pursuing a playoff berth, but if there was any doubt after the Porziņģis deal that they were essentially flipping the page to next season, it was eliminated with Barnes's departure. Dallas was three games below .500 and four games out of the Western Conference's eighth seed. The plan was that it'd be the last time for a long time that the Mavs missed the playoffs.

Voulgaris had been privately pushing Cuban to move on from Barnes, as well as Matthews and Jordan, for much of the season. Voulgaris's vision was to create the flexibility to replace the established veterans with players who would play off of Dončić and enhance the prodigy's brilliance. An argument could be made that Barnes, who had been a high-caliber role player on a championship team with the Golden State Warriors before Durant was recruited to replace him, could have fit well in that plan. Voulgaris doubted it, though. He didn't believe that Barnes could adjust to a complementary role in Dallas after being the Mavs' go-to guy for two years. He wanted role players who had better feel for passing. Plus, Voulgaris pointed out, Carlisle kept calling plays to put the ball in Barnes's hands, the same sets the Mavs ran for Nowitzki for years. So Voulgaris persistently lobbied Cuban to part with Barnes, a difficult sell at first.

"But I think what actually happened, what actually was the impetus for that, what made him do it, was that comment that he made about AAU versus European basketball," Voulgaris said. Cuban had put his foot in his mouth while gushing about Dončić to reporters before a late December road game against the LA Clippers. While raving about Dončić's remarkable basketball intelligence, Cuban made a ridiculous, unnecessary comparison to how elite prospects develop in America.

"When you're gifted like he is and you actually learn the game—if you look at the basketball education of kids starting at 11 years old in Europe, particularly Slovenia, which is basketball-ridiculous versus the United States—if we took our best kids and seven years before they're McDonald's All-Americans sent them over to Slovenia to get an education, the league would be a thousand times better," Cuban said. "They just learn how to play basketball, where our guys learn how to dunk and put together mix tapes. That's a big difference."

Cuban then cracked a joke about sending his 9-year-old son to Slovenia, with the infamous phrase that Fox News host Laura

Ingraham used to belittle LeBron James's social and political commentary serving as the punch line: "'Dad, where you shipping me?' 'Shut up and dribble.'"

It was a silly thing for Cuban to say for several reasons. One was that Dončić left Slovenia for the formative years of his basketball development, which he spent in Spain with Real Madrid. But the factual inaccuracy wasn't the most concerning issue. Cuban's off-the-cuff comments went viral on social media, generating criticism for having racial undertones by being disrespectful of the basketball culture in this country. Cuban offended Black players on the roster, most prominently Barnes, who went public with his displeasure.

"As a statement, I don't agree with it," Barnes said in a statement issued to Marc J. Spears, a veteran NBA reporter for the ESPN site then called *The Undefeated*, which covers the intersection of race, sports, and culture. "As a joke, I don't find it funny. And frankly I think it doesn't reflect what makes the NBA special.

"The great thing about our league is that players come from all over the world. We are raised in every background imaginable and bring unique perspectives because of it. We should celebrate that. We bring those perspectives on each other, on issues in our communities and we aren't afraid to learn from and share those perspectives. That's our strength."

Cuban confronted Barnes before the Mavs' next game, interrupting his individual warm-up session on the Warriors' Oracle Arena court. They engaged in a brief, tense conversation that neither party wanted to discuss with the media. The awkwardness lingered, according to Voulgaris.

"Mark started hanging around the team less, being in the locker room less," Voulgaris said. "He had to apologize to them. At the time, I was like, 'Oh, I was finally able to convince Mark to move off some of these guys,' but I think it was less to do with that and more to do with Mark's standing amongst the veteran players."

In the span of a week, the Mavs had traded every one of their regular starters except for Dončić. The returns of the deals were an All-Star who wouldn't suit up until next season and the hope of making another major addition in free agency. Sure, the Mavs had a history of whiffing with their big swings in free agency, but those occurred during the tail end of Nowitzki's prime and afterward. Now, they could sell the possibility of playing with two young stars.

Dončić, however, wouldn't be an active participant in the recruiting process. Stars wooing their peers often sets up the kind of player movement that shifts power in the league, but Dončić didn't have the relationships that frequently grow in the AAU and summer camp circuits or during Team USA stints. Nor did he have the interest, planning to spend his summer back home in Slovenia, aside from visiting an island off the coast in nearby Croatia. He just wanted to hoop and hang out. He didn't have the expertise to figure out how to put an NBA contender together, nor did he want the stress.

The Mavs paid Dončić to play basketball, and he did his job quite well. He figured it was the front office's job to build the roster. If they wanted to keep him in the loop, fine. But Dončić, unlike a lot of other NBA superstars, didn't care about having input or being involved with personnel moves.

"Luka wasn't really excited about much other than winning games, Fortnite and busting balls," Procopio said. "It was like, yeah, OK, let's go. I just think Luka deals with what's in front of him. I don't think he thinks ahead like that. Like, in a game, he's seven steps ahead. In roster building and things like that, he just [thought], 'Whatever team you give me, I'm going to bust your ass, so whatever. Moe, Larry and Curly or five All-Stars? It doesn't matter. I'm going to destroy you.'"

This was a roster teardown to fast-track the construction of a contender, a plan that seemed feasible because Dončić was so damn good so soon. "If Luka would have taken a more traditional trajectory and gone through your typical rookie season, you may not have seen some of these moves," Nelson said after the trade deadline. "That was definitely a factor with the timing."

Nelson acknowledged that, as high as he was on Dončić before the draft, he didn't anticipate him dominating games as a teen and doing things at his age that were "in a lot of ways unprecedented." It typically takes years to build a true contender around even the brightest prospects. A team hadn't won a title with its best player on a rookie deal since (cue the groans in Dallas) Dwyane Wade's Miami Heat in 2006. The Mavs firmly believed that Dončić could be next if they made the right moves around him.

"Seeing this young man every single day kind of push the envelope, it's exciting, it's inspiring," Nelson said. "It's taken our franchise and really opened up a lot of doors. We're ridin' the Luka wave and the Kristaps wave and trying to surround those guys with the right young core. The future is really, really bright."

CHAPTER 6

DIRK PASSES THE TORCH

A FEW WEEKS REMAINED IN DONČIĆ'S ROOKIE SEASON WHEN HE rubbed the sleep out of his eyes and headed to the team's morning meeting at the St. Regis San Francisco. He arrived a few minutes early and saw Procopio sitting in the hallway, scribbling in a spiral notebook. Dončić's curiosity was piqued, so he asked what Procopio was doing.

Procopio was updating his handwritten rankings of the NBA's best active players. "Let me see," Dončić demanded. He'd had a poor performance the night before in Sacramento, going 4-of-19 from the floor as the Mavericks lost for the 16th time in 19 games since the trade deadline, but Dončić's confidence had not been damaged.

Dončić scanned past the top names—LeBron James, Steph Curry, Kevin Durant, James Harden, Giannis Antetokounmpo—and quickly got annoyed. He shot Procopio a perturbed look after finding "L. Dončić" in the 22nd spot. Procopio had actually just drawn an arrow, indicating that he was moving Dončić up a couple of spots, putting him 20th, between Devin Booker and Kemba Walker and a few spots ahead of his new teammate Porziņģis.

"That's not fuckin' bad," Procopio said a few years later. "He's a rookie—20th best player in the league, and I thought he could probably get higher than that. He got fuckin' pissed, like wouldn't talk to me. 'This guy's better than me? This guy's better than me? Are you fuckin' kidding?!'"

As Nowitzki said many times that season, usually with a wry smile: "Luka is a very confident young man." The Mavs had two priorities for the final two months of the season after all the predeadline wheeling and dealing: lay the foundation for the Dončić-led future and bid a proper farewell to Nowitzki. The storybook tale would have been Dončić soaking up as much wisdom as possible from Nowitzki, the Euro legend twice his age, but that's not quite what happened—at least not that season.

THE ROOKIE SENSATION ENJOYED A FRIENDLY RELATIONSHIP with Nowitzki, but the pupil-mentor dynamic didn't really develop during their brief time together as teammates. Nowitzki was willing, eager even, to play that role, but he didn't want to be pushy or overbearing. He let Dončić know that he was always available and would gladly answer any questions, but Nowitzki wasn't going to force unsolicited advice down the kid's throat, especially as Dončić made the transition to the NBA seem easy.

Their paths from Europe to NBA stardom couldn't have been more different aside from the Dallas connection. Nowitzki played for the Würzburg X-Rays, his hometown team that competed in Germany's second division, before going to the NBA. He struggled mightily most of his rookie year and admits wondering whether he belonged in the NBA, even pondering if he should return to Germany midway through that season. Dončić, on the other hand, won titles and MVPs for one of EuroLeague's most prestigious clubs in

Real Madrid. He had no doubts about whether he could play in the NBA, establishing himself as a star almost instantaneously.

"He is not under my wing because he's not under anyone's wing," Nowitzki said during the 2019 All-Star Weekend, when he served as the honorary coach of Dončić's Rising Stars team. "It is not some guy coming in and being intimidated and figuring things out. He is a really good player who believes in himself and it shows. I want him to do great, but he doesn't need me to hold his hand. It is hard to believe he is 19."

The Mavs would have been ecstatic if Dončić wanted to pick Nowitzki's brain about the extreme commitment to diet and conditioning that allowed the big German to play for 21 seasons and climb to the sixth spot on the NBA's all-time scoring list. That wasn't a topic that at all interested Dončić, whose diet usually consisted of large portions of meat and potatoes, avoiding vegetables altogether.

"It's OK to go to McDonald's, but you don't want to live there," Nelson said. "Those are the things that we're kind of working through, and it's a work in progress." The Mavs did manage to gently persuade Dončić to hire a personal chef to help with his dietary decisions.

Dončić's physique remained a bit puffy even as he lit up the league. As Clippers coach Doc Rivers said, half kidding, in February: "The sky's the limit for him. Wait until he gets in shape."

Dončić's lack of focus in practice aside from scrimmage action frustrated the coaches, but it was tough to complain about that while he put together one of the best rookie seasons in NBA history.

"Hated working out," Procopio said. "Low energy, just didn't want to do it, but you get him in a game and he'll figure shit out." As a rookie, Dončić was required to arrive at the team's facility by 9:00 a.m. on practice days. He would routinely walk in a minute or two before, shout, "Hey, Pro!" across the gym, and flip off Procopio, which was Dončić's playful way of declaring that he was on time but not happy about waking up that early.

The media (and Mavs PR department) also would have loved if Dončić learned from Nowitzki about how to handle being the face of a franchise. Again, Dončić had zero interest. Nowitzki was shy early in his career, when his English was rough, but grew into one of the NBA's great spokesmen—insightful, humorous, and generous with his time well beyond his league-mandated obligations. Dončić wanted to keep media to the bare minimum, and it wasn't because of a language barrier. He spoke English quite well, as many Slovenians do. Dončić also didn't give any extra time to the occasional Slovenian reporter who traveled across the world to cover him. Like everyone else, the Slovenians had to ask Dončić questions in a scrum instead of getting a one-on-one with their countryman. But it's not as if Dončić needed reporters to boost his popularity. He finished second among Western Conference players in the All-Star fan voting, trailing only LeBron James, narrowly missing out on the rare rookie All-Star selection after the votes from coaches and players were tallied. When the Mavs arrived at hotels on the road, even in the early morning hours, there were routinely dozens of fans waiting with the hopes of getting Dončić to scrawl his autograph.

"It's Luka-mania. It's real," Nowitzki said in early January. He had been one of the NBA's best players of his generation but never generated the same buzz as Dončić, a highlight waiting to happen with a much flashier game than Nowitzki's.

It was a difficult season for Nowitzki, who missed the first 26 games, didn't travel with the team much while recovering from his April ankle surgery, and was a shell of himself once he got on the floor. He hobbled through an unofficial retirement tour that he really didn't want, which is why he didn't make his retirement plans official until after the Mavs' final home game. But Nowitzki approached it with his typical humility and humor. He laughed along with everyone else as assistant coach Darrell Armstrong, a former teammate, poked fun at his stiffness by dubbing him "Big Mummy."

Nowitzki knew how much he'd miss the camaraderie of playing on an NBA team, so he especially relished the jokes in the locker room and training room. This was something he had in common with Dončić, who has a big personality, even though he was determined to be as boring as possible with the media. Nowitzki didn't mind being the butt of a bunch of Dončić's jokes, which was the primary way they connected as teammates.

"Every time I mention the past, he's like, 'You're so old, you're so old.' He doesn't listen," Nowitzki said with a chuckle during the Mavs' trip to Miami in late March, a time to reminisce due to the rivalry between Nowitzki's Mavs and retirement-touring Dwyane Wade's Heat. "He's a young man, but he's an old soul, I guess. I don't know. He doesn't want to hear some of my old stories. Porziņģis shows a little more respect towards me than Luka does. Luka is reckless at times."

BAREA WAS PROBABLY THE LONG-TERM MAVS VETERAN WHO HAD the biggest impact on Dončić's rookie season. Dončić formed a quick bond with Barea, an affable Puerto Rico native, often speaking Spanish to each other and listening to rapper Bad Bunny. It might have helped that Barea let Dončić off the hook from carrying a Hello Kitty backpack, a harmless rookie rite of package that Smith followed with a variety of kid-themed bags the previous season. Barea figured Dončić's pro experience and production earned him an exemption. "He's a different rookie," Barea said with a shrug. "He won't follow the rules, but he's cool about it."

Barea also served as an interpreter of sorts for Carlisle and Dončić. Barea, who was in his eighth season playing for Carlisle over two stints in Dallas, had earned the coach's respect enough to tell him if his tone was too harsh or his nitpicking had gone too far. Barea would also boil down Carlisle's pointed criticism to only the essential information for Dončić, encouraging him to focus on how the coach was trying to help instead of the manner in which the messages were delivered.

But Barea ruptured his Achilles tendon in a January 11 road win over the Minnesota Timberwolves, muting the celebration of another spectacular performance by Dončić, who put the finishing touches on a 29-point, eight-rebound, 12-assist night with three buckets in the final 88 seconds, the last one a deep three to put the Mavs up for good. Barea didn't travel the rest of the season as he dove into a challenging rehab process and wasn't a regular at practices or film sessions. Carlisle lost his preferred liaison.

Procopio was the other regular intermediary between Carlisle and Dončić that year, often being asked to sit in on their one-on-one meetings. That was awkward given that Procopio, who uses movie references almost as often as expletives, told people all season that he was "on the green mile" with his contract expiring. But Dončić had a good relationship with Procopio, as did many players, in large part because he was hilarious, barking a relentless barrage of one-liners in his thick Boston accent while running his player development workouts. Procopio, a self-described "short, fat fuck" who stands at 5-foot-7, weighs well north of 200 pounds, and was known around most of the league by the nickname "Sweetchuck," which he got due to his childhood resemblance to a nerdy "Police Academy" character, had a lot in common with the superstar who was a foot taller than him and less than half his age.

"The guy wasn't complicated," said Procopio, whose résumé included working for renowned skills trainer Tim Grover and as Kobe Bryant's volunteer strategic game management coach, aka personal scout. "He loved basketball, loved competing, loved video games and loved eating, and that's a guy I loved. That's a perfect fit, besides the video games!"

Procopio and Dončić had something else in common: they couldn't stand Carlisle. Procopio had a Darth Vader ringtone for Carlisle in his cell phone. He felt like Carlisle picked on him for sport, but that didn't make him unique in the organization. A lot of Mavericks employees often felt intimidated and/or disrespected by Carlisle, from the business cubicles to the locker room.

"When I was there, the only guy he couldn't fuck with was Dirk, and he still fucked with him because Dirk wasn't confrontational like that," Procopio said. "If he thought he could punk you, he'd punk you. That's how he was. He was like a bully from an '80s movie. Remember Chet from fuckin' *Weird Science*? He was like that. He was like Johnny from *Karate Kid*. He was like the guy from *Teen Wolf*. He was all those guys."

Mejri, whom Dončić considered to be somewhat of a big brother, was among those who felt unnecessarily targeted by Carlisle. There was a public glimpse of the Carlisle-Mejri dynamic during a January win over the Wizards the previous season. Mejri, a gregarious guy off the floor who teammates joked morphed into a fiery character they called "The Mej" during game action, got tossed after picking up two quick technical fouls. The second T was an especially quick whistle, and Mejri briefly pleaded his case to Carlisle before leaving the court. The coach's response wasn't sympathetic. "You've got two fucking points, get the fuck out of here!" Carlisle shouted, pointing toward the tunnel to the locker room.

That exchange went viral, and Carlisle quickly realized it was a bad look for him. He made a point after the next day's practice to tell reporters that he had a discussion with Mejri and "apologized to him for behavior that was really emotional, uncalled for and unprofessional on my part." But within the team, the behavior wasn't considered uncharacteristic for Carlisle, who was always demanding and often abrasive. Mejri continued to frequently feel belittled by Carlisle, typically in front of the team, throughout his tenure in Dallas. That, like Carlisle's approach with Smith, planted seeds of discontent with Dončić. "It wasn't really about how Rick treated Luka," a player on that roster said regarding the early tension in that relationship. "Luka hated how Rick treated other people."

However, Dončić didn't enjoy most of his own interactions with Carlisle, either. Carlisle recognized Dončić's potential, as well as the importance of his development to the franchise, and poured himself into pushing the rookie. It's rarely comfortable to be Carlisle's focal point, especially as a young player.

"If you ever saw *Tommy Boy* with Chris Farley, he's trying to explain how to make a sale and why he messes up sales," Procopio said. "He takes a little biscuit and he strangles the biscuit into little pieces. That's what Rick sometimes does with young players, in the sense that he really wants to impress them, really wants to develop that relationship and he strangles it at first."

For the first time in Dončić's life, basketball wasn't much fun. He tried to create joy—finding some in the trick shots before and after practices, the bets on half-court shots, competing and creating against the world's best players in games—but it was hard. He had never dealt with so much losing in his life, and it was painfully obvious by the Mavs' trades that they were basically punting on the rest of the season. "Fuck this tanking shit!" Voulgaris recalled Dončić grumbling at one point, apparently suspicious that the Mavs were attempting to delay payment on the top-five-protected pick they owed the Hawks from the draft-night deal.

Winning wasn't a priority at that point, but that didn't mean Carlisle was willing to let any details slip, especially for Dončić. Carlisle harped on Dončić's shot selection and decision-making, which several people within the organization considered counterproductive micromanaging. "He is Mozart. Why are you telling him how he should be writing a symphony?" Voulgaris said. "Like, let's just figure this out and let's let him learn on the fly." Carlisle also hammered Dončić on issues such as his inattention to detail on defense and effort lapses, trying to prevent him from forming poor habits as the Mavs played out the string of his rookie season.

"Luka took a pounding that year in meetings and film sessions and practice," Procopio said. "To his credit, he got pissed—he was red faced and wasn't happy about it—but he respected elders and coaches. He wasn't Jimmy Chitwood dealing with coaches, but he respected. I thought he would erupt, and he didn't. That ended up changing."

THE CELEBRATION OF NOWITZKI'S CAREER BECAME A WELCOME distraction down the final stretch of the season. While he made a point not to announce his intention to retire, it was widely assumed that this season would be his last. The Mavs all but confirmed that by launching a "41.21.1" marketing campaign in mid-March with a tweet considered cryptic by some, although it was easy to decipher—Nowitzki's jersey number, followed by seasons played, all for one franchise.

The Mavs' home finale against Phoenix on April 9 had to be the most anticipated game ever between lottery-bound teams in the last week of the season. Dončić had sat out four of the previous five games as the Mavs protected him from injury with nothing at stake, but there was no way he would miss this one. He was in the starting lineup alongside Nowitzki, wearing a pair of Nike PG2 player exclusives with customized paint jobs to honor Dirk. Nowitzki's number was painted on both shoes, with "Thank You, DIRK" on the right heel and a portrait of him on the left heel. Nowitzki wore customized Nikes of his own with "LOYALTY" across the right toes, "LEGACY" on the left.

Dončić dished to Nowitzki for a mid-range jumper on the Mavs' first possession of the game, setting the tone for Dallas force-feeding the 40-year-old legend in his final home game, when videos commemorating Nowitzki's career were played during every break. Nowitzki attempted the Mavs' first eight shots of the game and scored their first 10 points, a great way to start a retirement party. He managed to get up 31 shots in 33 minutes, both by far season highs, including the 7-footer's second dunk of the season. Dončić celebrated that moment with the sellout crowd by gleefully hopping up and down with both hands over his head while Nowitzki hung on the rim for a few seconds. Nowitzki finished with 30 points, eclipsing Michael Jordan as the oldest player in NBA history to score that many in a game.

The 120–109 win was essentially an opening act for the planned postgame ceremony. The Mavs surprised Nowitzki by secretly inviting several of his childhood hoops heroes: Charles Barkley, Scottie Pippen, Shawn Kemp, Larry Bird, and fellow German Detlef Schrempf, all of whom made brief speeches. So did Carlisle and Cuban, the latter of whom promised Nowitzki "the most biggest, bad-ass statue ever"—pausing for a roar from the crowd—"and we'll put it right in front of the arena." The microphone was finally passed to Nowitzki, who with misty eyes acknowledged what was apparent: "As you guys might expect, this is my last home game."

Dončić's eighth triple-double of his rookie year—21 points, 16 rebounds, 11 assists—was a mere footnote from that night. That was fine with him, as he was happy to play a part in a night that was all about giving Dirk his due. Nowitzki was an exception in the modern NBA, a legend whose loyalty to a franchise was unwavering, earning a deeper kind of adoration from a city and fan base. Dončić witnessed that, soaking it in, for one final time.

"I wish I could spend more days with Dirk," Dončić said in the locker room. "I wish he would be younger and we could play together. But it was great. This one year was amazing for me, one of my best years. It's just been amazing, being with Dirk."

Dončić sat out Nowitzki's swan song the next night in San Antonio, where the Spurs paid their respects to a longtime in-state rival who had matched up against them in several playoff series. Nowitzki failed to hold back tears as a two-minute pregame tribute video, featuring highlights of many of those matchups against Tim Duncan's Spurs, played on the AT&T Center scoreboard screens. He put the finishing touches on his career by scoring 21 points. His last bucket, a jumper from the top of the key, was tightly contested by center Drew Eubanks despite Spurs coach Gregg Popovich frantically waving him off from the sideline, wanting to give Nowitzki a good look for his goodbye. San Antonio was up double figures, but the score didn't really matter.

Popovich clapped and cheered when Nowitzki's shot rattled in anyway, then called a time-out. That allowed Nowitzki to sub out and receive one last standing ovation. Dončić and Porziņģis, wearing their tailored suits sans ties while watching from the bench, enthusiastically joined in on the applause and the line of hugs for Nowitzki. They were 46 seconds away from the fate of the franchise symbolically becoming their shared responsibility.

"WE'RE LOOKING TO TAKE THIS SITUATION TO A WHOLE DIFFERENT stratosphere," Nelson said after exit interviews the following afternoon. The Mavs believed they could vault into contender status if they made the right offseason moves, confident that Dončić was destined for superstardom. Carlisle raved about Dončić being "the best rookie I've seen since LeBron James, Larry Bird, Magic Johnson and Michael Jordan," and it really wasn't hyperbole. Dončić, who received 98 of 100 first-place votes to easily win Rookie of the Year, averaged 21.2 points, 7.8 rebounds, and 6.0 assists per game. The only other rookie in NBA history to match or exceed those numbers? Oscar Robertson.

"I think the important thing is everyone in this organization now knows he can play basketball," Bill Duffy said of his prized client. "That's no longer a mystery. So now what do we do? We build on top of that and get some players in here and get this thing cranked up."

Dončić's summer plans, at least the ones he was willing to share publicly: "Turn off all my social media. You're not going to find me." He just wanted to head home to Slovenia and relax.

A Mavs contingent—Carlisle, Mosley, and veteran center Dwight

Powell—made an early May visit to Dončić's hometown of Ljubljana. The bond between Mosley and Dončić strengthened during
that trip, a significant step toward Mosley emerging as the star's
most trusted confidant within the organization, which was particularly important with Procopio's prediction of the end of his Mavs
tenure coming true. Dončić looked good during the workouts on
that trip, an encouraging sign that he was taking the conditioning
aspect of his development seriously.

Dončić spent some time in Dallas later that month to work out
at the team facility. A couple of weeks later, Cuban joked that he
"actually saw an ab, so it was a step in the right direction.... There
may have been two. But he's definitely in better shape." Dončić,
back in Europe, replied to *The Dallas Morning News* reporter Brad
Townsend's tweet with Cuban's comments: "6 pack coming soon
@mcuban," using four crying/laughing emojis as punctuation.

Cuban and the Mavs front office had plenty on their own plate
to execute their plan of constructing an instant contender around
Dončić and Porziņģis. Plan A, endorsed by both of Cuban's duel-
ing advisors Nelson and Voulgaris, was signing Kemba Walker to
a max deal worth $141 million over four years. He was eligible for a
supermax deal (five years, $221 million) from Charlotte after mak-
ing third-team All-NBA, but the Hornets had no interest in making
that kind of investment in the star of a team that missed the playoffs
the previous three seasons. So Walker was very much in the free
agency market. The Mavs envisioned Walker, still in his prime at 29,
as a scoring guard who could mesh with Dončić, able to space the
floor but also capable of taking some of the playmaking burden off
of Dončić's broad shoulders.

The Mavs felt good about their odds of landing Walker when
Dončić made another American trip to claim his Rookie of the Year
trophy at the NBA awards ceremony in Santa Barbara, California,
on June 24. That optimism faded quickly and drastically over the
next few days, as intel circulated throughout the league indicating

that the Boston Celtics had emerged as the strong front-runners for Walker. The Mavs knew they were out of the running well in advance of Walker making his commitment to Boston official minutes into free agency. It was a disappointment at the time that ended up being a bullet dodged for Dallas, as knee trouble marred the previously durable Walker's run in Boston, which ended after two years when the Celtics traded him in a salary dump. (Walker did eventually end up in Dallas, playing nine games for the Mavs during the 2022–23 season on a nonguaranteed minimum deal, his last NBA contract.)

The Mavs still made headlines in the opening hours of free agency—aside from Porziŋ́gis formally agreeing to his five-year max deal—but for a bizarre reason. Dallas agreed to be the third team in a sign-and-trade deal that delivered Jimmy Butler to Miami from Philadelphia, but somehow, the parties involved disagreed on what exactly the Mavs had agreed to in the trade. The Heat thought they were sending Goran Dragić to Dallas. That was the 76ers' understanding as well. Same with Duffy, who was also Dragić's agent. It made sense. Dragić wasn't as prolific as Walker, but he was only a year removed from being an All-Star and would have fulfilled the Mavs' wish for a veteran scoring guard who was also comfortable playing off the ball. He had a deep history with Dončić, having known Luka since he was a little kid and serving as his mentor and roommate during Slovenia's EuroBasket title run two years earlier. The Mavs could have taken Dragić's $19.2 million salary on his expiring contract into their cap space, acquiring him without giving up an asset.

Just one little problem: the Mavs refuted reports that they agreed to take Dragić in the deal. There was some dispute about whether that was true or the Mavs had changed their minds, but they were adamant that they believed they were getting forward/center Kelly Olynyk and forward Derrick Jones Jr. from Miami instead, although that combination's salaries weren't high enough for the trade math to work according to the league rules. The trade blew up, salvaged by the Heat and 76ers the next day with a four-team deal that didn't include Dallas.

Such strange scenarios happen when a front office is as disorganized as Dallas's. Cuban ultimately called the shots, as he had since buying the team two decades earlier, and Nelson's influence tended to ebb and flow, a trend that continued with Cuban valuing Voulgaris' voice. Voulgaris believed that Nelson was intentionally excluding him from meetings in the weeks leading up to free agency. "I was like, 'Fuck this, I'm not sitting around here,' so I went to Greece," Voulgaris said. He kept the same hours while overseas despite the different time zones, communicating with Cuban while Nelson handled the vast majority of discussions with agents and other teams, but wasn't in the loop on everything. For example, as the Miami/Philadelphia/Dallas sign-and-trade saga was unfolding, Cuban informed Voulgaris that they expected to sign Grizzlies restricted free agent guard Delon Wright.

"Mark's like a toddler," Voulgaris said, "so if you leave him unattended for a few minutes, you don't know what's going to happen."

The Mavs pivoted to prioritize quality role players, at least one who would be a starter, a strategy that Nelson dubbed "splitting our aces." They had some interest in Patrick Beverley, a pesky defender repped by Duffy, but not enough to compete with the three-year, $40 million deal he got to re-sign with the Clippers. Dallas homed in on Danny Green, a three-and-D wing who was fresh off helping the Raptors win the championship and had also won a ring with the Spurs, as their top target. The Mavs put a three-year, $36 million deal on the table for Green and waited for his decision. Green had no reason to rush, as a lot of business around the league was put on hold while his two-time title teammate Kawhi Leonard pondered whether to return to the Raptors or sign with one of the LA teams. Once Leonard chose the Clippers, who secured the Finals MVP by fulfilling his wish of a blockbuster trade for Paul George, the Lakers swooped in to get Green on a two-year, $30 million deal. The Mavs, like many times in recent years, made for good leverage.

Dallas didn't come out of their summer shopping empty-handed. They added some scoring punch by getting Seth Curry, Steph's little brother who played well for the Mavs in 2016–17, to return to Dallas on a four-year, $32 million deal. They ended up agreeing to a sign-and-trade deal with the Grizzlies, giving up two future second picks for the right to give Wright a three-year, $29 million deal. And they signed Serbian giant Boban Marjanović, a situational, journeyman center beloved by teammates at every stop, to a two-year, $7 million deal.

Those weren't the sort of additions that would vault the Mavs to a different stratosphere, but there were still plenty of positive summer vibes about the franchise's direction. Optimism abounded for a franchise that had landed two young centerpiece talents in the previous year. Plus, Dončić and Porziņģis provided tantalizing glimpses of their summer conditioning work on their Instagram accounts. Porziņģis showed off his beefed-up biceps, resembling Ivan Drago from Rocky. Dončić looked lean.

An Instagram post published by Dončić on August 8 generated the most buzz. He posted three pictures of himself working out with weights in Slovenia, the lead pic featuring him walking on a driveway with heavy weights and that electric blue Porsche Panamera in the background. He was svelte. If he lit up the league while a bit pudgy, what would this version of Dončić do? His teammate Courtney Lee summed up the consensus take with his contribution in the comments: "Skinny luka bout to be a problem."

CHAPTER 7

A BAD MOTHAFUCKA

LeBron James approached Dončić in the middle of the court at the American Airlines Center, offering the customary NBA postgame dap-and-wrap seconds after the final buzzer sounded at the end of a spectacular duel between the longtime face of the league and his potential successor. It was just more than a year earlier that Dončić had waited outside the home locker room at the Staples Center following their first meeting to get an autographed jersey from James, his favorite NBA player as a kid who consumed the far-away league via highlights. Dončić saw James walking his way and appreciatively took a few steps toward his foe.

It was November 1, 2019, the fifth game of the season for both teams, and the Lakers' 119–110 overtime win was every bit as entertaining as had been anticipated when it was scheduled as a prime-time ESPN matchup. James, still the league's premier superstar in his 17th season, dominated with 39 points, 12 rebounds, and 16 assists. Dončić, who at 20 was not even old enough to buy a beer in America yet, was almost as awesome with 31 points, 13 rebounds, and 15 assists.

They briefly embraced, big smiles on each of their faces, as they were surrounded by photographers and cameramen, one of whom was broadcasting live on ESPN. As a national audience eaves-dropped, James concluded the quick conversation by telling Dončić: "Keep going. You a fuckin' bad mothafucka."

"Thank you!" Dončić replied as he giddily glanced back at James after making eye contact with another approaching Laker. He had essentially just been anointed by King James, accepted as his peer among the NBA's elite.

"That was just some crazy stuff for me," Dončić said later in the locker room. "I've been following him—he was my idol since the beginning. Now I can play against him, play a game like that. The words he said after the game were just something real special for me."

Anthony Davis, fresh off successfully forcing a trade to the Lakers following a monthslong standoff with Pelicans management, put on a pretty good show that night, too. He had 31 points, 14 coming during the fourth quarter and overtime as Davis served as a strong Robin to James's Batman. Porziņģis, on the other hand, faded into the game's background. He finished with 16 points, only 4 of which were scored after halftime, with none in the overtime period.

Dončić starring while Porziņģis struggled to meet expectations—his own, much less the fan base's—became the early theme of the Mavs' season. Porziņģis had practiced with the Mavs in the final weeks of the previous season, but he was chipping off the rust of a 20-month layoff from game action while adapting to a new system. But the most difficult challenge for Porziņģis was adjusting to being a distant second in Dallas's pecking order. Porziņģis believed he'd be half of a superstar duo for the Mavs, anticipating a 1A, 1B situation. It quickly became apparent, beyond a shadow of a doubt, that the Mavs were Dončić's team. "I wouldn't trade him for anybody in the league," Carlisle declared on media day before the beginning of training camp.

Carlisle had realized that everything the Mavs did for the foreseeable future should (and would) revolve around Dončić, giving a player with 72 games of NBA experience the most power in the organization, whether or not he wanted to wield it. The coach lavished Luka with praise publicly and lightened up on him privately, letting Dončić's lapses slide in practices and film sessions, in an attempt to repair their relationship. Carlisle also excused Dončić's frequent arguing with referees, even when the emotional outbursts went too far, and emphasized lobbying refs on his temperamental star's behalf. And Carlisle handed Dončić the reins of the offense, giving him creative freedom even when it meant the coach had to bite his lip to avoid barking at the superstar for hunting highlights. "I like to be an entertainer. Sometimes it's good to be, sometimes it's too much," Dončić admitted.

"Guys like Dončić, Bird, Jason Kidd, Magic Johnson—sometimes they get bored and they want to get into a creative state and do some things to kind of break up the monotony," Carlisle said. "But the important thing is to understand that there's a time and place for everything. The most important thing is not to compromise your opportunity to win. I give him the trust to figure those things out. Special players need to be trusted. You have to." Carlisle paused, then repeated himself for emphasis, or perhaps to make himself believe it: "You have to."

Carlisle had only ceded offensive control like that once before in his coaching career, empowering Kidd after some friction over play-calling in the early stages of their relationship. At that point, Kidd had already ranked second all-time in assists, a pure distributor who sought autonomy in the strategic aspects of setting up his teammates. Dončić was a brilliant passer in his own right but ball dominant, and the decision to hand him the keys was based on a relatively small sample size of production and a ton of potential.

"Luka gets to blossom more," Cuban said days into the season. "He can see the court and makes everyone else better, so we don't have to call plays as much. In terms of Rick and Luka, teams go through cycles. We're in a different part of our cycle now. The team grows up. The coach grows up. The coach's relationship and what they expect from players all changes. That's part of the process. As Luka demonstrates not just that he makes things happen but he can make everyone else better, why would Rick jump in? Because that's the ultimate player."

That made Porziņģis the highly paid headliner of Dončić's supporting cast. Carlisle, with some significant input from Voulgaris and offensive coordinator Stephen Silas, decided that Dallas would employ a five-out offensive system to open up the floor for Dončić to operate. So Porziņģis, playing his preferred position of power forward, spent a lot of possessions spacing the floor as a spot-up threat on the weak side while Dončić played pick and roll with the center as his partner. Porziņģis had to be weaned off the steady diet of post-ups and mid-range jumpers from his All-Star season in New York, when he averaged 22.7 points per game on mediocre efficiency for a losing team.

Remember the Dirk-and-Nash comparison Carlisle made after the Porziņģis trade? Carlisle regretted it. The large Nowitzki section of the playbook, borrowed by Barnes for a while, was definitely not getting passed down to Porziņģis.

"The first conversation I had with Rick was, 'Hey listen, we don't really want you to be in the post that much. We want you to shoot from outside,'" Porziņģis recalled. "I was like, 'OK, but that's a big part of my game. You're kind of taking it away from me.'"

Porziņģis wasn't pleased. He was savvy enough to understand that he couldn't make a media fuss about it, knowing he'd already been labeled a malcontent after his messy divorce with the Knicks months earlier. However, there were moments that Porziņģis couldn't mask his discontent on the court. And it didn't take long to manifest.

A prime example occurred during the Mavs' preseason finale.

After setting a screen for Dončić near the top of the arc, Porziņģis took a couple of steps toward the free throw line and pivoted to seal Kawhi Leonard, who had switched onto him. Porziņģis made eye contact with his point guard and reached out with his right hand, asking for the rock. He wanted to go to work, just like Dirk had done from that area of the floor so many times over the years.

But Dončić kept dribbling, slowly shuffling out to the right wing. He wasn't going to give up the ball, which he bounced a couple of times with his left hand while waiting for Porziņģis to get out of the way. Dončić took a step back and a couple more dribbles, waving off Porziņģis with his right hand, pointing to the area on the opposite side of the floor where he wanted his supposed co-star to relocate. Porziņģis got the message after a few awkward seconds, shooting a look toward Carlisle on the sideline as he walked out to the left wing with his back to the action before turning around and spectating. Dončić, who took a total of 15 dribbles and was the only player to touch the ball on the possession, drove into the teeth of the Clippers' defense and committed a turnover after colliding with LA center Ivica Zubac in the paint. Preseason results are meaningless, but the moment raised antennas in the organization about the on-court rapport of the two young franchise cornerstones.

As Dončić DAZZLED, BOLTING OUT OF THE GATES WITH TRIPLE-doubles in half of the Mavs' first 14 games, Porziņģis frequently felt left out and frustrated. They attempted to create chemistry between them, or at least the appearance of it, smiling and joking through three-point competitions during the media access periods at the end of practices. But their lack of productive communication—along with the occasional bad body language, words muttered under their breath, and side-eye exchanges—became a concern within the team.

"We were bumping heads, especially early on," Porziņģis said a couple of years later. "Then I kind of felt like, 'Man, I can't keep doing this because it's not helping me.' And nobody else would say anything. Some people tried to talk to me, like, 'Hey, go talk to him.' [I thought] he will understand at some point. It's not my job to, like, try to get everybody on the same page. I already have enough to worry about myself—my game, what I'm doing."

But it was impossible to make a decent case that Dončić didn't deserve to have the ball in his hands as often as possible. He was absolutely dominant, taking the massive step from Rookie of the Year runaway winner to early MVP favorite. Dončić won the Western Conference's Player of the Month after averaging 30.8 points, 9.9 rebounds, and 9.6 assists in the first 18 games of the season, leading Dallas to a 12–6 record while the Mavs' offense hummed along as the most efficient ever in the NBA.

"This guy can do anything he wants to on a basketball court," Carlisle said after Dončić had 42 points, 11 rebounds, and 12 assists in a November 18 win over the Spurs, joining LeBron as the only players ever to record a 40-point triple-double before turning 21. "And you know, he's having just one of those magical runs right now, and it's a phenomenal thing to watch. It's a phenomenal thing to be a part of. His teammates, we're all just kind of along for the ride."

Dončić stuffed the box score even on his occasional off nights. That triple-double against the Lakers started a streak of 20 consecutive 20–5–5 nights for Dončić, breaking Michael Jordan's record for the longest such run in NBA history. The only downside for Dončić was he didn't like being asked about putting up such ridiculous numbers.

"I mean, it's a lot of stats going on. I think it's a little bit too much stats, you know," he said sheepishly, not wanting to come across as arrogant. "You can't compare nobody to Michael Jordan. He's one of a kind. Those are just stats."

Meanwhile, Porziņģis struggled to establish any sort of rhythm. Carlisle attempted to ease the pressure for Porziņģis—not an easy task for a 7-foot-3 man nicknamed "Unicorn" who had a freshly inked max contract—by noting that Celtics forward Gordon Hayward needed a full season, sandwiched by two summers and training camps, to regain his form after coming back from a serious leg injury.

"Look, I'm not saying it's going to take that long for KP," Carlisle said when the Knicks and New York media horde visited Dallas on November 8. "But what I am saying is that we all have to manage expectations about this. He's got to do the same, which is not easy."

But rust wasn't the biggest problem for Porziņģis. He was uncomfortable playing an offensive role that was much more restricted than he anticipated, and he was disappointed and discouraged by his inconsistency.

Porziņģis's first game against his former franchise was somewhat of a personal bright spot, despite the Mavs managing to lose to a New York team that arrived at the American Airlines Center with a 1–7 record. Porziņģis had 28 points on 11-of-22 shooting, although he went scoreless in the final 10 minutes and fouled out with 30 seconds remaining. (Dončić missed a potential tying step-back three that he attempted with a foot on the Mavs' half-court logo with 18 seconds remaining. He criticized himself postgame for "a bad decision," while Carlisle reiterated how much he trusts Dončić in those situations.)

Carlisle praised Porziņģis postgame, reinforcing some talking points from their private conversations in the prior days: "He really just moved and played within the system and allowed the game to come to him. When a player like him does that with a guy like Dončić on the floor, really good things are going to happen for him."

Porziņģis admitted he'd been "overthinking a little bit." He described his refreshed approach as, "Be aggressive, but be relaxed." This felt like progress.

"The guy is a bona fide superstar!" Cuban gushed pregame a few nights later in Boston. "He's putting up ungodly numbers and he's still rusty. Can you imagine where he's going to get to?"

Well, Porziņģis got to a spot on the bench for the final nine minutes of that night's loss to the Celtics. Carlisle attributed that decision to a "tough night" for Porziņģis, who finished with 4 points on 1-of-11 shooting. "Of course I want to be out there, but can't blame him," Porziņģis said, but he also acknowledged frustration with how he was—or wasn't—being utilized.

"Sometimes I'm not going to get the ball as much as I'd like to, and that leads to me maybe forcing some things and so on," Porziņģis said. "It's a work in progress. I know Coach is trying to do the best job he can to get me the ball in the offense and utilize my skills, and I also got to do a better job of making sure I'm effective in those situations."

By the standards of Dončić's typical approach with the media, he was quite talkative on the topic of Porziņģis's poor performance, making a point to publicly support his teammate after a low point. "This happens to great players. They have bad nights," Dončić said. "I think the next game he's going to have at least 30 points. He keeps working. He just came back from injury. These things are normal. We all believe in him."

The harsh truth was that opposing defense's best hope of defending Dončić at that point was for Porziņģis to also be on the floor. Porziņģis was frequently guilty of forcing bad shots, especially after not touching the ball for several possessions. He cluttered the Mavs' flow and spacing by going away from the game plan and calling for post-ups. The loss in Boston dropped Dallas to 6–4; in that 10-game stretch, the Mavs scored 123.9 points per 100 possessions when Dončić played without Porziņģis, but only 102.3 with Porziņģis in the game. That was the difference between an offense that would have been the most efficient the NBA had ever seen—by a margin of several points—and one that would have ranked dead last in the league that season. "It humbled me a little bit," Porziņģis said a few weeks later.

Massaging Porziņģis's ego became an organizational priority again, but it was done within the context of persuading him to embrace the role envisioned for him. That wasn't easy, considering Porziņģis's scoring average was down several points from his All-Star season in New York while his field goal percentage was poor, hovering around 40 percent. He was cajoled to be patient about his offensive production and pour himself into doing the dirty work, stuff like rebounding and playing great help defense, things that help a team win but don't land a player any endorsement deals or All-Star votes. Cuban and Carlisle, in particular, emphasized praising Porziņģis for playing hard and contributing in less obvious ways than lighting up the scoreboard like Dončić, as Dallas got on a roll while riding Luka's cape.

"I think the most underappreciated change has been KP," Cuban said during that stretch, when the Mavs sandwiched a loss to the Clippers with a couple of five-game winning streaks. "I don't think there has ever been a max-out player like that who has changed his game to fit what's needed for the team as quickly as KP has."

Nobody had to work very hard to hype Dončić as he put up MVP-caliber numbers in wildly entertaining fashion, leading to a bidding war among shoe companies for the NBA's most high-profile sneaker free agent, whose Nike deal signed in Spain had expired. It took some effort to spread the credit for Dallas's success to Porziņģis. For example, after Dončić finished a rebound shy of a 42-point triple-double in a November 29 win over the Suns, Carlisle raved about Porziņģis being "spectacular," despite scoring only 2 points and missing all eight of his shots from the floor. But Porziņģis's 13 rebounds and three blocks in that win served as proof that he was buying in. He was averaging more than nine rebounds per game—a couple more than his best season for the Knicks—and the advanced stats ranked him among the league's most effective rim protectors.

"I'm looking for opportunities for how I can play better, now that I'm not shooting the ball as much and maybe not as involved in the offense," Porziņģis said. "Throughout my career, a lot of times maybe my energy was based on if I score or not, and that leads to everything else. Now, it's not that I've changed my mindset. I'm still a scorer, but if it's not going in and things aren't going my way offensively, I'm still there for the rest of the other stuff. That's a big change for me."

No, Porziņģis still didn't like his offensive role, but he wasn't pushing against it anymore. He had accepted that he'd play second fiddle to Dončić, who had elevated to a stratosphere that was beyond Porziņģis's wildest imagination. Porziņģis recognized that he'd have to adjust to playing with Dončić, not vice versa.

"I didn't expect—nobody expected—Luka to be hooping like *this*," Porziņģis said after an early December win over the Timberwolves. "Luka runs the show. He's been playing incredibly effective. I'm there to support him in any way I can—stretching the floor or whatever so he can do his thing. Now, I feel like he's getting a better feel for me also—when to feed me a little bit, when to get me the ball and run some plays for me. I think it's going in the right direction."

THE SUPERSTAR-SIDEKICK DYNAMIC HAD BEEN DETERMINED AND wasn't subject to change. It would still require maintenance, such as some minor tweaks that Carlisle made in consultation with Dončić to get Porziņģis more touches. It helped to have vets like Barea and Lee, who had good relationships with both Dončić and Porziņģis and nudged them into bonding by playing cards on the team plane and taking part in group dinners, but there might still be some bumps in the road.

"We've got a group of guys that are still at the stages of their career where they're trying to establish themselves," Carlisle said in his office after the win over the Timberwolves. "No matter what I say or anybody on the coaching staff says, these guys are going to have to go through certain growth stages on their own. Look, it's not a big problem, but there's an awareness. And it's getting better and better."

The Mavs had as much sizzle as any team in the league when they arrived in Mexico City for a December 12 game against the Detroit Pistons, one of those regular-season matchups the NBA schedules abroad to market the game internationally. The early awkwardness between Dončić and Porziņģis had seemingly dissipated, glimpses of synergy replacing the side-eye moments. It was sort of fitting that the Mavs made a trip to Mexico, given that one way Dončić and Porziņģis bonded was by speaking to each other in Spanish, the language they learned as prized teen prospects. They also took comfort that they could speak it on the court without others understanding, allowing them to openly discuss strategy, among other things. (When asked who they wouldn't want to understand their conversations, Porziņģis said with a grin, "The opposite teams. Sometimes the coach.")

Dončić showed off his flawless Spanish during a brief, enthusiastic pregame speech at mid-court, charming the crowd of 20,064 at Arena Ciudad de México. It consisted mainly of pleasantries, and Dončić drew a roar by concluding with "¡Viva México, güey!"— rough translation: Long live Mexico, dude. With that, Dončić handed the microphone to Pistons forward Blake Griffin, who laughed at having such a tough act to follow. "Hola, Mexico," Griffin said, smirking as the crowd laughed.

The Pistons were just as overmatched against Dončić after tip-off. He picked apart the Pistons with flair, putting on a show for an arena packed with people who had never before seen an NBA game. His prettiest highlights from a 41-point, 12-rebound, 11-assist performance—his second 40-point triple-double and the third ever by a player younger than 21—were a pair of passes to Porziņġis that displayed the feel the duo was developing. They were both lobs for dunks, coming off well-timed cuts from the corner by Porziņġis, taking advantage of Dončić driving into the teeth of the defense and drawing a few defenders before flipping a pass up high for his 7-foot-3 teammate to finish.

"I think we're getting better and better every day," Dončić said that night, when five of his assists fed Porziņġis, who finished with 20 points. "He's going to get better. I'm going to get better. And with us two, the team is going to get way better."

The Mavs were already pretty damn good, sitting at 17–7 almost a third of the way into the season. It was premature to declare that Dallas was a legitimate contender, but the Mavs had provided plenty of reason to believe it was a possibility, despite failing to fulfill their ambitious free agency plans. They were in third place in the Western Conference standings, behind only the Lakers and Clippers, teams that had formed proven superstar partnerships over the summer.

Ninety seconds into the next game, Dončić stepped on Heat guard Kendrick Nunn's foot while driving to the basket. His right ankle rolled over so violently that Dončić's sock above his Jordan Jumpman Diamond low-tops touched the hardwood. He hobbled to the baseline and sat down on the concrete behind the courtside seats, grabbing the high ankle area in excruciating pain. The American Airlines Center crowd sat in hushed shock, fearful that the phenom might have suffered a serious injury. A negative X-ray result minutes later provided some relief, but the ankle sprain would sideline Dončić for a stretch.

The timing was especially unfortunate for a couple of reasons. Dončić was on the verge of finalizing a lucrative endorsement deal with the Jordan Brand that would eventually include a signature shoe, one of the premier perks of superstardom. And the Mavericks had just begun one of the most difficult parts of their schedule, a five-game gauntlet through a series of Eastern Conference contenders, including three games on the road. Suddenly, Dallas needed Porziņģis to play a starring role, at least temporarily, although he downplayed the need to make drastic alterations without Dončić.

"We want to keep this offensive system going," Porziņģis said after the loss to the Heat on the night Dončić went down. "I don't want to, just because I want to get my own buckets, mess up the spacing and things like that. So we'll keep doing what we're doing."

The Mavs managed to split the four games that Dončić missed, getting a pair of tough road wins in large part because Porziņģis rose to the challenge, while Jalen Brunson capably filled in as the starting point guard. Porziņģis had 26 points, 12 rebounds, and two assists in Milwaukee as the Mavs snapped the Bucks' 18-game winning streak. He had 22 points, 18 rebounds, and three blocks to lead the Mavs to a win in Philadelphia. As much as the Mavs needed Porziņģis's star turn, there were quietly some worries about how it might impact the reprogramming of his game that had required so much care over the previous few months.

Dončić returned the night after Christmas, 12 days after he sprained his ankle, for a nationally televised home game against the Spurs. Porziņģis started slow, missing his first six shots from the floor, when TNT color commentator Chris Webber had apparently seen enough.

"As a great player, this is where Porziņģis needs to make himself known," Webber told the TNT audience early in the second quarter. "You can't be 7-foot and just stand behind the three-point line. If you're the man on your team, you must demand the ball and get going to work."

Webber, a five-time All-Star as a power forward/center during his playing career, harped on that point for the remainder of the game. He had plenty of opportunity, as Porziņģis had an off shooting night, going 4-of-15 from the floor with more than half his attempts coming from three-point range. But it was, frankly, lazy analysis. First of all, Porziņģis was definitely not "the man" on Dončić's team in Dallas. Second of all, the Mavs had the league's top-rated offense despite Porziņģis's inefficiency on post-ups. At the time, he was averaging 0.54 points per possession on post-ups, according to numbers that were readily available to anyone who took the time to log on to the NBA's advanced stats website. Dumping the ball to Porziņģis on the block was one of the worst ways for the Mavs to use a possession, especially if Dončić was on the floor. But that didn't stop Charles Barkley and Shaquille O'Neal, who made the Hall of Fame by bullying defenders on the block, from wholeheartedly agreeing with Webber during TNT's halftime show.

Carlisle, who had put so much effort into getting Porziņģis to accept and adapt to the Mavs' system, couldn't afford to allow this narrative to gain steam. So Carlisle pounced after the Mavs' 102–98 win when he was asked about the TNT broadcast's lobbying for Porziņģis to post up.

"The post-up's not a good play anymore," Carlisle said, starting a soliloquy on the subject that lasted almost three minutes. "It's not a good play. It's not a good play for a 7-3 guy. It's a low-value situation."

Carlisle pointed out that the Mavs' internal advanced statistics showed that Dallas was a "historically good offensive team" and when any of their players posted up, the efficiency "diminished exponentially." He acknowledged, "It's counterintuitive. I understand that, but it's a fact.... We've gotta realize that this game has changed."

Carlisle took some pretty significant liberties by declaring that Porziņģis, shooting 33.5 percent from three-point range for the season at that point, was "a historically great all-time three-point shooter with unbelievable efficiency." But you couldn't blame Carlisle for sprinkling some sugar on Porziņģis, whom he also praised for attacking closeouts for dunks and improving his reads on drives.

He specifically pointed out a lob Porziņģis tossed to Dwight Powell in the second quarter. "I mean, that's pretty fucking cool if you ask me," Carlisle said. He was presenting a case as if he was getting Porziņģis's back, but Carlisle was really defending his offensive system. Which was a pretty ridiculous position for him to have to take, considering that system aided a 20-year-old's emergence into an MVP candidate for the best offensive team in the league.

"Look, we gotta get off this thing," Carlisle said. "We gotta treat KP with some respect. He's a historically great player, and quit criticizing him because he's 7-3. That's what everybody's doing. I don't care who it is. I don't care if it's people on TV or anybody else."

Perhaps Porziņģis agreed with Webber's premise, as Barkley and O'Neal did. He certainly entered the season with that line of thinking. But the Mavs had been rolling, and he wasn't going to rock the boat now.

"Obviously, I'm always looking to score and I want to be aggressive, but I want to do what's best for the team," Porziņģis said, minutes after Carlisle's passionate anti-post-up speech went viral. "And if that's the way we're effective and we're good on offense, I'm with it. If we're winning, I'm with it. Imagine we're No. 1 [-ranked offense] with me shooting, what, 40 percent? Something like that from the field. So once I become more efficient with my own shots and my own stuff, then those numbers will go up even more as a team. So as long as we're winning, we'll stick to it and I'll do what's right."

A reporter in the scrum around Porziņģis's locker began asking a question about Dončić's return, but Porziņģis politely interrupted. He sensed that his last comment could be perceived as passive-aggressive and wanted to make it clear that he had no controversial intent.

"That sounded a little bit off, what I said at the end," Porziņģis said. "But you know what I mean. I'm willing to do whatever it takes to win. That's what I want to say. I'm with whatever Coach wants us to do."

This had been a masterful coaching job by Carlisle and his staff. They installed an offensive system that empowered their prodigious talent and produced unprecedented success. Mosley, who ran Porziņģis's individual workouts and eventually took over that role with Dončić, handled much of the psychological challenges with Porziņģis and managed any tension between the two with assists from Barea and Lee. The Mavs had a lot of momentum but still plenty of room for improvement, particularly from Porziņģis.

Then Porziņģis pushed the pause button. He was a late scratch for the New Year's Eve game in Oklahoma City, pulling himself from the starting lineup minutes before tip-off due to soreness in his right knee. That had been considered his "good" knee, meaning it wasn't the one with the surgically repaired ACL. He ended up sitting out 10 straight games, getting a platelet-rich plasma injection during his absence to help alleviate the pain and stiffness.

Porziņģis was rusty upon his return, going 4-of-17 from the floor in a 110–107 home loss to the Clippers on January 21. "If I played just a little bit better, we would have won the game," Porziņģis said. "This loss is on me. That's how I feel." But the loss isn't why it felt so glum in the Mavs' locker room that night. Powell's Achilles tendon had popped when he tried to drive to the basket in the first quarter. Dallas's starting center—and Dončić's favorite pick-and-roll partner—was done for the season.

As a result, Porziņģis's role changed significantly. Carlisle responded to the loss of Powell by shifting Porziņģis from power forward to center. It wasn't that much of a difference defensively, as Porziņģis often guarded centers so he could protect the paint, but it was a drastic adjustment offensively. This ended up being a silver lining for Porziņģis, featuring him much more often in the primary actions, usually pick and roll or pick and pop with Dončić, instead of serving as a floor spacer on the weak side. It might take some time, but the Mavs had a little less than half the season remaining to prepare for the playoffs.

A week later, however, Dončić went down in a scrimmage as practice was winding down. He rolled that right ankle again, even worse this time. The Mavs were about to embark on one of the busiest stretches of the schedule with six games in the next nine nights, and Dončić was ruled out for all six.

Dončić ended up missing seven games, and the Mavs slipped to seventh in the competitive Western Conference standings after going 3–4 in his absence. Once again, however, Porziņģis starred without Dončić. Porziņģis averaged 28.8 points in the five games he played during that span, sitting out the other two because he rested on back-to-backs as a precaution due to his sore knee. This time, though, Porziņģis kept cooking after Dončić returned. The duo combined for 60 points, 25 rebounds, and 13 assists in a blowout over the Kings before the break, when Dončić made his first All-Star Game appearance and Porziņģis took a beach vacation. They resumed with a 57–20–13 combined line in a rout of the Magic.

The Mavs seemed far past the pressing issues of Porziņģis's fit and friction with Dončić from earlier in the season. There was a togetherness about the team, which partied hard to celebrate Dončić's 21st birthday when the NBA schedule-makers gave him the gift of a game in Miami. The celebration started with a postgame dinner at South Beach's Papi Steak and continued well into the wee hours of the morning at Liv, the club that hosted the Mavs' championship party nine years earlier. Dončić missed the next game—officially due to a sprained left thumb that only sidelined him once—but Porziņģis picked up the slack with 38 points, 13 rebounds, four assists, and five blocks in a road rout of the Timberwolves.

This was still Dončić's team, but his days as the Mavs' lone star had seemingly ended. The "Unicorn" had arrived. This was the version of Porziņģis the Mavs hoped they would get when they made the trade with the Knicks, which seemed like a steal at this point, particularly with Tim Hardaway Jr. establishing himself as an effective third scoring option who feasted on open threes created by Dončić. Porziņģis was playing the best basketball of his career, averaging an efficient 27.7 points, 11.0 rebounds, and 2.4 blocks over a six-week span.

"Everyone's caught up in the offensive stats, but for me, it's a combination of his offensive production and what he's doing defensively and rebounding," Carlisle said after another dominant all-around performance by Porziņģis in a March 6 win over the Grizzlies. "It's ridiculous."

"It took me a little bit of time to figure some things out and feel really comfortable out there," Porziņģis said that night. "Now, it feels natural. It feels organic. It feels just in the rhythm of the game. I know where my shots are going to come from and when I can be aggressive. It feels much more just simple and natural. I'm in a good rhythm now and want to keep that going."

Five nights later, in early March 2020, the brakes were slammed on the whole league—and the whole country—as the coronavirus pandemic hit America. As the Mavs were playing the Nuggets in Dallas, news broke that Utah Jazz center Rudy Gobert had tested positive for COVID-19, prompting commissioner Adam Silver to suspend the NBA season "until further notice." In a surreal scene, the Mavs played out the win over the Nuggets as fans in the packed American Airlines Center gawked at their smartphones in shock, just as Cuban did while seeing the news for the first time early in the third quarter, a moment captured live by an ESPN camera.

"This is crazy. This can't be true," Cuban said on the ESPN broadcast early in the fourth quarter. "I mean, it's not within the realm of possibilities. It seemed more like out of a movie than reality."

CHAPTER 8

BUBBLE BLISS

Most of the Mavericks' bags were still packed in their rooms at the Grand Floridian, the Walt Disney World resort that would be their home for their stay in the NBA bubble, when the social-distancing dance party started the afternoon of July 9. It was a goofy, made-for-Instagram moment (posted by Maxi Kleber) to break up the monotony of a mandatory two-day quarantine, but the fun was genuine.

As techno music thumped, the camera started out on Kleber, who was wearing a pair of white headphones, bopping to the beat and pretending to play DJ with water bottles and Styrofoam cups on the balcony outside his room. Then it panned to Dwight Powell, unable to play but in the bubble to rehab and provide moral support, waving a white towel and hyping up the imaginary crowd below. To Kleber's right, Dorian Finney-Smith, a hilariously mustachioed J. J. Barea, and Luka Dončić danced in a row on balconies of their own, making believe that they were in a club somewhere instead of stuck in a room and staring at the Seven Seas Lagoon.

There was a lot of complaining about bubble life among the 22 teams that participated in the NBA's season restart while a deadly pandemic raged. The circumstances required the league to invest $180 million to create a controlled environment, preventing the spread of the coronavirus by keeping family, friends, fans, and all but the most essential team employees out of the bubble, preserving $1.5 billion in revenue by allowing the NBA to conduct an abbreviated end to the regular season and the entire playoffs. None of the moaning came from the Mavericks, however, who made the most of their surroundings from the day they arrived at Disney.

"A lot of people have been complaining, but where I'm from, I think it's good food, good living," Finney-Smith said via Zoom after one of the Mavs' first bubble practices during the three-week ramp-up before the games began. "So I can't complain at all."

For some players, the bubble was bliss. Dončić, a dude who just wants to hoop and hang out, fell into that category. So did Boban Marjanović, the joyful giant who had quickly become Dončić's best friend on the team despite being a decade older. It was somewhat of a summer camp for big kids, at least for those who approached the bubble with that mindset during an especially heavy time in the real world.

"We have more fun in the bubble than other teams," Marjanović said, recalling the memories with a huge smile.

The NBA couldn't replace the comforts of home for players who had become accustomed to living a life of luxury, but the league made great efforts to provide entertainment outside of the gym. Dončić and the Mavs took full advantage. They played Ping-Pong, tennis, pickleball, Spikeball, cornhole, video games, golf, pool volleyball, and on and on. "Luka's good at everything, geez," Hardaway said with a sigh, having heard plenty of Dončić's trash talk during their competitive diversions. They also frequently went fishing, which reminded Dončić of days spent on the Croatian seaside. But it was purely for fun and relaxation, not food. "I don't like fish," Dončić said. The Mavs frequently gathered at the resort pool, basking in the sun while bonding over beers. Plus, there was plenty of food and snacks. "I'm fan of ice cream," Marjanović said. "It was ice cream there." Dončić also enjoyed some meals with Marjanović, Dragić, Nuggets star Nikola Jokić, and other Balkans from around the league, dinners that stretched into the wee hours of the morning as they drank, joked, and sang Serbian songs. "That's his element right there," Mavs Assistant Coach Darrell Armstrong said.

In a way, the bubble allowed Dončić a chance to recapture some of the adolescence he gave up by going to Real Madrid as a kid. He didn't hesitate when asked, as the Mavs' 54-day stay was ending, what his best memories of the bubble were. "Just hanging out with the guys," Dončić said. "I think it brought us closer."

As Marjanović put it, "Everybody was living out dreams, and we played basketball." Dončić found joy in the practice gym, too. He didn't suddenly become fond of noncompetitive drills, but Dončić was elated to be back on the court with his teammates after months apart, time he mostly spent training back home in Slovenia.

There was also a benefit to the practice courts being converted ballrooms. It expanded the possibilities for Dončić to come up with different trick shots, a favorite post-practice pastime. For example, he stood behind the basket and lofted a high-arching shot over the backboard, banking it off a relatively low-hanging ceiling beam and into the hoop. Dončić enjoys placing wagers on these sorts of shots, as he does with the half-court shooting contests, although he has a reputation for never settling his debts. "He's full of money but never pays," Armstrong cracked. Dončić insists he always pays up at the end of a season, but the trick shots are really about pride. After making a miracle shot, Dončić would excitedly ask, "Did you get it?" to Jason "Chopper" Chinnock, the photographer and videographer documenting the bubble for the Mavs.

Dončić put on some spectacular shows when the bubble's bright lights were on as well. The rest of the regular-season schedule was condensed into eight "seeding" games, and the Mavericks were all but locked into the seventh spot in the West after a 153–149 overtime shoot-out loss to the Rockets in the bubble opener. That turned the next two weeks into tune-up time for the Mavs, but Dončić didn't need to chip off any rust after the layoff. He had three triple-doubles in Dallas's first five games at Disney World, then rested for one game and most of another in preparation for the playoffs.

Dončić's performance just before he took a game off created a buzz throughout the bubble and beyond. He was the best player on the floor in a 136–132 overtime win over soon-to-be two-time MVP Giannis Antetokounmpo and the Bucks, who had the NBA's best record. Dončić finished with a 36–14–19 line, his league-leading 17th triple-double of the shortened season and the first time in NBA history anyone had recorded that many points, rebounds, and assists in a game. Antetokounmpo's analysis of Dončić: "One of the most talented guys I've ever played against."

Dončić's final dime came on the kind of highlight that is so stunning, so sensational, it causes spontaneous, hilarious laughter. Dončić ran a high pick and roll with Kleber from the top of the arc, coming off the screen with a left-hand dribble while his defender trailed, drawing help from Antetokounmpo. When Antetokounmpo committed, Dončić widened his path, creating another foot or so of space for Kleber's roll. Then Dončić delivered a no-look bounce pass *between his own legs* that Kleber caught in stride before rising for an and-one dunk. Porziņģis, who had fouled out with 26 points and 11 rebounds, reacted on the bench by standing up and applauding while shaking his head and exhaling hard. "I don't know what I did," Dončić said with a shrug on his postgame Zoom. "I just did it."

Dončić WAS A UNANIMOUS SELECTION TO WHAT EVERYONE hopes will be the only All-Bubble team ever, honored for averaging 30.0 points, 10.1 rebounds, and 9.7 assists in his seven appearances in seeding games. Porziņģis, who sat out of two of the final three games as a precaution, was a second-team selection after putting up averages of 30.5 points and 9.5 rebounds. With their co-stars clicking, a Dallas team that broke the NBA record for offensive efficiency (115.9 points per 100 possessions) seemed like a rather dangerous seven seed.

"They're terrific," Clippers coach Doc Rivers said after his team's first-round matchup with the Mavs was set. "Best offensive team in history, right? And they have one of the young stars. They're a two-star team now, I mean—Porziņģis is playing great. I look at that, and that's a tough matchup in the first round. That's what it is."

But there's a big difference between a dangerous seven seed and a bona fide contender, which is what the Clippers were considered from the moment they made the blockbuster trade for Paul George that simultaneously sealed Kawhi Leonard's free agency commitment. With all due respect to the titles Dončić had won in Europe, he had yet to play a single minute in the NBA playoffs. Nor had Porziņģis. Leonard, on the other hand, had won his second NBA Finals MVP after leading the Raptors to the title the previous season. LA's starting lineup had a combined 265 games of NBA playoff experience; the Mavs had 15, all from Hardaway. The Clippers swept the three regular-season meetings with the Mavs, winning by double figures on the two occasions that Leonard and George both played, including once in the bubble. LA was heavily favored (-560 odds) to win the series.

Dončić quickly proved that his inexperience was irrelevant, breaking the scoring record for an NBA playoff debut with 42 points in Game 1. He also had seven rebounds and nine assists but described his performance as "terrible," pointing to his 11 turnovers.

"Eleven turnovers, never had that much," grumbled Dončić, who tended to be the most talkative with the media when he was criticizing himself. "I just want to win. I am really proud of this team—we fought, we fought 'til the end. We tried. I am really proud."

But Dončić was a bit player in that game's biggest storyline: the controversial ejection of Porziņģis a few minutes into the third quarter. Porziņģis got booted as the fallout from a minor confrontation that started when Clippers forward Marcus Morris Sr. put his hands on Dončić after the whistle.

After Dončić was called for a palming violation, Morris grabbed his shoulders from behind with both hands, tugging forcefully enough to knock him off balance. It's the sort of thing an antagonist does to a star—especially one with a reputation for being hotheaded—to try to set a tone for a series. Dončić, not surprisingly, didn't appreciate it and muttered a few words at Morris before attempting to walk up the floor. Morris instantly transitioned from proclaiming his innocence to antagonizing Dončić again, leaning on him and chirping.

Porziņģis instinctively opted to protect his co-star, walking over a few steps to get between Dončić and Morris. Morris responded with a shove to Porziņģis's chest. There was the typical NBA dustup scrum, with some holding and grabbing as referees, coaches, and other players intervened to make sure nothing ugly occurred. It was all pretty calm as on-court confrontations go, but it merited a replay review by the refs. The ruling: double technicals for Morris and Porziņģis, the latter of whom got hit for "being an escalator to the altercation," crew chief Kane Fitzgerald said in a postgame pool report.

The problem: Porziņģis had been called for a technical foul midway through the second quarter, when he punched the air in frustration after being called for a foul on a clean block of George's layup attempt. A second T meant he was automatically tossed. "Man that was BOGUS AS HELL MAN!!!! Cmon man," LeBron James tweeted at the time, adding a face-palm emoji. Dirk Nowitzki tweeted that the ejection was "super soft." It was also an instant momentum shift. The Mavs had a 71–66 lead when Porziņģis prematurely exited. LA outscored Dallas by a 21–11 margin the rest of the third quarter and pulled out a 118–110 win.

"I saw him getting into Luka's face and I didn't like that," said

Porziņģis, who had 14 points and six rebounds in 20 minutes before his ejection. "That's why I reacted. That's a smart, smart thing to do from their part. I've just got to be smarter and control my emotions the next time."

Not that a playoff loss was worth it, but Porziņģis's eagerness to intervene on Dončić's behalf provided further proof that a bond was forming between the Mavs franchise cornerstones. "I knew KP had my back—he did it for me, he did it for his teammate," Dončić said. "He had my back. I appreciate that. I don't think it was fair to get him out of the game, especially in the playoffs. We had to play without him, which was tough."

The Mavs felt confident that they could compete with the Clippers as they bussed back to the Grand Floridian that night. That was apparent from Game 2's opening tip less than 48 hours later. Dallas jumped out to a 15–2 lead with Dončić assisting or scoring on every point during the spurt, starting with an alley-oop to Kleber on the opening possession. Porziņģis had popped up on the morning injury report as questionable with right knee soreness, but he got rolling early, hitting a pick-and-pop three when Dončić flipped him a behind-the-back feed and slashing for a dunk when Dončić hit him on an inbounds play. "Let's go!" Dončić yelled after drilling a dancing-with-the-dribble, step-back three right in front of Rivers, who responded by calling time-out to calm his veteran team.

The Clippers cut into the lead, making the game competitive again, but didn't find any solutions to their Dončić dilemma for the rest of the half. He had 22 points, six rebounds, and seven assists with only one turnover by halftime, an even more impressive performance than his record-setting playoff debut. He torched Morris time and time again. George didn't fare any better. Leonard, a former Defensive Player of the Year, didn't even bother Dončić. Reggie Jackson and Lou Williams, a couple of small, offensive-minded guards, might as well have been traffic cones.

But the Clippers found some hope in the final seconds of the half. Dončić, defending on the perimeter, slid his feet in front of a dribbling Leonard a beat too late and was called for his third foul. It took all of 52 seconds into the third quarter before he picked up his fourth for reaching in and raking LA big man Ivica Zubac across his left forearm. Dončić reacted with shock, directing an astounded look and exaggerated shrug toward ref Sean Wright, then slowly walking away with his hands on his hips. Then Dončić turned and wagged a finger toward Carlisle, informing his coach that he didn't want to check out of the game. Carlisle concurred, taking a chance by allowing Dončić to play until the midway point of the quarter, when he normally subbed out to rest. But Dončić didn't have the same aggression. His rhythm was thrown off. He didn't record a field goal or an assist in the quarter.

Fortunately for the Mavs, Dončić's supporting cast picked up the slack. Porziņģis stayed aggressive, scoring 6 of his 9 points in the quarter from the line. Hardaway got hot. So did Seth Curry, Rivers's son-in-law, after coming off the bench when Dončić rested. Dallas closed the quarter with a 13–2 run to push its lead back to 13 points.

Dončić stayed on the floor for a grand total of 23 seconds at the start of the fourth quarter. He got whistled for his fifth foul when he hacked Clippers center Montrezl Harrell while defending him under the basket in transition—an incredibly dumb play for someone with such a high basketball IQ. Carlisle didn't have much choice but to pull Dončić at that point, saving him for crunch time. But the Mavs maintained their lead with Trey Burke, picked off the scrap heap because Jalen Brunson had shoulder surgery, running the point. Dallas cruised to a 127–114 win to even the series, despite its superstar being limited to nine minutes in the second half.

"We've just got three left," Dončić said, referring to how many more wins the Mavs needed to pull off the series upset. "I think we can fight with them. Any series we go in, we're going to believe we can win, for sure. If you don't believe it, you're not supposed to be here. You've got to believe it."

Only George Mikan, the NBA's original superstar, had scored more points in the first two playoff games of his career than Dončić's 70. The Clippers had clearly tired of all the talk about the Wonder Boy's brilliance and cranked up the physical and psychological attacks on Dončić in Game 3. "Bitch ass white boy," Harrell barked at Dončić midway through the first quarter. Harrell had just slammed his body backward into Dončić to create space for a layup, contact that Dončić was complaining about to an official, when a TNT close-up captured those words coming out of Harrell's mouth. Less than a minute later, Harrell swung a right elbow into Dončić after the Mavs superstar made a pass in the lane. Dončić retaliated with an elbow of his own after the Clippers grabbed a rebound, resulting in double technical fouls.

Maybe the Clippers' tactics took a toll, or perhaps Dončić just had an off night, but he struggled to score for the first time all series. His first shot, a lefty layup off a pivot move, was blocked by Zubac. His second, a three from the left wing, was an airball. The tone was set. Dončić was inefficient in the paint (3-of-8), from three-point range (1-of-6), and at the free throw line (4-of-10). He missed six straight shots from the floor before finally getting a jump hook to go down with 6:27 to go in the third quarter. Dončić responded by raising his eyes and his hands toward the rafters, thanking the basketball gods for finally letting one fall. Cruel twist: it ended up being his last shot attempt of the game.

A handful of possessions later, Dončić sat down in the paint, clutching his left ankle in pain as play continued around him. He got caught defending Leonard, who lit up the Mavs all night, in a transition cross-match. Dončić was knocked a bit off balance by inadvertent contact to his left leg after Leonard, who has the physique of a pass-rushing outside linebacker, drove to the basket. Dončić's left ankle took an ugly twist, and down he went.

When a foul was whistled five seconds later, Dončić rolled onto his hands and knees before hobbling off the floor to the baseline.

He sat down, grabbing his left ankle with his right hand, putting his head into the shooting-sleeve-covered elbow on his left arm that rested on his knee. Barea and Casey Smith, the Mavs' director of player health and performance, rushed off the bench to check on the face of the franchise. After briefly lying on his back, left knee near his chest and still clutching that ankle, Smith helped Dončić to his feet. Dončić brushed off Barea's offer of a shoulder to lean on as he exited toward the tunnel, hopping on his right foot the whole way as he navigated up a ramp and into the Mavs' locker room.

After being evaluated by Smith, Dončić hobbled back onto the floor with a little more than two minutes left in the quarter. He stood next to Barea at the end of the bench, gritting his teeth while putting some pressure on the ankle and jogging in place, testing the pain level. Smith came over to consult with Dončić again, and they decided that he was available to return. The Mavs needed a miracle after Clippers reserve guard Landry Shamet banked in a buzzer-beating transition three to stretch LA's lead to 17 at the end of the quarter.

Dončić was willing but nowhere close to able. He hobbled and limped as he moved and spent much of his time when the Mavs had the ball standing in the corner as a decoy. He recorded his 10th assist a minute into the quarter on a basic bounce pass to Curry off of a curl. He grabbed his 10th rebound off a Harrell missed free throw with 9:37 remaining, an uncontested board that Dončić hopped maybe two inches off the floor to get. That sealed a bit of history, as only Magic Johnson and LeBron James had playoff triple-doubles at a younger age, but it was certainly not a celebratory moment. Dončić fouled Williams 35 seconds later, helpless defending him on the perimeter after a pick-and-roll switch, and immediately glanced at Carlisle with his right hand up to call for a sub.

Dončić walked straight to the end of the bench, putting his head in his hands with his elbows on his knees. Seconds later, he leaned all the way over with his head down, grabbing that left ankle again. Smith came over, gently placing his hand on Dončić's shoulder and telling him to head to the trainer's room to start treatment right away. Dončić stood up and gave a frustrated swat behind him with his right hand, knocking over the chair, before walking into the tunnel with his hands on his hips and Smith trailing. He had about 40 hours to attempt to recover for Game 4, an afternoon tip.

"It's not that bad," Dončić said after the 130–122 loss, perhaps trying to give himself hope. He had missed stretches of seven and four games when he sprained his other ankle during the regular season. "Honestly, I had luck it's my left ankle. It's not my right. It's a little sprained."

ABOUT 35 MINUTES BEFORE GAME 4, THE MAVS RECEIVED SOME bad injury news, unrelated to Dončić: Porziņģis was a late scratch. Porziņģis was coming off a 34-point, 13-rebound performance in Game 3, but the pain and stiffness in his right knee grew progressively worse. It locked up on him during warm-ups, forcing Carlisle to scramble to adjust his game plan and the Mavs to make arrangements for Porziņģis to get an MRI postgame.

Dončić was officially considered a game-time decision, but there was little doubt that he would play. The question was whether he could be effective. The early indications weren't exactly encouraging. He had two turnovers, one technical foul, and only one bucket in the first eight minutes. And Dončić grimaced after that bucket, limping and grabbing his ankle after getting back on defense. The T was the consequence for yelling at ref James Williams and angrily pointing to the other end of the floor, where Dončić thought he was fouled on a floater. Carlisle had filled the 7-foot-3 Porziņģis's spot in the starting lineup with 6-foot Burke, essentially giving up hopes of trying to defend the Clippers and attempting to simply outscore them. But the Mavs' offense was in mud, and the Clippers took a 23–11 lead when Leonard made the technical free throw with 4:03 left in the quarter.

Bad got worse, as the Clippers' lead ballooned to 21 during the 3:48 that Dončić rested to open the second quarter. But Dončić found his rhythm midway through the quarter, scoring on a few paint attacks, taking advantage of Harrell's inability to protect the rim. (Dončić and Harrell squashed their beef pregame, when Harrell approached to apologize for his Game 3 insult. Dončić readily accepted, saying later: "There's a lot of emotions on the court, especially this is playoffs. Sometimes you say things you don't want to say. He apologized. I respect that, so no problems.") Burke got going, too, hitting a few quick jumpers, two off dimes from Dončić, who had a hockey assist on the other. Dončić hit a pull-up three to slice the lead to 6 with 2:06 to go in the half and pounded his chest a couple of times. Game on.

Dončić conducted a high pick-and-roll clinic in the third quarter. Rivers kept switching up the Clippers' coverage and changing centers (Zubac, Harrell, JaMychal Green). None of it mattered. Dončić scored 13 points—on six paint buckets, including an and-one—and accounted for 12 more on assists while playing the entire quarter. The Mavs took the lead and pushed it to 8 points. Any pain Dončić felt was overpowered by adrenaline.

"I obviously wasn't 100 percent," Dončić said later, "but I think I was good."

The Mavs were poised to pull off the biggest playoff comeback in franchise history. They bumped the lead to 10 while Dončić caught his second breather of the game, sitting out the first 3:27 of the fourth quarter. They led by 8 after Hardaway hit a pull-up three with 2:44 remaining. Then the Clippers, the heavy favorites playing an opponent missing a star, made their comeback. With Leonard playing smothering defense on Dončić, Dallas's only points down the stretch came on a pair of Hardaway free throws. LA tied it up in the final minute and had a chance to win it on their last possession, but Leonard's contested 22-footer clanked off the right side of the rim and into Dončić's hands.

Dončić, playing hurt, had 36 points, 16 rebounds, and 12 assists. The Mavs needed more. On to overtime—and the biggest stage of his NBA career so far.

"Look, we know this kid has got a flair for the dramatic," Carlisle said postgame. "He's a performer as well as a great player. He's a guy that lives for these moments and is completely fearless."

The margin was never more than 2 points either way during the extra period. Dončić didn't score until hitting a twisting floater off the glass to tie it up with 50 seconds remaining. Then he gave the Mavs the lead by driving and spinning for a layup the next possession, making him the youngest player in NBA history with a 40-point playoff triple-double. But the Mavs still needed more, as the Clippers responded with a corner three from Morris off a Leonard drive-and-kick dish to go up by a point.

Dončić's feet were on the corner of the NBA's Jerry West half-court logo when he caught the inbounds pass with 3.7 seconds remaining. He had Jackson on him—the result of a Kleber screen that made Leonard settle for switching off the opposing superstar—and attacked immediately. He took one dribble and two big strides toward the left wing, Dončić's favorite area of the floor. He planted his left foot with that sore ankle and dribbled between his legs, left to right, and accelerated forward just enough to get Jackson to backpedal. Dončić tapped the brakes, crossed back over to his left, and eased into a comfortable step-back from a couple of feet beyond the arc. Jackson tried to contest, but he was too small to bother the much bigger Dončić. The buzzer sounded and red lights on the backboard's edges went off with the ball in the air, framing the splash of the net.

"Bang! Bang!" ESPN play-by-play man Mike Breen shouted, using his trademark call. "It's good!" Dončić, who backpedaled as his eyes followed the shot's path, turned toward the bench at mid-court, clenched his fists, and pounded his chest once before being mobbed by his teammates and coaches.

"I can't explain the emotions I had," Dončić said. "Not only when the ball goes in but when I see the whole team running toward me. That was something special, one of the best feelings I ever had as a player. Just something special."

Not just special. Historic. Only one player had ever put the finishing touches on a 40-plus-point playoff performance by hitting a make-it-or-lose buzzer-beater: Michael Jordan, when he made "The Shot" over Cleveland's Craig Ehlo in 1989. The 43–17–13 line was Dončić's second triple-double in his first four playoff games, joining Magic Johnson as the only players to pull off that feat.

Michael. Magic. LeBron. Luka. That's the kind of legendary, singular-name-only company this kid was keeping.

Dončić went from game-time decision to having a game that will be discussed in reverential tones for generations to come. He logged 46 minutes, the most of his career at that point, on a bad wheel and won the game in the final second.

"Listen, there was nothing that was going to keep him from staying in the game," Carlisle said. "He kept telling me that he was good, as many minutes as we needed him. I didn't even try to get him out before the quarter breaks. That would have been a fistfight, and I wasn't into that today. Look, we needed him out there. We needed him out there."

THAT MAGIC DIDN'T CARRY OVER FOR THE MAVERICKS INTO Game 5, a 154–111 rout by the Clippers. Porziņģis sat out again, Carlisle exited early after getting two quick technicals midway through the fourth quarter, and Dončić had a mere mortal outing with an inefficient 22 points, eight rebounds, and four assists. The most memorable moment of the game was another Morris-Dončić extracurricular encounter. Early in the third quarter, as Dončić awaited an inbounds pass underneath the basket Dallas was defending,

Morris marched in from the left wing and—*whoops!*—stepped right on Dončić's tender left ankle, knocking off his shoe.

It was either quite a coincidence for Morris, who'd made antagonizing Dončić his mission the whole series, to land on the world's most scrutinized sprained ankle or a blatant cheap shot. Morris proclaimed his innocence in a postgame tweet—"It was a mistake deal wit it," it read in part—but Dončić was suspicious, to say the least.

"I have my own thoughts. I hope it wasn't intentional," Dončić said postgame. "Tell me what you think." Dončić paused for a moment, looking at the Zoom screen while raising his eyebrows, tilting his head, and smirking.

"I don't want to talk to him," Dončić said when asked if Morris offered any explanation. "He's just saying a lot of bad stuff to me all the game. I just don't want to talk to him. I just want to move on. Like I say, everybody is going to have their own opinion. I just hope it wasn't intentional. If that was intentional, that's really bad."

The Mavs also requested for the league office to review an uncalled landing space violation on a three-pointer Dončić made over Morris about 90 seconds later, again putting Dončić's sore ankle at risk.

Any benefit of the doubt that Dončić might have given Morris disappeared late in the first quarter of Game 6. Morris cocked back his right hand and smacked Dončić across the head and neck after the Mavs' star drove to the basket, resulting in Morris's ejection and a $35,000 fine.

"It was a terrible play. What can I say?" Dončić said. "It's two games in a row he did something like that. I really hoped the first game it wasn't on purpose, but looking back on the foul this game, you know what I think."

There wasn't much more drama as the Clippers closed out the series with a 111–97 win. Dončić was brilliant with 38 points, nine rebounds, and nine assists, but he didn't have enough help to pull

off an upset over one of the league's elite teams, especially with Porzingis out again. "I'm proud of our team, how we fight," Dončić said.

Dončić had solidified his status as the NBA's premier young
player, a likely face of the league at some point in the not-too-distant
future. In training camp, he had said that the Mavs making the playoffs was his goal, but he was willing to publicly declare much bigger
dreams after the significant steps Dallas took during the season.

"My goal at the start of every season is to win a championship,"
Dončić said. "There's no other goal. So that's going to be mine."

Porzingis had tried to practice in the days between Games 5
and 6, but his knee locked up again. The Mavs announced that he
had a torn meniscus and would miss the remainder of the series.
The Mavs' medical staff wanted to see how Porzingis's knee would
respond to treatment over the next few weeks before determining
whether an operation was necessary.

"I'm looking forward to just picking it up where I left off and keep
playing that high-level basketball," Porzingis said. "And I'm looking
forward to the next things we can accomplish as a team."

Porzingis had surgery six weeks later. The hope was that Dončić's
sidekick would be ready for training camp, whenever that might
be. The harsh reality: Porzingis had seen his peak in a Mavericks
uniform.

CHAPTER 9

"LIKE CLIMBING UPHILL NONSTOP"

DONČIĆ HAD CHANGED OUT OF HIS UNIFORM, PUTTING ON A GRAY T-shirt and blue practice shorts, and returned to the American Airlines Center court by the time Carlisle began his postgame Zoom media availability following the Mavericks' 2020–21 home opener. Reporters in the arena, confined to an area at the top of the empty lower seating bowl due to pandemic procedures, watched as Dončić got up shots with assistant coaches rebounding and passing him the ball. He definitely needed the work.

"Ugly night," Carlisle said after sitting down in front of the computer camera. "There's not a whole lot else to say."

Carlisle looked down at a printout of the box score from that night's 118–99 loss to the Charlotte Hornets, which dropped the Mavs to 1–3 to open a shortened season that started more than two months later than normal due to COVID-19-related complications. He cringed a little as his eyebrows raised, deepening the worry lines in his forehead.

There were a lot of unsightly stats on that sheet of paper. Maybe the most hideous: minus-27 in the plus-minus column for Dončić, who played only 24 minutes because the game was such a blowout. He exited the game for good with 2:55 remaining in the third quarter, chin down as he trudged to the end of the bench after Carlisle called a time-out with Dallas trailing by 31. On the Mavs' previous possession, Dončić missed a step-back three by about a foot, his second airball of the night.

"Look, it's clear Luka doesn't have his rhythm yet, and everybody's working through something at this point in time," Carlisle said. "But the thing that we can't work through is the idea or the fact that in this league this year, you've got to step on the floor playing with full force all the time or you're going to get your ass beat."

Carlisle would have preferred that the conversation steer clear of Dončić, knowing he'd need to choose his words carefully. However, four of the five questions Carlisle fielded focused on Dončić.

Dončić's conditioning, or lack thereof, was an especially sensitive subject. It was clearly a factor in one of Dončić's worst performances of his career, as he was dreadfully sluggish defensively against the Hornets, and his 12 points in the loss matched his lowest total from any game in the previous season that he played for more than two minutes. But Carlisle opted to avoid the issue when asked directly about it.

"Listen, I'm not going to get into a thing about conditioning or whatever," Carlisle said. "This is a team game. It wasn't fun. You know, let's keep our eye on the ball."

Dončić reported to training camp noticeably heavier, so much so that his round cheeks and puffy upper body became fodder for social media memes. "I mean, people on Twitter say every stuff," Dončić said during the preseason, uncomfortably attempting to laugh it off. "But it's true. I mean, I'm not in my best shape. I will get there for sure. But, you know, I've never been a muscular guy, so what can I say?"

He looked more like he should be playing left guard for the Cowboys than point guard for the Mavericks. He was still officially listed at 230 pounds, a weight he's probably never played at in the NBA, but after spending a few months in Slovenia, Dončić actually tipped the scales at 263.

With the Mavs off to a slow start, the two primary discussion points were when Porziņģis might return from his offseason knee surgery and concerns about Dončić's conditioning. On the rare occasions that Dončić's bosses discussed him being out of shape, they made excuses for him. Cuban attributed the issue to Dončić's plans to train and play with the Slovenian national team being canceled because of the pandemic. Carlisle blamed the NBA season starting earlier than anticipated amid the COVID uncertainty, as if packing on several extra pounds was ever part of the plan. It was telling that Carlisle—a notoriously demanding coach who once called out Chandler Parsons for being overweight in the preseason after he signed a max contract with the Mavs—preferred to sound nonsensical rather than risk publicly criticizing Dončić.

Dončić sweated through his T-shirt during his shooting session that lasted about half an hour after that December 30 rout at the hands of the Hornets. Mosley and player development coach God Shammgod helped conduct the entire workout. Shooting coach Peter Patton observed during the latter stages. All hands are on deck when a superstar struggles, and Dončić was 2-of-21 from three-point range in the first four games, missing his last 10 attempts.

Why was he having such a hard time finding a groove? "I don't know, I just think my legs are really tired," Dončić said in his postgame Zoom a couple of minutes after finally leaving the court. "But it's not an excuse."

Citing tired legs, particularly in an early-season game following two nights off, is a pleasant way for a player to admit to being in poor shape. "It was hard to practice in Slovenia," Dončić said. "Everything was closed, but the gyms were open, so there's no excuses." Then Dončić made an excuse, or at least downplayed concerns, by noting that training camp and the exhibition schedule were shorter than usual. "We've just got to stay together," Dončić said. "Normally, we'd still be in preseason."

In other words, he wasn't too worried about it. His conditioning issues were apparent, but the Mavs had much bigger concerns. The good vibes from the bubble were long gone. It was a generally glum time in the NBA—games had to be played without fans in the stands to start the season, and players essentially were able to leave their homes or hotel rooms only to practice, play, travel with the team, and follow the relentless COVID-19 testing routine—but the Mavs were especially miserable. There were cold feuds playing out in the front office and the coaching staff, featuring passive-aggressive power struggles and suspicions of backstabbing. Dončić's relationship with Carlisle was deteriorating to the point that the 21-year-old was often blatantly, occasionally profanely, disrespectful of his coach.

Plus, Porziņģis had fully participated in practice the previous day for the first time since the bubble. The revised target date for his return of January 1 was out of the question. Porziņģis ended up being cleared to make his season debut on January 11, but that night's home game against the Pelicans was postponed due to a COVID outbreak among the Mavs. When Porziņģis made his season debut a couple of nights later, Dallas was down five rotation players due to COVID protocols: Brunson, Finney-Smith, Kleber, Powell, and Josh Richardson, the shooting guard acquired in an offseason deal that sent Seth Curry to Philadelphia in an attempt to upgrade the Mavs' defense. The Mavs managed to win in Charlotte that night, but it wasn't long before the passive-aggressive tension between Dončić and Porziņģis began bubbling again.

A big part of the problem was that Carlisle was incapable of managing the dynamic between Dallas's pair of young franchise cornerstones. The primary thing that Dončić and Porziņģis had in common at that point was a resentment of their coach, but they didn't bond over that.

"I was just being professional and getting my work in, but it's like climbing uphill nonstop, that kind of feeling," Porziņģis said later. "I didn't have the feeling that I want to go to war for this guy. The energy then, it is what it is. We just didn't have that kind of chemistry that we wanted to have."

It didn't help that the Mavs had moved on from Barea and Lee, two veterans who didn't play much the previous season but were crucial elements of the team's chemistry. Barea was waived upon his request before the preseason began, once he realized that the guaranteed one-year deal he signed for the $2.6 million veteran's minimum was meant as a farewell gift from Cuban, not a spot on the roster or even the chance to compete for one. That's a decision the Mavs ended up regretting because Barea was missed in helping manage the relationships among Dončić, Porziņģis, and Carlisle. Lee's roots in Dallas didn't run nearly as deep as Barea's, but he had a similar personality and behind-the-scenes impact, which is why the Mavs had brought him to the bubble after he suffered a freak calf injury moving furniture that required surgery. After Lee replaced Barea on the roster for the preseason, Carlisle offered him a role on the coaching staff, recognizing the need for a locker room liaison that he trusted. But Lee declined, hoping to catch on with another team. So a lot of Carlisle's communication with his unhappy stars went through Mosley, even though Carlisle had concerns that Mosley was angling to replace him—suspicions that were shared by others in the organization.

"I told Rick, 'This guy's coming for your job,'" said Voulgaris, who Nelson thought was gunning for *his* job.

During one early-season game, Dončić questioned Carlisle's authority by shouting at him during a time-out, "Who's in charge— you or Bob?" That was a reference to the belief held by several players and staffers that Voulgaris dictated Carlisle's lineups and rotations. Carlisle valued Voulgaris' data and input but always had final say. However, the coach didn't necessarily mind the perception that Voulgaris called some shots. In fact, Voulgaris suspects that Carlisle intentionally planted seeds of that possibility back in Dončić's rookie season. Carlisle scheduled a meeting with Wesley Matthews to inform him of the Mavs' intention to start giving Finney-Smith some of the defensive assignments on opponents' best scorers, a role the veteran took great pride in filling. Carlisle called Voulgaris into his office before the meeting with Matthews, and that discussion ran over for about 25 or 30 minutes while Matthews waited in the hallway. After Voulgaris exited, Carlisle informed Matthews of the plan, a pretty clear sign his days in Dallas were numbered.

"Carlisle is so tactical," Voulgaris said years later. "From my perspective, it was either the biggest bullshit thing anyone has ever done to me or it was a complete coincidence, and I don't think there's very many coincidences with Carlisle. ... From my perspective, it was like [Carlisle said], 'OK, this is out of my hands, but this is what the numbers are saying.' And I'm the numbers.

"I think that's a lack of leadership from the top. Also, Carlisle's like that, as big of a bully as he can be. But around players, especially players who were making a lot of money, he would be like, 'We can't tell this guy [the truth].'"

For all of Dallas's dysfunction, the Mavs did have one great thing going for them: Dončić, as a first-team All-NBA player still on his rookie contract, provided the best bang for the buck of any player in the league. As he expected, Dončić didn't take long to morph back into MVP-candidate form as he worked off some of the extra off-season weight. Dallas won its next five games with Dončić in the lineup after that horrific home opener, and he averaged a 30-point triple-double during that span, culminating with Porziņģis's season debut.

Dončić was spectacular again in the next game, putting up 28 points, 10 rebounds, and 13 assists to give the Mavs a chance at a road upset in Milwaukee despite its depleted rotation and an out-of-sync performance by Porziņģis. But the final minute of the 112–109 loss provided the ESPN national audience a peek at the decaying dynamic between Dončić and Carlisle.

With 7.8 seconds remaining, after a Porziņģis brick likely sealed the defeat, Dončić showed up Carlisle in the middle of the floor. He was in disbelief that Carlisle hadn't called a time-out when fill-in center Willie Cauley-Stein grabbed a long offensive rebound with 20 seconds remaining and Dallas down 2 points. Cauley-Stein handed off to Burke, who had just missed a three off a feed from a double-teamed Dončić. Burke dribbled underneath the basket and found Porziņģis on the right wing. Porziņģis, who had made only 6 of 18 shots in the game, launched a long three over Antetokoun-mpo's contest that clanked off the backboard on the other side of the hoop. Dončić watched from above the top of the three-point arc, a foot on the half-court logo, and threw a temper tantrum after the Mavs committed a foul to stop the clock.

Dončić yelled toward the Dallas bench, angrily clapped, and then yelled again into his hands while bending over in dismay. He stood up, staring at Carlisle on the sideline about 25 feet away, and repeatedly shrugged in exaggerated fashion, flapping his arms while shouting some more. He took a couple of steps toward the sideline and then turned to walk down the floor for Khris Middleton's free throws. Then, he yelled at Carlisle again, forming a *T* with his hands while shaking his head, just in case anybody wondered whether he thought the coach should have used the Mavs' final time-out. Dončić continued complaining after Middleton made the first free throw, walking from the lane to the middle of the floor while looking at Carlisle. Dončić gestured toward the other end of the floor, put his hands in a *T* once more, and flapped his hands in frustration. Carlisle bit his lip.

Carlisle used that last time-out after Middleton made the second free throw, stretching the Bucks' lead to 4. Dončić stomped toward the bench with his chin down, shaking his head. He gave a few reserve teammates and Mosley low fives, then extended his arms and hollered a few more words when he walked past Carlisle, who had his back turned while in discussion with a couple of other assistant coaches. "This is where he's got to move on," former coach/color commentator Jeff Van Gundy said on the ESPN broadcast.

It's rare in the NBA to see a star exhibit such passionate displeasure with his coach, but this didn't stun anyone within the Mavericks organization. According to several players and staff members, it wasn't unusual for Dončić to shout "stupid motherfucker!" toward Carlisle during time-outs. Carlisle privately, sheepishly joked that he had developed selective hearing loss to avoid fiery confrontations with the face of the franchise.

As difficult as it was for Dončić to control his emotions in the heat of the moment, he consistently avoided criticizing Carlisle in the media. He cooled off before his postgame Zoom in Milwaukee, saying "everything would be good" if the shot went in, and that time-out usage is a coach's decision. Carlisle expressed no regret about his strategy—there is a legitimate argument against allowing the Bucks to set their defense during a time-out—and said he was "not going to get into that publicly" when asked if he had discussed the matter with Dončić. At least they agreed on one thing.

"If we talk, we're going to talk," Dončić said. "It's not going to be in the media. It's between us."

Dončić's very public pouting after that decisive possession also could have been perceived as disrespectful of Porziņģis, given that he missed the critical shot. Porziņģis's place in the Mavs' offensive pecking order would again surface as a passive-aggressive point of contention. Porziņģis felt more like a distant afterthought than a second option.

"It's a team game, so we have to find ways how to play for each other so we can feed off of each other's energy," Porziņģis said after a 117–101 home loss to the Bulls on January 17. He agreed with Dončić's sentiment that the superstar got caught up in stats during a 36-point, 16-rebound, 15-assist outing.

"The second half, I played terrible," Dončić said after joining Oscar Robertson, James Harden, and Wilt Chamberlain as the only players in NBA history with 35–15–15 lines. "That's on me, that game. I was being selfish a little bit because I had 30 points in the first half. That wasn't me in the second half. I've got to do way better."

It was one of the rare occasions that Dončić and Porziņģis were on the same page that season. After his occasional prolific scoring performances, Porziņģis would sometimes casually mention something along the lines of "the ball actually moved tonight."

Dončić used the word "terrible" again in a postgame Zoom a dozen days later, but this time it was a one-word description of Dallas's performance in a 120–101 road loss to the Utah Jazz. It was the Mavs' fourth straight loss, including two to the Jazz despite All-Star guard Donovan Mitchell's absence, and seventh in nine games dating back to the Milwaukee trip. When asked to elaborate, Dončić—in a rare talkative moment with the media—ripped into Dallas's dismal competitive desire.

"I've never felt like this," Dončić said. "We've got to do something because this is not looking good. We've got to step up and just talk to each other and play way better than this. It's mostly effort."

Asked what specifically needed to change, Dončić said, "Right now, it's looking like we don't care, honestly, if we win games or not. We just got to [have] more energy, more effort, dive for every ball, box out, everything. There's a lot of things we could improve, and I know we will. I know we will, and that's all that matters."

Some sluggishness from the Mavs was understandable, considering the circumstances. Finney-Smith, Richardson, and Powell returned from extended stretches in the league's health-and-safety protocols just in time for the two-game stop in Salt Lake City's high altitude. Kleber, who got the sickest among the several Mavs infected during the COVID outbreak, remained out. But Porziņģis, in particular, had a couple of listless performances in Utah, where the Mavs were outscored by 42 points in his 57 minutes over the two games.

Porziņģis's poor defense became a lingering problem, a stark contrast to the previous season when his rim protection was one of the primary reasons the Mavs were average instead of awful on that end of the floor. Two months into the season, Porziņģis ranked second to last among the league's rotation players in defensive efficiency, as Dallas allowed 119.3 points per 100 possessions with him on the floor. The Mavs were a game under .500 at that point—8–9 when Porziņģis played, 7–7 when he didn't. He was struggling to move and felt like he'd rushed back from his offseason knee surgery, but it was difficult to discern whether limited mobility or a lack of motivation was Porziņģis's most glaring problem.

"It was more health than anything else because I'll always push myself," Porziņģis said later, reflecting on a miserable time in his career. "But also, at the end, we're human. If you're not getting the ball, you're not going to play crazy defense. It's just the nature of every player out there. You're not going to play hard defense if you're not touching it when you think you should be touching it."

As quietly as possible, the Mavs began gauging Porziņģis's value in the trade market. They discovered that it was negative, as the rest of the NBA had the same significant concerns about Porziņģis's durability and dollars. He was owed $101 million over the next three seasons, with the player option on the last year, a contract that was considered an albatross around the league. Dallas would have to dangle a first-round pick to even generate serious discussions about moving Porziņģis—but they still owed a pair of picks to the Knicks from the trade to get him, so that was out of the question. The Mavericks would have to make do with Porziņģis.

But it's awfully hard to keep trade talks about a max player hushed in the NBA, even if the discussions don't pick up any steam. In late

February, more than a month before the trade deadline, *Bleacher Report* reported that the Mavs had "sniffed around" on potential Porziņģis deals, as an anonymous assistant general manager put it. The story also included a blunt quote from a Western Conference executive that partially explained why there wasn't a market for Porziņģis: "It looks like it's impossible for him to get in a stance. He looks like a scarecrow out there. You don't expect him to necessarily be great from the jump, but I've watched Porziņģis a couple of times this year, and I'm not sure the guy can guard anybody."

Cuban adamantly denied that the Mavs had explored the market for Porziņģis. Carlisle also attempted to shoot it down. "There's nothing that's been explored," Carlisle insisted. "I know Mark's denied it. I'm denying it. He's a Maverick and we expect him to be here." Of course, telling the truth would have only made matters worse. The Mavs knew they'd have to live with Porziņģis, so it made sense to pretend they wouldn't have it any other way. Not that Porziņģis necessarily bought the spin.

"It kind of like came out, and it is what it is," Porziņģis said later that week, when he was ready to return after missing three games due to lower back tightness. "I don't know what's going on behind the scenes, and I shouldn't be too worried about it. It can only distract me at the end of the day."

It was an intentionally terse comment. It was awkward, but Porziņģis didn't want to pretend. This was reality.

THE MAVS SOON HAD SOME SUCCESS, CLIMBING BACK INTO THE playoff picture as Dončić put up numbers that made him an MVP candidate again, but they weren't a harmonious team. Carlisle's relationships with both Dončić and Porziņģis continued to be distant and strained. Dončić and Porziņģis didn't communicate much with each other, either, on or off the court. Porziņģis's body language—such as leaving his hands up for a few extra seconds if he was wide open when Dončić took a tough shot—often spoke volumes. Even a high five between them was so rare that such an event became notable. Carlisle did his best to pretend that there were no problems with the pair, refusing to discuss the issue publicly and attempting to avoid it privately. Carlisle often referred to the relationship between the two as "evolving," which was a rather optimistic description.

Porziņģis made the tension impossible to ignore after an April 7 road loss to the Rockets, who were en route to the NBA's worst record in the wake of James Harden forcing a trade. Porziņģis had 23 points on 10-of-19 shooting but didn't get any shots in the fourth quarter, when Dončić took eight of his 26 field goal attempts. Asked why he wasn't involved in the offense in the final quarter, Porziņģis paused for six seconds, forming a pained smirk.

"Good question. It's just the plays that we were running," Porziņģis finally said. After another brief pause, he added, "Happened before also."

A play-calling complaint is typically directed at the coach, and Porziņģis probably intended for Carlisle to get a good share of the blame, but Dončić had as much control of the offense as any player in the NBA. Porziņģis could have dimmed the spotlight on the dynamic between Dončić and him after a win over the Giannis-less Bucks the next night. The Mavs made a point to feed Porziņģis in the fourth quarter, when he had 11 of his 26 points, but all was certainly not well.

"Yeah, we're trying to play together and help each other," Porziņģis said when asked directly about the appearance of awkward tension between Dončić and him. "We want to win. At the end, we all want to win here—and that's it. We have to keep playing and keep playing together and keep playing well and help each other."

Carlisle picked a bizarre time to finally address the tension. He called Dončić and Porziņģis into the cramped coach's office in the visiting locker room at Memphis's FedExForum the following week. This was minutes after Dončić hit one of the most miraculous shots of his career: a buzzer-beating three to beat the Grizzlies that he made between two defenders, flipping the ball up with his right hand as he stumbled toward the paint. "It's kind of lucky, but we'll take it," Dončić said afterward. As he raised his hands triumphantly with a big grin on the baseline, most of his Mavs teammates ran to mob Dončić. Porziņģis was an exception, standing in the spot above the top of the three-point arc where he was when Dončić released the shot. Porziņģis pointed in Dončić's direction, but his shoulders were turned toward the sideline, hardly sharing the exuberance felt by the rest of the Mavs. The impromptu meeting in the coach's office was brief and unproductive, as Dončić and Porziņģis sat there and wondered why Carlisle wanted to finally discuss their dynamic at that moment.

THE MAVS NEEDED A STRONG FINISH TO AVOID THE NBA'S PLAY-in tournament, a new concept that featured the teams that finished between seventh and 10th in each conference playing extra games to earn the final two playoff spots. "I don't understand the idea of a play-in," Dončić said when the Mavs were seventh in the West standings in mid-April. "You play 72 games to get into the playoffs, then maybe you lose two in a row and you're out of the playoffs. So I don't see the point of that."

The idea had been unanimously approved by the NBA's Board of Governors, but hours after Dončić's critical comments, Cuban wished he had a mulligan. "In hindsight, this approach was an enormous mistake," Cuban said via text message.

It ended up being a nonissue for the Mavs, who cleared the play-in by a couple of spots, winning seven of 10 games Porziņģis missed due to an ankle injury and knee soreness down the stretch. The Mavs' reward for finishing fifth in the West was a rematch with the Clippers, who blatantly tanked in the final week of their regular season to get the matchup they wanted. The strategy might have been motivated more by pushing a potential meeting with the Lakers to the West finals instead of the second round, but the Clippers clearly didn't mind facing the Mavs again in the first round.

That was fine with Dončić, too. He came out on fire in Game 1, putting up 24 points and six assists by halftime. The Clippers opened the series with Patrick Beverley, a scrappy, yappy defender who'd missed the final five games of the series against Dallas the previous year due to injury, guarding Dončić. That didn't last long. "You're too fucking small!" Dončić yelled in the 6-foot-1, 180-pound Beverely's face after bullying him for an easy layup early in the first quarter. It was an accurate statement. Dončić spent the rest of the half picking on a much bigger target, Ivica Zubac, constantly calling for the 7-footer's man to set a high screen and torching the center on switches, lighting up LA with a variety of step-back threes, Dirk-esque one-legged fadeaways off the dribble, and drives.

The second half started with more of the same—a Dončić trip to the line after a Zubac foul, a spinning onelegger over the helpless big guy, then a step-back three before Clippers coach Ty Lue mercifully substituted to go small. But LA didn't have a solution to the Dončić problem until Carlisle pulled his star from the game midway through the quarter with the Mavs up 6. Dončić had just picked up his third foul, committing a silly take foul instead of running back on defense, but he adamantly disagreed with Carlisle's decision. That was readily apparent to the 6,117 fans in the COVID-condensed Staples Center crowd and everyone watching on TV.

Dončić gestured to Carlisle right after the whistle was blown, informing the coach that he wanted to stay in the game. When Dončić heard the horn sound, signaling a sub, and saw Brunson heading to the scorer's table to replace him, he shot a shocked glare toward Carlisle. Then Dončić dropped his head and clenched his fingers, squeezing the air as if he were crushing something in his hands. He shook his head as he walked to the bench and shouted at Carlisle when he passed the coach. Dončić didn't stop at his seat at the end of the bench, stomping another 10 steps until he reached the short wall at the bottom of the arena's lower bowl. He leaned against the wall, rested his head on top of his arms, turned his back to the floor, and remained there for most of the Clippers' ensuing possession. When he returned to the bench, Dončić stood and again shouted in Carlisle's direction before finally taking his seat. Nobody on the Mavs' bench blinked. Dončić's blowup was business as usual.

Carlisle's decision disrupted Dončić's rhythm, as the superstar didn't score the rest of the game, but it didn't bite the Mavs. Dallas pulled out a 113–103 win, taking a lead in a playoff series for the first time since the 2011 title run. Dončić finished with a 31-point triple-double, with seven of his 11 assists going to Hardaway and Finney-Smith, who combined for 39 points.

Porziŋģis had a clutch three and a dagger dunk, but he scored only 14 points on 4-of-13 shooting. His job on most possessions was essentially to stay out of the way while Kawhi Leonard guarded him, as the Clippers made taking away the Dončić/Porziŋģis pick and roll their priority. That was a smart strategy considering that, for all of the interpersonal discomfort between Dallas's star duo, the Mavs scored an average of 1.18 points per possession during the regular season when Porziŋģis set a ball screen for Dončić. According to Second Spectrum tracking, they were the league's most efficient pairing that ran at least 300 picks.

Carlisle praised Porziŋģis for being "patient" after the win. "There were a couple stretches that I think he got a little frustrated and took a couple of shots that may not have been the best shots, but in the end, I loved his discipline," Carlisle said.

Carlisle wasn't so pleased with Porziŋģis's discipline a couple of days later, when clips of Porziŋģis visiting an LA strip club emerged on social media. Under normal circumstances, that wouldn't be a big deal, especially two nights before a game. But the NBA was still operating under a different set of rules due to the pandemic, including one that prohibited players from going into bars, clubs, lounges, or similar establishments. Porziņģis, who was fully vaccinated by that point, had put his status for Game 2 in jeopardy. The league office announced a $50,000 fine with no suspension the morning of the game, but there were internal discussions about pulling Porziņģis from the starting lineup, using the rule infraction as cover for a change they had considered anyway.

"Looking back, Rick was trying to get me to say that [Porziņģis] shouldn't start because of the strip club thing," Voulgaris recalled. "He wanted it to be my idea. He kept saying, 'What should we do here? What should we do here?' I'm just like, 'I don't know. Do whatever you want.' He was like, 'What do you think we should do?' I'm just like, 'What do I think? I don't think he should be playing in this series. That's what I think, but obviously you guys aren't prepared to do that.'"

Porziņģis started and helped the Mavs shock the basketball world by winning a 127–121 shoot-out in Game 2 to go up 2–0 in the series. It was an offensive clinic by Dallas, led by Dončić, who had 39 points and seven assists, negating Leonard's 41-point performance. Hardaway had another huge game, scoring 28 points and hitting six threes, further justifying Carlisle's overdue late-season decision to replace Richardson, whose shaky jumper resulted in poor spacing, in the starting lineup. Porziņģis only got 12 shots but scored 20 points. The Clippers seemed to be in serious trouble.

"I'm not concerned," Lue said dismissively. "They won two games on our home floor and now we got to return the favor."

The Mavs returned to Dallas with a major home-court advantage. With the vaccine widely available and COVID cases dwindling, the Mavs were allowed to boost Game 3 attendance to 17,705 fans, still shy of the American Airlines Center's capacity but more than three times the size of their largest regular-season crowd. There was an electric sense of anticipation for Dončić's first home playoff game, and he immediately gave the fans what they paid to see. Dončić scored the first 8 points of the game—a one-legged fadeaway followed by a pair of step-back threes, all exploiting switches onto Zubac. He dripped with cockiness, wagging his finger at the Clippers bench after the first step-back and shouting that Zubac couldn't guard him. It was another brash but accurate statement, which is why Lue called time-out to sub for Zubac after Dončić's third bucket and didn't play the center with the starting lineup the rest of the series.

Dončić scored or assisted on the Mavs' first 20 points, at which point they led by 14. Dallas's lead had swelled to 17 when Brunson got off the bench to give Dončić a rest with 4:58 remaining in the quarter, which followed Carlisle's normal substitution pattern. Dončić didn't protest at the time, but that decision was ripe for second guessing after the Clippers went on a 14–0 run to get right back within striking distance. It's not as if Dončić cooled off. He had 11 points in the first quarter, 26 by the half, and finished with a new career playoff high of 44, plus nine rebounds and nine assists. But he didn't get enough help, especially from Porziņģis, who had a dud with 9 points on 3-of-10 shooting, missing all four of his shots off post-ups against smaller defenders. And the Dallas defense got torched, as Leonard and George combined for 65 points and LA shot 57.9 percent from the floor. The Clippers got on the board with a 118–108 win.

Several times in the second half, Dončić grabbed the area of his neck and left shoulder. He received treatment during time-outs and when he rested. Dončić acknowledged postgame that he started feeling pain in the neck at halftime and it shot down the nerves toward his left arm in the second half.

"It's just weird," Dončić said. "Just some massage, some ice and hopefully it will be good." But the pain got worse the next day, prompting the Mavs to list Dončić as questionable for Game 4 with the official diagnosis of a cervical strain.

Dončić played, straps of black kinesiology tape covering his neck and shoulder, but he was seriously hurting. He grabbed his neck and grimaced several times throughout Game 4, often doubling over in pain. He couldn't turn his neck to his left, just a slight problem for a point guard who relies on extraordinary vision to pick apart defenses. Not surprisingly, Dončić performed poorly, finishing with 19 points on 9-of-24 shooting from the floor and missing all five free throw attempts.

How much did the injury impact him? "I don't think that matters right now," Dončić said after the 106–81 series-tying rout. "We lost. Injuries are part of basketball, but I was 100 percent. I played terrible, so just gotta move on to next one."

THE TWO DAYS OFF BETWEEN GAMES, WITH AROUND-THE-CLOCK treatment from Casey Smith and the rest of the Mavs' medical staff, did wonders. By the time Game 5 tipped off, Dončić was ready to put the Mavs on his back along with a superhero cape. He had 19 points and four assists in the first quarter, playing every second. Dončić was up to 27 and eight by halftime; 40 and 12 by the end of the third, when the Mavs led by 14. He faded in the fourth—and the Mavs were fortunate to survive a Clippers rally that ended with Leonard airballing a potential tying three over Finney-Smith with seconds remaining—but he finished with 42 points and 14 assists in the Mavs' 105–100 win.

"He's just one of the toughest players I've ever seen, ever been around," Carlisle said. "He's just a warrior-type guy that happens to be one of the very best players in the world."

Dončić made or assisted on 31 of the Mavs' 37 buckets. He also attempted 37 shots from the floor. "I shot some shots that I shouldn't have shot," Dončić said. "Honestly, I think it was too much."

Porziņģis took only six shots, making half, including a clutch three. The Mavs' counter to the Clippers' small-ball starting lineup—going massive with 7-foot-4 Marjanović at center—made Porziņģis more of a perimeter bystander than ever.

"Yeah, just stretching the floor," said Porziņģis, who stood in the corner on most offensive possessions. "As I said, doing what's best for the team, what's necessary for the team, what they're asking me, and that's it. And staying ready, staying ready if I do need to be involved and making a shot or doing whatever. Just that's it. Just here to do whatever we need to to win."

The Mavs had a prime opportunity to close out the Clippers at home, even leading by 4 entering the fourth quarter of Game 6. But Leonard didn't let the series end in Dallas, as the two-time NBA Finals MVP had arguably the greatest playoff performance of his career, scoring 45 points on 18-of-25 shooting in addition to shouldering a large share of the defensive responsibilities on Dončić. The deciding sequence occurred when Leonard scored on three straight possessions while hunting Dončić on switches. Leonard hit a pull-up in Dončić's face, a step-back three over the Mavs' superstar, and then another step-back three over Finney-Smith when Dallas scrambled out of the switch.

"I mean, he destroyed us," said Dončić, whose 29 points and 11 assists weren't enough. "He had a hell of a game. And that's what he does."

So this strange series, in which neither team had managed to win at home, would come down to Game 7 in LA. Dončić responded with a historic performance, scoring 46 points and dishing out 14 assists—accounting for 77 points, the most ever in a Game 7, according to the Elias Sports Bureau. But it didn't matter, not even enough to make the finish dramatic. The Clippers cruised to a 126–111 win to eliminate the Mavs. Dončić had huge numbers—averages of 35.7 points, 7.9 rebounds, and 10.3 assists in the series—but a hollow feeling.

"I mean, nothing yet," Dončić said when asked what he proved during the series. "We made the playoffs twice since I've been here. We lost both times. At the end, you get paid to win. We didn't do it."

Dončić also had a disgruntled sidekick. Porziņġis was embarrassed by his mediocre production in the series after averaging 13.1 points and 5.4 rebounds. He wasn't the only key Dallas player to have a disappointing series. Brunson, who finished fourth in the NBA's Sixth Man of the Year voting, had his playing time cut drastically over the course of the series, contributing only 2 points and one assist during his 10 minutes in Game 7. But the spotlight shined much brighter on Porziņġis with his max contract than on Brunson, a second-round pick still on his rookie deal, and the diminished role reinforced Porziņġis's concerns that he was nothing but a bit player in the Luka show.

"How do I feel? I mean, I'm good," Porziņġis said after Game 7. "I tried to put in the work, tried to work hard. I do my part, listen to the coaches, what I'm asked to do, and that's it."

Porziņġis said the right things about trying to "focus on what I can control"—a phrase he used twice—and looking forward to working during the offseason. "Whatever I do, it seems like it's always something," Porziņġis said, lamenting the scrutiny on him. "I just try to be as professional as I can." The truth was, he hoped to get traded over the summer, but he was savvy enough to know he couldn't say that, not so soon after his bitter divorce with the Knicks.

"He's a great player," Dončić said when asked about Porziņġis during exit interviews the next day. "I don't know what we're going to do next year with the roster. We have a couple free agents. In the NBA, every year, you have new teammates. I don't know what's going to happen. But he's a great player."

For the first time in Carlisle's 13-year tenure in Dallas, his job security seemed uncertain. The franchise hadn't won a playoff series since their championship run 10 years before, but the coach couldn't be blamed for that. It was fair to question, however, if Carlisle was the right man for the job going forward, primarily because neither of the Mavs' best players enjoyed playing for him.

"That's a question you'll have to ask Mark," Carlisle said in the wake of the Game 7 loss. "I obviously do [believe I'm the right man for the job]. But I'd text him and see what he has to say about it."

Was Carlisle fishing for a public vote of confidence? Perhaps. But Cuban's text reply minutes later was rather lukewarm: "Let me tell you how I look at coaching. You don't make a change to make a change. Unless you have someone that you know is much, much, much better, the grass is rarely greener on the other side."

CHAPTER 10

THE FALLOUT

TWELVE DAYS AFTER THE GAME 7 LOSS, CUBAN SUMMONED SEV-
eral of his most trusted basketball advisors to his spacious bunker suite at the American Airlines Center. The Mavericks were
in crisis mode after one hell of a messy week. Carlisle had just
resigned, less than 24 hours after the Mavs announced that they
had "mutually agreed to part ways" with Nelson, who was actually
fired by Cuban a few days earlier. Voulgaris, who had been working
remotely the previous two months, had no intent to return after
his contract expired that offseason. He'd been the focal point of
an explosive article published by *The Athletic* earlier that week that
described Voulgaris as the Mavs' "shadow GM," detailed some of
the franchise's behind-the-scenes drama from that season, and
portrayed his presence as a looming, irritating threat to Dončić's
long-term desire to stay in Dallas. "Total bullshit," Cuban tweeted
in response.

However, the harsh truth was that the Mavericks had stumbled
into chaos. This was a franchise whose structure had crumbled a
few years into the career of its young, generational superstar, having

failed spectacularly in its ambitious quest to quickly build a sustainable contender around Dončić. Cuban, who had vacancies to fill at head coach and lead basketball executive, sought help finding a path forward.

So Cuban called a meeting with five men he knew had the Mavs' best interests at heart. Nowitzki, the legend who hadn't had a formal role in the two years since he retired, was in the room and ready to serve in a "special advisor" role. So was Michael Finley, the former All-Star who'd returned to the franchise as a front office executive eight years earlier and was now the highest-ranked person left standing in the basketball operations department. They were joined by a few people who weren't famous but had long been part of the franchise's fabric: Keith Grant, the assistant GM who had been with the franchise since it was founded in 1980; Casey Smith, hired as head athletic trainer in 2004 and since promoted to director of player health and performance; and Don Kalkstein, the team's sports psychologist for more than two decades.

The departures of Nelson and Carlisle seemed sudden and surprising, given their long tenures and, in Carlisle's case, Cuban's recent vow to stay the course. But the unceremonious exits weren't shocking to those familiar with the turmoil that had been simmering for the previous few seasons. The team's culture had been corrupted by infighting and scheming similar to Game of Thrones storylines. The fallout had finally begun.

SEVEN MONTHS EARLIER, PANDEMIC SAFETY MEASURES HAD PREvented the majority of the Mavericks' scouting department from joining the team's top decision-makers in person during the 2020 draft, which had been pushed back months into mid-November. The scouts joining via Zoom received quite a surprise as Dallas went on the clock with the 18th overall pick: Voulgaris, not Nelson, was running the show.

Voulgaris's growing influence on Cuban, who had been the Mavs' ultimate personnel shot-caller since the day he bought the team in January 2000, was well known within the organization and the cause of much grumbling from those loyal to Nelson. The Mavs had been trying to trade up into the lottery—dangling Jalen Brunson as bait, along with the 18th and 31st overall picks—for weeks, with Tyrese Haliburton as the target. Nelson made the calls to other teams, never finding a taker, but it was Voulgaris and his analytics department that ranked Haliburton as the best player in the class and convinced Cuban to aggressively pursue a pick high enough to take him.

Nevertheless, after Haliburton went off the board at No. 12 to the Kings, Nelson anticipated that he'd make the call on the 18th pick. Minutes before the Mavs went on the clock, Nelson reached out to Villanova forward Saddiq Bey's representatives to inform them that Bey would be Dallas's pick. Voulgaris instead selected Arizona wing Josh Green. (Kentucky's Tyrese Maxey and TCU's Desmond Bane were still on the board and have emerged as star guards for the Sixers and Grizzlies, respectively, but they weren't part of the discussion in the Dallas organization at the time.)

The story of how Voulgaris ended up in charge varies based on who's telling it. Some believe that Voulgaris pulled a coup, getting the green light from Cuban at the last moment. Voulgaris insists that Nelson stormed out of the room right before the Mavs' pick.

"He flipped out on me like, 'Why aren't you the GM of the team if you're so smart?'" Voulgaris recalled.

The significance of the moment was not subject to any debate. It was a major blow to Nelson's standing in the organization that he had worked for since 1997, arriving along with his father Don as the coach/GM's right-hand man—and then not just surviving his father's messy divorce with Cuban in 2005 but getting promoted to replace him as the Mavs' top basketball executive.

"I think the writing was on the wall for him at this point," said

Voulgaris, an outsider whose perceived arrogance rubbed a lot of basketball lifers in the organization the wrong way. "He realized that the team is no longer his, like very clearly."

Nelson had plenty of experience engaging in power struggles during his nearly two-decade tenure as the Mavs' president of basketball operations. His level of influence on Cuban's personnel decisions had ebbed and flowed with external and internal threats. It started with Dan Fegan, the agent whose client list included many Mavericks over the years. Fegan was known to have so much sway with Cuban that rival agents and executives would sarcastically refer to Fegan as "your boss" during conversations with Nelson.

Then, in 2013, Cuban hired Gersson Rosas away from the Rockets as general manager to work under Nelson. That arrangement lasted only three uncomfortable months before Rosas resigned just before the season began, frustrated by how little impact he was allowed to have on the team's basketball operations. "He kind of had the opportunity to stay 90 days, see what happened," Cuban said, spinning Rosas's Dallas tenure as a trial period of sorts, a ridiculous premise for an executive who soon returned to the rival Rockets. "He made his choice. I wish him the best." Nelson had successfully run off a potential successor.

Yet another threat arrived when Chandler Parsons—one of Fegan's clients—landed on the Mavericks' payroll on a maximum contract. Parsons signed that contract in 2014 while partying with Cuban in an Orlando nightclub and frequently socialized with his billionaire boss. Parsons also enjoyed a perk usually reserved for superstars: significant input on personnel decisions. Cuban has angrily denied that Parsons had more power than Nelson, but both Parsons and Nelson believed that to be the case at times. Parsons would privately boast about being a player/GM and mapped out the Mavs' infamous plan to pursue DeAndre Jordan and a three-and-D wing—settling on Wesley Matthews after Danny Green showed no interest in leaving San Antonio—in the summer of 2015. Parsons recruited Jordan for months and hung out with him every day for two weeks leading up to free agency. Nelson was responsible for handling the logistics of the official pitch to Jordan and called Parsons to ask whether he wanted to attend. "Donnie, I am the fuckin' meeting!" Parsons barked before hanging up the phone.

NELSON, ALONG WITH CARLISLE, SMITH, AND NOWITZKI, managed to convince Cuban not to give Parsons another massive contract the next summer, when he opted out of the final year of his deal despite undergoing season-ending knee surgeries in both of his years in Dallas. After Parsons left for another max deal in Memphis, Nelson told people, "I've got my team back."

Voulgaris ended up being the last in a line of real or perceived threats to Nelson. There had been a sense that Nelson's power within the organization, or how much Cuban valued him, had been drastically diminished well before that draft night.

"I wanted to be a part of something. I wanted to win basketball games," Voulgaris said after his contract had expired. "Changing the organizational structure of the Dallas Mavericks was never something I was interested in unless I was going to be the guy in charge, and I wasn't even sure. I never actually wanted to be the guy in charge until it became clear that the guy in charge didn't want me around. And then I was like, 'Oh, OK, now it's competitive....'

"Just to be very clear, the first two years or whatever, Donnie was very pleasant around me when I was there. It's just, you hear certain things, you learn certain things, you're told certain things. It was a very gossipy workplace, very gossipy. It was like a sewing circle over there."

There were some secrets, however. Only a select few knew that Nelson had gone to Cuban in August with an allegation that Jason Lutin, Cuban's chief of staff, had "sexually harassed and sexually assaulted" Nelson's 29-year-old nephew in a Chicago hotel room during an informal meeting regarding job possibilities at the 2020 All-Star Weekend. This was either right before or right after—again, the stories conflict—Nelson and his agent had initiated discussions with Cuban about a 10-year contract. Nelson never had a contract with Cuban—working as an at-will employee, an extreme rarity for an NBA executive—and wanted that to change. Cuban offered $66 million; Nelson countered at $77 million. The talks stopped soon thereafter. An internal investigation cleared Lutin, a gay man who at the time was still in the closet, of any wrongdoing.

Lutin wasn't a public figure, but he was a power broker behind the scenes. Lutin was a fundraiser for the Obama campaign when Cuban hired him as chief of staff, overseeing all of his companies. There was speculation at the time that Cuban had aspirations to run for president, but that fizzled following the Mavs' 2018 scandal. It was Lutin who recommended the hiring of Cynthia Marshall as the Mavs' CEO, recruiting her to lead the cleanup of the franchise's corporate side. He became good friends with multiple Mavs players, most prominently Dwight Powell, helping make the center's charitable foundation a huge success. He was also a strong ally of Carlisle, sitting next to the coach's wife at home games and next to Carlisle on flights when Lutin traveled with the team. Founded or not, a lot of people throughout the organization considered a strong bond with Lutin to correlate with job security. "Lutin's the real puppet master around that team," Voulgaris said.

The accusations became public in March 2022, when Nelson filed a lawsuit against the Mavericks claiming that he was "fired in retaliation" for reporting Lutin's alleged misconduct to Cuban. Nelson's lawsuit, a 46-page filing, included several examples of how Cuban's "micromanaging and meddling" repeatedly resulted in mismanagement of the Mavs' roster. It also repeatedly referenced the *Sports Illustrated* exposé from 2018. "Given the Mavericks' checkered history, Cuban decided he could not endure the reputational risk and likely NBA sanctions if Lutin's sexual harassment was revealed," the lawsuit claimed. (Nelson's lawsuit notably omitted the Mavs' most recent sexual misconduct scandal. Tony Ronzone, the Mavs' director of player personnel who worked closely with Nelson, was fired in the wake of a July 2020 *Sports Illustrated* story accusing him of sexual assault. The Mavs originally responded with a scathing 800-word rebuttal to the "one-sided, incomplete and sensational form of journalism" and then refused to comment on Ronzone's dismissal.)

"This lawsuit—and its utterly fictitious Petition—represents the final desperate effort of Nelson's lengthy scheme to extort as much as $100 million from the Dallas Mavericks," read the Mavericks' legal response to Nelson's suit filed the following day. "Long before filing this lawsuit, Nelson demanded that he receive, in effect, blackmail payment in exchange for his promises not to expose the sexual orientation of a former Mavericks front-office employee or to assert other claims which he promised would embarrass Defendants and certain individuals, including Mark Cuban. When his demands were not met, and his own conduct was revealed, Nelson's desperation intensified." The response further stated that Nelson was "terminated for performance issues and unrelated misconduct," citing the amount of time Nelson spent on his many outside business interests, an under-the-table sale of his ownership stake in the G League franchise Texas Legends that didn't follow NBA guidelines, and unspecified "serious allegations that Nelson had violated the Mavericks' Respect in the Workplace policy" days before he was fired. The suit was dismissed with prejudice on Halloween 2024 after the parties agreed to confidential terms.

THAT'S THE LEVEL OF DRAMA AND DYSFUNCTION THAT OCCURRED at the highest levels of the Mavericks organization—and it trickled down to the coaches, players, and assistants. Carlisle and Voulgaris, for instance, believed that Mosley was using his bond with Dončić to position himself as Carlisle's successor. A common route to job security in the NBA—and perhaps even a promotion—has long been to establish a connection with a superstar; Mosley had that with Dončić. It was a mutually beneficial relationship. Mosley knew how to push Dončić's buttons to get the best out of him during workouts. He's 6 feet 8 and stays in phenomenal shape from his mixed martial arts training, so Mosley could play physical defense and challenge Dončić during their frequent one-on-one battles. Mosley also developed a feel for when to talk trash to stoke Dončić's competitive fire and when to make a joke to lighten the mood. "That's my guy," Dončić usually says with a big smile whenever Mosley's name is brought up.

Carlisle and Voulgaris, on the other hand, were definitely not Dončić's guys. "He is the most powerful person in the whole organization," Voulgaris said later. "If he doesn't like you, you're gone, no matter who you are." Carlisle and Voulgaris developed a mutual distrust of Mosley, who declined to be interviewed for this book and abided by Carlisle's policy preventing assistants from talking to the media unless granted his permission in rare cases.

Procopio, although he wasn't still part of the organization at that point, offered a different viewpoint, shared by some other current and former staffers: "That's what most assistants do to keep assistant jobs. I don't think there's anything wrong with it at all. At least Jamahl wasn't faking it. You get a lot of these coaches that are lazy as fuck and won't do anything, but the press comes in the last 15 minutes [of practice] and they sprint like they're fucking Usain Bolt to work out the best player. Then they fake to be nice people and they're really not nice people. Jamahl is really that hardworking, and the second thing is he's a genuinely good person. I think he was just trying to get the best [out of Dončić]. Was he doing a little politicking to help his job search? Yeah, for sure, but I don't think it was an undermining thing."

But Carlisle, well aware that coaches who have friction with the face of a franchise typically end up looking for another job, wasn't fond of having his potential replacement on his staff but couldn't fire Mosley. So Carlisle lobbied for Mosley as a candidate for other head coaching jobs, helping him land interviews with the Cavaliers, Knicks, Pacers, and Pelicans.

"He's obviously, in my opinion, ready for this kind of opportunity and I think this is something that he'll thrive in," Carlisle said before an April 2 game in New York. He was confined to his hotel room due to what turned out to be a false positive COVID-19 test result, so Mosley served as acting head coach that night, although Carlisle still handled the pregame media availability. After the Mavs' 99–86 win, which players celebrated by mobbing Mosley and dousing him with water bottles as he entered the locker room, Dončić gladly campaigned for his guy.

"He's got the things that are needed for a head coach," Dončić said. "He can be the head coach, for sure."

The head coach? Did Dončić mean to intentionally imply that Mosley could be the Mavs' head coach? Or was it a case of a player not being precise with his words while speaking his fourth language? With Zoom media sessions, when reporters were only unmuted when called upon to ask a question, those kinds of follow-ups usually didn't happen. Dončić probably didn't mind, especially in this instance.

The biggest obstacle to Mosley becoming the Mavericks' head coach might have been how much Cuban valued Voulgaris's opinion. Voulgaris doubted whether Mosley had the X's and O's acumen to excel in the job. He blamed the schemes used by Mosley, Dallas's defensive coordinator, for much of the Mavs' struggles on that end of the floor, despite Carlisle having ultimate authority.

At the urging of Cuban, Voulgaris was much more visible that season. He was a frequent courtside spectator, which was especially noticeable with no or few fans in arenas. He stuck out even more because he usually had an open laptop, and Voulgaris was informed that players found that to be odd and unsettling, as was his lack of emotion. Voulgaris was taken aback during an early February home game against the Warriors when Dončić yelled at him, "Don't fucking tell me to calm down." Dončić apparently thought that Voulgaris made a downward motion with his hands that was directed toward him. Voulgaris said any such motion or comments came from Cuban, who was seated next to him.

"[Dončić] apologized to me profusely in the elevator after he blew up at me courtside, when Mark was yelling at him and he didn't want to blow up at Mark, so he made believe that he thought it was me," Voulgaris said. Cuban didn't sit by Voulgaris anymore after that night, and Voulgaris soon started leaving his laptop in his office.

Voulgaris drew the ire of Dončić again late in an April 16 home loss to the Knicks. He left his courtside seat with the Mavs trailing by 10 points in the final minute. It wasn't unusual for Voulgaris to retreat to his office near the end of the games, where he would often look up data before his postgame meeting with Carlisle, but Dončić took notice and umbrage on this occasion. He openly complained in the locker room that Voulgaris had quit on the team, which was relayed to Voulgaris in a panicked, post-midnight phone call from Carlisle.

"It was such a non-event that I didn't think it was a big deal, and the fact that it became a big deal led me to believe that this is just not worth it to me," Voulgaris said, figuring that it'd be easily explained to Dončić after he had cooled off the next day, likely by Mosley.

Voulgaris showed up to the American Airlines Center again two nights later, when the Mavs played the Kings. When Voulgaris walked out onto the sideline during warm-ups more than an hour before tip-off, Mosley's one-on-one workout with a player suddenly became much more animated.

"Immediately, it turned into hand clapping, feet stomping,"

Voulgaris recalled. "Like, 'We play 'til the final whistle! We never quit! Don't ever quit on the game! We ain't done yet.'"

Voulgaris assumed Mosley's comments were meant for him to hear. He figured at that point that any relationship he had with Dončić was doomed, so he decided he was done being around the team. Voulgaris informed Carlisle and Cuban that he would work remotely if they wanted his services the rest of the season.

"If I'm distracting that fucking guy, I don't need to be around," Voulgaris said. "Whatever the case may be, no matter how I see it, it doesn't matter at the end of the day. He is the fulcrum of the team. So I was like, 'Cool.' Plus, I was trying to find a way out of this job to begin with."

So Voulgaris started counting down the days until his contract expired in the fall while continuing to communicate with Carlisle on a daily basis about analytical data and basketball strategy. Voulgaris looked forward to being done with the Mavs' "high school drama," as he called it, but ended up in the middle of a media circus despite his silence at the time.

"I didn't want to continue working for the team," Voulgaris said, "but I didn't want to go out like that."

THE SEQUENCE OF EVENTS IN THE WAKE OF THE MAVS' SEASON ending—the viral story villainizing Voulgaris, Nelson's supposed "mutual" departure, and Carlisle's resignation, all over a span of three days—was widely misconstrued as a domino effect. Carlisle's exit, in particular, had nothing to do with the proverbial dumpster fires in the front office. This was a calculated decision by Carlisle, made in the best interests of his career. He knew that his days in Dallas were numbered.

Carlisle had planned to visit Dončić in Slovenia later that month, hoping to watch his national team practice and perhaps find a way to bond with the star away from the stress of an NBA season. That trip got canceled after Carlisle was informed by a third party that Dončić didn't want him to come. The reason given was that Dončić didn't want any distractions as the Slovenian national team prepared for an Olympic qualifying tournament, but his wishes squelched hope that Carlisle could salvage his rocky relationship with the superstar.

Carlisle, who had two seasons remaining on his deal, had attempted to initiate a conversation with Cuban about a contract extension. Cuban quickly shot down that idea. Carlisle would go into the next season on the hot seat if he stayed in Dallas.

Dončić never asked for Carlisle's departure. He didn't have to, as all parties understood that a divorce was inevitable. Carlisle seized control of the timing, stepping down early in the annual cycle of NBA coaching changes. He announced the end of his 13-year tenure with the Mavs by typing out a one-paragraph statement on his phone's notes app and texting it to ESPN's Adrian Wojnarowski. "Dallas will always be home, but I am excited about the next chapter of my coaching career," the statement concluded, making it clear that Carlisle was resigning, not retiring.

Rumors quickly spread within NBA circles connecting Carlisle to two jobs: Milwaukee and Indiana, in that order of attractiveness. The Pacers had just fired first-time head coach Nate Bjorkgren after his rookie year went poorly and wanted an experienced replacement. Carlisle, who'd maintained a good relationship with Indiana owner Herb Simon after stints as both an assistant and head coach for the Pacers, was at the top of the list. The Bucks job wasn't open, but it was widely expected that Mike Budenholzer would be fired if Milwaukee didn't have a playoff breakthrough, and the Bucks were trailing the Nets 3–2 in the Eastern Conference semifinals when Carlisle stepped down. But the Bucks beat the Nets that night and won again in Game 7. Days later, a week after his resignation in Dallas, Carlisle finalized a four-year deal worth $29 million plus incentives to return to the Pacers.

"You never want to get to a point where you ever feel like you're overstaying your welcome, and I just felt like this is the right time," Carlisle said over the phone after accepting the Pacers' offer. "I just have such great respect for Mark and everyone there, and I'm fortunate to move on to another great opportunity."

Carlisle said that he'd concluded that his departure from Dallas would be "mutually beneficial" and gushed with praise of Dončić. "I just sent him a message thanking him for three amazing years," Carlisle said. "I learned many things from him, and I told him that I'm glad I'm only going to see him twice a year. I mean it in the most complimentary way, of course. I think he's the best young player in the world. I think these three years set up as a major springboard for the next 10 for him. I expect him to be an NBA champion. I expect him to be a multiple MVP winner. I just have an amazing level of respect for his abilities and his grasp of the game. He's truly a once-in-the-generation type player." (Dončić had a one-word reply to Carlisle's lengthy text: "Thanks.")

Then, unsolicited, Carlisle weighed in on who he thought the Mavs should hire to replace him: "My hope is that Jason Kidd will be the next coach of the Mavs because he and Luka have so many things in common as players. I just think that it would be a great situation for Luka, and I think it would be an amazing situation for Jason. I'm the only person on the planet that's coached both of those guys and that knows about all of their special qualities as basketball players. To me, that just would be a great marriage, but that's just an opinion."

The endorsement of Kidd was widely perceived as a passive-aggressive slight of Mosley within the NBA coaching community. As president of the National Basketball Coaches Association, that perception was problematic for Carlisle, especially coupled with public criticism of the Pacers for not legitimately considering any minority candidates before hiring Carlisle.

Carlisle had some inside information on the Mavs' coaching

search, or lack thereof. Kidd had been reported as a candidate, along with Mosley and others, but Cuban and his five-man advisory committee had already decided Kidd would be the Mavs' target during the meeting they held in the wake of Carlisle's resignation. Kidd had mixed results as a head coach—a 183–190 record in a one-year stint with the Nets and a three-and-a-half-season run with the Bucks— but was immensely respected among the men huddling in Cuban's bunker suite. All but Finley were part of the title team in 2011, when Nowitzki starred and Kidd served as the veteran leader and coach on the floor. (The bitterness Cuban felt about Kidd reneging on a verbal agreement to re-sign with the Mavs to go to the Knicks in 2012 had long been water under the bridge.) They believed in Kidd's extraordinary basketball intelligence and his ability to earn Dončić's trust and respect with his Hall of Fame pedigree as a point guard. They were confident that Kidd, who'd won another ring as a Lakers assistant coach the previous season, had learned a lot about coaching since taking the Brooklyn job immediately after retiring as a player.

Cuban told reporters that the Mavs needed to hire a lead basketball executive before focusing on the coaching position, but that was a fib. The internal discussions were about who could run the franchise's basketball operations department and would fit well with Kidd. The focus soon narrowed to an outside-the-box candidate: Nico Harrison, Nike's vice president of North America basketball operations.

Harrison had deep connections with players (including Dončić) throughout the league—past, present, and future—often dating to their high school years. He had rapport with all of the power agents. He was widely respected by the many coaches, executives, scouts, and others in the basketball industry who had participated in Nike's clinics and other grassroots programs. He had managed a multibillion-dollar business and could provide structure that the Mavs' front office had been sorely lacking. He was known to have a good eye for talent, although scouting for potential shoe deals is different than building an NBA roster. He had never worked for a team, but Harrison had discussed executive positions with other organizations before.

Harrison and Kidd had been tight for years and had talked about working together as a coach/executive combo. Finley, who would be the new GM's right-hand man, and Nowitzki knew Harrison well and had confidence he could thrive in the role. Harrison was the Mavs' man, part of a package deal with Kidd. Their deals were agreed to in principle on June 24, hours after Carlisle's endorsement of Kidd, and officially announced four days later.

Dončić wasn't heavily involved in the process and didn't want to be. "I'm not the one making decisions there," he said the day after Nelson's firing during a press conference with the Slovenian national team program. However, Cuban had kept him in the loop and was confident that he was comfortable with his new bosses, at least on the organizational flowchart. If Dončić wanted veto power, he could have had it. It's one of the many perks of being a perennial first-team All-NBA talent.

But it was awkward that Mosley—who probably would have been Dončić's pick—was passed over and would be moving on. Mosley, after toiling as an assistant for 14 years, did finally get his opportunity to be a head coach. The Magic hired Mosley on July 11 after Carlisle, who was proud to be the president of the coaches association, strongly lobbied Orlando ownership and management on his former assistant's behalf. "Congrats my guy," Dončić tweeted with a few "raising hands" emojis, responding to the news of Mosley's new gig.

Dončić had not offered any public comment about the Mavs' hiring Kidd or Harrison. He declined to answer questions about the Mavericks while competing with the Slovenian national team, saying he wanted to keep his focus on the Olympics. Kidd and Dončić had cordial conversations via FaceTime and text, but any in-depth discussions would wait until after the Slovenian program's first Olympics appearance. Kidd soon hired Igor Kokoškov, who had stepped down as Slovenia's coach but was still close with Dončić, as an assistant, making sure the Mavs' superstar had a familiar, friendly face on the coaching staff.

ONE MAJOR PIECE OF BUSINESS FOR THE MAVS THAT SUMMER would be signing Dončić to a contract extension, but that was a mere formality. He had become the first player to qualify for a super-max extension of his rookie contract—the result of his two All-NBA selections—and that deal would be worth more than $200 million over five seasons. The system is designed to make sure teams can keep the stars they draft for at least a second contract. Only the Mavs could offer Dončić the supermax (worth 30 percent of the salary cap in the first year, as opposed to 25 percent for a normal max), and Dallas would have had the right to match any offer Dončić received if for some wild reason he decided to become a restricted free agent when his rookie deal expired. If he was determined to become an unrestricted free agent, he could have done so, but at a massive cost. It would have required playing on a one-year qualifying offer of $13.4 million after his rookie deal expired.

So Luka, you plan to sign that supermax? "Um…I think you know the answer," Dončić said the day after the season ended, smiling at first and then laughing. "I think you know the answer."

The pressing question for the revamped Mavs brass: How would they manage to build a championship-caliber roster around Dončić? Cuban candidly discussed that issue during a late June appearance with alumni from prestigious Dallas private school St. Mark's, comments he probably didn't anticipate would be made public. "Trust me, nobody wants to get Luka more help than I do. What do we need is really the question, and we need a second scorer," Cuban said.

A few weeks later, however, Kidd insisted the Mavs already had a suitable co-star in Porziņģis. "I think he's excited, he's ready to work, and I think you're going to see a different KP," Kidd said at the July 15 press conference officially introducing Harrison and him. "This is a positive summer for him. He's healthy. I think he's really excited about this opportunity. I think he's a perfect fit for Luka."

Cuban seconded Kidd, calling Porziņģis "unfairly maligned" and seemingly blaming Carlisle for Porziņģis's postseason dud. "During the playoffs, he did exactly what he was asked to do. Exactly," Cuban said. "He put team first, and he put his own personal statistics [aside], knowing that people were going to give him a hard time. Because, as he said to me and others, he just wants to win."

The revised messaging was that the Mavs already had the core of a contender. It was the culture that needed work.

"I'm excited to get my hands, and watch Jason get his hands, on the roster," Harrison said. "Because I really believe that when you change the culture, when you bring in some new leadership and constant communication, I think the whole team is going to rise up. Like overnight. I really believe that."

The Mavs still had a chance to make a major upgrade, one last big swing in free agency while Dončić was a remarkable bargain on a rookie contract. Their target: Kyle Lowry, a five-time All-Star point guard who was two years removed from helping the Raptors win a title as Kawhi Leonard's co-star. Lowry was 35, certainly not a long-term fit next to Dončić, but his blend of skill, smarts, tough- ness, and leadership could fill most, if not all, of the Mavs' needs. Dallas dealt Josh Richardson, the previous summer's prized trade acquisition who lost his starting job late in the season, to Boston in a salary dump to clear the books to make Lowry a big offer. But Lowry chose to go to Miami instead, opting to join his Team USA buddy Jimmy Butler with the Heat.

The Mavs had a new coach and a new GM, but it was the same old free agency bridesmaids tale in Dallas. The Mavs pivoted to re-sign Tim Hardaway Jr., their (distant) second-leading scorer in the playoffs, to a four-year, $75 million deal. Their only significant offseason addition was Reggie Bullock, a three-and-D wing they signed with the mid-level exception. It was a summer of massive change for the Mavericks, but the core of the roster remained the same. So did the doubts about whether Dončić had enough help.

"Well, when you got a guy like Luka, he's going to win championships," Harrison said early in his tenure. "So, hopefully, he wins them in Dallas and I'm a part of it."

The Mavs had some time to get the roster right around Dončić, but the clock was ticking. His supermax extension would run through the 2026–27 season, but the final year is a player option, a perk that had once been a rarity in a rookie max extension. From the end of the 2011 lockout until 2020, only three of the 17 rookie max extensions signed included player options. Those went to Indiana's Paul George, Cleveland's Kyrie Irving, and New Orleans's Anthony Davis—all of whom forced trades before the end of those deals. But Utah's Donovan Mitchell and Boston's Jayson Tatum both successfully pushed for player options in 2020. That set the precedent for stars of a certain status, so it wasn't subject to negotiation for Dončić and Bill Duffy.

The Mavs patiently waited for Slovenia's Olympics run to end, respecting Dončić's wishes, before formally presenting his contract extension. And they made a major production of that, sending a contingent of Cuban, Harrison, Kidd, Nowitzki, Finley, and Smith to Ljubljana to let Dončić sign the contract and celebrate in his hometown. "The food, the wine—the wine, the wine, the wine—was amazing," Cuban said, chuckling between Dončić and Harrison at a press conference to officially announce the deal. "We had a good time with it."

That trip was the first face-to-face time Kidd and Harrison had with Dončić since they were hired. It was symbolic that they hopped on a 12-hour flight halfway around the globe to make it happen. "To confirm to Luka how important he is to us," Cuban said. "This is just the beginning. We want him to know we're there for him, whether it's here in Slovenia, in Dallas or anywhere in the world."

Nothing mattered more to the Mavericks than Dončić's comfort and happiness. After a summer of major change, the franchise's top priority remained the same.

CHAPTER 11

KDOR NE SKAČE NI SLOVENC

Dončić had made a pit stop in Dallas after the Game 7 loss to the Clippers, participating in the Mavs' exit interviews, before hopping on a private jet to his hometown. The lone silver lining to the Mavs' early elimination was that Dončić could be back in Slovenia for all of the national team's training camp and exhibition schedule leading into the Olympic qualifying tournament in Lithuania at the beginning of July, a little more than three weeks after Dallas's season ended.

As much as Dončić could have used some time to decompress and rest, there was nowhere else in the world he would rather have been. It's a sense of pride and brotherhood that brings him back to the Slovenian national team every summer.

"To me, it's a lot of feelings when you represent your country," Dončić said later. "You basically give up your summer to play for your country. I really respect everybody that does that. It's really hard. At some point, you have to go to practice, but you want to be on a beach somewhere. But I always enjoy it, every moment, playing for my national team."

His national team. That distinction mattered, because Slovenia was not the program that would have provided Dončić the easiest path to international glory. With a Spanish passport in his possession, Dončić could have chosen another route as a teen.

Years earlier, as the new kid in Madrid, Dončić wasn't lonely for long. He basically became an honorary Hernangómez *hermano*. Willy and Juancho Hernangómez were older than Dončić—by five and three years, respectively—but Dončić always played with older age groups and bonded with the brothers, who were Madrid natives.

Soon, Dončić was spending the night at the Hernangómez home about 15 minutes away from the Real Madrid campus more often than he slept in his dorm room. They'd go to practice in the mornings and then live the typical teenage life—going to the movies and the mall, playing video games, and watching hoops. Whether he spent the night or not, Dončić usually stayed for dinner.

"His family wasn't in Spain, so most of the days he was with me and my brother and my parents in the house, eating all of the food. Eating all the Spanish jamón," Willy Hernangómez recalled, smiling fondly. "My mom, every day, had to cook jamón for him, because he loved it. My mom would be like, 'Luka, again? You ate all the jamón!' It was super fun. For me, he's part of my family."

Dončić remained part of the Hernangómez family after his mother moved to Spain following his promotion to Real Madrid's top team, and they got an apartment together. Willy was Dončić's road roommate during his first season as a real pro. Dončić would go on vacations with the Hernangómez brothers, too.

If anyone could have recruited Dončić to play for the Spanish national team, it would have been the Hernangómez brothers. But they never even discussed the matter.

It was a popular topic in some Spanish publications as Dončić rose to prominence with Real Madrid. It was an option for Dončić because he had a Spanish passport and had never played in an official FIBA event for the Slovenian national program, only the under-16-friendly tournament in Hungary. It would have been an opportunity for Dončić to join an established powerhouse. Spain had medaled in the previous five EuroBaskets—including three golds—and the last three Olympics.

There was also some scuttlebutt about Dončić playing for Serbia, as his family on his father's side is of Serbian descent. Serbia had also established itself as a world basketball power, winning silver medals at the 2014 World Cup and the 2016 Olympics, losing to the United States on both occasions. But Serbia wasn't a serious consideration for Dončić, either.

"The Slovenian national team, that was the only option for him," his father, Saša Dončić, said in a 2017 Eurohoops.net interview, months before Luka made his official debut with the Slovenian program at EuroBasket. "I read a lot of things in some newspapers, but officially nobody asked. Never. Nobody asked for which team he would play. This is only some story for some journalists."

For Dončić, representing his country meant more than maximizing his odds of winning medals. He was proud to be Slovenian, so he'd play for Slovenia. His strong sense of loyalty made it that simple.

"Luka always loved Slovenia," said Zoran Dragić, Goran's brother and a forward on the Slovenian national team. "He feels himself here with the national team. It's like he's with his brothers. He needs that."

There's a comfort that comes with the culture of his youth. He gets to speak his native language and eat his favorite foods, such as ćevapi, a Balkan sausage dish.

"It's so fun," said Vlatko Čančar, the Denver Nuggets reserve forward who is Dončić's Slovenian teammate. "I feel like it means a lot to him going back home and being around your people, speaking your language, eating your food. That's his way, with all the mental stresses he has during the season, just to flush them away."

The Slovenian national team, composed of professionals who spend their seasons scattered in leagues around the world, has a special kind of competitive camaraderie that extends well beyond the court. "We don't see each other during the year, and summer is when we can be together," said Luka Rupnik, a reserve guard who is one of Dončić's closest friends. The vibe is similar to what the Mavs managed to create in the bubble, but with the sense of brotherhood that comes from being from the same small country. They pass the downtime during training camps or tournaments by competing.

The Slovenians play a lot of cards, usually poker or Tablić, a fishing-style game popular in the Balkans. "Everybody talks shit, so it's even more hungry," Zoran Dragić said, smiling. They also tend to add to the stakes by putting a little money on the line, especially when Dončić is playing, whether it's cards or anything else. Dončić wants to wager on everything—cards, Ping-Pong, trick shots, and whatever goofy game pops into his mind.

"Like in the documentary when Michael Jordan throws the coin against the wall," Čančar said, referring to a scene in *The Last Dance* when Jordan wagered with his security guards. "Any game, he would try to put money on it."

The Slovenian teammates also tend to be passionate about Ping-Pong. They'll often set up tournaments on off days. When Goran Dragić was on the team before the 2017 EuroBasket MVP retired, some of the veterans gave him the nod as the best Ping-Pong player on the roster. Dončić would disagree.

"If you ask Luka, he will say he is," Rupnik said. "Whatever he does, he's the best—at least, that's what he'll say." Rupnik shrugged and added, "It's true most of the time."

Dončić's combination of confidence and competitiveness makes for a lot of fun on the occasions when he doesn't win, however rare they may be. His Slovenian teammates take great pleasure in taunting Dončić when he loses. Rupnik, Edo Murić, and Klemen Prepelič are especially effective at getting under his skin, drawing howls of laughter from other teammates.

"I hope he reads this—he gets so pissed off," Čančar said, cracking up in the visitors' locker room at the American Airlines Center before facing the Mavs. "He can win 10, but if he loses one, he will be pissed off. That's just the nature of him. He's that competitive. And obviously when you have guys who know how to put gas on the fire, it's gonna be even more bad."

The basketball is serious business, of course. Slovenia, part of the basketball-mad former Yugoslavia, has a rich hoops history for such a small country, otherwise known for its beauty—a blend of caves and castles, lakes and mountains. The nation produced five NBA first-round picks over a seven-year span in the late '90s and early 2000s. Slovenia emerged as one of the best basketball programs in Europe during that span but didn't break through to win a Euro-Basket medal until Dončić debuted, serving as Goran Dragić's teenage sidekick during their undefeated championship run in 2017. That team was the subject of a documentary, 2017, which filled movie theaters in Slovenia.

Unlike a lot of NBA stars, who consider whether to play for their national teams on a case-by-case basis, Dončić's commitment is unconditional. If Slovenia is playing a meaningful game, Dončić intends to be in the starting lineup, as long as he isn't injured and there isn't a conflict with the NBA schedule.

Asked whether he'd prefer an NBA title or an Olympic gold medal, Dončić doesn't hesitate to say the latter. "You play for your country and that's something," he said. "But I wouldn't mind both." There's something special for Dončić about playing with "SLOVENIJA" across his chest. As much as Dončić enjoys the atmosphere of playing in packed NBA arenas, nothing can match seeing and hearing sections full of Slovenians, waving the country's white, blue, and red flag, wearing the nation's bright green scarves, and chanting.

Kdor ne skače ni Slovenc

Hej! Hej! Hej!

Rough translation: Anyone who does not jump is not a Slovene. Hey! Hey! Hey!

"This is just the culture of Slovenia," Zoran Dragić said. "We just breathe like one and have crazy fans that support us."

Because of FIBA's bizarre qualifying system, which has critical games that conflict with the NBA and EuroLeague schedules, Slovenia didn't qualify for the 2019 World Cup. Dončić had to wait until 2021—delayed a year by the pandemic—to put on the Slovenian uniform in another major event: an Olympic qualifying tournament in Kaunas, Lithuania.

THE TOURNAMENT STARTED IN LATE JUNE, JUST A FEW WEEKS after the Mavericks were eliminated from the playoffs. Dončić flew home immediately after exit interviews in Dallas to join his teammates in training camp under coach Aleksander Sekulić, who had been promoted after serving as an assistant under Kokoškov. Dončić was the Slovenians' undisputed leader after Goran Dragić's decision to retire from the national team after the EuroBasket title (temporarily, it turned out, as Dragić returned for one final run in 2022). At stake was the Slovenians' hope to clinch the program's first Olympic bid.

That would require winning four games in five days. Dončić and Slovenia cruised through the first three games—beating Angola by 50, Poland by 35, and Venezuela by 28—to set up the anticipated final against host Lithuania. Slovenians made up just a small slice of the sellout crowd at Žalgirio Arena. The rest of the 15,415 seats were filled by rowdy Lithuanians, banging drums while wearing green, yellow, and red—tie-dyed, in many cases. They hoped to watch Jonas Valančiūnas and Domantas Sabonis, the quality NBA starters who formed a towering tandem for the Lithuanian national team, bully the smaller Slovenians. (Slovenia, recognizing its need for size, had added American 7-footer Mike Tobey to the roster as its one allowed naturalized citizen. Tobey, who plays professionally in Europe, said he first heard of the country of Slovenia "when they asked me to get a passport." Good scouting: he quickly formed pick-and-roll rapport with Dončić and feasted on Luka lobs the next few summers.)

The scene at Žalgirio Arena had all the ingredients of an intimidating atmosphere. But Dončić made himself right at home. He delivered an epic performance, putting up 31 points, 11 rebounds, and 13 assists, doing so with ferocity and flair. He snarled and shouted at the hostile crowd after overpowering Lithuanian defenders on and-one drives. He flipped a couple of no-look, behind-the-head dimes to teammates for threes as the Slovenians pulled away in the second half. And Dončić smiled widely as the final seconds expired, standing at mid-court and turning toward the Slovenian section, raising his arms up high to encourage his countrymen to roar even louder as they celebrated the historic moment.

"He was born with how to handle pressure," Rupnik said later. "He didn't really care. In Lithuania, it was just another day at the office for him."

Arvydas Sabonis, Domantas's dad and a European basketball legend, presented Dončić the MVP trophy in a brief postgame ceremony on the court. After a few cordial words and a handshake, Dončić waved to the crowd and pumped his fist as he walked toward his teammates. They mobbed him at mid-court. They lifted him off his feet, bouncing him up and down as he joyously raised his arms toward the rafters again.

"I don't care about the MVP," Dončić said at the postgame press conference. "We won here. We're going to the Olympics, the first time in our country. It's amazing. I think every kid dreams about being in the Olympics. I did, too. So, here we are."

The Olympics in Tokyo—or nearby Saitama, where the basketball games were played—were a far cry from the charged atmosphere the Slovenians experienced in Kaunas. There were still strict pandemic protocols in Japan, preventing fans from attending games and events. The only people allowed in Saitama Super Arena were players, coaches, team staff, media, and some arena workers. Yet Dončić, who frequently feeds off the energy of a crowd, still managed to generate some extra motivation from the stands during Slovenia's Olympic opener against Argentina.

An Argentinian staff member sitting opposite his team's bench shouted something seconds into the game that Dončić considered disrespectful. He's known to listen for anything that might give him an edge, from trash talk to simple strategy that he takes as a slight, such as going under the screen while guarding him on a pick and roll. Whatever this anonymous Argentinian said, Dončić heard what he wanted to hear.

"He was speaking something in Spanish, and Luka of course understood, and it just fueled him," Rupnik recalled. "It was like the first or second play. You cannot do that. He did it, and obviously he felt bad for it in the end."

Dončić splashed threes on three straight possessions in the opening minutes to set the tone for a historic performance. He repeatedly glared toward the offending Argentinian staffer after scoring, sometimes barking in that direction—and Dončić scored a lot. He had 17 points in the first quarter, 31 by halftime. "Una bestia," Manu Ginóbili, one of the stars of Argentina's 2004 Olympic gold-medalist squad, wrote in a halftime tweet gushing about Dončić. Translation: a beast.

Dončić had 48 points by the time he took a seat with 4:35 remaining in a game that Slovenia led by 26. The Olympic record of 55 points, set by Brazilian legend Oscar Schmidt, was within reach.

Sekulić offered to sub Dončić back in to make a run at the record. Dončić declined despite encouragement from his teammates, satisfied with a convincing win over Argentina and a statement made. "This shows the character that he has, that he came here to do something for Slovenia, not himself," Sekulić said after Slovenia's 118–100 win, in which Dončić was 18-of-29 from the floor, 6-of-14 from three-point range, and filled out the box score with 11 rebounds, five assists, and three blocks.

"He is the best player in the world, including the NBA," Argentina head coach Sergio Hernández said. "If there was any doubt in my mind, there is no doubt anymore. He is the best player in the world, and it's an honor to be there in the game with him."

Regardless of whether fans were allowed in the stands, the Olympics was the sort of big stage that Dončić craved, especially since it was Slovenia's first bid. He was more than ready for the moment.

Host Japan had no hope of slowing down Dončić in Slovenia's second game, as he had 25 points, seven rebounds, and seven assists while playing only 26 minutes in a 116–81 rout. Spain, the European power loaded with current and former NBA talent (and several of Dončić's former Real Madrid teammates), made it much more difficult in the group play finale. The Spaniards double-teamed and trapped Dončić on a regular basis and employed a variety of junk defenses, doing anything possible to get the ball out of his hands. They succeeded in that mission, limiting Dončić to only 12 points on 2-of-7 shooting, but Dončić dominated in other facets with 14 rebounds and nine assists to lead Slovenia to a 95–87 comeback win.

"Even when we were down by 12 points, we believed we could win," Zoran Dragić said afterward. "This is like a big family. We breathe like one, and today we show that even if we are so small country, we have hell of a player."

Slovenia advanced to face Germany in the quarterfinals, which was Dončić's third win-or-go-home game in a span of less than two months. He had certainly proven himself under pressure with the 46-point, 14-assist performance in the Game 7 loss to the Clippers and the 31-point triple-double to take the Olympic bid from Lithuania, but Slovenia didn't need a superhero outing to get past Germany. Dončić had 28 points, eight rebounds, and 11 assists in a 94–70 win as Slovenia improved to 17–0 with him in uniform, dating to the EuroBasket title run. "When you have Luka, it's easy. Everything's easy," Sekulić said after Slovenia punched its ticket to the semifinals, guaranteeing that it would play for a medal.

Facing France, however, was far from easy. The Frenchmen were uniquely suited to defend Dončić, featuring three-time NBA Defensive Player of the Year Rudy Gobert as the 7-foot-1 anchor and Nicolas Batum, the 6-foot-8, 230-pound wing who'd guarded Dončić for much of the Mavs' recent series against the Clippers. Relying on that duo, France was determined to take away Dončić's drives. The strategy succeeded, for the most part, as Dončić made only five of his 18 shots from the floor, and France led by double figures with a few minutes remaining in the third quarter.

But Dončić had one of the best passing performances in Olympic history, highlighted by a dime he bounced between Gobert's legs to Tobey, whose 23 points were fueled by France's commitment to slowing Dončić down. Dončić dished out 18 assists—two shy of the Olympic record—with only one turnover. Six of those assists came in the fourth quarter, allowing Slovenia to stay within striking distance and pull within a point when Dončić fed Prepelič for a three with 33 seconds remaining.

Slovenia got a stop, and Dončić grabbed the rebound. It was his 10th of the game, giving Dončić a 16–10–18 line and the Olympics' first triple-double since LeBron James in 2012. More importantly, it gave Dončić and Slovenia 20 seconds to generate a game-winning shot. He walked the ball up the court, directing traffic as he crossed the half-court line with Batum crouched in front of him. Tobey set a screen to the left of the "TOKYO 2020" half-court logo. France switched, putting Gobert on Dončić, who tried to work his way to his favorite sweet spot on the left wing.

Gobert damn sure wasn't going to let Dončić get a step-back three. The big man was well aware that was the shot Dončić wanted. Like everyone else interested in the NBA, Gobert had seen the highlight of Dončić's left-wing step-back beating the Clippers in the bubble dozens of times, among the many other occasions Dončić hit big shots from that spot. Gobert cut Dončić off several feet beyond the three-point arc as Batum clogged up the middle of the court, sagging off Prepelič and double-teaming when Dončić tried to drive to his right.

With five seconds on the clock, Dončić threw a bounce pass to Prepelič on the right wing. Prepelič immediately attacked, driving to his right as Batum slid to recover. The 6-foot-3 Prepelič darted into the lane for a layup—only to have Batum, blessed with a condor-esque 7-foot-1 wingspan, reach from behind to swat the ball off the glass. Final: France 90, Slovenia 89.

As Batum and the French celebrated, Dončić shouted at a ref one last time for the day and then slumped over the scorer's table. He made his way to Slovenia's bench area, sitting down and draping a towel over his hung head, before Batum approached, squatting in front of Dončić and looking his opponent in the eye before offering some affirmation. They exchanged hugs before parting ways.

"He told me he hates playing against me in a good way," Dončić said during his postgame press conference, when he had ice wrapped on his left wrist as a precaution after crashing into a plexiglass table on the sideline while hustling defensively. "I really respect him. He's a really class act, and that was a really nice comment."

Batum succinctly summed up his respect level for Dončić, only 22 years old at the time: "He's the present. And he's next."

Slovenia still had a chance to claim bronze, which would have been the nation's first Olympic medal in a team sport. Australia, a program loaded with NBA talent that was seeking its first Olympic medal in basketball, stood in the way. The 107–93 loss to the Boomers was a frustrating end to a fantastic run for Dončić and the Slovenians.

For the first time that summer, Dončić wasn't the most dominant player on the floor. Australia guard Patty Mills, the NBA veteran who earned a championship ring as a key reserve for the San Antonio Spurs, scorched Slovenia for 42 points and nine assists. Dončić, playing with his left wrist and forearm heavily taped, produced 22 points, eight rebounds, and seven assists, but it wasn't a pretty performance. He committed eight turnovers and made only seven of 20 shots from the floor. He also drew his fifth technical foul in six Olympic games for arguing a no-call at the halftime buzzer.

"At some point, we were a little bit too emotional both games, especially me," Dončić said postgame, his eyes visibly red. "We've got to learn from that. This is not the way I should be behaving. I've got to learn from that, but at the same point, we're playing for our country, which is 2 million people. We wanted to give them a medal, and it was something very emotional for us."

After the loss, Dončić sat on the floor by Slovenia's bench area, draping a towel over his head again. Prepelič leaned over and attempted to console Dončić, who was clearly distraught. He had time to gather his emotions before the postgame press conference, when Dončić downplayed concerns by saying his "wrist is going to be fine" but acknowledged that he was exhausted, mentally and physically.

"I need a couple of days off from basketball," Dončić said. "I've had every day basketball since the beginning of NBA season. A lot of games, so I need a couple days off."

A couple of days later, Dončić welcomed the Mavericks' contingent to his hometown, touched by their gesture. They celebrated Dončić's contract that night, and he officially signed it the next morning at the Ljubljana hotel where Cuban and the Dallas crew stayed. Hours later at the press conference, Dončić referred to Dallas

The day after the 2018 NBA draft, Dončić's first afternoon in Dallas featured a press conference and photo shoot along with (from left to right) then–Mavs president of basketball operations Donnie Nelson, second-round pick Jalen Brunson, coach Rick Carlisle, and vice president Michael Finley.

(*Steve Chavera*)

As a nine-year-old, Dončić joins his father, Saša (center, grasping the trophy), and his teammates in celebrating Union Olimpija's championship of the Liga UPC Telemach, the Slovenian pro league. Marko Milić, a future Mavericks assistant coach, is to the far left. Future NBA star Goran Dragić is standing behind Luka, who years later would become his teammate for the Slovenian national program.

(*Vid Ponikvar / Sportal Images*)

Dončić and team captain, Sergio Llull, pose with the Copa del Rey trophy the day after Real Madrid claimed the prestigious cup in February 2017. Llull missed most of the next season with a knee injury. Dončić filled his shoes as Real Madrid's leading scorer and the EuroLeague's MVP.

(*Jorge Sanz / Pacific Press*)

Dončić smiles and shrugs during a series-clinching win over Panathinaikos Superfoods that sent Real Madrid to the 2018 EuroLeague final four. "I've never seen him nervous," Real Madrid coach Pablo Laso once said in Spanish.

(COOLMedia / NurPhoto)

Dončić, eighteen at the time, scored 12 of his 27 points in the final six minutes as Slovenia eliminated Kristaps Porziņģis and Latvia in the EuroBasket 2017 quarterfinals. "You could see he's starting to take over in the sense of, OK, he knows he's really good," Slovenian forward Vlatko Čančar said. "He was not afraid of nobody."

(Vid Ponikvar / Sportida)

Dončić soaks in the adulation of Slovenian fans at Sinan Erdem Dome in Istanbul after the country's EuroBasket 2017 title. "It's a lot of feelings when you represent your country," Dončić said later.

(Vid Ponikvar / Sportida)

Dončić and Goran Dragić embrace after Slovenia won the nation's first EuroBasket championship. "Mark my words, he's going to be one of the best in the whole world!" tournament MVP Dragić said of his teenage teammate after the title game.

(Vid Ponikvar / Sportida)

Dončić, shown after clinching the Liga ACB championship on his final night in a Real Madrid uniform, left for the NBA as the most decorated teen prospect in European hoops history.

(Peter Sabok / NurPhoto)

The Atlanta Hawks technically drafted Dončić, which is why he wore their cap when he met NBA commissioner Adam Silver onstage. But Dallas and Atlanta had agreed to a trade minutes before the pick, as the Mavericks gave up their next first-round pick to move up two spots to take the number one player on their board.

(Steve Chavera)

Dončić and Trae Young were swapped for each other on draft night, linking the two star playmakers for the rest of their careers. Dončić and the Mavs blew a 26-point lead to Young's Hawks in their first meeting, leading to a fiery team meeting the next day.

(Steve Chavera)

Dennis Smith Jr. and Dončić became fast friends, but the Dallas brass had doubts about the basketball fit between the two young lottery picks from the moment they drafted Dončić. The partnership didn't last long.

(Steve Chavera)

Mavs director of player development Mike Procopio served as a valuable sounding board—and source of comedic fodder—for Dončić during his rookie season. "He loved basketball, loved competing, loved video games, and loved eating, and that's a guy I loved," Procopio said. "That's a perfect fit, besides the video games!"

(Steve Chavera)

Dončić thrived during his three seasons playing for Rick Carlisle, but the star and coach had a strained relationship.
(Steve Chavera)

Dončić spent one year as Mavs legend Dirk Nowitzki's teammate, but it wasn't as pupil and mentor. "He is not under my wing because he's not under anyone's wing," Nowitzki said. "I want him to do great, but he doesn't need me to hold his hand."
(Steve Chavera)

Dončić and Dirk Nowitzki walk into the American Airlines Center together before the final home game of Nowitzki's career. Nowitzki officially announced his retirement during a postgame ceremony that night.
(Steve Chavera)

Dončić asked LeBron James for his jersey after the first time they faced each other. After they met early in Dončić's second season, James sought out Dončić to tell him he was a "bad motherfucka."
(*Steve Chavera*)

The Mavs planned for Dončić and Kristaps Porziņģis to be their franchise cornerstones for a generation. It didn't work out that way. The duo played only two and a half seasons together.
(*Steve Chavera*)

Dončić's first two NBA playoff appearances were first-round exits at the hands of Kawhi Leonard and the Los Angeles Clippers.
(*Steve Chavera*)

Dončić led Slovenia to the basketball program's first Olympic berth, fulfilling one of his childhood dreams. He had a 31-point triple-double against the host team in Lithuania in the title game of an Olympic qualifying tournament to earn the bid.
(*Alfredas Pliadis | Xinhua | Alamy Live News*)

Mark Cuban was part of a Mavs contingent that traveled to Dončić's hometown of Ljubljana to formally present him with a five-year, $215 million supermax contract in August 2021. Dončić referred to Dallas as his "second home" during the press conference after signing the deal.
(*Luka | Dakskobler | Sipa USA | Alamy Live News*)

Since being hired as the Mavs' head coach in July 2021, Hall of Fame point guard Jason Kidd has shown a good feel for when to push Dončić and when to pat him on the back.
(*Jeff Chiu | Associated Press*)

Dončić argues a call with referee Nick Buchert during game four of the Mavs' 2024 first-round series against the Clippers. Dončić has struggled throughout his career with his tendency to become distracted by his frustrations with officiating.
(*Jeffrey McWhorter | Associated Press*)

Dončić and costar Kyrie Irving embrace after the Mavs' game-three win over the Timberwolves, a moment that exhibited the bond the duo developed during their first full season together. "Just working with him, just playing with him, it's a pleasure no matter what," Dončić said. "He's always positive energy, always."
(*Gareth Patterson | Associated Press*)

Celtics star Jayson Tatum drives past Dončić during Boston's game-three win in the 2024 NBA Finals. Dončić described his first Finals appearance, a five-game loss for the Mavs, as a learning experience.
(*Tony Gutierrez | Associated Press*)

as feeling like a "second home" and suggested he could be "second Dirk," another all-time great who'd spend his entire NBA career in a Mavericks uniform.

Dončić's disappointment in missing out on an Olympic medal had already dissipated. He beamed with pride about his national team's accomplishments that summer. And, for all the happiness he expressed about his situation in Dallas, Dončić expressed hope that the Mavericks could replicate an essential element of Slovenia's success.

"I know we made some great moves in free agency, but one of the most important things that a team needs to win is chemistry that the team has off the court," Dončić said. "Like for example, in Slovenia, we had amazing chemistry the whole time, and I think that led to us winning games. And I think that's what we need in Dallas."

CHAPTER 12

PARTING WAYS WITH THE "PERFECT CO-STAR"

Dončić and Porziņģis didn't talk or text from the time they departed Dallas in early June until they returned before training camp in late September. However, they did resume the habit of tapping the like button on each other's Instagram posts over the summer. Cuban trumpeted that development as a "telltale sign" that the relationship between the Mavs' franchise cornerstones was fine, indicating just how distant Dončić and Porziņģis had become during the previous season. They made a mutual, unspoken decision not to dwell on the past under the previous coaching regime, greeting each other cordially and exchanging pleasant small talk the first time they saw each other at the Mavs' practice facility that fall.

"We left it behind, and pretty much that was it," Porziņģis said. "Just had a good first conversation—'Hey, how you doing? You good? Dah, dah, dah.' New beginning."

They never did discuss the issues that created the iciness between them. Dončić preferred to pretend that the friction was fiction. "I think that's more [what the] media did to us," Dončić said during the preseason. "Not us. Just the media saw it like that. I don't know. We're good. He's in a way better place now, I think, especially mentally." That last point was undeniably true. Porziņģis, perhaps even more so than Dončić, had been miserable playing for Carlisle and felt a massive sense of relief when the coach resigned. But the Mavs couldn't be more successful under Kidd if the chemistry problems between Dončić and Porziņģis persisted.

"We both realized we're going to need each other," Porziņģis said over lunch at a Dallas restaurant early that season. "We had our ups and downs earlier, little things that happened. Luka's young, I could have been smarter in some situations, and it kind of just builds up. There was nobody really for us to just fix it. It kind of kept going, kept going. The vibe wasn't getting any better. But beginning of the season, he came in, we said what's up to each other and here we go. We needed, like, fresh air around us. That was the big thing."

Kidd made it a priority to make Porziņģis feel valued again, understanding the psychological struggle Porziņģis had endured. Kidd, along with Casey Smith, flew from Slovenia to Riga, Latvia, after Dončić's press conference to visit Porziņģis for a few days in his hometown. There and in Dallas, Kidd consistently delivered the message that Porziņģis wanted to receive, such as predicting that Porziņģis would be an All-Star again that season. Kidd declared that "there is no bad shot" for Porziņģis, giving him permission to post up and fire away from mid-range. Those are the sorts of shots that Carlisle, armed with convincing analytical evidence, discouraged Porziņģis from taking as the Mavs became more and more of a heliocentric offense with Dončić dominating the ball.

"I don't know if anybody told Picasso that he has to use all the paints, but I just want to remind him that he can rely on his teammates," Kidd said of Dončić on media day. "His teammates are going to be there to help him. I'm very excited to have this opportunity to work with a young Picasso whose paintings have been incredible up to this point and are only going to get better."

Kidd, in particular, pushed for Dončić to trust Porziņģis, the guy the coach called "the perfect co-star for Luka" months earlier. Porziņģis had developed optimism about that possibility. "Luka's one of the best players in the league," Porziņģis said. "Talent-wise, he's incredible. I also realize I'm not going to have many chances to play with a guy like that and try to win it all.... Luka's so good that it's super easy to play with him. If you're cool with him and he wants to get you involved, he will get you involved. The important thing is we're looking out for each other now. He's looking out for me."

Kidd placed an emphasis on communication between players and himself, which was both an adjustment from his previous stints as a head coach and a course correction from the Carlisle era. "It's different. He's a good leader," Porziņģis said of Kidd. "It starts with him; it trickles down. He's calling me out, calling Luka out when we need to be called out. It's what it needs to be—addressing the issues, addressing the little problems and things that need to be addressed, not letting them slip by and then it's too late."

Kidd wasn't just willing to listen. He forced players to use their voices and followed through on what they said, even if it meant getting mocked for employing tactics typically utilized by junior high coaches. That was the case after the Mavs' win over the rebuilding Rockets in their home opener, when all 15 active players on the Dallas roster got into the game by the end of the third quarter, which is practically unheard of in the NBA. Kidd explained postgame that the team's new leadership council had requested full roster participation in the game, and he fulfilled the request to promote team unity. It was a feel-good win, other than the fact that Porziņģis left the game early due to lower back tightness, an ailment that sidelined him for the next week.

"The more you talk, the better," said Dončić, a member of the leadership council along with Porziņģis and Tim Hardaway Jr. "Especially with these meetings, on the court, off the court, talking solves things, so I think it's a good idea."

However, there were some delicate subjects that Kidd struggled to discuss with Dončić during the developmental stages of their relationship. In particular, Kidd had a difficult time figuring out how to communicate his concerns about Dončić's poor conditioning without putting himself at risk of alienating his superstar. Dončić had reported to camp weighing more than 260 pounds again, clearly having enjoyed a lot of ćevapi and beer in the six weeks between the supermax press conference in Slovenia and returning to Dallas. Over the first six weeks of the season, Kidd would privately ask former coaches he crossed paths with for advice on how to get through to Dončić without jeopardizing the foundation of the relationship he was attempting to build.

Dončić is such an immense talent that he can still produce All-Star–caliber numbers while out of shape. That was the case in this instance, as he averaged 25.4 points, 8.1 rebounds, and 8.5 assists per game during the season's first six weeks, highlighted by a game-winning buzzer-beater to punctuate a 33-point performance against the Celtics. But the slight dip in scoring, as well as efficiency, wasn't indicative of the drop in Dončić's performance. He had been absolutely dreadful defensively. He frequently loafed through defensive possessions, essentially resting because he wasn't conditioned well enough to play hard on both ends of the floor while managing a major offensive workload. Frequently, Dončić failed to even run back on defense, although that was due to his incessant complaining to referees at least as often as the conditioning concerns.

It didn't help that Dončić had suffered a sprained left knee and ankle in the final minute of a November 15 home win over the Nuggets, when Denver guard Austin Rivers fell in the lane and into the back of Dončić's leg. That caused Dončić to miss the next three games—all losses—and complicated any effort to get extra conditioning work. Dončić sat out again due to lingering soreness in the ankle on December 4, when the Mavs lost at home to the Grizzlies on the second night of a back-to-back with Porziņģis also sidelined due to a left knee contusion.

The first game of that back-to-back prompted Kidd to publicly call out Dončić for the first time as his coach. His griping at the referees in a 107–91 home loss to the Pelicans reached ridiculous levels, even by Dončić's standards. Dončić and the Mavs had embarrassed the Pelicans in New Orleans a couple of nights earlier, setting a franchise record by shooting 68.7 percent from the floor in a 139–107 rout. The Pelicans, not surprisingly, were determined to prevent a repeat performance and responded by playing physical defense on Dončić.

"You know he got a little frustrated early on, and we tried to build off of that," Pelicans forward Garrett Temple said. Dončić was awarded nine free throws—higher than the norm for him, but not nearly as many as he believed he deserved. Dončić had animated discussions with the officiating crew of Tony Brothers, Jacyn Goble, and Brandon Adair throughout the game, often while the ball was still in play. He repeatedly showed the referees marks on his arms from being hit, which Dončić frequently does to accompany his complaints. "Why do you hate me?" Dončić asked at one point. It was an extreme example of one of Dončić's biggest flaws: a tendency to be overwhelmed by frustration and focus more on the three refs than the five opposing players on the floor.

"I would lean toward playing five-on-five a bit more," Kidd said after the loss when asked about Dončić's constant arguing with the referees. "You're not going to get any calls. Officials, they tend to not stop the game to change calls. You have to understand there's a point in time in games—dead balls—to be able to talk to officials. While the game is going on, transition defense is one of the things we've talked about that we have to get better. If we're lobbying for calls during live play, it puts us in harm's way.... Just some things have got to be a little bit more important."

Dončić's next game, at home against the Nets, was a national broadcast on TNT. Color commentator Reggie Miller harped on Dončić's conditioning throughout the game, stating that "this is the heaviest I've probably ever seen Luka look," and pointing out that Dončić was "plodding up and down" instead of running the floor. "You have the keys to the kingdom if you're Dončić, right?" said Miller, a Hall of Fame shooting guard. "And he is a superstar, a superstar in the making already. But he could be so much better. And he will get better. But to me, he's got to trim down. He really does. And he's got to get better defensively, as well."

It was harsh criticism. It was also fair, as Dončić admitted after the 102–99 loss, which dropped Dallas to 11–12 on the season. "I think that's my thing. People are going to talk about it, yes or no," Dončić said. "But I know I've got to do better. I had a long summer, and then I relax a little bit. I had Olympics, took three weeks off and then I relax a little bit. Maybe too much. And I've just got to get back on track."

Kidd played coy, claiming he wasn't sure whether Dončić was out of shape because he hadn't been around him before. He told reporters those questions were better asked to Dončić. But Kidd later expressed his gratitude to Miller for delivering his message.

"Jason Kidd said thank you, because it's almost—and you know this very well as a parent—you can say everything you want to your kids and it goes in one ear and out the other," Miller said on *The Dan Patrick Show* that spring. "But when they hear from somewhere else, and it's the same message, they're like, 'Oh OK, I get it.' So he understood, and he knew, and Jason Kidd had been kind of verbalizing to him: 'You've got the kingdom at your feet, young man, but you've got to get in better shape and you've got to stay off the officials.'"

But things got worse for Dončić and the Mavs before they got better. A couple of games after being called out, Dončić rolled his tender left ankle again in a game against the Pacers, the anticipated awkward reunion with Carlisle that was delayed due to the coach testing positive for COVID. Dončić hobbled for the rest of the game after stepping on an Indiana player's foot while grabbing an offensive rebound in the third quarter. The Mavs lost for the fourth time in five games, 106–93, scoring only 13 points in the fourth quarter. "It sucks right now to be us," Porziņģis said.

The next day, the decision was made to shut Dončić down indefinitely. The official reason given by the team was to give Dončić's ankle time to heal, but much of the motivation for sidelining Dončić was to make conditioning his primary focus. A week and a half later, the Mavs had seen enough progress for Kidd to reveal their plan for Dončić's return. Dončić would sit out again that night against the Timberwolves, missing his fifth straight game, and hopefully be back in the starting lineup 48 hours later against the Bucks.

The Mavs sure could use some good news on the health front. Coronavirus was spreading like wildfire throughout the league, and the outbreak had hit Dallas's roster especially hard. That afternoon Hardaway joined Maxi Kleber, Reggie Bullock, and Josh Green on the Mavs' list of players out due to the league's health and safety protocols. Porziņģis, who was dealing with a sore toe, was also out against the Timberwolves. Dallas had to scramble to sign Theo Pinson and Marquese Chriss to 10-day hardship contracts and plug them right into the rotation without any practice time. Kidd mentioned that he told the team's injured players to go home after getting their treatment and work in pregame because of COVID concerns. "We're trying to stay away from each other as much as possible," Kidd said. A couple of minutes after tip-off, Dončić emerged from the tunnel at mid-court and plopped down between teammates on the Mavs' bench. Dončić tested positive the next day, delaying his return.

It was a surreal time in the NBA, with several players adhering to the league's health and safety protocols due to positive COVID tests every day. Teams were permitted to add a replacement via a 10-day hardship deal for each player who tested positive, preventing disruptions to the schedule, turning a lot of NBA games into glorified pickup runs. The Mavs cycled through seven hardship additions over a span of 10 days in late December. Geographical proximity played a significant role in some of the personnel decisions, such as when Dallas signed former All-Star guard Isaiah Thomas in large part because his Seattle home was a short flight to Sacramento, where the Mavs were on a two-game visit. Thomas got the phone call while grocery shopping, hopped on the next flight, played 13 minutes that night, and tested positive the next day. So ended his short, strange trip with the Mavs.

THE MAVS CLAWED TO KEEP THEIR HEADS ABOVE WATER DURING Dončić's extended absence, going 5–5 in the 10 games he missed before finally returning on January 2 in Oklahoma City. Brunson, the Mavs' sixth man when Dončić had been available, starred as the starting point guard, averaging an efficient 21 points and 7.4 assists per game during the stretch. He never returned to the bench role, starting alongside Dončić the rest of the season.

Brunson also played a critical role in the identity the Mavs managed to create amidst the COVID chaos. He emerged as a leader, an extension of the coaching staff, helping communicate the details of the team's schemes that new players needed to learn on the fly with no practices or shootarounds. Pinson, an exuberant personality who was plucked out of the G League, instantly established himself as an essential part of the team's cultural fabric. His relentlessly positive spirit—usually expressed rather loudly—rubbed off on the rest of the Mavs. He became such a valued teammate that the Mavs signed Pinson to a two-way deal after they could no longer keep him on a hardship contract. There was so much that the Mavs couldn't control, but they were excelling at the things that they could: effort, energy, attitude, attention to detail. Their superstar followed suit upon his return.

Dončić didn't hit the ground running. Most players coming back from COVID needed some time for their lungs and legs to feel normal again, and that was especially true for Dončić. "Weird feeling, but I'm just happy to be back," Dončić said postgame in Oklahoma City. "My chest was burning. I think slowly it's going to come back. When I shot, the feeling was weird. I didn't know if it was going to go in or out. There was one shot that feels amazing—I said, 'You shot it great and it's going to go in,' and it was an airball."

It wasn't a pretty performance for Dončić, who scored 14 points on 14 shots and committed seven turnovers, but it was a win. An ugly win, 96–85, but the standings don't have a column for style points. The Mavs' ability to win such a muddy game was a source of pride, proof of the drastic defensive improvement under Kidd and fiery assistant coach Sean Sweeney. It suddenly became a trend, as Dallas won with defense while Dončić took some time to rediscover his rhythm and Porziņģis sat out seven games due to his own COVID case. The Mavs went 10–2 in the first dozen games after Dončić's return, despite Dončić shooting poorly for the first couple of weeks. He was a force as a rebounder and facilitator and was fulfilling the Mavs' need for him to "participate" on defense, to borrow the term that Kidd began using around that time.

Dončić had returned to superstar form by the time Carlisle's Pacers made their annual visit to Dallas for the Mavs' final home game of the month. It was also the Mavs' first game after All-Star starters were announced, and Dončić felt snubbed by his omission. There were plenty of legitimate reasons for the fans, players, and media who voted to leave him off the ballot, but Dončić felt disrespected, the sort of thing he seeks for motivational fuel.

Tears streamed down Carlisle's cheeks when a two-minute tribute video played on the American Airlines Center's scoreboard screens during pregame introductions. Carlisle, whose wife and teenage daughter remained in the home he kept in Dallas, was overwhelmed with emotion from the fond memories of his 13-year tenure with the Mavs.

Then Dončić seemed to take great delight in providing Carlisle an up-close reminder of the future the coach would miss out on.

Dončić accounted for 26 points in the first quarter, three more than the entire Indiana team. He had 22 points and six assists by halftime, finishing the first half with quite a flourish. In the final seconds of the second quarter, Dončić speedily dribbled up the left sideline, turned his back and got Pacers defender Justin Holiday to bite on a fake spin move, and took one more dribble and a couple of side steps to the left corner to launch a three. After the ball splashed through the net as the buzzer sounded, Dončić stood still in that corner, staring across the court at his teammates celebrating in the Mavs' bench area as his bottom lip protruded, a blend of a snarl and satisfied smirk. He turned his head to the right to look across the court toward Carlisle and held the pose for a beat. Then Dončić formed a pretend pistol with his index finger and thumb and fired an imaginary shot in that direction. He finally dropped the bottom lip and busted out a big smile as he high-fived teammates on his way off the floor.

Carlisle got a small measure of comedic payback late in the third quarter, when his shout into referee J. B. DeRosa's ear resulted in a palming violation on Dončić, a call rarely made in the NBA. Dončić responded by turning toward DeRosa with the ball cradled under his left arm and his head tilted, looking shocked and disappointed. "Oh, hell no!" Dončić yelled. DeRosa couldn't stifle a laugh. After he tossed the ball toward another ref, Dončić repeatedly pointed at DeRosa as he walked up the floor and briefly pointed at Carlisle, lecturing the ref for letting Carlisle make a call.

"Hey, you gotta try to find some ways to slow the guy down," Carlisle said postgame with a chuckle and bemused smile. "I mean, even if you have to just beg for a call."

The rebuilding Pacers certainly didn't have any other solutions for Dončić. He finished with 30 points, 12 assists, and that lone turnover before resting the entire fourth quarter of the Mavs' 132–105 win. "If he's not the best player in the world, he's right on the cusp," Carlisle said. "He's just so, so good." Carlisle praised the Mavs as "a well-oiled machine" and made a point to declare that Dallas was "a real threat in the West and in the big picture."

At the end of the game, as Mavs players, coaches, and staffers lined up to chat with Carlisle, all eyes on media row shifted to Dončić. It would have been a storyline if Dončić avoided any postgame interaction with his former coach. Perhaps Dončić realized that. He got in the back of the line and had a nice moment with Carlisle, exchanging hugs, smiles, and pleasantries before they left the court. "Being with him my first three years, I learned a lot of things," Dončić said postgame. "He helped me in other ways, too. So, it was a special moment."

DONČIĆ'S DOMINANCE WASN'T THE ONLY FAMILIAR DEVELOPMENT during Carlisle's return to Dallas. There was an unfortunate footnote: Porziņģis exited in the second quarter due to right knee soreness. As it turned out, that was the last time he wore a Mavericks uniform.

Porziņģis was diagnosed with a bone bruise in the knee, an injury that would sideline him for weeks. It reinforced doubts that the Mavs could rely on him. It had also become apparent that Porziņģis, who was putting up respectable numbers by averaging 19.2 points, 7.7 rebounds, and 1.7 blocks in the 34 games he had played that season, was not enhancing Dončić's brilliance. The Mavs were averaging only 103.7 points per 100 possessions with them both on the floor, which was less efficient than the league's lowest-ranked team offense. Lo and behold, Voulgaris and Carlisle had a point about Porziņģis's post-ups and mid-range shots.

Perhaps Kidd had to learn the hard way or at least give Porziņģis a shot to prove he could thrive playing his preferred style. Maybe Kidd realized all along that it wouldn't work and played the long game by pumping up Porziņģis, hoping to boost his trade value. Not that the latter logic paid off.

The hope that Porziņģis could be the second star the Mavs need to make a championship run—or the ticket to such a star in the trade market—had passed. Dallas made overtures earlier in the season about swapping Porziņģis for Kyrie Irving, but Brooklyn wasn't interested, even though the perennial All-Star guard wasn't playing due to his refusal to comply with New York City's vaccine mandate. The Mavs, as quietly as possible, made finding a trade partner for Porziņģis their priority as the February 10 trade deadline approached.

The Mavs still held out hope of landing a superstar to pair with Dončić. That was the primary reason Cuban hadn't given the green light to offer contract extensions to Brunson or Finney-Smith. They were in the final seasons of their contract and eligible for four-year, $55.5 million extensions, but new deals would have made them ineligible to be traded before the deadline. Any deal for a star would certainly have included at least one of them, and likely both. That type of deal didn't materialize.

Finding a trade partner in a Porziņģis deal became rookie GM Harrison's priority in the days leading up to the deadline. Talks with Toronto gained some traction. Raptors GM Masai Ujiri had been dangling Dončić's hometown mentor Dragić, who had an expiring contract with an $18.6 million salary, and a first-round pick in his search for frontcourt help. The Mavs proposed including shooting guard Gary Trent Jr. in the deal. He was making $16 million in the first year of a three-year deal, enough to comply with the league's trade rules. He would have been a great fit for the Mavs as a 23-year-old wing who shot the three well and was a solid defender. That deal was too rich for the Raptors, who instead sent Dragić and the pick to

San Antonio for a package headlined by journeyman power forward Thaddeus Young.

With an hour remaining before the 2:00 p.m. CT deadline, the Mavs seemed stuck with Porziņģis—but that changed when Harrison and Wizards GM Tommy Sheppard touched base. Washington desperately wanted to dump a couple of players—guard Spencer Dinwiddie and forward Dāvis Bertāns—whose salaries happened to match up with Porziņģis's money. Dinwiddie had quickly worn out his welcome in the Wizards' locker room after signing a three-year, $54 million contract that summer, but Dallas assistant coach Jared Dudley and Pinson were teammates of his in Brooklyn and vouched for Dinwiddie. The Mavs brass figured Dinwiddie could add some scoring punch the second unit had been missing since Brunson became a full-time starter. Bertāns was a one-dimensional player who had been a bust since signing a five-year, $80 million deal during the 2020 offseason. The hope was that the three-point specialist might benefit from being set up by Dončić, but make no bones about it, Bertāns was considered a bad contract. But bad midsize contracts are much easier to move than bad maximum contracts, and it helped that only $5 million was guaranteed in the final season of Bertāns's deal.

The consensus within the Mavs' front office, including Cuban and Harrison, was that the deal made sense even though it'd be a public relations dud. They did cough up a second-round pick when Washington asked for a sweetener, but a year before, the Mavs couldn't get anyone to answer a phone call about Porziņģis without dangling a first rounder. The deal was agreed to about 25 minutes before the deadline. "Flexibility and depth," Harrison said that night when asked why the Mavs were motivated to make the trade, not putting much effort into PR spin. The harsh truth is the Mavs determined it was time to get out of the Porziņģis business and pounced on their only opportunity to do so.

It was an unceremonious divorce with a player that was supposed to be a franchise cornerstone. Porziņģis stepped out of line at a Dallas sandwich shop to take Harrison's call informing him he'd been traded. He wasn't stunned. He didn't believe Cuban when he denied reports about the Mavs exploring Porziņģis's value in the trade market the year before, and Porziņģis had heard the rumors in the days leading up to the deadline that Dallas was discussing deals involving him again.

Dončić described news of the deal as "shocking," but he'd been briefed about the possibility. Dončić didn't feel the need or desire to be deeply involved in front office business. He was taking his normal game-day afternoon nap in the final hour before the trade deadline.

"Obviously, we're going to miss KP," Dončić said that night. "We were building something great here. It didn't obviously work out. I wish him the best, and we've got two new guys who are welcome. Bertāns is a great shooter. Dinwiddie can put the ball on the floor and he can score. The NBA is a business."

That business had Brunson and Finney-Smith wide awake as the trade deadline approached and passed. Brunson's initial reaction to news of the Porziņģis trade was to make sure he wasn't included in the deal. After the deadline passed, the Mavs put four-year, $55.5 million extensions on the table for both Brunson and Finney-Smith, the most Dallas could offer at the time. Brunson declined, confident that he could get significantly more as an unrestricted free agent that summer. Finney-Smith accepted. He figured he might have been able to get more in free agency, but he was happy in Dallas and ecstatic to commit to a contract for life-changing money, having scrapped for his spot in the league as an undrafted player. "Man, my mama worked at Church's my first three years in the league," Finney-Smith said with a huge smile that night. "I tried to make her quit. So I'm just happy she can finally kick up her feet and chill."

Arena workers had to scramble that afternoon to remove the Porziņģis giveaway posters from the American Airlines Center seats. His departure was at the front of fans' minds as they filled those seats that evening. Not that the fans were necessarily distraught to see Porziņģis go, but the franchise was back at square one in the search to find Dončić's co-star—and still owed the Knicks a first-round pick from the trade that brought Porziņģis to Dallas.

It didn't take long, however, for Dončić to command the crowd's full attention. He swished a step-back three over Clippers center Ivica Zubac on the Mavs' opening possession, and the massive grin on Dončić's face as he backpedaled down the floor gave a pretty clear answer about whether he was bothered by the day's developments. Dončić kept smiling and exploiting switches against the 7-footer throughout the first quarter, scorching the Clippers for 28 points on 10-of-13 shooting, including seven-of-ten from three-point range. He was well on the way to the first 50-point game of his NBA career, finishing with 51 points in a 112–105 win. "MVP! MVP!" the crowd chanted during Dončić's trip to the free throw line in the final minute.

It was a timely reminder of just how rare of a talent the Mavs had to build around. Perhaps the pressing question wasn't, How could the Mavs find a co-star? Maybe it was whether they needed one.

"That's a good question," Kidd said that night. "You always want talent to win championships. We'll see. I'm the coach who has to put them in a position to be successful, get paid, find a way to win. As we go through this journey, we'll see if we come across a No. 2 guy. It could be the team that we have where there is no real second star. You've just got guys who play roles at a very high level. And you've seen teams win championships that way, too."

Lone-star teams rarely win titles in the NBA, but it happened before in Dallas when Dirk Nowitzki was surrounded by high-quality role players who complemented him well. "Yeah, you had one superstar and the rest were burgers," Kidd said with a grin, using Nowitzki's favorite endearing insult for Kidd and the rest of his teammates on that 2011 championship squad. Could that be the blueprint to build a contender around Dončić?

"I don't know. I think you've got to ask Nico, but I trust them," Dončić said, deferring as usual to Mavs management when asked about personnel decisions. "They see the basketball like a GM, Mark's got the president part. So I trust them, whatever move they make. I think I have great teammates."

CHAPTER 13

WE BELIEVE, MAN

"The vibes are immaculate," Jalen Brunson frequently said, almost as often as he posted it on social media. His catchphrase became a slogan of sorts for the Mavericks in the post–New Year's portion of the 2021–22 season. The team won and had fun doing it.

Brunson shined in his first opportunity as a full-time starter. He established himself as the Mavs' clear second option, thriving in a complementary role and while running the offense with Dallas's second unit when Dončić rested. Brunson, who replaced Porziņģis on Kidd's leadership council, was also a bedrock of the team's culture, his steady, cool demeanor supplementing Dončić's emotional tendencies. Kidd occasionally mentioned that one of his goals was to get Brunson "paid," but Brunson blocked out the potential distraction of his pending free agency, intently maintaining his focus on the present with the Mavs.

Dinwiddie, ecstatic to escape Washington and eager to disprove his reputation as a problem in the locker room, embraced the sixth man role and excelled in it. He flourished as a secondary ball handler, almost always paired with either Dončić or Brunson, and raved about how much a clear, simplified role benefited him. Dinwiddie provided offensive punch off the bench and some clutch scoring, highlighted by hitting game-winning threes off dishes from Dončić in consecutive games during a March road trip through Boston and Brooklyn.

"It's a credit to him, because as a superstar it's within your power, within your control," Dinwiddie said after the win over the Nets. "You can make people feel wanted, you can make them feel not wanted. You can trust them, not trust them."

Finney-Smith, Bullock, and Kleber spaced the floor and took the toughest defensive assignments, keying Dallas's improvement from ranking 21st in defensive efficiency the previous season to seventh. They never complained about how often or infrequently they touched the ball, the sort of selflessness that's a rare commodity in the NBA. Powell, who started at center and usually cheered from the bench as Kleber closed games, exhibited the same approach as a big man who set solid screens and always rolled hard to the rim even when he went long stretches without receiving a pass.

The Mavs had a blast on the bench. That was primarily the domain of Pinson, who rarely played but was constantly heard. He'd be on his feet almost the entire game, shouting out instructions like a coach, talking trash, and serving as the league's "best hype man, culture guy, whatever you want to call it," as Dinwiddie described him. Marjanović ranked high on that list as well. Boban enjoyed being Dončić's best buddy. They were essentially inseparable on the road, hanging out and speaking Serbian along with Kokoškov, the assistant coach who had known Dončić since their EuroBasket title run together years earlier.

"The Luka that I was coaching was just a kiddo," Kokoškov said later, referring to the teen he coached on the Slovenian national team. "It was like I never coached this guy."

This guy was the driving force of Dallas's success and a legitimate MVP candidate despite the slow start to the season. After his few weeks off in December, when he focused on conditioning and then battled COVID, Dončić was as dominant as ever. He averaged 29.8 points, 9.7 rebounds, and 8.7 assists per game after his January return, and the Mavs went 35–12 in the regular season after the calendar flipped to 2022—the NBA's second best in that span behind only the Phoenix Suns. Dončić had slimmed down, dropping into the 240s, taking his diet much more seriously even if he still sipped on the occasional beer or two.

"I think he was humbled a little bit," Cuban said during a radio appearance on *The Ticket* in Dallas. "I think he didn't like being called out for his weight and other things. And it finally clicked that there's a level of discipline that's required. All athletes at his level go through it at some level, where things are just easy and you're always used to being the best. And you're always used to getting all the accolades. And then when something doesn't go according to what you would expect, it makes you reconsider.

"And I think what people don't realize about Luka, he is smart. You know, I'm not talking about Harvard MBA smart. I'm talking about street smart. I'm talking about common sense. I'm talking about dedication and effort. He knows what he needs to do, and it finally clicked that if he's going to be the best—and I know he wants to be the best—that there's certain things he has to control. And once he got a handle on those things, it's just been, Katy bar the door. He's just been unstoppable."

THE VIBES WERE INDEED SO IMMACULATE THAT DONČIĆ EVEN laid off the referees for a little while after he picked up his 14th technical of the season (not counting one rescinded by the league office) for complaining midway through the fourth quarter of a March 9 blowout loss to the Knicks, putting him two shy of an automatic one-game suspension. Dončić had avoided a suspension by the slimmest possible margin the previous season, when he had two technicals rescinded. "He's always crying," Hall of Famer Walt Frazier said in an exasperated tone on the Knicks' TV broadcast. "He's gotta be the biggest crybaby in the league."

Dončić vowed postgame that a suspension "won't happen," adding that he intended to appeal what he considered a "crazy" technical. He had vowed plenty of times to cool his act with officials, but this time he had a plan. He figured out a way to ease the frustration he felt when he believed the refs got it wrong.

"It's a funny thing—I just start singing a song in my head," Dončić said the next week. He grinned, proud of himself for finding a solution. "One of my favorite songs I pick and just start singing and let it pass." For the record, he usually picked a Slovenian or Serbian folk song.

Dončić was whistled for only one technical foul over the next month, and that was for a relatively innocuous between-quarters exchange of words with Timberwolves forward Taurean Prince. By Dončić's standards, it was a remarkable run of calm. But Dončić just couldn't resist the urge to protest a no-call in the second-to-last game of the regular season.

The Mavs were up 23 points over the blatantly tanking Trail Blazers at the end of the first quarter, when Dončić was appalled at a no-call. Portland's Elijah Hughes hacked Dončić on his left shoulder from behind and undercut him as he attempted a half-court shot before the buzzer, but the whistle didn't blow. Dončić sat on the court where he landed, raised his arms in a dismayed shrug, stared at ref Tom Washington, and asked why a foul wasn't called. Dončić didn't get a satisfactory answer, and he responded by lying flat on his back and covering his face with his hands for a few seconds. After getting up, Dončić immediately made his way across the court to confront crew chief Tony Brothers, a veteran ref with a no-bull rep who had ejected Kidd from a game a week earlier. Finney-Smith got in between them, attempting to nudge Dončić toward the Mavs' bench. That didn't work. As Mavs reserve guard Frank Ntilikina and the head of the Mavs' security staff arrived to assist Finney-Smith, Brothers decided he'd heard enough, calling a technical foul on Dončić. "When I was walking toward the table, he was 15 feet in the backcourt still complaining so he got a technical for continuously complaining," Brothers said in a postgame pool report, when he acknowledged that Dončić did not use profanity.

Dončić had his palms raised in confusion as he was ushered back to the Mavs' bench area. He turned toward Brothers with his mouth wide open and eyebrows raised, then pressed his hands together like a praying emoji in front of his face. He then settled into a pose with his hands on his hips and a bewildered smile, shocked that Brothers dared to call him for a T that would trigger a suspension for the regular-season finale.

"If you ask me, I think 100 percent it should be rescinded, because it wasn't a tech at all," Dončić said after the 128–78 win. "No warning, no nothing. I just asked him, 'How is that not a call?' Hopefully, it will be [rescinded], so I can play Sunday."

That regular-season finale against the Spurs had potential to impact playoff seeding. The Mavs were a half-game behind the third-place Warriors and owned the tiebreaker, but Golden State controlled its fate because it had two games remaining. Despite the stakes, Kidd didn't seem too concerned about Dončić's availability.

"It is what it is. It's over with," Kidd said postgame. "We'll get ready for San Antonio. If he can play, he plays. If he can't, he moves on to the playoffs. It's not a big deal."

The league office surprisingly gave Dončić a reprieve, rescinding the technical foul the next day, allowing Dončić to avoid the suspension. The counter reset for the playoffs, when seven technical fouls triggered a one-game suspension. "I'm telling him six," Kidd cracked before the regular-season finale.

Golden State had won the previous night, meaning the Mavs-Spurs result would only matter if the Warriors lost that afternoon in New Orleans, with the games tipping off at the same time. It was apparent by halftime, when the Warriors led by 20, that the Mavs would be locked into the fourth seed. Kidd opted to play the regular rotation through the third quarter anyway, treating the game like a "dress rehearsal" with several days off before the first round began. That meant Dončić playing the entire quarter before calling it a night, and a regular season. It didn't go according to plan.

Dončić felt sharp pain in his left calf when he attempted to push off it after delivering a pass. He ended up hobbling off the floor with 2:24 remaining in the quarter, helped by Casey Smith. His regular season was over, and his availability for the playoffs was suddenly in jeopardy.

The official diagnosis: a strained left calf. That was confirmed by an MRI the next day, when a picture circulated on social media of Dončić wearing a protective boot on his left leg and walking alongside Smith into a Dallas hospital entrance. The Mavs revealed as little information as possible while following the NBA's rules on reporting injuries. "Day to day," Kidd said following the next practice, claiming not to know the severity of Dončić's strain or to even understand the difference in grades. The Mavs had enough information to be optimistic that Dončić would be available at some point in the first round, but there was a competitive advantage in playing coy.

The Game 1 result—a 99–93 home loss for the Mavericks—amplified concern about Dončić's status. Dončić wore a black graphic hoodie and designer sweats and watched from the Mavs' bench, munching popcorn from a cup during the fourth quarter, as the Dallas offense sputtered without him. Brunson, bearing the responsibility to fill Dončić's role as the primary offensive creator, scored 24 points but was inefficient. He went 9-of-24 from the floor, and the rest of the Mavs weren't much more accurate, shooting a woeful 38.2 percent as a team. "We missed a lot of easy looks, a lot of great looks," Brunson said postgame, refusing to use Dončić's unavailability as an excuse. "We just missed them."

Dončić didn't practice in the two days between Games 1 and 2 but showed progress. He jogged on the treadmill and did some light court work, such as standstill shooting and low-speed off-dribble moves, during the media availability access period at the end of practices. Once the media was ushered out, Balkan music blasted through the walls, an indication that Dončić's workouts continued. It seemed that Dončić would play at some point in the series. The media, and the Jazz, were left guessing as to when that might be. It wouldn't be Game 2, as he was listed as doubtful before being ruled out hours before tip.

Dončić inadvertently dropped a hint to the Jazz during his commute to the arena when his Ferrari zipped in front of one of Utah's buses in traffic. "That's a stick shift, right?" a Jazz assistant coach muttered as he stood at mid-court and watched Dončić go through a three-quarter speed workout during his normal pregame window. That meant that Dončić's left calf was comfortable enough to press the clutch with that foot. "He's not very far away."

Dallas didn't need Dončić to even the series. Brunson was brilliant, scoring a career-high 41 points without committing a single turnover. He made six threes and an assortment of off-dribble floaters and pull-up jumpers in a 110–104 win, abusing several Utah players who attempted to defend him. "He's going to make a lot of money," Kidd said postgame. "I don't know if he needs an agent, but I'll put my name in the hat."

Kleber busted out of a monthslong shooting slump to go 8-of-11 from three-point range. Kleber had shot only 18.8 percent from three-point range after the All-Star break, struggling as he dealt with ankle soreness before resting the final four games of the regular season. Utah's game plan was to have three-time Defensive Player of the Year Rudy Gobert help off of Kleber to clean up messes made by the Jazz's poor perimeter defenders. So much for that.

With Kleber cooking, Gobert swapped assignments down the

stretch to defend Finney-Smith, who hit a dagger three after Brunson blew by Donovan Mitchell, drew the big man into the paint, and dished to a wide-open Finney-Smith in the corner. The Mavs set a franchise postseason record by making 22 threes—17 of which were wide-open, according to ESPN Stats and Information tracking, the most in a playoff game in at least a decade. This was a painfully familiar scenario for the Jazz, who'd been shredded in the second round of the playoffs the previous year when the Clippers played a five-out style.

The Mavs had all the momentum without Dončić playing a minute yet. For the first time in the series, it seemed like a realistic possibility that he could be ready for Game 3. He made explosive movements off his left leg for the first time in the recovery process during an individual workout the day after Game 2, passing that test and getting cleared for the next day's practice. "I don't know if I'm going to be 100 percent," Dončić said after that workout. "I think that's tough right now. But if I'm ready and there's no risk of [aggravating the] injury, I'll be out there."

The Mavs privately planned for Dončić to sit out one more game, erring on the side of caution with their superstar. After the morning shootaround in Utah, Dončić went through an extensive on-court workout under Smith's watch—full-speed, full-court ballhandling and shooting. "Feeling great," Dončić said as he exited the arena afterward. Barring a setback, he'd be back for Game 4.

Once again, Brunson and the Mavs handled their business without Dončić that night. Brunson had 31 points and six assists in the 126–118 win, despite needing to retreat to the locker room for the last 4:38 of the second quarter to get treatment on his back, the result of Jazz wing Royce O'Neale ramming into Brunson at full speed from behind, striking with his elbow first. It was a blatant cheap shot but didn't get a whistle, which so angered Brunson that he earned only his second technical foul since high school for yelling at the refs as he gingerly walked off the floor. It was also the Jazz's best, maybe only, hope of slowing down Brunson, whose Wikipedia page was soon edited to add the title, "Utah Jazz owner."

Utah's fans were just as ornery, booing the Jazz on their home floor at halftime when the Mavs led by 17. Mitchell scored 28 of his 32 points in the second half to help the Jazz slice the lead to 1 midway through the fourth quarter, but Brunson and Dinwiddie took turns torching the Utah guards down the stretch as Dallas pulled away and took the series lead despite Dončić wearing his warm-ups and watching from the bench.

"What I don't understand is they say Luka doesn't have help," Rick Brunson, Jalen's dad and a former NBA journeyman, said while sitting in the lobby of the team's Salt Lake City hotel the day before Game 4. "Then when Luka is down and not just [Jalen], but the guys are performing well, then Utah is a bad team. It just doesn't make sense to me, but what it does is fuels my son to keep proving that he belongs in this league. Not just that he belongs, but he can play in this league."

The Jazz were reeling. Utah's whole season had been a slog. Their playoff failure the previous season, when the Jazz had the NBA's best regular-season record but got bounced in the second round despite building a 2–0 lead over the Clippers, lingered like a cloud over the team. That produced a now-or-never kind of pressure for a core that made six straight playoff appearances but never broke through to the conference finals.

The strained chemistry between franchise cornerstones Mitchell and Gobert—which barged into the headlines at the beginning of the pandemic when the former blamed the latter for infecting him with coronavirus—continued to be an incessant storyline. Gobert poured gasoline on that fire mid-season when he questioned the Jazz's "winning habits" and went out of his way to praise Phoenix's All-Star shooting guard Devin Booker for "playing his ass off defensively," a pretty transparent jab at Mitchell. Gobert was just as annoyed by the widely believed perception that Mitchell planned to push his way out of Salt Lake City sooner rather than later to play in a bigger market. The presence of two high-profile Knicks executives at Game 1 in Dallas—William "World Wide Wes" Wesley next to New York's All-Star power forward Julius Randle in a courtside seat, Allan Houston seated right behind the Jazz bench—provided an awkward reminder of that threat. There were also persistent rumors about coach Quin Snyder looking to leave Utah at the end of the season. And now, the Jazz trailed 2–1 in a first-round series, with the opponent's MVP candidate ready to join the festivities.

The return of Dončić in the middle of the series temporarily disrupted Dallas's rhythm, however. He had 30 points, 10 rebounds, and four assists during his series debut in Game 4, but he described his performance as "a little janky." Dončić admitted that "getting my wind back" was an issue after the 13-day layoff, especially in Salt Lake City's high altitude. He struggled for most of the fourth quarter, missing four of his first five shots while dominating the ball as the Mavs' offense sputtered. Then, with the game on the line, Dončić rose to the occasion. He methodically worked his way to the left block off a pick and roll to hit a wrong-footed floater that gave the Mavs the lead with 1:13 remaining. On Dallas's next possession, Dončić went one-on-one against Gobert after getting a switch, sizing up the big man while playing with the ball, crossing over right to left and dribbling back between his legs a couple of times. Suddenly, Dončić picked the ball up and launched a step-back three. Gobert got a good contest, but it didn't matter.

As the ball splashed through the net, Dončić pivoted, staring and sneering at a fan who had been bad-mouthing him all afternoon. When Snyder called time-out, Dončić strutted in the fan's direction, shouting and snarling at him, then let some folks in the baseline seats hear it as well as he slowly made his way toward the Dallas bench. It felt like a dagger, putting the Mavs up four with 39.1 seconds left. It wasn't.

Mitchell followed his own shot on the ensuing possession for a putback, plus an ill-advised foul by Dončić. Just like that, the Jazz were within one. Powell, fouled after a double-teamed Dončić delivered a bounce pass to him in the middle of the lane, missed both free throws while the rowdy crowd, clad in their yellow freebie T-shirts, roared. Then the Jazz's franchise cornerstones ran a perfectly executed pick and roll, ending with Mitchell lofting a lob to Gobert for a two-handed finish to put Utah up one with 11 seconds to go. "Metaphoric on some level," Snyder said postgame.

The Mavs still had time to screw up Utah's storybook moment, but the Jazz made damn sure that Dončić didn't get a shot to do it. The strong message in Utah's time-out huddle: "Make someone else beat us." As soon as Dončić touched the ball, receiving a pass from Brunson just to the left of the half-court logo with 5.5 seconds remaining, the Jazz sent an extra defender at him. Danuel House Jr. and Bojan Bogdanović bracketed Dončić as he dribbled, forcing him to give up the ball, while Gobert zoned up between two Mavs on the opposite side of the floor. Dončić fired a chest pass to Dinwiddie on the right wing with less than a second remaining. It was the pass that Gobert, well aware of Dinwiddie's pair of March buzzer-beaters, anticipated. Dinwiddie managed to get the shot off over Gobert, but it was well short. Tie series.

"Man, fuck the talk," Gobert grumbled during his TNT walk-off interview. He'd heard enough of what he referred to as "the noise" swirling around the Jazz. For that matter, he was tired of the relentless trash talk coming from Pinson and the Mavs' bench mob, who had relentlessly mocked the big man as he missed half of his 18 free throw attempts that afternoon. Gobert sensed that people were eager to write the Jazz's obituary—for the era, not just the season. But the fight wasn't over.

The Jazz apparently didn't pack that sentiment on their flight to Dallas for Game 5, a 102–77 blowout win for the Mavs. Dončić put on a show, scoring 33 points in 33 minutes, shimmying for the home crowd after a step-back three that put the Mavs up 28 late in the third. Dončić attempted to put an exclamation point on the rout by driving and rising to dunk midway through the third, but Jazz backup big man Hassan Whiteside met him in front of the rim and delivered a routine hard foul. Dončić flailed as he landed off balance and ended up flat on his back. He immediately sat up and expressed displeasure with Whiteside, who reached down toward him with palms open as if to say, "What was I supposed to do?" There was really no reason for a confrontation, but the unwritten rule is to always have your superstar's back, so Finney-Smith rushed in from the wing to push Whiteside away. Whiteside shoved back, and an NBA brouhaha ensued, which means a lot of shoving and shouting and mean-mugging and no punches thrown. Bullock got in Whiteside's face before Mavs security and coaches got in the middle to de-escalate things. Dallas defensive coordinator Sean Sweeney bolted into the fray, stepping in front of Whiteside like he was boxing out for a rebound and putting his hands up, ready to hold off any Maverick who approached. "But nobody saw him because he's tiny," Dončić cracked afterward about Sweeney, a diminutive former Division III point guard with a red-haired flattop and fiery personality to match.

The whole scene was silly, but Dončić appreciated the gesture by his overprotective teammates. It was a glimpse of the bond that the Dallas squad had developed over the season. "Amazing, man," Dončić said. "They had my back. Both of them, anybody, we had each other's back. That's what great teams do. I would go with these guys to war. This is a special team."

The Mavs played just well enough in Game 6 to close out the Jazz with a 98–96 win, holding their breath as Bogdanović's open three in the final seconds bounced off the back rim. "Oh, man, I thought, 'He don't miss a lot of those.' My heart stopped," Dončić said postgame. It was Bogdanović's last moment in a Jazz uniform. He was the fourth starter Utah traded that summer, including Gobert and Mitchell, as the Jazz went into rebuilding mode in the wake of Snyder's resignation. The Mavs had put the Jazz out of their misery.

Somewhat fittingly, Brunson hit a three off a Dončić feed that gave the Mavs the lead for good. The national discussion that night focused on Dončić advancing in the playoffs for the first time in his NBA career, but this series wasn't about him. Brunson starred when Dallas desperately needed him to. Finney-Smith, Bullock, and Kleber, in particular, also shined in their roles.

"There's a lot of trust," Kidd said. "We accomplished something, but this series is over. Now, we have to get ready for Phoenix."

ON TO THE SUNS, WHO FOLLOWED UP A TRIP TO THE NBA FINALS by winning 64 games in the regular season, eight more than any other team. Phoenix was heavily favored over Dallas. So much so that in the predictions published on ESPN.com, every reporter and analyst picked the Suns to win the series. That lopsided image featuring 21 Suns logos and blank space in the Mavs' column went viral on NBA Twitter. It also made its way into the Mavs players' group chat.

As the Mavs' morning shootaround before Game 1 wrapped up at Phoenix's Footprint Center, Dončić entertained himself by flinging up two-handed shots while sitting in a courtside seat. Kidd was about to handle his usual media obligations at mid-court, and I walked by Dončić en route to the scrum, pausing while he got up a shot and then passing him.

"Hey," Dončić said to get my attention. This was quite a surprise. I'd been covering this guy for four seasons, and this was the first time he ever initiated a conversation. Heck, I could count on one hand the number of times he appeared interested in any of our discussions, almost all of which were in group settings with other reporters. "I saw you picked the Suns."

Ah, it made sense now. I'd caught wind that some Mavs players were (playfully?) perturbed about my pick, as I was the ESPN face they saw on a regular basis. I thought I was being respectful by being one of the few who predicted the series to last seven games. Dončić raised his eyebrows and cocked his head toward me. I laughed and told him that I apologize if he feels disrespected that I expect them to lose a competitive series against the team with the league's best record.

"I thought you worked for Mavs?" Dončić replied. I briefly informed him about the drastic difference between covering a team and being an employee. "OK," he said, nodding his head. "We'll see."

Our chat, which lasted maybe 30 seconds, was over. A tremendously entertaining series was about to start.

NOTHING HAPPENED THAT NIGHT TO MAKE ANYONE WHO PICKED Phoenix change their minds. The Suns led for all but the first 14 seconds, scoring the first 9 points of the game. Phoenix's lead was in double digits for most of the game, peaking at 21 points when Suns backup center JaVale McGee picked Dončić's pocket on the perimeter and rumbled for a tomahawk dunk on perhaps the most surprising one-man fast break of the postseason. It was a more convincing win than the 121–114 final score indicated.

The Suns' defensive strategy was essentially to dare Dončić to beat them by himself, rarely sending an extra defender at the Mavs' superstar. Dončić did plenty of damage, frequently muscling Defensive Player of the Year runner-up Mikal Bridges to get wherever he wanted to go on the floor. He finished with 45 points on 15-of-30 shooting, 12 rebounds, and eight assists. The problem: Dončić outscored the rest of the Dallas starting lineup, which combined for only 39 points. "We've just got to get someone to join the party," Kidd said after the loss.

Dallas also had to figure out how to slow down the Suns, whose game plan was to go after Dončić as often as possible on defense, forcing him to exhaust energy on that end of the floor. According to ESPN Stats and Information tracking, the Suns scored 24 points on 10-of-18 shooting when Dončić was the primary defender in Game 1. "I think our defense lost us the game today," Dončić said postgame. "Our start on the defensive end was terrible, and we've got to change that. I know we can play way better defense."

Terrible took a turn for the worse in Game 2. The Suns mercilessly picked on Dončić defensively en route to a 129–109 rout. They relentlessly hunted Dončić by having the man he was defending set a ball screen, and it worked over and over and over again; the Suns scorched the Mavs for 71 points in the second half. Chris Paul and Devin Booker, the Suns' star backcourt duo, basically took turns, combining for 41 of their 58 points after halftime.

Second Spectrum tracking had Dončić as the screener defender 19 times in the second half with the Suns averaging 1.81 points on those possessions. Simply put, running actions that targeted Dončić was a layup, figuratively and often literally. The 77 on his jersey might as well have been a bullseye. Booker and Paul, seated side by side during their postgame press conference, turned toward each other and smirked when asked about the strategy. "Tough matchup to guard," Booker said of Dončić, "but he's going to have to guard a little bit."

Dončić had another brilliant offensive performance, scoring 35 points and dishing out seven assists, but it didn't matter. The Mavs were outscored by 28 points in his 36 minutes. Dallas waved the white flag with 4:41 remaining, subbing out Dončić and the rest of the starters after a Booker three that was the Suns' 11th bucket in a span of 13 possessions.

"We need to do a better job of helping him," Kidd said. "They're bringing him up into everything. We knew that coming into the series. We knew that in the last series. We did a better job of protecting one another, not just Luka. We've got to get back to protecting one another for Game 3 back at home."

Dončić didn't want to discuss X's and O's adjustments. His solution was simple, albeit easier said than done: "I've just got to play better defense. That's it."

It might have been a humbling trip to Phoenix, but Dončić's confidence had not been dented. "We believe, man," he said, shrugging his shoulders with his arms crossed. "They've got to win four, so it's not over yet."

A few minutes into Game 3, Dončić dove on the floor to fight for a loose ball under the Mavs' basket. He clawed to keep Suns center Deandre Ayton from picking up the ball, which ended up in Powell's hands. Message sent: Dončić was serious about doing his share of the dirty work. "When you see your best player doing that, it kind of sets a mood," Finney-Smith said after Dallas's 103–94 win.

Brunson broke out of a mini slump with 28 points—6 more than he had combined in the two road losses to open the series—to lead the Mavs in scoring. Dončić didn't have a great shooting game (10-of-25 from the floor), but he finished with 26 points, 13 rebounds, and nine assists. More importantly, he made good on his vow to drastically improve on the defensive end. "He participated, too," Kidd said. "It puts us in a different position when that happens." The Suns couldn't just keep picking on Dončić. Booker and Paul had more turnovers (12) than buckets (11) as Dallas snapped an 11-game losing streak against the Suns that dated back to November 2019. Paul, whose 37th birthday was spoiled, committed seven turnovers by halftime.

"It wasn't like us," Booker said. "You can credit them. They came out and played hard, played desperate. But that's that. We got a series."

Dončić started Game 4 hot, scoring 12 of the Mavs' 37 points as they jumped to a dozen-point lead in the first quarter, and excelled as a distributor all afternoon. He dished out 11 assists, feeding teammates for eight of the Mavs' 20 threes, including five of Finney-Smith's eight triples. But Dončić's most impactful moment of the game occurred when he crashed to the floor 94 feet away from the Mavs' basket.

Paul, playing well below his Hall of Fame standards again, missed an open short jumper in the final seconds of the first half and followed his shot. Dončić, who is seven inches taller and roughly 70 pounds heavier than Paul, was positioned for an easy rebound. But Paul made the inexplicable decision to try to go over Dončić's back to fight for the ball despite already having three fouls. Dončić made damn sure to draw the whistle, flying to the baseline floor like he'd been blindsided by a much bigger man. It was a foul worth much more than the two free throws Dončić made on the other end. Phoenix coach Monty Williams had taken a risk by leaving Paul on the floor in foul trouble to finish the half, but the coach didn't expect one of the smartest basketball brains of all time to make such a silly decision.

Paul's line in the second half: no points, one rebound, one assist, and two fouls in three minutes, 58 seconds. He had to watch the final 8:58 from the bench after getting called for his sixth foul, disqualifying the Suns' best closer, a player who had led the league in fourth-quarter scoring that season. The Mavs cruised down the stretch to a series-tying 111–101 win.

Dončić took great pleasure in getting the best of the "Point God" at Paul's own game. Paul, a master thespian himself with an acting resumé that includes many State Farm commercials and countless flops, sarcastically asked Dončić if he pushed him that hard after that foul late in the first half.

"No, not that hard," Dončić quipped, "but it was a smart play."

"Yeah, I know," Paul responded according to Dončić, who beamed with pride as he recalled the exchange. Dončić busted out a smile that was brighter than the multicolored tropic-themed shirt he wore postgame, kidding that he stole it from Finney-Smith's closet.

The Suns got plenty of payback in Game 5 back in Phoenix, rolling to a 110–80 rout to take the series lead. Phoenix blew the game open in the third quarter, outscoring Dallas by 19 as the Mavs had almost as many turnovers (12) as points (14) in the quarter. The Suns were on a 16–0 run when Finney-Smith released some frustration by bodychecking Booker as the Suns star went up for a transition layup midway through the quarter. The hit sent Booker sprawling into the baseline underneath the Suns' basket, and he rolled over to lay face down with his head resting on his left forearm. He stayed in that position for 20 seconds, as if he were in excruciating pain, as the referees went to review the play, which resulted in Finney-Smith being assessed a flagrant foul. But Booker had a big smile on his face as he rolled back over. As teammates helped him up, he looked at a courtside fan who was recording the scene on his cell phone and boasted about his embellishment: "The Luka special!"

Booker and the Suns had plenty to say and celebrate the rest of the game. Even garbage time was eventful. Dallas's Marquese Chriss and Phoenix's Bismack Biyombo were both ejected after a confrontation with 2.3 seconds remaining that started when Chriss delivered a hard foul to prevent Biyombo from throwing down a disrespectful dunk—an attempt that violated the NBA's unwritten rules about running up the score. Chriss chased Biyombo into the tunnel that leads to the Suns' locker room before security from both teams prevented that situation from escalating. Other Phoenix and Dallas players exchanged words on the court after the final buzzer.

"Everybody acting tough when they up," Dončić said after walking through the tunnel toward the visitors' locker room, a towel draped over his neck. He wasn't talking to anyone in particular, but he wanted to make sure his message was heard loud and clear. He repeated himself as cameras rolled. "Everybody acting tough when they up."

At that point in NBA history, the team that won Game 5 in a tied series had advanced 82 percent of the time. The odds were stacked even higher against the Mavs, given that the Suns were the top overall seed and would play Game 7, if necessary, at home. Not that

Dončić gave a damn. His confidence hadn't diminished a bit, and his determination had only increased. Nobody really needs more motivation in the playoffs, but this series against the Suns had become personal.

That was evident by the Game 6 response in Dallas: a 113–86 rout for the Mavs that featured plenty of bravado, primarily from Dončić, becoming bolder and bolder as the lead ballooned. Dončić stared down at Booker after an and-one drive with a little more than four minutes remaining in the first half, when Booker attempted to challenge Dončić around the basket as a help defender and ended up on his butt several feet away as the ball went through the net. It was still a close game then—Dallas went up 6 when Dončić made the free throw—but the Mavs were on the verge of seizing control. Less than a minute and a half later, Dončić got a switch and swished a three over Ayton from the left wing, a few feet in front of Suns coach Monty Williams, to push the lead into double figures. The Suns were in serious trouble now, and Dončić made sure they knew it—staring down the bench as he snarled and exaggeratedly nodded his head.

Dončić had a similar celebration after his dunk pushed the lead to 20 midway through the third quarter, prompting a Suns time-out. It was his second drive for a dunk right down the middle of the Phoenix defense in the span of a few possessions, a sign that the Suns were ready to board the flight back home for Game 7. After landing, Dončić shot a satisfied look toward his teammates on the bench and then strutted out to half-court, staring at the Suns' bench and nodding the whole way. "Yeaahhhh!" he shouted at his opponents as the sellout crowd roared. "Yeahhhh!"

"I like when people trash talk to me," Dončić said after his 33-point, 11-rebound, eight-assist, four-steal performance. "It gets me going. It's fun."

Somebody would get the last words a few days later. On to Game 7 on a Sunday afternoon at the Footprint Center—the biggest stage of Dončić's NBA career so far. "He couldn't wait for that game to start," Kokoškov said. "That's a talent, too, just feeling comfortable and excited about such a big game."

Dončić put on a show from the opening possession, dancing with the ball on the left wing after Ayton switched onto him before driving down the lane and pirouetting into a pretty one-legged fade from just inside the free throw line, a shot that surely made Nowitzki proud as he watched from his courtside seat. That bucket gave the Mavs the lead for good. Dončić's next shot was a step-back three over Ayton from the left corner. He barked back at a fan as the ball splashed through the net and laughed as he jogged back on defense. He felt it. Dončić had a dozen points by the end of the first quarter, and Dallas led by 10. Then it really got ugly for the Suns.

As Dončić took his usual rest to start the second quarter, Dinwiddie kept cooking, matching his first-quarter scoring total with 8 points as Dallas pushed the lead to 15. The Suns' offense was stunningly discombobulated, going scoreless for three and a half minutes before Dončić checked back in midway through the fourth quarter. He went right back to work on the next possession, swishing a fadeaway over Ayton that was almost identical to the first shot, grinning as he backpedaled down the floor. Dončić and Dinwiddie took turns torching the Suns for the rest of the quarter, slicing through the Phoenix defense off the dribble over and over again before Dončić put the finishing touches on the scoring flurry with a pair of off-the-bounce threes on back-to-back possessions. Dončić laughed as he backpedaled down the sideline after swishing the first of those threes. He was toying with the Suns now, having just executed a beautiful spin move before stepping back to shoot over Cam Johnson. There wasn't a defender within 10 feet when Dončić released the next shot. Johnson skidded across the court on his back after losing his balance when Dončić gave him a bump while dribbling backward between his legs. "Oh, no he didn't!" Reggie Miller uttered on the TNT broadcast. Dončić curled up his bottom lip and glared toward the corner, where that fan who had talked trash in the opening minutes was sitting.

Halftime score: Dončić 27, Suns 27. The rest of the Mavs chipped in 30 points, including 21 by Dinwiddie. Phoenix fans booed, knowing full well that the Suns couldn't come back. The 30-point deficit was the largest ever at halftime of a Game 7. The game, the series, was over. The second half was a mere formality.

Final score: Mavs 123, Suns 90. Dončić finished with 35 points and 10 rebounds, spending the entire fourth quarter celebrating on the bench. Dinwiddie scored 30, joining Dončić as the first pair of teammates to put up 30-plus apiece in a Game 7 since Shaq and Kobe two decades earlier.

"He's the type of guy who wants to throw a knockout punch," Dinwiddie said of Dončić after the blowout. "So I give him credit for that. He's never scared of the moment."

The Mavs didn't just pull off a monumental upset. They humiliated the heavily favored Suns in historic fashion. It was the most lopsided Game 7 road win since the Philadelphia Warriors blew out the St. Louis Bombers (don't feel bad if you didn't know that franchise ever existed) by 39 in 1948. Booker was about as bad as Dončić was brilliant, going 3-of-14 from the floor with four turnovers while the Suns were outscored by 41 in his 37 minutes. Paul's first bucket came when the Suns were down 40. Ayton, the first pick in Dončić's draft, got benched after playing only 17 minutes and argued with Williams about it in the fourth quarter.

"No one gave us a chance," Kidd said before poking a little fun at the predictions. "A lot of people said it was going to be a blowout. Well, they were right, but they didn't have us on the winning side."

When Dončić walked into the interview room for his postgame media session, he pointed at me and said, "Told you so." It was a good-natured jab, but he made his point: doubt him at your own risk.

"You can't get this smile off my face right now," Dončić said after sitting down in front of the microphone. "I'm just really happy.

Honestly, I think we deserve this. We've been playing hard the whole series. Maybe a couple of games here we weren't ourselves, but we came here with a statement in Game 7. We believed. Our locker room believed. Everybody believed. So I'm just happy."

Dončić's mood hadn't changed a couple of days later, following the Mavs' practice at the Chase Center in San Francisco the day before Game 1 of the Western Conference finals against the Warriors. He actually admitted that he wasn't quite as confident as he'd portrayed entering the previous series.

"Honestly, I never expected to be here," Dončić said. "I'm living my best life. This is the dream. I was worried before Game 7. I said, 'This might be my last game of the NBA season,' but I wasn't ready [for the season to end]. I wanted to play basketball. Tomorrow [is] another basketball game that I will enjoy. I get to play in this floor. So I'm just happy to be playing basketball, man. It's a pleasure for me."

THE WEST FINALS WEREN'T MUCH OF A SERIES. THE MAVS ENDED up being a speed bump in the Golden State dynasty's road to the Warriors' fourth championship of this era. Game 1 was a 112–87 blowout win for the Warriors. In Game 2, Golden State rallied from a 19-point second-quarter deficit for a 126–117 win, despite 42 points and eight assists from Dončić. That made Game 3 at home essentially a must-win for the Mavs, but Golden State pulled out a 109–100 victory to put Dallas on the brink of elimination, with Andrew Wiggins's poster dunk over Dončić in the fourth quarter as an exclamation point.

No team in NBA history has come back from a 3–0 deficit to win the series, and the Mavs might as well have waved a white flag during the postgame press conferences. Kidd referred to the Mavs' playoff run as "just the beginning of this journey" and referenced the "great lesson learned" by facing a dynasty that features three future

Hall of Famers in Stephen Curry, Klay Thompson, and Draymond Green. Dončić gushed about Golden State's chemistry and how well the Warriors fit together and understood their roles. He scored 40 in the Game 3 loss, unfortunately joining an exclusive list of players to score 40-plus in consecutive playoff losses (LeBron James, Magic Johnson, Michael Jordan, Jerry West, and his buddy Booker). But Dončić, who had 19 points in the fourth quarter as the Mavs attempted to muster a rally that never really got rolling, blamed himself for playing "very bad" in the first half. He acknowledged that he was still figuring out how to balance individual brilliance with putting his team in position to win a championship.

"I'm still learning," Dončić said. "I think after this season is done, whatever we are, I think we're going to look back and learn a lot of things. It's my first time in the conference finals in the NBA. I'm 23, man. I'm still learning a lot."

The Mavs' season was done four days later. Dallas avoided the embarrassment of a sweep with a 119–109 Game 4 win on its home floor, leading by as many as 29 and holding on after Golden State got within single digits down the stretch. Dallas bowed out with a 120–110 loss in Game 5, when Dončić assessed his performance as "terrible." He especially struggled in the first half, going 2-of-12 from the floor with three turnovers and frequently failing to get back on defense, a major factor in the Mavs falling behind by as many as 25 points. But Dončić emphasized how proud he was of his team and the massive progress the Mavs made in their first year under Kidd.

"I think this year we made a huge, huge step, maybe a couple steps," Dončić said. "I think we are in a great way. Obviously there's a lot of things to do, but I think, like I say, we made a huge step, and I think we are on a great path."

Without singling out Dončić, Kidd publicly challenged his superstar to take the next tough steps. "Now it's about, What is our appetite come next season?" Kidd said. "Are we going to tiptoe into the season or are we going to be hungry? Then, are we going to train this summer to understand what it means to play into May and June? Because it's a long season."

The deep playoff run had provided tangible hope that the Mavs had a formula in place for a perennial contender with Dončić as the face of the franchise. "Yes, without question," Cuban said during his round of interviews in the Chase Center hallway in the wake of the Mavs' elimination. "Hard-playing, physical, multitalented, being able to complement Luka. Knowing how to play with Luka—that probably is No. 1." The roster had flaws—Warriors big man Kevon Looney's 18 rebounds in the closeout game hammered home the need for an upgrade at center—but the Mavs' decision-makers didn't feel the need to make massive changes. Specifically, they insisted that there was no desperation to acquire another star to pair with Dončić.

"The superteams haven't really worked," said Cuban, who continued to express confidence that the Mavs would keep Brunson in free agency, as he had since the trade deadline. "I think there's good reasons why. In this league with a lot of space, a lot of people—we saw Spencer, we saw JB just be able to get to the rim and score. Now, we need guys to fill all the other roles. We'll work to fill those roles, because that's what a J. Kidd team is—playing hard, playing physical, outcompeting, and playing harder than the other teams."

Harrison echoed that stance during the next day's exit interviews: "I don't think it's just about having All-Stars. There's tons of teams—and I'm not even going to waste my time mentioning names—that have a bunch of All-Stars, and they were sitting at home watching us play [in the Western Conference finals]. You need to keep upgrading the roster, but I don't think it's about just getting a bunch of All-Stars. I think it's about getting people that fit together—starting with Luka—and people that can fit around him. I think that's more important than just getting All-Stars."

It had indeed been a rough season for the NBA's so-called superteams. Brooklyn dealt with all kinds of drama—including James

Harden's mid-season trade demand—before being swept in the first round despite the presence of Kevin Durant and Kyrie Irving. The Lakers, two years removed from winning a title, didn't even make the playoffs as Russell Westbrook proved to be as bad of a fit as the skeptics had believed alongside LeBron James and Anthony Davis, who both missed significant time due to injuries. Maybe the Mavs, with a perennial MVP candidate still approaching his prime and a collection of quality complementary pieces, were already on the best path.

"We've definitely got enough in this locker room to do something special," Finney-Smith said during the conference finals. "We're here. We're a top-four team in the NBA. You can try to find another star, but you never know how that's going to mesh with Luka or the other personnel. It's an adjustment to play with somebody like Luka, too, and I feel like JB adjusted well and Spence, too. The bunch of stars shit don't even work anymore. Fit matters."

CHAPTER 14

BRUNSON BOLTS

MINUTES AFTER THE MAVS' SEASON ENDED, CUBAN INDICATED that Brunson's return was a sure thing—casually dropping "obviously after re-signing JB" while discussing offseason plans during a live interview on Bally Sports Southwest. Throughout the Mavs' playoff run, as Brunson's value in the upcoming free agency market seemingly soared, Cuban repeatedly reminded reporters that the Mavs had the guard's Bird rights, meaning the franchise could exceed the salary cap to keep him, as well as offer larger annual raises and a longer contract than other suitors.

"We can pay him more than anybody," Cuban said when asked a follow-up question specifically about Brunson. "I think he wants to stay, and that's most important."

Brunson's eyebrows lifted when he saw Cuban's comments while scrolling through social media in the early morning hours. He had avoided discussing his future contract throughout the season, even as Kidd frequently mentioned that one of his goals was to "get Brunson paid." That price went up throughout the playoffs, as Brunson starred in Dončić's early absence and proved himself as the clear No. 2 option for a West finals team. When Brunson saw what Cuban had to say, he thought the billionaire would back it up with a big contract offer, finally making a commitment to the former second-round pick whom the Mavs had repeatedly dangled as trade bait.

"Hey, JB about to get that bag," Finney-Smith declared that night, taking his turn speaking to the media before Brunson. Brunson still deferred, saying he was just focused on getting to play with this group of teammates and appreciating their accomplishments. He said he'd think about free agency later.

"He's boring as shit to interview," Jalen's father Rick Brunson had said with a booming laugh the previous month, crediting (or blaming) his son's college coach. "He learned that from Jay Wright. You ask him a question, it's, boom, boom, boom, boom, boom—same answers. It's a Villanova thing. Jay Wright programmed him. He didn't get that from me."

That was one of the first things Rick Brunson, who played for eight teams during his nine-year NBA journeyman career, blurted out when we sat down in a couple of chairs in a hallway at the Grand America Hotel in Salt Lake City the morning after the Mavs' Game 3 win over the Jazz. As players, coaches, and staffers walked past, several laughed and shook their heads at the sight of Rick Brunson chatting with a reporter. "Uh-oh," some of them half joked.

His son was the breakout star of the playoffs' first round, carrying the Mavs to a 2–1 series lead over the Jazz while Dončić recovered from his calf strain, and Jalen's pops had some stuff he wanted to publicly get off his chest. Brunson had no interest in discussing his pending free agency, but his dad was eager to get the family's side of the developing story on the record.

"We've got to figure out if Dallas wants him. Not words," Rick Brunson said. "Ain't no discount. So don't put it on us. Don't tell me you love me. Show me."

The Brunsons certainly didn't feel love from the franchise the previous summer. Jalen, who had just finished fourth in the Sixth Man of the Year voting, was eligible for a four-year extension of his rookie deal for a total value of as much as $55.5 million. It was a reasonable deal for a 24-year-old who had proven he could be part of a playoff team's core, had a great relationship with the face of the franchise, and consistently lived up to his "immaculate vibes" catchphrase in contributing to the locker room culture. The Brunsons believed it was a mere formality that the deal would be put on the table and planned to pounce on it, ecstatic about Jalen enjoying the security of a guaranteed contract that his dad never had. They'd looked at houses in Preston Hollow and other nice Dallas neighborhoods, as Jalen was eager to get a backyard with grass for his dog to roam.

Father and son had discussed the extension offer they were sure was on the horizon while relaxing on the beach during the Brunsons' annual summer vacation at the Round Hill Hotel in Montego Bay, Jamaica, the homeland of his mother's side of the family. They decided that they'd even accept a little less than the maximum that Dallas could offer if the Mavs wanted to negotiate. Fifty million was a nice round number that would work for them. "I gave 'em a discount!" Rick Brunson said later.

But the Mavs—communicating through Brunson's CAA agents Aaron Mintz or Sam Rose—weren't ready to make that kind of commitment. "When I first got the phone call—[the Mavs said], 'We really want to think about it'—it fucked my whole vacation up," Rick Brunson grumbled.

The explanation was that Dallas had just undergone massive organizational change—hiring a new head coach and general manager—and wanted time to evaluate the roster. Harrison had said they wanted to wait until training camp opened in September. When that time came, the Mavs still didn't offer the extension.

There were a few major factors in the Mavs' decision to defer. With the Mavs' limited assets, it was likely that Brunson would have had to be included in any package to pursue a co-star for Dončić. If Brunson signed an extension, he wouldn't have been eligible to be traded before that season's deadline. Cuban was also worried about adding to the Dallas payroll, as every single dollar would be multiplied in luxury tax payments in accordance with the league's collective bargaining agreement. For the first dozen years of Cuban's control, he brashly blew into the luxury tax, when the payments were dollar for dollar over the limit. But he had avoided it since the Mavs' 2011 title run, as the tax payments became more punitive. That wouldn't be feasible once Dončić's supermax contract kicked in, but Cuban was determined to limit the damage to his wallet. He also didn't believe there would be much of a market for Brunson if he did hit free agency, privately pointing out that the teams set up to have salary cap space the next summer had all made heavy investments in young guards. Cuban believed at the time that the best deal Brunson could get in free agency was the mid-level exception, which would have been $45.1 million over four years.

Rick Brunson let it be known that his son wouldn't be willing to entertain contract discussions during the season if an extension wasn't offered before the October 21 opener. The Brunsons didn't stick to their guns, though. According to them, they went back to the Mavs' front office in early January—after Brunson had kept the Mavs afloat during Dončić's absence and seized a full-time starting role—and informed Dallas's decision-makers that he'd sign the extension if it was put on the table at that point.

"They looked the other way," Brunson said later. "They had every right in the world to do so. I don't blame them for making any business decisions. That's on them."

Speculation soon started to swirl around the league about Brunson bolting for the Knicks in free agency, even though New York would have to dump several players to create enough salary cap space. He would be an unrestricted free agent—unlike most players coming off their rookie deal, whose teams have the right to match any offer—because his original agent negotiated for the final year of that contract to be nonguaranteed instead of a team option, a major flub by Donnie Nelson and Cuban. That agent was Leon Rose, Brunson's godfather who was now the Knicks' president.

The Brunsons' family ties with the New York franchise ran deep. New York coach Tom Thibodeau had also known Jalen since he was born. Thibodeau's relationship with Rick dated to the elder Brunson's high school days in Salem, Massachusetts, when Thibodeau coached at Salem State and would work out local teenage prospects. Thibodeau was an assistant coach in New York and Houston when Rick played for the Knicks and Rockets and hired him as an assistant when Thibodeau got head coaching jobs in Chicago and Minnesota. Sam Rose, Brunson's lifelong friend and one of his agents, is Leon's son.

"I just think this New York thing is too tied to his family to overcome," Harrison texted to Cuban in early February.

But the Mavs opted not to act on inquiries about Brunson—including from New York—leading up to the February 10 trade deadline. Dallas discussed dumping injured shooting guard Tim Hardaway Jr.'s fresh four-year, $75 million contract, which would have required attaching future draft compensation, a move that would have created enough cap space to offer Brunson a larger extension. Brunson's agents passed on word that a five-year, $87 million offer would be accepted. However, Dallas didn't deal Hardaway. Instead, they meekly offered Brunson the four-year, $55.5 million extension. Finney-Smith excitedly signed his identical extension offer at the time, but Brunson turned it down, rightly believing that he had "outgrown" that number.

"That was a 30-second conversation," Rick Brunson said. "I wasn't on the phone, but how I got the message was, 'You guys wouldn't be interested in that deal now, would you?' That's how it was said to me. I just laughed."

So Brunson played out the rest of the season, steadily building his value. That three-game stint as the Mavs' primary initiator against the Jazz provided a glimpse of Brunson's ability to be the man in high-stakes situations. But Brunson was happy to be Dončić's sidekick, a role he had to patiently earn over the years as the Mavs acquired other guards, such as Seth Curry, Delon Wright, Josh Richardson, and Trey Burke, who cut into his minutes.

The Mavs had a two-pronged challenge in their search for a co-star to complement Dončić. They had depleted their trade assets with the Porziņģis trade that had yet to be paid off, and Dončić was so ball dominant that some proven stars wouldn't want to play with him. But maybe the Mavs already had a suitable co-star in the low-maintenance Brunson, who didn't mind operating in Dončić's shadow.

"The main challenge is probably ego," Brunson said during those conference finals. "When a person has the ball in his hands for that long, people can get upset. People want the ball or people say they need a rhythm.... I learned how I need to play without a rhythm. I don't need a rhythm. It's Luka Dončić. Shit's not changing. It's *Luka Dončić*. I've come to the conclusion that he's an amazing player, he's going to do a lot of great things, and this organization is going to build around him. I've grown into the mindset of, How can I fit that mold? How can I be successful in my role or in whatever role they want me to be in? My dad also said it's how it's going to be. Certain guys have that aura about them. It's not whatever they say goes, but it's revolving around them—and rightfully so. I've just kind of learned how I can be effective off of that."

But Rick Brunson, who readily admits that his son had blown past his expectations for him, couldn't help but envision how Jalen would handle the opportunity of having his own offense to run. "It's a great fit [in Dallas], but at the end of the day, my son is no different than the next man," the elder Brunson said in that Salt Lake City hotel hallway. "You try to raise them the right way in terms of understanding the game, but everyone wants what Luka has. I don't care who you are. Everyone wants that feeling of, 'Hey, I can do this, too.' I don't always think the grass is greener on the other side, but we'll sit down this summer and go through all the pros and cons of staying here or going somewhere else."

A week after the Mavs' season ended, Rick Brunson agreed to reunite with Thibodeau, accepting a deal to become an assistant coach for the Knicks. Meanwhile, according to Jalen Brunson, he heard "crickets" from the Mavs in the weeks leading up to his free agency, which caught Brunson by surprise after Cuban publicly expressed such confidence in keeping him. On draft night, a week before free agency officially opened, New York's Rose executed some financially motivated wheeling and dealing—shedding the 11th overall pick and Kemba Walker's $9.2 million salary. It was apparent that the Knicks were maneuvering to make room under the salary cap to sign Brunson.

"We weren't shocked that they did that," Harrison said that night regarding the Knicks' planned pursuit of Brunson. "Honestly, until he tells us he doesn't want to be here, we're optimistic. We haven't heard otherwise, so we're optimistic. We have to be."

Cuban considered a fair offer for Brunson to be "Fred VanVleet money," or a five-year, $105 million deal, using the then–Toronto Raptors point guard's $21 million salary as the benchmark. (This was a year before VanVleet opted out of the final season of his contract to sign a three-year, $129 million deal with the Houston Rockets.) Cuban had taken a similar approach with Steve Nash 18 years earlier, when Kings point guard Mike Bibby's contract was the line-in-the-sand standard before the future Hall of Famer left Dallas for Phoenix in free agency.

The Knicks needed to trim more payroll to make a competitive offer to Brunson, and in the worst-case scenario, Cuban figured he could get a first-round pick out of them by cooperating in a sign-and-trade deal. That possibility went poof when the Knicks dumped the $19 million combined salaries of Nerlens Noel and Alec

Burks in a deal with Detroit a couple of days before free agency opened, sending the Pistons a pair of second-round picks and $6 million in cash. ESPN reported that night that the Knicks were widely anticipated to give Brunson a four-year deal worth more than $100 million.

The Mavs still scheduled a meeting with Brunson and his representatives in New York on June 30, the night negotiations could (wink-wink) begin. A handful of Dallas teammates who had formed close friendships with Brunson—including Maxi Kleber, Dwight Powell, and Dorian Finney-Smith (but not Dončić, who was with the Slovenian national team)—planned to attend along with Cuban, Harrison, and other members of the front office. The Brunson family braced themselves for Cuban to attempt to outbid the Knicks in a last-ditch effort to avoid a painful repeat of history by losing their second-best player for nothing. The Mavs could offer up to a maximum of $175.5 million over five years.

"Yo man, I know what [Cuban is] doing. He's going to come to New York and say, 'Here goes a max deal,'" Rick Brunson recalled telling his wife and son. "I'm thinking the guy got money coming off his ass. So he's coming with a max deal and then going to say, 'What you going to do?'"

Jalen Brunson's response, according to his dad: "This, I'm taking it."

"And guess what I said? 'Gotta do it!'" Rick Brunson said.

The Mavs, with the advantage of Texas's lack of a state income tax, could have forced Brunson to make a difficult decision by at least matching the annual salary offered by the Knicks. But Cuban and the Mavs weren't willing to budge. The meeting was canceled, with each side initially claiming the other called it off—not that it mattered. (Cuban and Brunson agreed that the Mavs canceled the meeting a couple of years later, when they briefly, awkwardly discussed the final days of Brunson's free agency when Cuban appeared on *Roommates Show*, a podcast Brunson co-hosts.)

Brunson formally agreed to a four-year, $104 million deal with the Knicks that night. They had nearly doubled the extension Brunson was willing to sign the previous summer, as he pointed out to his dad as they relaxed on the beach in Jamaica again days later.

"Personally, deep down in my gut, I was like, 'Man, I'm out of here [in Dallas],'" Rick Brunson, who felt the Mavs repeatedly disrespected his son, said about his attitude as free agency approached. "But I knew I had to convince him that, 'Yo, you're better than this. You can have your own team.'

"But I tell you this, this is a conversation we had: if Dallas offers the same money or more, I don't know if he leaves. Come with the money. Make it hard! You didn't. You made it easy."

The Knicks drew some criticism for a perceived overpay, but Brunson's contract proved to be a bargain. He quickly established himself as a star in New York, breathing life into one of the league's flagship franchises that had been floundering for most of the previous two decades.

Months after it became clear the Mavs had made a massive mistake, Cuban publicly blamed Brunson's dad for meddling in the negotiations. Not that Rick Brunson took offense after his son got much more money and a larger role on a winning team. "Yeah, I'm the fucking father," Rick said. "You protect your kids, and you tell your kids the truth."

This was a classic case of revisionist history by Cuban. He claimed that the Mavs couldn't have outbid the Knicks because they were never told what the offer was, even though anyone with an Internet connection and casual interest in the NBA was aware of the range in advance of free agency. That reporting factored into the NBA office's decision to find the Knicks in violation of the league's tampering rules, which comes with the slap-on-the-wrist punishment of losing the next year's second-round pick.

"We didn't know what the bid was," Cuban said. "They never gave us a number. Knowing the numbers now, I would've paid it in a heartbeat, but he wouldn't have come anyway. There's just no possible way that it was about money."

Cuban also insisted that Brunson never indicated in January that he would sign the extension at that point, disputing the accounts from father (before free agency) and son (afterward on multiple occasions). Cuban went so far as to queue up the early February texts from Harrison to show reporters during the impromptu courtside media availability, much to the shock of the Mavs' GM. I asked Cuban to scroll up so we could see the texts from early January, matching the extension-talk timeline provided by the Brunsons. Cuban didn't appreciate the line of questioning.

"Bullshit! That's fucking bullshit, Tim!" Cuban barked at me. "And you are a moron if you listened to those motherfuckers."

Cuban had quite a different tone in the days after the summer transaction-cycle smoke cleared. His spin then was that the Mavs had upgraded their roster despite losing their second-leading scorer. Cuban specifically pointed to the trade for Christian Wood and the return of Hardaway, who had missed the second half of the season, as reasons why Brunson's departure wasn't that big of a deal.

"I wish Jalen the best. He's a great guy," Cuban said during the Las Vegas Summer League. "I mean, it'd be one thing if I didn't like him and I thought he was just a jerk, but he's really, really a good, good, good guy with a heart of gold. So I wish him nothing but the best. We changed our team and we got a lot bigger. We're gonna be able to score—we lost Jalen at 17 a game, but we pick up Timmy at 18, 17 a game and Christian at 17, 18, 19 a game. So we're going to be fine."

The Wood trade was a polarizing move within the organization. Simply put, Kidd wanted nothing to do with Wood despite his talent, which gave Kidd something in common with other coaches from Wood's previous six NBA stops. Rockets coach Stephen Silas pleaded with Houston GM Rafael Stone to get rid of either troubled guard Kevin Porter Jr. or Wood to give the coach a fighting chance at establishing a decent culture in the final season of his contract.

Stone had been trying to trade Wood, who averaged an efficient 19.9 points and 9.9 rebounds per game during his two seasons in Houston, for a year with no takers. Stone pounced when the Mavs offered the No. 26 overall pick along with four nonrotation players—all but one of whom the Rockets waived despite owing the next season's salary, the exception being Boban Marjanović, everyone's favorite teammate who would be especially missed by Dončić. The Mavs' rationale for making the trade was as much about clearing roster spots—used to re-sign hype man Theo Pinson and add veteran center JaVale McGee, who was promised a starting job—as adding a center/power forward with great skill and a lousy reputation.

Wood had proven that he could put up good numbers on bad teams but was widely considered by executives, scouts, and coaches around the league to lack the acumen and attitude to contribute to a winner. He would have an opportunity to disprove that perception playing with Dončić in Dallas, but it would have to come on Kidd's terms. That meant coming off the bench, which Wood claimed was news to him after Kidd confirmed the plan on media day before training camp opened.

Wood considered himself to be an All-Star–caliber player, likely in large part because his agent Adam Pensack told him that was the case. For that matter, Pensack told that to anyone who would listen, frequently and often abrasively reaching out to everyone from beat writers to fan bloggers who covered the team. Pensack also aggressively pushed the crackpot conspiracy theory that Dallas had an "agenda" in bringing Wood off the bench: deflating his value during his contract year so the Mavs could keep him at a lower price the next summer. But the consensus opinion around the league was that Wood, who had a reputation as a poor defender, was best utilized as a bench scorer.

Kidd didn't want to close games with Wood, either. Wood got off to a strong statistical start, but Kidd subbed for him late in the Mavs' first three tight games. That became a topic of conversation in the media and behind the scenes, which annoyed Kidd. Then, when the Mavs managed to blow a 16-point lead in the final 3:57 of regulation in an October 29 home overtime loss to the Oklahoma City Thunder, Kidd went out of his way to point out that Wood was on the court as Dallas crumbled in crunch time.

"We left C. Wood out there with that group and it didn't go well on either end," Kidd said. The Mavs became only the second team in a 25-season span to lose a game it led by at least 16 in the final four minutes of the fourth quarter. It was a stretch to dump the debacle entirely on Wood, who sat out all of overtime as the Mavs were outscored by 6 points, but Kidd clearly was determined to get his point across.

Kidd had been on board with the signing of McGee, who'd won a title as the Lakers' backup big man when Kidd was an assistant coach in Los Angeles, but it quickly became apparent that move was a complete bust. McGee's promise of a starting job lasted about two weeks before Powell, the center the Mavs were determined to replace during the offseason, reclaimed the role.

AT THE BEGINNING OF THE SEASON, THE MAVS' MANY FLAWS were overshadowed by Dončić's brilliance. He scored more than 30 points in each of the first nine games, the second-longest such stretch to start an NBA season, trailing only Wilt Chamberlain in 1962–63. Dončić averaged 36.0 points per game on 52.4 percent shooting during that 6–3 stretch, despite every opposing defense scheming to try to force him to give up the ball. Without Brunson to share some of the playmaking duties, Dončić was carrying a historically heavy burden that didn't seem sustainable.

"If we keep this up, then he will not be human if he gets past Christmas," Kidd said on November 10, the night after Dončić's 30-point streak ended. "So one or the other is going to show: he's human or not, and we believe he's human."

Dončić indeed proved to be mortal, and the Mavs' roster around him was mediocre at best. After that 6–3 start, Dallas lost seven of 10 games, going 3–1 when Dončić scored at least 30 during that stretch. That became a recurring theme: the Mavs were tough to beat as long as Dončić looked like the MVP, they were mediocre when he was mortal, and couldn't win when he rested, which was half of every back-to-back because of his massive workload.

Two months into the season, with the Mavs floating around .500, Kidd relented and inserted Wood into the starting lineup. Wood had driven the coaching staff mad with his struggles to grasp even simple defensive assignments, much less schemes, often looking at teammates with a bewildered shrug after the opponent scored. In one game against the Nuggets, Wood guarded the wrong guy for a couple possessions in a row, confusing Bruce Brown for Christian Braun.

"C. Wood, you've got Braun!" assistant coach Sean Sweeney shouted from the bench.

"I know!" Wood retorted, motioning toward Brown.

"The white guy!" Sweeney yelled with exasperation, clearing up the confusion.

The Mavs soon reeled off a season-best seven wins in a row with Wood starting—highlighted by his 30-point performance in a Christmas Day victory over the Los Angeles Lakers—but the success felt like fool's gold. The winning streak required production from Dončić that was ridiculous even by his standards against a pillow-soft stretch of schedule, featuring four games against the West's two worst teams, whose front offices were focused on lottery positioning in hopes of landing French phenom Victor Wembanyama.

Dončić had his second career 50-point game, as well as eight rebounds and 10 assists, in a December 23 win in Houston, the first of three matchups against the Rockets in an 11-night span. He played 42 minutes in the 112–106 victory, including every second of the second half. Dončić hit the dagger three with 19 seconds remaining, swishing the catch-and-shoot 30-footer to end a possession that began with the Rockets trapping him near half-court to force the ball out of his hands. He celebrated by mean-mugging the Toyota Center crowd while hopping sideways toward the Dallas bench during the Rockets' time-out. "Just too much Luka," Silas bemoaned postgame.

After a 124–115 win over the Lakers—who were missing All-Star center Anthony Davis—the Mavs got another break with the Knicks in town, as a hip injury sidelined Brunson for his Dallas return. New York lost another key starter 96 seconds into the game when R. J. Barrett lacerated his finger. And Dallas still trailed by double digits entering the fourth quarter, despite Dončić being in the midst of a monster performance.

The Mavs needed a miracle after Miles McBride's free throws bumped the Knicks' lead back to 9 with 34 seconds remaining. How slim were the Mavs' odds? According to ESPN Stats and Information, teams trailing by at least 9 in the last 35 seconds had been 0–13,384 over the previous two decades. And Dončić delivered.

After Wood hit a three with 26 seconds remaining, Dončić immediately tied up Quentin Grimes, won the jump ball, and slashed in for a putback, despite being bumped by Immanuel Quickley. The free throw was Dončić's 50th point. More importantly, it made it a one-possession game with 15 seconds remaining.

Dallas was down 4 after McBride split a pair of free throws a few seconds later. Coming out of the time-out, Spencer Dinwiddie hit a three off of Dončić's inbounds pass, giving Dončić his 10th assist of the night and first 50-point triple-double of his career. It was a 1-point game with 8.3 seconds remaining. McBride extended the deficit to 3 when he made both free throws after the Mavs fouled him again to extend the game.

Grimes fouled Dončić on purpose with 4.2 seconds remaining, hacking him as soon as he crossed the half-court line to prevent a potential game-tying three. Dončić made the first free throw, tying his career high with 51 points, a milestone that didn't mean much in the moment. McGee checked in for the first time all night, as everyone in the arena knew that Dončić needed to intentionally miss and the Mavs had to grab the offensive rebound, a desperate strategy that rarely works. His line drive skimmed the back of the rim and caromed off the backboard, then the ball bounced off two Knicks' hands before Dončić retrieved it with a foot outside of the paint and instantly flipped in an off-balance 11-foot shot as he fell to the floor. He rolled over, got back up, and broke into an impromptu, goofy dance, chopping his feet and waving his arms with his eyes and mouth wide open. Dončić celebrated more after Quickley's heave missed at the buzzer, so caught up in the moment that he lost track of the score, believing for 30 seconds or so that his prayer of a putback had won the game. "Goddamn," Dončić grumbled, his smile disappearing as he realized that overtime was about to begin.

Dončić found enough fuel for five more minutes. He scored 7 more points and grabbed three more rebounds in the overtime period, helping the Mavs pull away for a 126–121 win. He finished with 60 points, 21 rebounds, and 10 assists—the first 60–20–10 night in NBA history. He had 38 points, 15 rebounds, and six assists after halftime, resting only the final four seconds of the third quarter and final eight seconds of overtime. He checked out of the game to a standing ovation.

"I'm tired as hell," Dončić told Bally Sports Southwest's Jeff "Skin" Wade during the on-court postgame interview, smiling and shaking his head as he collected his thoughts. "I need a recovery beer."

Dončić had a 35–12–13 line against the Rockets—his league-leading eighth triple-double of the season—in the Mavs' next game a couple of nights later and got to rest the final 8:07 with a comfortable lead. From there, it was on to San Antonio for a New Year's Eve matchup against the rebuilding Spurs, whose legendary coach Gregg

Popovich had playfully declared, "We're holding Luka under 50!" Dončić proved Popovich wrong, scoring 51 points, and the Mavs needed every one of them to squeak out a 126–125 win. Dončić became the first player ever with at least 225 points, 50 rebounds, and 50 assists in a five-game stretch, packing three 50-point performances in that span. He celebrated by sipping a Hazy Little Thing IPA on the team bus.

THE MAVS WERE 22–16—A SEASON-BEST SIX GAMES ABOVE .500—after opening January by grinding out a road win over the Rockets. Beating the West's last-place team this time required Dončić to log 41 minutes, including all but a dozen seconds of the second half. He had another monster stat line with 39 points, 12 rebounds, and eight assists, but his off shooting night (10-of-26 from the floor, 1-of-9 from three-point range) indicated that Dončić was fighting fatigue while carrying the Mavs on his back. He averaged 41.7 points, 11.0 rebounds, and 9.9 assists in 39.8 minutes per game during the franchise's longest winning streak since the 2010–11 championship season.

Reality smacked the Mavs a few nights later as their streak was snapped with a blowout loss at home to the Boston Celtics. The only silver lining was that the score was so lopsided that Dončić sat out the entire fourth quarter, which began with the Mavs down 24. But this started a stretch of Dallas dropping nine out of 13 games, including going 0–3 when Dončić was given the night off to rest.

Midway through that funk, there was a silly local controversy about a mural outside of St. Pete's Dancing Marlin, a bar and grill in the Deep Ellum section of Dallas. Local artist Preston Pannek painted Dončić, surrounded by some of his remarkable stat lines, holding up a sign that read, "PLEASE SEND HELP." Cuban, in reply to an email from the artist, wrote that he considered the mural to be "disrespectful." Pannek shared the email with several local media outlets as he launched a publicity tour—then painted over the mural upon the request of Dončić via his publicist.

Dončić was sensitive to the public perception that he didn't believe in his teammates, but for the first time in his career, he showed an eagerness to be involved in private discussions with the front office about personnel decisions. He had been strongly indicating to Harrison and vice president of basketball operations Michael Finley behind the scenes that he wanted the roster to be upgraded before the February 9 trade deadline. I reported that on January 18, when Trae Young's Hawks were in town, as part of an article comparing the challenges faced by Atlanta and Dallas to build around the stars who were swapped for each other on their draft night.

A perturbed Cuban messaged me demanding a correction. The reporting was accurate—and was information known by executives with other teams for weeks—so I refused. I told Cuban that I would report any on-record comment that he made.

Cuban replied: "Tim MacMahon got it dead wrong. Luka has never suggested, asked, demanded or discussed changes to the roster." Seconds later, contradicting himself, Cuban added: "Luka and Nico have a great relationship. They talk almost daily. Luka knows exactly what we have going on and is very supportive."

After the Mavs lost again that night, allowing 130 or more points for the third straight game with a defensive effort that Kidd compared to a "shootaround," Dončić downplayed his desire for roster changes. But, he acknowledged, "I talk to Nico and I talk to Fin more than I used to" in communication "that just stays between us." Frankly, anyone with eyeballs recognized that Dallas needed to improve the personnel around Dončić to have any hope of contending. The Mavs had been searching for a legitimate co-star since the first months of his career and were months removed from losing Brunson, the player who came closest to filling that void, for nothing in return.

The problem was finding a deal, as Dallas had limited trade assets. Aside from Dončić, who was obviously untouchable, Dorian

Finney-Smith was the only Dallas player who generated significant interest from other teams—but he wasn't valuable enough to be the centerpiece of a package for a star. Attempts to shop Wood and Tim Hardaway Jr. went nowhere, even before Wood broke his thumb in the loss to the Hawks. The Mavs had only two first-round picks available to trade—less than the going rate in a package for a proven star—because they still owed a protected first-round pick to the Knicks as the final payment of the Porziņġis deal. Harrison had attempted to initiate trade talks with the Bulls about shooting guard Zach LaVine, but Chicago wasn't willing to entertain the idea—a decision the Bulls regretted a year later when they shopped LaVine and failed to find a market for him.

Six days before the trade deadline, a door cracked open for Dallas: Kyrie Irving requested to be traded after his contract extension talks with the Brooklyn Nets broke down. Irving was a perennial All-Star in his prime—often referred to as the most skilled guard to ever play the game—the type of talent who would be far too valuable for the Mavs to make a competitive trade offer for under normal circumstances. But nothing about Irving's three-and-a-half-season tenure in Brooklyn had been normal.

IRVING'S ARRIVAL IN BROOKLYN AS PART OF A FREE AGENCY PACKage deal with Kevin Durant in 2019—both stars bolting from contenders, Irving in Boston and Durant in Golden State—sent shock waves throughout the league. The Nets, long an irrelevant franchise, were suddenly the NBA's next superteam. Brooklyn pushed in all of its chips early in the 2020–21 season when disgruntled former MVP James Harden successfully forced a trade from the Rockets to the Nets, who suddenly had as potent of an offensive trio as had ever been assembled in the NBA.

That trio played a grand total of 16 games together due to injuries, off-court drama, and trade demands.

Irving sat out the first thirty-five games of the 2021–22 season after refusing to comply with New York City's COVID-19 vaccine mandate, meaning he wasn't permitted to play home games. The Nets' management opted not to allow Irving to play road games, either, until they reversed their stance midway through the season. Harden grew frustrated and demanded to be traded again, forcing his way to Philadelphia. In the summer after being swept by the Celtics in the first round, Irving and Durant both made, and then rescinded, trade requests.

Early in the 2022–23 season, the Nets suspended Irving indefinitely for posting a link on social media to *Hebrews to Negroes: Wake Up Black America*, a film that features antisemitic tropes, and refusing "to unequivocally say he has no antisemitic beliefs, nor acknowledge specific hateful material in the film" in a media availability session, according to the team statement announcing the punishment. The suspension lasted eight games and eroded any remaining trust between Irving and Nets management.

There was no doubt that Brooklyn would grant Irving's trade request this time. The Nets, who had forfeited seven years of first-round draft capital (three picks, four swaps) in the failed Harden trade, needed to recoup some value months before Irving entered free agency. However, as talented as Irving was, many of the league's executives labeled him as toxic. His trade value had been drastically depressed. For Dallas, this presented a prime opportunity.

All of the Mavs' major stakeholders—Cuban, Harrison, Kidd, and most importantly, Dončić—were aligned in making a play for Irving. Harrison had known Irving since he was 16 and had signed him to a prized signature shoe deal with Nike, a lucrative contract the company terminated in November due to the controversy. Irving grew up in New Jersey as a fan of Kidd, who led the Nets to the franchise's only two NBA Finals appearances and had also formed a relationship with him in recent years, attending Kidd's Hall of Fame ceremony. Harrison and Kidd were confident that their bonds with Irving could allow him to feel comfortable and focus on basketball in Dallas. Nobody questioned his ability to perform on the court.

The primary competition in the market was the Lakers, the league's most disappointing team, sitting in 13th place in the West standings and in serious jeopardy of not even making the play-in tournament. LeBron James made it clear he wanted to reunite with his co-star from the Cavaliers' title team. The Lakers were looking to move on from Russell Westbrook, the ill-fitting former superstar who had worn out his welcome with the franchise and was in the final season of his contract.

The Lakers' proposals centered around Westbrook and their 2027 and 2029 first-round picks. The Mavs offered Finney-Smith, Dinwiddie, a pair of future second-round picks, and their 2029 first rounder. Brooklyn GM Sean Marks didn't drag out the process, making his decision on a Sunday afternoon 48 hours after Irving's request and four days before the trade deadline. The Nets, who wouldn't benefit from being bad due to the Rockets' controlling their first-round picks, chose the deal they believed would allow them to continue to be competitive.

Irving (along with out-of-rotation veteran Markieff Morris) was headed to Dallas. At least for the rest of the season. The Mavs made the deal with the understanding that any contract discussions with Irving would wait until the summer, when he'd be an unrestricted free agent. The Lakers would be able to pursue Irving again then if they so desired, or if James got his way.

"Definitely disappointing. I can't sit here and say I'm not disappointed on not being able to land such a talent," James told ESPN's Michael Wilbon in a TV interview after the Mavs acquired Irving. "Someone that I had great chemistry with, and know I got great chemistry with on the floor—that can help you win championships."

Seven months after Brunson's departure, the Mavs landed a marquee star to pair with Dončić. How Dončić would fit with such an accomplished scorer was to be determined—and the subject of some skepticism around the league. But, for the moment, the NBA was buzzing about the Mavs again.

"Mark Cuban is into names," Rick Brunson said later. "He's not into game, he's into names. He's into those big names. That's your prerogative. Guess what? He got what he wanted. He liked Jalen. He didn't love Jalen. Which is fine. You know that he ain't the most likable in terms of, he don't sell tickets. He wants names that sell tickets. With Kyrie Irving, he got what he wanted. He got another star. That's selling tickets."

If Brunson had signed a second contract with the Mavs, he might have been rerouted to Brooklyn when Irving became available. As it played out, even with Irving's trade value diminished, Dallas gave up two starters who were key contributors to the Mavs' West finals run, as well as a future first-round pick that had lottery potential if things didn't pan out and Dončić eventually departed.

But Dallas filled its glaring need for a co-star. The Mavs (28–26 at the time of the trade) had scored at a league-best rate (118.7 points per 100 possessions) when Dončić was on the floor and a league-worst rate (106.8) when he wasn't. Irving's presence would prevent that sort of offensive plummeting when Dončić rested. Kidd proclaimed Irving's acquisition as a move that would "help put us in a position to win a championship," pointing to Dončić's success sharing the backcourt with Brunson as the baseline.

"Nothing against JB," Kidd said, "but Kai is at a different level."

CHAPTER 15

ANOTHER CO-STAR, ANOTHER TANK

THE DEBUT OF THE DALLAS'S NEW SUPERSTAR DUO WOULD HAVE TO wait several days. When the Mavs acquired Irving, Dončić was recovering from a bruised right heel suffered in a scary fall during a win over the New Orleans Pelicans that week. Irving joined the team in Los Angeles two days after the trade for a Tuesday practice and press conference—saying he was happy to be with a franchise where he was "really wanted" after feeling "very disrespected" in Brooklyn—and was in the starting lineup the next night against the Clippers. Dončić flew from Dallas to LA the afternoon of the game, midway through a five-game road trip, happy to have a front-row seat to watch the Mavs' new marquee attraction.

Irving didn't disappoint, scoring 24 points and dishing out five assists to lead Dallas to a 110–104 road win over an LA team that had twice eliminated Dončić from the playoffs. The Mavs scored 41 points in Irving's first quarter in a Dallas uniform. It was a strong statement that the Mavs' offensive woes when Dončić sat had been solved.

The Clippers mounted a comeback, but Irving put the exclamation points on his dazzling Mavs debut with a classic Kyrie moment for the dagger bucket with 77 seconds remaining. After blowing by Paul George near the half-court logo, Irving weaved to his left when Kawhi Leonard peeled off his man to pick him up. "The Klaw" recovered well enough to contest what appeared to be a southpaw layup attempt by Irving, who contorted his body in midair, switched the ball to his right hand, and softly kissed a shot off the glass just before landing.

It was the sort of spectacular blend of ballhandling and finishing that fuels debate about whether Irving is *the* most skilled player in the history of the game. Dončić, as he'd done on several occasions that night, responded with a standing ovation. Cuban also hopped out of his seat in the second row of the bench and applauded.

"Amazing," Dončić said as he walked toward the Crypto.com Arena exit postgame. It was a brief, accurate summary of Irving's performance and Dončić's way of brushing off an attempt to get him to elaborate on the long-awaited arrival of a legitimate star to play alongside him. Cuban, on the other hand, didn't need any prodding to pontificate about it. He held court in the hallway outside the visitors' locker room, basking in the Mavs' moment in the NBA spotlight.

"He's a Hall of Famer, so why would you do it any other way when you get a chance to get somebody [of] his quality on the court? He's a superstar," Cuban said of Irving. "Why wouldn't you take that chance?"

Putting aside Irving's recent tumultuous history, which followed him from Cleveland to Boston to Brooklyn, there was the matter of his pending free agency. He had vowed to be "all-in" for the rest of the season with the Mavs but made no promises beyond that, saying he didn't want the "ruthless" aspects of NBA business to become a focal point. Cuban dismissed concern about the possibility of Irving's departure over the summer.

"We got those Bird rights—and I know what you can bring up!" Cuban said, chuckling as he realized he had used the same line regarding Brunson. "But I don't think it's a similar set of circumstances."

It was a stance Harrison echoed several days later during a press conference before Irving's home opener. It was the first time Irving met with the Dallas media at large, and he politely but firmly requested not to be asked about free agency until the end of the season. He didn't want to deal with "unwarranted distractions," as he did in his second and final season in Boston, when his looming free agency lingered over the Celtics like a black cloud before he bolted for Brooklyn.

"I don't see the risk involved. I actually see the risk in *not* doing the deal," Harrison said. In other words, if the Mavs had passed on this chance to pair Dončić with another star, they wouldn't have been assured another such opportunity would arise.

By the time Irving had finished his postgame routine of weight lifting and treatment in Los Angeles, his impressive Mavs opener had been bumped to second on the list of NBA headline stories. New Suns owner Mat Ishbia, following a Cuban-esque playbook of micromanaging basketball operations, made a massive splash by negotiating a deal for Irving's former teammate Kevin Durant on the night before the trade deadline. A reporter blurted out a question about the Durant deal to Irving before he'd even settled into his seat in the cramped visitors' press conference room.

"I'm happy we got the win," Irving responded, smiling and shaking his head. "Can we start with our team first? Start with our team."

That conversation quickly moved to the potential of his partnership with Dončić. The Mavs would still be "Luka's team," as Kidd put it, but Dončić would be asked to adapt and share the ball to a degree that he hadn't since his teenage years playing next to Sergio Llull with Real Madrid and Goran Dragić with Slovenia. Irving was accustomed to playing off another superstar, having done so with

James in Cleveland and Durant in Brooklyn, and expressed eagerness to team with "one of those bad Europeans" for the first time.

"I'm sure when No. 77 gets back, it will be even more enjoyable to see and play out there," Irving said. Dončić sat out the front end of a back-to-back in Sacramento, and the Mavs got off to another scorching start, scoring 45 points in the first quarter en route to a 122–114 win. Dallas had won five of six to move up to fourth in the West standings and seemed to have upward mobility as they welcomed Dončić back into the mix.

"I never played with a guy like Kyrie, so it's obviously going to be a work in progress," Dončić said. "But I think it's going to be fine. We both can play on the ball. For me, I think it's going to be a learning process, for sure. Outside of my first season, I didn't play off the ball. But with a guy like him it's going to be different."

The Mavs lost the stars' first game together 133–128 in overtime, when Sacramento's De'Aaron Fox scored 14 points of his 36 in the extra period to match Dallas's total. After missing the previous four games, Dončić appeared fatigued. He finished with 27 points but didn't score in the fourth quarter or overtime until a meaningless layup with seconds remaining.

Dončić regretted attempting a tightly contested step-back three that would have tied the game on the previous possession. He said he should have put the ball back in the hot hands of Irving, who had made all three of his shots in overtime, including a pretty off-dribble side-step three seconds earlier. Irving took no issue with Dončić's shot selection, expressing respect and understanding of his new co-star's confidence.

It was the rare occasion that Dončić was in a good mood after a defeat. "It's only our first game together, but it's so fun to play with this guy," Dončić said. "He's an amazing basketball player, and I think it's going to be really fun. First game, it was really fun."

Irving put on a sensational show in his Dallas home debut a couple of nights later against the Minnesota Timberwolves. Irving scored 26 of his 36 points in the fourth quarter, the highest-scoring quarter of his surefire Hall of Fame career, making 11 of his 12 field goal attempts in the final frame. He carved up the Minnesota defense off the dribble—a full-speed pull-up three after zigzagging through traffic was especially jaw-dropping—while carrying Dallas back from an 18-point deficit to make it a one-possession game in the final seconds.

Once again, like in Sacramento, the Mavs needed a three in the final seconds, and Irving had the hot hand. Coming out of a time-out with 14.8 seconds left, lanky Timberwolves forward Jaden McDaniels deflected the inbounds pass to Dončić, who had to retrieve the ball in the backcourt. Dončić threw a crosscourt pass to Irving, who took a hard right-handed dribble toward the top of the three-point arc. He appeared primed to launch another pull-up but thought better of it with Anthony Edwards crowding him and tossed the ball back to Dončić on the right wing. Dončić, smothered by McDaniels, stumbled as he passed the ball back to Irving, who pump-faked to try to create separation from Edwards, took a dribble, and got double-teamed by McDaniels. Irving faked a pass toward Dončić, momentarily froze with indecision, and had the ball squirt out of his hands for a turnover. As the buzzer sounded, Dončić had a pained grin.

"I'm still trying to emotionally recover, man," Irving said in his postgame media availability, covering his head in his hands. "It's still so raw. Ah, man. I would have liked to at least get a shot up."

The new duo had been too deferential to each other, an indication of their mutual respect. It was the kind of growing pain that comes when two stars attempt to mesh their games on the fly. It was also a sign of things to come, as the Mavs continued to struggle in clutch situations despite having two of the league's elite offensive creators. The fun didn't last long as Dallas dropped six of eight beginning with the overtime loss to the Kings.

Dončić's frustration became a focal point after the Mavs managed to blow a 27-point lead at home against the Lakers in a February 26 ABC Sunday afternoon showcase game, the worst collapse of the NBA season at that point. Dončić, even by his standards, was animated with the referees—frequently while the ball was in play. After dominating the first quarter, Dončić had as many turnovers as buckets the rest of the game, going 5-of-14 from the floor in the last three quarters and making an egregious mental blunder that cost the Mavs a chance to tie the score in the final minute.

Coming out of a time-out with Dallas trailing by 3 with 18.1 seconds remaining, Irving threw an inbounds pass toward the backcourt, giving Dončić a chance to separate Lakers forward Jarred Vanderbilt and catch the ball. But Dončić forgot that he could go into the backcourt to retrieve the pass, smacking the ball forward to save what he wrongly believed would have been a violation, gifting Anthony Davis a steal to seal the Lakers' comeback win. "It's my bad," Dončić said postgame, admitting that he forgot the rule.

"As a team, we've got to mature," Kidd said after the loss. "We've got to grow up—if we want to win a championship. There's no young team that's ever won a championship, mentally or physically."

It was a stretch to describe Dallas as a young team. After all, four of the Mavs' starters that afternoon were 30 or older. The exception was Dončić, who was a couple of days away from his 24th birthday. This was Kidd's way of calling out the face of the franchise without singling out Dončić by name.

"We were playing at a high level on both ends, offensively and defensively, and then we just got a little distracted with the whistle," Kidd said. "We've just got to be better with that."

Asked if he allowed his disagreements with officials to become a distraction, Dončić acknowledged, "It's probably true."

Dončić's fiery disposition again found the spotlight a week later, when the Mavs came up short in another ABC Sunday afternoon showcase game. The 130–126 loss to the Phoenix Suns followed a familiar recent pattern for Dallas—poor defense and clutch failure.

In this case, after Kevin Durant hit a go-ahead pull-up jumper with 11.7 seconds remaining, Dončić had a chance to answer. But Dončić's short floater rimmed in and out before Durant grabbed the rebound—and that's when Dončić got feisty with his playoff pal Devin Booker.

After Dončić fouled Durant to stop the clock with 3.5 seconds remaining, he crouched over in the lane, elbows on his knees and head in his hands. He was appalled that he'd missed such an easy look, a fitting end to an 8-of-23 shooting performance. Booker took the opportunity to make a case to a referee that the reason that Dončić was so open on the floater was because he committed an offensive foul, pushing off and leaving Josh Okogie sprawled on the baseline. Booker stepped close to Dončić as he made his point, appearing to troll his foe without directly addressing him.

"Shut the fuck up!" Dončić snapped at Booker. They exchanged a few more words before Dončić aggressively approached Booker. They went nose to nose, bumping chests and tussling before being separated by other players and security officials. The incident resulted in double technical fouls and some more fuel to the heated rivalry between the All-Star guards.

"You guys say you don't want everybody to be friendly-friendly," Booker said after scoring 36 points, one fewer than Durant. "Here you go. We got some smoke."

"It's fine. It's just a competitive game," said Dončić, who was assessed his 14th technical of the season—two shy of triggering an automatic one-game suspension with 17 games remaining on the schedule. "It's all good. Just next time, don't wait until there's three seconds left to talk."

The game had been billed as a potential playoff preview for franchises that had faced each other the previous postseason, and both had traded for stars as Brooklyn's supposed superteam broke up. Suddenly, however, the playoffs didn't seem like a sure thing for Dallas. The Mavs were only a game above .500 and had slipped into a tie for seventh in the West standings—play-in territory. And their situation was about to get much worse.

WITH THE MAVS DESPERATE TO BUILD SOME MOMENTUM, DONČIĆ played both ends of a back-to-back for the first time in a few months the following week. He didn't finish the second game, a loss in New Orleans in which he picked up his 15th technical foul of the season, hobbling off the floor late in the third quarter. Seconds later, he was ruled out due to a left thigh strain, an injury Dončić said had nagged him for a couple of weeks and made pushing off that leg "really hard." He missed the next five games.

Then Irving was a late scratch before the Mavs' next game—a road loss to a Memphis team missing soon-to-be-suspended All-Star guard Ja Morant—due to right foot soreness. Irving missed the next two games as well, sitting out a home loss to the Grizzlies and a road win over a San Antonio team trying to tank its way to the top pick. Irving returned to lead the Mavs to a St. Patrick's Day win over the Lakers in LA, scoring 38 points and feeding Maxi Kleber for the game-winning buzzer-beater three. The Mavs dogpiled Kleber at mid-court, a celebration that Dončić enjoyed while staying on his feet, mindful of not aggravating his strained thigh during the much-needed joyous moment.

The good times were temporary, as the Mavs followed up their first two-game winning streak since Irving's first two games by losing again to the Grizzlies. That dropped Dallas to .500 with 10 games remaining in the regular season, putting them in the middle of a pack of teams separated by a game and a half in a section of the West standings that stretched from sixth to 12th place. "Just understand, we're getting better," Kidd said that night. "It's just a matter of, Can we be healthy in time to make a stretch run? And if we're not, that's just the season. No one's dying."

Dončić was cleared to return for a home game against Golden

State, which was clinging to the West's final guaranteed playoff spot, but Irving needed the night off to rest his sore foot. Once again, the Mavs came up short in crunch time. And once again, Dončić took umbrage with the officiating. After arguing for a foul with 1.7 seconds remaining when he missed a layup while Dallas was trailing by 3, Dončić made a money gesture by rubbing the thumb and fingers together on his left hand, insinuating the officials were on the take. He wasn't whistled for a technical, which would have triggered a suspension, but the NBA did hit Dončić with a $35,000 fine. It ranked a distant second in referee-related controversy in the loss that dropped Dallas to the bottom half of the West play-in scenario.

Mark Cuban filed an official protest of the Warriors' 127–125 win due to a bizarre sequence that he referred to as the "worst officiating non call mistake possibly in the history of the NBA," while airing his grievances on Twitter that night. Golden State's Kevon Looney made an uncontested dunk coming out of a time-out late in the third quarter because the Mavs mistakenly believed the previous out-of-bounds call was ruled in their favor and lined up on the other end of the floor, a misunderstanding they blamed on the officials. Cuban marched over to the ESPN play-by-play booth at the end of the quarter to declare that he'd protest the game if the Mavs lost by 2 points or less. He did so knowing the league wouldn't rule in his favor, but he wanted to raise a public stink. Not that it provided any comfort.

"The mood is not good, obviously," Dončić said after logging 41 minutes in the loss. "Every time you lose, it's bad. We've got to focus what's next. We've got to be focused on winning."

What was next, mercifully, was a home-and-home matchup with the miserable Charlotte Hornets—a team that was en route to an early lottery pick and missing three starters, including face-of-the-franchise LaMelo Ball. The schedule had gifted the Mavs a get-well opportunity. But they botched it in humiliating fashion, hearing boos from the American Airlines Center home crowd while trailing by 18 midway through the third quarter. "We probably should have been booed in the first quarter," Kidd said, using descriptive terms like "awful" and "dog shit" to describe the 16-point-favorite Mavs' effort in the 117–109 loss, the largest upset in terms of the betting line in the entire NBA season.

Dončić's expression was dour on his way to the arena's interview room an hour later. He wore a black T-shirt with white lettering that read, "ALL I NEED IS SUVO MESO AND RAKIJA"—referencing smoked beef and brandy popular in the Balkans—but it would take much more than that to lift Dončić's spirits. He admitted that he had never been so frustrated in his NBA career.

"I think you can see it with me on the court," Dončić said after a low-energy outing in which he still managed to produce 34 points, 10 rebounds, and eight assists. "Sometimes I don't feel it's me. I'm just being out there. I used to have really fun, smiling on court, but it's just been so frustrating for a lot of reasons, not just basketball."

Asked what else was bothering him, Dončić said, "You know I don't talk about my personal life."

Irving wrongly took the brunt of the blame from outsiders; he hadn't been the root of any off-court issues and had actually been a positive influence on some of the team's younger players. But he clearly hadn't impacted their ability to win, either.

"We're still feeling each other out in a way of getting used to each other's efforts and attitudes and temperament," Irving said that night. "And that's a real thing. It's a human thing. That's a human element. Whether people believe in basketball or not, there's a very fine line between winning basketball games and everyone being on the same page, and losing basketball games and things splintering and pointing fingers."

The Mavs lost again two days later in Charlotte. Dončić got called for a technical foul for cussing at a ref while complaining about a no-call but avoided the automatic suspension when the league office rescinded the tech upon review—the second straight season his 16th T got waved off after the fact. But the Mavs' season continued to spiral out of control. A month and a half after their blockbuster trade, Dallas had to make up ground just to make the play-in tournament.

By the time the Mavs wrapped up their five-game road trip, their outlook was bleak. They went 1–4 on the trip and had lost seven of eight overall, falling to 11th in the West standings. With three games remaining on the schedule, Dallas's most likely season-ending scenario was to miss the play-in and land at 11th in the lottery odds—the worst-case scenario, considering Dallas owed New York a top-ten-protected pick as the final payment for the Porziņģis trade.

Internal discussions among the Mavs' brass turned to tanking the rest of the season by shutting down core players, positioning an asset-depleted Dallas franchise to add a lottery pick. The idea leaked to the media. It was embarrassing for a franchise featuring two All-Stars—and in an ethical gray area, to put it politely, although one occupied by multiple teams every season. But the biggest problem was that the Mavs' front office hadn't consulted Dončić before the trial balloon was floated—and Dončić detested the plan.

"I'm playing tomorrow," Dončić declared. "When there's still a chance, I'm gonna play. So that's not gonna happen yet."

It was rare that Dončić made himself available to the media after a home practice, but he wanted to get that point across. Dončić also discussed what had gone wrong during what he described as "a very disappointing season," after being West finalists the previous year. He bemoaned the team's lack of chemistry, especially when compared to the previous year's squad, adding that "it's a long process" to build it. He acknowledged, with a pained grimace, that the Mavs missed Brunson "a lot," in the locker room and on the court. He pointed out the obvious: the Mavs' offense wasn't the problem; their 25th-ranked defense was a disaster. "Whoever it is, anybody can score on us," Dončić said.

One reason the Mavs were so bad defensively, of course, is because Dončić had been dreadful on that end of the floor. He took accountability for that and admitted that he struggled with fatigue. The organization was concerned about Dončić's weight and conditioning again, amplified by his historically heavy workload in the wake of Brunson's departure. He mentioned how infrequent his breaks from basketball had been over the last few years between his commitments to the Mavs and the Slovenian national team.

"But that's not an excuse," Dončić said. "I'm still young, age-wise, but it's a lot of basketball. But I gotta be way better. I'm the leader of this team. The one to blame is me."

But giving up wasn't an acceptable option to Dončić, regardless of the potential benefits down the road. He understood that Dallas had "little chance" of qualifying for the play-in, which would then likely require the Mavs to win two road games just to claim the West's eighth seed. But he was too proud to care about the percentages. As long as the Mavs' playoff hopes were mathematically alive, Dončić vowed to compete.

Cuban, who had kept a much lower public profile since hiring Harrison, opted to hold an unannounced courtside session with reporters before the next night's home game. His primary objective was to deflect blame for the departure of Brunson, who had emerged as the face of a Knicks franchise that was preparing for the playoffs. Once Cuban made his case that it was all the fault of Brunson's meddling father—presenting the old text from Harrison as evidence—the growing media crowd moved on to more pertinent topics regarding the Mavs' future.

There was the pressing issue of Irving's pending free agency. The Mavs had stumbled since pulling off the deal to get him, but re-signing Irving remained a priority, in large part because Dallas had no realistic path to acquiring another star anytime soon.

"I'd love to have him stay for sure," Cuban said, although he hedged when asked if the Mavs could be outbid for Irving, saying he didn't know. "I'd love to have him. I want him to stay for sure, and I think we have a good shot. I think he's happy here."

Then there was the matter of Dončić's happiness, or lack thereof. The subject dominated the conversation about the Mavs throughout the league because it was a potential domino that could change the balance of power in the NBA. The Mavs got the gift of unwavering loyalty from Dirk Nowitzki, the face of the franchise for a generation, but Cuban acknowledged that Dončić's commitment to Dallas couldn't be taken for granted.

"Look, players don't talk like that, just like, 'Hey, I'm here for the next 17 years,'" Cuban said. "He'd like to be here the whole time, but we've got to earn that."

How could the Mavs do that? Cuban's suggested solution was easy to say and difficult to do.

"Win championships," Cuban said. "It's amazing how that cures all. I mean, before Giannis won, everybody was like, 'Where's he going? Where's he going? He's not staying. He's not staying.' Jokić, while they haven't won, da, da, da, da, da. Dirk before [the Mavs won the 2010–11 title], right? There's no great player, no superstar, where they don't question, 'What are you gonna do if you haven't won yet?'"

A few hours later, Irving scored 19 points in the fourth quarter as the Mavs pulled out a win over the Kings. Dallas's slim play-in hopes were still flickering. "Just desperation basketball," Irving said postgame. "It's not like it's the first time I've been in a must-win game, so it felt good."

But over the next 36 hours or so, Dallas decision-makers determined that the two remaining dates on the Mavs' schedule were must-*lose* games. If Dallas dropped their last two games, they'd have about an 80 percent chance of keeping their pick entering the lottery. If they won both, they still needed the Thunder to lose one just to squeak into the play-in. The call was essentially announced when the Mavs updated the official injury report the morning of their April 7 home game against the Bulls. Irving, Tim Hardaway Jr., Josh Green, Maxi Kleber, and Christian Wood were all downgraded to out due to minor injury issues or rest. This was a bumbling, transparent tank job. Timing was of the essence, as the Mavs and Bulls were tied for the 10th-best lottery odds.

But the timing was also awkward. It was the second annual "I Feel Slovenia" night at the American Airlines Center, and Dončić had missed the inaugural edition the previous season, disappointing hundreds of his countrymen who had flown in for the festivities celebrating their homeland. A compromise was reached: Dončić would play the first quarter before calling it a season.

Dončić ended up playing one offensive possession into the second quarter, scoring on a post-up and then committing an intentional foul so he could check out of the game. The intention was to allow fans to shower Dončić with a standing ovation as he concluded the greatest individual statistical season (32.4 points, 8.6 rebounds, and 8.0 assists per game) in franchise history. Instead, the crowd responded with a smattering of confused clapping.

Dončić changed into sweats at halftime and watched from the bench as the Mavs blew a 13-point lead. He seemed loose and relaxed in the seconds before the Mavs were officially eliminated from play-in contention. He covered his mouth and chuckled to teammates before the game's final possession, when a couple of Mavs on two-way contracts missed three potential game-tying three-pointers, none of which drew iron.

"It's not so much waving the white flag," Kidd said after the 115–112 loss, attributing the choice to Cuban and Harrison, although the coach was fully on board with it behind the scenes. "Decisions sometimes are hard in this business, and you have to make hard decisions. We're trying to build a championship team, and sometimes you got to take a step back."

The decision was made despite Dončić's public protest a few days prior. The Mavs' front office could live with making Dončić mad for a moment if the scheming helped the franchise bounce back from this debacle of a season. The real disaster would be if Harrison and his staff failed to make the drastic roster upgrades the Mavs desperately needed and, as a consequence, couldn't make a realistic case that the franchise was on the path toward contention. They had limited assets for this roster reconstruction, and the lottery pick would rank as the best among them.

"Once we didn't control our own destiny, it was like, all right, we can't be foolish," Harrison said later, well after the league office's investigation reached the obvious conclusion, resulting in a harshly worded statement and a $750,000 fine. "The worst-case scenario was we were 11 versus being 10—and you don't make the play-in and don't get your pick. Then I think I would probably look more foolish than doing it the opposite way."

THE MAVS CONDUCTED THEIR MEDIA EXIT INTERVIEWS IMMEDI-ately after a bunch of backups wrapped up this season to forget with a blowout home loss to the Spurs, whose more traditional tank job had already secured them a bottom-three record, maximizing their odds to win the lottery that ultimately delivered Wembanyama to San Antonio. Dončić didn't talk after the previous game, when the Mavs pulled the plug, and didn't have much to say about that matter other than that he "didn't like that decision." However, he down-played the threat of him leaving Dallas in the near future. He wasn't fond of ESPN reporting that the organization feared Dončić could request a trade as soon as the summer of 2024 if the Mavs didn't make major progress the next season.

"It was funny, you know, because I didn't know that was true," Dončić said sarcastically. "I didn't say it."

Dončić didn't have to say a word about a trade request for the Mavs' front office to operate with that sense of urgency. That's the reality of the modern-day NBA. The sense from people who knew Dončić well was that he genuinely enjoyed Dallas and wouldn't look for reasons to leave, but the Mavs had to make sure those reasons— like another losing season—weren't smacking him in the face.

"I think our job really to keep Luka happy, if you will, is surrounding him by the right players to help him win," Harrison said a couple of days later. "And I think Luka's a talent that deserves that."

But Dončić wanted to ease the pressure, at least publicly, before heading back to Slovenia for the summer. "I'm happy here, so there's nothing to worry [about]," Dončić said.

Of course, Dončić wasn't happy about the Mavs' 38–44 record and missing the playoffs for the first time since his rookie year. "Some things got to change, for sure," Dončić acknowledged. It was an embarrassing way to end the season for a perennial MVP candidate, especially after Irving's mid-season arrival created so much excitement. But Dallas went 7–18 after the duo's debut together, falling from fourth in the West to an early vacation. The Mavs were only 5–11 in games Dončić and Irving played together, which is the worst winning percentage (.313) for a pair of teammates who were both All-Stars since the ABA-NBA merger in 1976–77, according to ESPN Stats and Information research. But Dončić remained confident that the co-stars could form the foundation of a contender.

"I think it's a great fit," Dončić said. "Obviously people are going to say no [and] look at the results we are having, but like I said, chemistry and relationships takes time. I wish he can still be here."

Harrison reiterated during his season-ending media availability that re-signing Irving would be the Mavs' top summer priority. Harrison expressed optimism that it would happen, citing comments Irving had repeatedly made "about how he feels here, how he feels appreciated, how he feels accepted and allowed to be himself." Harrison firmly believed that the Dončić-Irving duo could work, despite evidence to the contrary.

"I really think it's the players around them…kind of knowing their role with having those two guys out on the floor at the same time," Harrison said, emphasizing the need for good defenders who had high basketball IQs to fill out the supporting cast. "I think that's the thing that we need to work on."

Irving opted out of the exit interviews with the media and managed to steer completely clear of the subject entering his free agency summer, leaving people to wonder whether his silence spoke volumes.

Irving mostly kept a low profile while living and training in Los Angeles during the offseason. But he raised eyebrows with a couple of very public appearances, attending a pair of Lakers home play-off games. His seats were directly across from the home bench. On both occasions, after LeBron James was introduced in the starting lineups, he jogged over to greet Irving. They exchanged hugs and their customized handshake from their days together in Cleveland. It sure felt like pre–free agency flirting, similar to Irving's infamous All-Star hallway chat with Kevin Durant months before they became a package deal headed to Brooklyn.

Speculation about the Lakers pursuing Irving had plenty of fuel. LA could have made a legitimate bid by bidding farewell to free agents point guard D'Angelo Russell and forward Rui Hachimura and making a smaller salary-dump trade or two. However, Lakers GM Rob Pelinka immediately hushed that conversation, declaring during his exit interview that the franchise planned to lean into continuity. Pelinka followed through on that plan, as the Lakers never showed any interest in signing Irving.

A few weeks before free agency officially opened, there were reports that Irving planned to recruit James to join him in Dallas. It was a juicy twist—if only it were even remotely feasible. James wasn't a free agent. Even if he shockingly decided to force a trade—leaving the entertainment empire he had built in LA just as his son Bronny entered his freshman year at nearby USC—the Mavs had no way to make an offer to the Lakers anywhere close to the appropriate value.

Reports before free agency about Irving intending to meet with the Phoenix Suns were just as silly. The Suns, who had just traded for Bradley Beal to play alongside Durant and Booker, could only offer the veteran's minimum. There just wasn't much of a market for Irving outside of Dallas, certainly not above the mid-level exception.

The Mavs were offering $120 million guaranteed over three years, plus another $6 million in incentives tied to games played and wins. Irving, whose agent is his stepmom Shetellia Riley Irving, officially agreed to the deal in the opening hour of free agency. The Mavs received some media criticism for bidding against themselves, but Harrison's goal wasn't to win the negotiation. It was to have a happy Irving on a roster that had flexibility to be upgraded. This deal accomplished that, awarding Irving a contract that reflected his production and status while providing the Mavs enough wiggle room within the salary cap rules to have their mid-level exception available.

"It wasn't too difficult of a process," Irving said when he finally met with the media again during the first week of training camp. "Had Dallas as No. 1 on my list. Obviously I looked elsewhere—salary cap opportunities, where I could fit in with other guys around the league—but there just wasn't much space. And me being 31 now, I had to have a different vantage point, and I felt like I could not just settle here but be happy to come back here and be welcomed back with a warm embrace."

CHAPTER 16

ROSTER RENOVATION AND THE PRAVI MVP

It was Christmas Day 2023 at Phoenix's Footprint Center, and Dončić made a beeline for the visitor's bench. He had just hit a floater over Devin Booker to put the finishing touches on perhaps the best Christmas performance in NBA history. The Suns fans who booed Dončić as he stepped on the court during warm-ups had long been silenced. After making his way through a line of high fives and backslaps from teammates and coaches, Dončić collapsed into a chair, exaggerating for effect.

Dončić saw Irving approaching and slumped into his seat, pretending to catch some sleep. He broke out in a grin as Irving, wearing a designer sweater and jeans, flapped his hands over Dončić's head, fanning the flames after Dončić scorched the Suns for 50 points and 15 assists in a 128–114 win that was 29.5 seconds away from being official. As Irving put his hands on Dončić's chest, acting like he was shaking him awake, the superstar cracked up with laughter.

The few seconds of rest were well earned. Dončić played 44

minutes, including all but that final half minute of the second half, as Irving sat out his ninth straight game due to a heel contusion, suffered in a freak incident when Mavs center Dwight Powell fell on him. Such a heavy workload had become routine again, as Dončić was averaging 40 minutes in December, putting up 37.3 points, 9.2 rebounds, and 11.6 assists per game so far to carry the Mavs. After wearing down the previous season, Dončić had made a commitment to improve his conditioning. He hired a full-time staff—the Slovenian national team's strength coach Anže Maček, as well as physiotherapist Javier Barrio Calvo and nutritionist Lucia Almendros from Real Madrid—that was paid out of his own pocket and routinely traveled with the team. His noticeably more svelte physique was being put to the test.

And Dončić wasn't getting much rest as usual at home, either. He had become a first-time father on December 1, when his childhood sweetheart and fiancée Anamaria Goltes gave birth to their daughter, Gabriela. Dončić scribbled his newborn baby girl's name on his Luka 2 shoes before every game.

"That's one thing—I'm happy in my life," Dončić said postgame when asked about his first Christmas as a father. "I can't go back home today—I wish—but tomorrow I can't wait to see her. So that's a big impact."

Dončić had plenty of reasons to be happy in his professional life, too. His co-star partnership had been put on pause due to Irving's injury, but the early-season results were encouraging. The Mavs were 10–6 when the tandem played together, winning twice as often as they did the previous season, and excelling in clutch situations. They had formed a friendship off the floor, a bond that was strengthened during the team's preseason trip to Abu Dhabi and Madrid. Irving would be back within days, as he looked good in an extended on-court workout after that morning's shootaround.

Rookie center Dereck Lively II, the lottery prize from the Mavs' late-season tanking, had returned that night from a sprained ankle that had sidelined him the previous four games and immediately reminded everyone why the Mavs were so excited about him. The 7-foot-1 Lively scored 20 points and grabbed 10 rebounds in the win, overwhelming the Suns with his blend of size, energy, and athleticism. He shot 8-of-9 from the floor with five of his buckets coming off of Dončić feeds, evidence of the trust the teenager had earned from the superstar much sooner than anybody expected.

Harrison and the Mavs' front office envisioned Lively developing into exactly the kind of big man that had been atop Dončić's personnel wish list—a springy pick-and-roll partner, rim protector, and rebounder. They compared him to Tyson Chandler, the epitome of the coaching phrase "star in his role" who was the finishing piece of the Mavs' 2011 championship puzzle and frequently showed up to the Mavs' practice facility to work with Lively on a volunteer basis. The Mavs were ecstatic to draft Lively after trading down to No. 12, dumping Dāvis Bertāns's bloated contract in the process. But Dallas didn't have huge immediate expectations for the kid who was a bit of a disappointment in his sole season at Duke, averaging only 5.2 points and 5.4 rebounds per game after arriving on campus as the nation's top recruit in his class. Lively was considered a project—high potential, but with patience required—a risk given the Mavs' urgent need to win. That's why Dallas explored the summer trade market for a starting center, engaging in discussions with the Hawks about Clint Capela and the Suns about Deandre Ayton.

But Lively showed dramatic improvement over the summer, when he stayed in Dallas to work and watch film daily with assistant coach Sean Sweeney and, often, Chandler.

"He's a sponge," Chandler said.

By the time training camp opened, Kidd had decided to give Lively a legitimate chance to win the starting job. The Mavs brought him off the bench for the season opener, not wanting to put too much pressure on him in a nationally televised game against No. 1 overall pick Victor Wembanyama. Lively outplayed him, posting a 16-point double-double in a road win, and instantly established himself as an essential piece of Dallas's core. With the Christmas win, the Mavs' record improved to 17–6 when Lively played; they were 1–6 when he sat out.

"I obviously knew he was going to be great, but the way he's performed since the first game, it's been amazing," Dončić said on Christmas night. "I didn't expect this impact [from] him, because he's been playing like he's been in the league for 10 years already, so I'm really proud of this guy. He works on his game, and he listens to me, so it's a great combo."

Things weren't going so well with Grant Williams, the former Celtics forward who was the Mavs' other significant offseason investment. Dallas surrendered 2030 first-round swap rights to the Spurs in the three-way sign-and-trade to get Williams, who the Mavs gave a four-year, $53 million contract to be a three-and-D glue guy. He started off so hot from three-point range, hitting 25 of his 46 attempts during the Mavs' 6–1 start, that his shortcomings on the other end of the floor after reporting to camp out of shape were overlooked. But Williams's shooting soon cooled, his defense continued to disappoint, and he wore on nerves with incessant yapping that comes off as charmingly obnoxious when he's productive and grating when he isn't. "Shut the fuck up!" Sweeney had shouted at Williams in a film session after the forward responded to some unfavorable clips by making strategic suggestions. Sweeney told Williams to focus on doing his job and let the coaches do theirs. Dončić chimed in from the back of the room: "He's right."

On Christmas, for the first time in a Mavs uniform, Williams wasn't part of the starting lineup. Kidd made it clear pregame that would be the plan moving forward, although he did so without mentioning Williams by name. Kidd instead praised a couple of the Mavs' bargain-bin free agency additions, guard Dante Exum and forward Derrick Jones Jr., and said they'd remain in the starting lineup when Irving returned. Williams was the odd man out.

Not that it dampened the enthusiasm during and after Dončić's holiday masterpiece. He talked trash to Suns fans and playfully taunted a couple of Suns assistants who had been on the Mavs' staff the previous season. There wasn't much anyone could say in retort as Dončić efficiently dissected the Phoenix defense, going 15-of-25 from the floor, 8-of-16 from three-point range, 12-of-12 from the line, and exploiting double-teams for several of his 15 dimes. "When you make a shot, the whole gym is quiet, so that's the best feeling in the world," said Dončić, who especially enjoys dominating in a road venue where he's treated like a villain.

Dončić accounted for 82 points overall, including 22 in the fourth quarter, matching the Suns' team total in the final frame, which began with Dallas down a point and ended with Dončić joking on the bench. He registered the fourth-ever 50-point performance in a Christmas game, when the league schedules its marquee teams. He became the first player since James Harden in 2016 to have 50 points and 15 assists in any game. He also passed 10,000 points in the first quarter, needing the fewest games to hit that milestone of any player since Michael Jordan.

But Dončić was particularly proud of his four blocks and three steals against the Suns. Everyone knew Dončić could put up gaudy offensive stats. He wanted to disprove the knock that he couldn't, or wouldn't, play defense.

"Nobody's going to ask me about my defense. OK, I see," Dončić complained, half kidding, as his postgame press conference wrapped up. As Dončić headed down the hallway toward the visitors' locker room, he claimed with a smile that he should be considered for second-team All-Defensive.

By the time the Suns and Mavs met again 30 days later in Dallas, Dončić's mood had dimmed. The Mavs were in "tape and bubble gum" mode as Harrison called it, referring to how Kidd had to patch together rotations as Dallas dealt with a series of injuries to key players. The Mavs had lost four of the previous six games—the two wins actually came during a three-game stretch Dončić missed due to a sprained ankle—to slip to eighth in the West standings. Now Irving was out again due to spraining his right thumb in a home loss to the Celtics a couple of nights earlier. It was the 44th game of the season, and the Mavs star tandem had played together in only half of them.

After that loss to the Celtics, Kidd mentioned that the Mavs got "a little bit frustrated with the officiating, and we lost our focus." He didn't single out anyone, but Dončić had complained to the refs all game and got whistled for a technical foul as the Mavs were unraveling midway through the second quarter. The message didn't have its intended effect.

As the Suns sliced into the Mavs' 16-point lead in the final minutes of the second half, Dončić's bickering at the officials became progressively more frequent. He became especially angry after rolling his sore right ankle on Kevin Durant's foot during the Mavs' last defensive possession of the half. After gritting his teeth and getting back on his feet, Dončić yelled at referee David Guthrie as he hobbled past half-court, continuing the conversation as he clutched his ankle and watched Tim Hardaway Jr. create and miss a pull-up jumper. Dončić barked at Guthrie again after the buzzer sounded, and the ref responded with the universal "enough" gesture, putting his hand up before walking to the other side of the court. That didn't deter Dončić, who pointed across the court at Guthrie and kept shouting before finally getting called for a technical foul.

Booker's free throw to start the second half tied the score, beginning a disaster of a quarter for Dallas. Williams, who received a T in the first half for initiating a minor skirmish with Durant in which Jusuf Nurkić intervened, was ejected a few minutes into the quarter after shouting in a ref's face while arguing for an offensive foul on Nurkić. That Booker free throw bumped the Suns' lead to 9, and it seemed to open the floodgates for him. Booker lit up the Mavs for 18 points over the next seven minutes as the Suns' lead swelled to 28.

It was bad enough that the Mavs were getting blown out on their home floor by one of their biggest rivals en route to Dallas's fifth loss in seven games. Dončić's frustration was simmering, as evidenced by his lagging effort and bad body language, and his ears were sensitive. There was a Suns fan sitting a couple of rows behind the mid-court media section who had occasionally heckled Dončić throughout the night, a 22-year-old Southern Methodist University student wearing a Booker "El Valle" jersey whose booming voice got a bit louder with every sip of Modelo.

"Luka, you're tired! Get your ass on the treadmill!" the heckler hollered as Dončić trudged up the court in the final minute of the quarter, his spiciest taunt of the night. Dončić stared him down. As Dončić jogged back on defense seconds later, he motioned across the court to the Mavs' vice president of security, pointed toward the fan, and made a gesture indicating he wanted the heckler ejected. When a time-out was called a couple of possessions later, Dončić reiterated the request. An arena usher soon came over to the fan, and after a brief conversation, the guy grabbed his tall boy and marched up the stairs toward the exit.

The officials and the heckler felt Dončić's wrath during the Mavs' 132–109 loss. During Dončić's media availability afterward, one particular reporter got his turn. When asked about his frustration leading up to his technical foul, which Kidd had called out as "a trend here unfortunately," Dončić changed the subject, taking umbrage with a tweet about the Suns' fan's forced departure.

"That was not the only thing he said, but I knew you would be the first one to point out something like that," Dončić said to me. "It's just funny, you always seem to be the first one to put some bad stuff about me."

Dončić contended that it wasn't fair to only mention the heckling that was the last straw. He claimed his request for the fan's ejection was the culmination of the guy "cursing me the whole first half, too." Asked why he didn't make the request earlier, Dončić said: "Because I never would eject a fan. They pay for tickets, but I had enough, you know. It's a little bit of frustration."

Dončić had unsuccessfully attempted to get a courtside fan ejected during a road loss to the Lakers a week earlier. This was further evidence of his growing frustration. In his mind at the moment, however, it was proof that he was being unfairly portrayed.

"That's fine," Dončić said. "I'll be the bad guy in the media. It's all right."

A night later, Dončić made an in-person appearance with TNT's *Inside the NBA* crew. It was planned in advance, as the Mavs had an off night in Atlanta before playing the Hawks, and All-Star starters were revealed on the show, a select group that would obviously include Dončić. But Dončić vs. the heckler (and the media, to a certain degree) had been the story that dominated the NBA discussion all day, so it couldn't be ignored. TNT's Ernie Johnson gently broached the subject at the end of the appearance.

"It was just a lot of emotions," Dončić said, mentioning hearing the heckler throughout the game, his frustration with losing, and turning his sore ankle again. "Probably shouldn't have done that. When I'm wrong, I admit it. So, probably shouldn't have done that. But it was just the whole game going on."

Dončić gave everyone something else to talk about the next night with a historic performance against the Hawks, the team that traded him on draft night. He scored 18 points in the first quarter, exploiting the soft Atlanta defense with a blend of slow-paced drives, mid-range buckets, and threes. He had put up that many points in the first quarter plenty of times. But it was soon apparent that Dončić was in the midst of a special performance.

The Hawks stubbornly kept defending Dončić with single coverage, and he kept scoring. He hit a step-back three for the Mavs' first bucket of the second quarter, then an off-dribble fadeaway from the free throw line. A couple of possessions later, after grabbing a defensive rebound, Dončić cruised coast to coast for a layup, taking six dribbles without even accelerating or changing direction—an embarrassing defensive effort by Atlanta that encapsulated criticism of the highest-scoring season in NBA history. A few minutes later, Dončić really caught fire. He had 30 after hitting another step-back three with more than five minutes remaining. He had 41 by halftime—the highest-scoring half in franchise history, not to mention Dončić's career. He was more than halfway to 81, the mythical total Kobe Bryant had scored against Toronto 18 years earlier, the most points by a player in one game in modern NBA history. And the Mavs needed every point. Halftime score: Hawks 66, Mavs 66.

After Dončić hit yet another step-back to start the second half—his sixth three of the night already—the Hawks finally started sending a second defender at him. That strategy didn't work, either. Dončić passed out of it time and time again, putting his teammates in position to play four-on-three, and the Mavs took the lead. As soon as he saw single coverage again, Dončić went back to scoring at will. He hit the 50-point milestone for the seventh time in his career with a pull-up three with a little less than five minutes remaining in the third quarter. He had 57 when he checked out of the game to catch his breath for the last 80 seconds of the quarter.

Dončić matched his franchise record of 60 in the opening minute of the fourth quarter, when he came off a screen set on the half-court logo, split a pair of helpless, reaching Hawks defenders, and hit an and-one floater. He hit a tough pull-up three over Atlanta forward Jalen Johnson just 23 seconds later, giving him 63 points—one more than Minnesota's Karl-Anthony Towns had four days earlier and what Booker would finish with that night. He stared at the State Farm Arena crowd from mid-court, smacked himself on the chest, and pointed toward the court, as if to say it was his house now. Dončić drove against Johnson the next possession and decelerated to create space to kiss a short floater off the glass. He wagged his finger at the crowd and talked a little trash while jogging back to the bench during the ensuing time-out.

By this point, most of the crowd was cheering for Dončić, wanting to witness history. The Hawks, on the other hand, decided that they'd rather not be on the wrong end. They started doubling Dončić again, holding him without a bucket for more than seven minutes, his only points in that span coming on a couple of free throws. Dončić pounced at a chance to get in the open court after retrieving a blocked shot by Lively, pushing the ball down the court as fast as he had all night and muscling in a layup despite being fouled from behind by Dejounte Murray. He strutted past the stanchion on the baseline after the whistle and again stared into the crowd. "Yeah!!" he roared. "Yeah!!"

Dončić made the free throw with 2:58 remaining, hitting the 70-point milestone and matching reigning MVP Joel Embiid's NBA season-high from earlier in the week. That put the Mavs up 10, but double-digit leads disappeared faster than ever in this video game version of the NBA. Atlanta scored on its next four possessions to make it a one-possession game again.

The Hawks were determined to make someone other than Dončić beat them. When Lively set a high screen for Dončić with 90 seconds remaining, Atlanta center Clint Capela and Murray both stayed with Dončić, who delivered a leaping two-handed pass over the rotating defense to an open Hardaway on the opposite side of the court. Hardaway missed, but Lively grabbed the rebound and tossed the ball back out to Dončić on the left wing. He pump-faked to get Trae Young to fly by and could have fired a three with Murray closing. But Dončić spotted Exum all alone at the top of the arc and flicked a pass to his teammate for the clutch three. On the most important possession of a record-setting scoring performance, Dončić made the right play and passed to a teammate. Twice.

Dončić delivered the dagger on the Mavs' next trip. He split the double by the eye in the Hawks' half-court logo, galloped into the paint, and finished through contact for another and-one. Once again, he stared into the stands and roared. He made the free throw, the final of his 73 points, tied for the fourth most in NBA history. Only Wilt Chamberlain (twice) and Kobe had more. Nobody ever scored 70 more efficiently than Dončić, who was 25-of-33 from the floor, 8-of-16 from three-point range, and 15-of-16 from the line, mixing in 10 rebounds and seven assists, too.

"He was letting everybody know that he's all right," Kidd said after the Mavs' 148–143 win. "And that we're all right."

The latter part of that statement didn't hold up well over the next week as the calendar flipped to February. The injury-depleted Mavs, still missing Irving among others, lost three of the next four games. They needed another epic Dončić outing to pull out the sole win, rallying from a 16-point halftime deficit for a 131–129 home win over the Magic, riding Dončić's 45-point, nine-rebound, 15-assist performance. And that victory came with more pain: Lively's nose was broken on a flagrant foul late in the fourth quarter, an injury that required surgery and caused the rookie to miss two weeks.

Harrison had already been working the phones hard to upgrade the roster before the February 8 trade deadline. There was one major difference leading up to this deadline from his previous two as the Mavs' general manager: he had autonomy as Dallas's basketball personnel decision-maker, a perk from Cuban's decision to sell the majority stake of the franchise.

Cuban had gone to great lengths to declare that he would remain in charge of basketball operations when the Adelson and Dumont families—the billionaires behind the Las Vegas Sands casino company—agreed to buy the majority share at a $3.5 billion valuation, plus some related real estate. Cuban, calling himself a "middle-class billionaire," admitted that he couldn't afford to solely fund an NBA contender. (Just in case anyone was wondering why Dallas had ducked the luxury tax for a dozen years.) So, Cuban claimed, he formed a "great partnership" with a deep-pocketed group who were "not basketball people," indicating that their motivation for the 10-figure investment was to strengthen their lobbying position for legalizing sports gambling in Texas, eventually leading to a new arena being built as part of a Venetian-style casino resort in Dallas. Cuban portrayed it as the best of both worlds for him—he cashed out and still got to call the basketball shots.

"Nothing's really changed except my bank account," Cuban said, chatting with reporters after wrapping up his three-point shooting session on the American Airlines Center court hours after the NBA officially approved the sale. "It's what the team needed on the court and off. I'll still be overseeing the basketball side of it, but having a partner like Patrick and Sivan [Dumont] and Miriam [Adelson] and their ability to build and to redevelop the arena and whatever comes next beyond that just puts us in a much better position to compete. That's all. That's what it comes down to."

As is often the case, Cuban wasn't telling the full truth. He acknowledged that there was "no contractual language" in the purchase agreement regarding his authority over basketball operations but indicated that he had a gentleman's agreement with new governor Patrick Dumont. That wasn't the case, however. Harrison reported directly to Dumont, who wanted to be informed about personnel decisions but empowered the GM to be in charge. Cuban retained a 27 percent share of the franchise and his courtside seats an arm's distance from the bench, but he no longer had control, essentially becoming the world's richest mascot. This change was enthusiastically welcomed by members of the front office and coaching staff. The basketball people could do their jobs without worrying about the (middle-class) billionaire owner's whims.

Harrison again received plenty of welcomed input from Dončić throughout the process. "Luka is ready to win, so he wants the right players around him," Harrison said. "So he'll let us know from his vantage point what those players are. For him, it's usually less about names and more about archetype."

Harrison was determined to fix the one offseason mistake the Mavs' front office made. He aggressively shopped Williams in discussions with other teams, making an upgrade at power forward the top priority. A name that was high on Harrison's list: Washington's Kyle Kuzma, who was averaging almost 22 points per game on a rebuilding team and had championship experience, having won a ring as a role player with the Lakers when Kidd was an assistant coach on that staff.

Days before the trade deadline, Harrison quietly agreed in principle with Thunder general manager Sam Presti on a deal that provided Dallas a late first-round pick in the 2024 draft. The pick provided ammunition the Mavs needed to get immediate help, as their 2027 pick was the only first rounder they could include in deals due to outstanding obligations from previous trades and the NBA's rule forbidding teams from giving up first rounders in consecutive drafts. Washington insisted on receiving two first-round picks in a package for Kuzma. The Mavs now could meet that price, having surrendered 2028 swap rights to Oklahoma City. The Thunder, who owned a historic stockpile of first-round picks from Presti's wheeling and dealing during the franchise's rapid rebuild, was eager to dip into its quantity for a swing at high-upside quality. As San Antonio did by getting the 2030 swap rights in Williams's sign-and-trade over the summer, Oklahoma City was making a low-risk bet on Dončić eventually leaving Dallas, which would make the payoff a likely lottery pick.

"Honestly, I don't worry about the bet that they're making, but I understand it," Harrison said later. "You need to understand where they're coming from, too. But for me, it's more focused on what we're trying to accomplish and that's really the thing that matters."

The Kuzma talks fell through because Kuzma didn't want to be traded to Dallas. Kuzma doesn't have a no-trade clause in his contract, but he told *The Athletic* after the deadline passed that Wizards president Michael Winger verbally gave him the option of going to

Dallas, which Winger confirmed. Kuzma said he declined because he didn't consider the Mavs to be a true contender. "I just felt like our timelines didn't line up," Kuzma said, a strange justification for preferring to stay on a team with the league's second-worst record. There were two popular theories around the league regarding the real reasoning behind Kuzma's decision: 1) he enjoyed being the go-to guy in DC and didn't want to be a distant third offensive option in Dallas, or 2) the rumors about Kidd's lack of job security concerned him.

"I'm excited about the trade deadline. It did work out pretty well," Harrison said. He shrugged off the fizzled Kuzma talks that "unfortunately" became public knowledge by noting that he engaged in discussions with "a whole bunch of teams." After Kuzma was taken off the table, Harrison got to the finish line on a couple of other deals.

One was again with the Wizards, but for Daniel Gafford, an athletic big man who would give the Mavs a rim-running tag team if Lively was healthy and insurance if the rookie was injured. Dallas sent Washington the pick they got from Oklahoma City and salary filler in third-team center Richaun Holmes.

Harrison then pivoted to Charlotte's P. J. Washington to upgrade at power forward, sending Williams, reserve guard Seth Curry, and a top-two-protected 2027 first-round pick to the Hornets to get him. Like Gafford, Washington was 25 years old and signed to a reasonable contract through the 2025–26 season. Harrison viewed the moves as adding a couple of core pieces for at least the Mavs' next three playoff runs.

But making the playoffs was far from a foregone conclusion. The Mavs had a 28–23 record and sat in eighth place in the West standings when the deadline passed, closer to falling out of the play-in tournament than getting home-court advantage in the first round. And several rival scouts and executives expressed skepticism that adding Gafford and Washington—role players from bad teams that ranked statistically as the worst defensive squads in NBA history (and were worse on that end with them on the floor)—moved the needle enough to justify the risk of giving up more first-round draft capital. In the span of a year, beginning with the Irving deal, the Mavs had given up first-round control of every draft from 2027 to 2030, trading two picks outright and swap rights to the others.

"They've put themselves in a very precarious position," a Western Conference executive said that night. "But that's the pressure put on you by having a superstar. You have to prove to them that you're all in on winning—and then you're in big trouble if it doesn't work and they decide to leave."

If Dončić decided to leave, the Mavs couldn't even benefit from being bad. The Brooklyn Nets had provided the case studies of how painful that situation can be: the picks they'd sent Boston for the win-now Kevin Garnett/Paul Pierce trade—which produced a grand total of one playoff-series win—resulted in Boston acquiring Jaylen Brown and Jayson Tatum. And the Rockets owned the Nets' first-round capital for years to come from the James Harden trade.

But Harrison doesn't operate with a defeatist mindset. He doesn't let worst-case scenarios lead him to a cautious approach. Dallas already had the most important piece in place—a superstar capable of leading a team to a title—when he was hired. Harrison's job was to maximize Dončić's chances of taking the Mavs to that promised land.

"It's always going to be a sense of urgency, no matter what. At least how I look at it," Harrison said. "When you come in, you have Luka, you got an MVP candidate every year. You got to surround them and give an opportunity. So I don't think it changes. It's just whether you can get it done or not."

THE FIRST IMPRESSION FROM GAFFORD AND WASHINGTON couldn't have been much more impressive. Hours after their introductory press conference, they received a roar of a welcome from the American Airlines Center crowd when they came off the bench midway through the first quarter. The next three Dallas possessions: Gafford alley-oop from Dončić, Gafford dunk off a 70-foot outlet pass from Dončić, Washington alley-oop from Dončić. The Mavs' newcomers contributed a combined 33 points and 14 rebounds in 41 minutes during a 146–111 rout of the second-place Thunder. Asked the next day about the input he has on trade talks, Dončić said, "You can see the impact they have, so I think it's really important."

That was Dallas's third straight win, a streak that started when Irving returned from his sprained right thumb. The Mavs stretched the winning streak to seven games by coming out of the All-Star break with a 123–113 victory over the Suns, when Dončić had 41 points, nine rebounds, and 11 assists. "Our health, our energy, everything's in a positive way right now," Kidd said. "I think the guys are having fun. You can see that energy on the floor."

That energy soon disappeared, as the Mavs lost five of their next six games to slip back to eighth in the West. The lone win during that stretch at least came on Dončić's 25th birthday, when he had a 30-point triple-double in Toronto, then celebrated with Irving well into the wee hours of the morning when Irving joined him as the last two left standing while listening to the Serbian folk band hired for the occasion. The Mavs had regressed to defending like they did while sliding into the lottery the previous season. Dallas had the league's worst defensive team over that six-game span. Dončić was producing monster lines—37-12-11, 38-11-10, 39-10-11—in losing efforts.

"It doesn't matter," Dončić muttered after joining Oscar Robertson and Russell Westbrook as the only players in NBA history to record three straight 35-point triple-doubles. "I just want to win, man. That's it."

The Mavs suffered a 137–120 loss that night to Rick Carlisle's

Pacers, the same team that snapped Dallas's winning streak in Indiana nine days earlier. Carlisle endured a couple of losing seasons in Indiana after his departure from Dallas as the Pacers renovated their roster, but he had a young, fun team on the rise now. All-Star point guard Tyrese Haliburton was thriving under Carlisle, who by all accounts had mellowed since his Mavs tenure. Kidd, on the other hand, felt the scrutiny as rumors continued to spread about his job being in jeopardy if Dallas had another disappointing finish.

"Rome wasn't built in a day; 2011 wasn't built in a day," Kidd said, referencing the championship the Mavs won when Kidd played point guard for Carlisle—repeating one of his talking points during his pregame media availability. "There's only a few of us in that locker room who have won at the highest level, and so it's for us to help these young men get through this tough time."

Irving, who won a championship with the Cavaliers in 2016, addressed his teammates in the locker room after the loss, telling them that he believed in them. So did reserve forward Markieff Morris, who won a ring with Kidd and the Lakers in 2020. Morris rarely played, but the veteran had a valuable OG-type role because his voice resonated in the locker room.

"We had a decision to make," Morris said later, recalling his comments that night. "The season was going to end like last year or we was going to turn it around right then and there. We had the pieces. At the time, I just think the guys needed to get some reaffirmation that we had a chance to do something great if we just put our heads down and we kept working and kept trusting J. Kidd."

Kidd had the most critical thing a modern NBA coach needs, which Carlisle had lost in Dallas: strong relationships with his stars. Irving's trust in Kidd helped him feel at home in Dallas, where Irving had emerged as the Mavs' emotional and spiritual leader, easing pressure on Dončić. And Kidd had Dončić's respect, allowing him to coach the superstar instead of needing to coddle him. That was evident in Dončić's willingness to adapt, such as him embracing Kidd's plan for the Mavs to play at a much faster tempo, as Dallas zipped from ranking 28th in pace the previous year to seventh this season. But Dallas desperately needed Kidd to fix the defense—ranked 23rd at the time—to have any realistic hope of a playoff run.

Kidd made a few personnel adjustments before the Mavs hosted the Heat a couple nights later. He inserted Gafford into the starting lineup over Lively, who Kidd was concerned had hit the "rookie wall," hoping for a jump start of energy. He also put Jones back in the starting lineup over Josh Green, giving the Mavs' best on-ball defender the task of guarding the opponent's best perimeter scorer every game. And Kidd handed the defensive reins back to Sweeney, the architect of Dallas's seventh-ranked defense two seasons earlier who had shifted to offensive coordinator over the summer.

The starting lineup now featured the Mavs' two stars and three high flyers acquired over the last six months (Jones, Washington, and Gafford). The Mavs snapped their losing streak by beating the Heat. Dončić had another 35-point triple-double, highlighted by a clutch step-back three over Jimmy Butler. A minute later, Irving hit another clutch three, the closing tandem that had been among the league's best coming through again. Lively grabbed an offensive rebound and assisted Irving for that dagger, epitomizing the big man's 23 terrific minutes off the bench, a remarkable display of focus and maturity by a rookie pulled from the starting lineup.

Dončić kept his triple-double streak rolling during the ensuing easy two-game East road trip—and showed that he clearly does care about historic numbers if they come in the process of winning. He didn't check out of a blowout win in Detroit until there was 3:14 remaining, calling time-out immediately after grabbing his 10th rebound, which gave Dončić an NBA-record six straight 30-point triple-doubles. The Mavs were blowing out the Bulls by 34 entering the fourth quarter, but he stayed in the game to chase 30 points. After Dončić missed step-back threes on three straight possessions, Kidd prioritized caution and pulled his star with 6:19 to play. Dončić settled for a stat line of 27 points, 12 rebounds, and 14 assists, his seventh straight triple-double, tied for the third-longest streak in NBA history.

Eleven of his assists in Chicago were to Gafford and Lively, who combined for 42 points on 20-of-21 shooting. Dončić had pushed to be paired with an elite finisher at center for the last couple of years. Now he had a pair of them, and they were flourishing off his feeds. Gafford hadn't missed a shot in four games, making 28 straight field goals—seven shy of Wilt Chamberlain's NBA record.

The Mavs won again at home against the Warriors, but Dončić's triple-double streak ended. His night ended early again, this time due to concerning circumstances. He felt tightness in his left hamstring, and he lasted only one possession after checking in during the fourth quarter. Kidd called time-out after Dončić signaled to the bench that he didn't want to risk it.

Kidd pretended postgame that he wasn't sure whether Dončić would be available the next night in Oklahoma City. More than an hour later, after the rest of the team had headed to Love Field to catch the flight, a horn, accordion, and voices blared a familiar tune in the hallway outside the Mavs' locker room. Dončić had just finished receiving treatment, and he was being serenaded by some guests of honor: the Slovenian folk-pop band Fehtarji playing a customized version of their hit song "Zetor," which Mavs fans recognize as the catchy tune that plays when Dončić checks back in to a home game. He wasn't going to Oklahoma City, but Dončić's giddy grin provided a hint that his hamstring ailment wasn't too serious.

The Mavs' modest winning streak was snapped by the Thunder with Dončić watching from home, as was Gafford's consecutive-made field goal streak, which stopped two shy of Wilt's. After a fortunate schedule break of a few days, Dončić was ready to return. Dallas's new starting lineup was still undefeated, and the Mavs had a measuring-stick opportunity in front of them.

The defending champion Denver Nuggets were in town for a Sunday afternoon showcase that would be televised in prime time in Europe.

It felt like a statement game for the Mavs midway through the fourth quarter on St. Patrick's Day. Dončić and Irving had been a potent one-two punch, but that came as no surprise. It was startling to see Dončić's Balkans buddy Nikola Jokić, the heavy favorite to win his third MVP, seem so frustrated by Dallas's defense. Gafford, Lively, Maxi Kleber, and Washington all took turns as the primary defenders on Jokić, and the Mavs did a masterful job of keeping the brainy big man out of rhythm by running a variety of schemes. And Dallas played physical defense, a recent change in their identity that leaned into the recent trend of leeway from referees—the result of the league office's desire to provide defenses a semblance of hope after Dončić's 73 put the exclamation points on a run of ridiculous scoring outbursts.

Dallas led by 13 after Dončić's driving layup with 6:50 remaining, but then the Mavs went cold and the Nuggets started clicking. The Nuggets took the lead on a Jamal Murray pull-up three with 28 seconds remaining, his third bucket in a 14–2 run. Dallas had gone more than four minutes without scoring from the floor before Dončić tied it up with a 30-footer off an inbounds play. The Nuggets ran a Murray/Jokić pick and roll, perhaps the most lethal half-court play in the league. Denver could have worked the clock to guarantee getting the last shot of regulation, but Murray couldn't resist taking an open look from the right elbow. He missed long, Hardaway grabbed the rebound, and the Mavs called time-out. They had 2.8 seconds—plenty of time to put the ball in the hands of one of their premier closers.

Dončić lined up a few feet inside Irving on the left side of the floor, away from the ball. When Dončić set a screen for his co-star, Denver's Aaron Gordon and Kentavious Caldwell-Pope switched. As Dončić popped to the top of the arc with Caldwell-Pope denying an angle for the inbounds pass, Irving sliced through the lane and got another screen from Washington on the block. Irving caught the inbounds pass from Kleber on the move in the right corner with Jokić switched onto him. Irving took a dribble to his left, then a hesitation dribble, picking up the ball as he crossed the three-point line toward the right elbow. For a slow-footed 7-footer, Jokić did a phenomenal job staying with Irving, who quickly recognized that he didn't have room to get off a shot with his right hand. He lofted a running, 20-foot lefty hook that Jokić couldn't reach. As the buzzer sounded, the ball swished through the net.

As the Nuggets' shoulders slumped, Irving held his left hand near his head, spreading his fingers and unleashing a triumphant shout. He strutted toward mid-court, pointed at his approaching teammates with both hands, and leaped into a chest bump with Morris before being mobbed in celebration. It took several seconds for Dončić to join the party. He had cut into the paint when Irving got the ball, making sure Caldwell-Pope wouldn't be in position to help, and was standing a foot away from the baseline when the shot went in. He covered his head with his hands in amazement, crouching and cracking up with laughter. Even Dončić was flabbergasted by the degree of difficulty that Irving made look smooth and easy.

"I couldn't believe it," Dončić said postgame. Maybe it was time to believe that the Mavs could be contenders. They were a season-best 10 games above .500 and Kidd had figured out on the fly how all the new puzzle pieces fit. Harrison's vision of an athletic, tough, smart supporting cast surrounding a pair of superstars had come to life.

IN THE LOADED WEST, THE MAVS WERE STILL IN PLAY-IN TERRItory, tied for seventh in the standings. But they had a clear path to a guaranteed playoff spot: an easy stretch of schedule entering a two-game visit to Sacramento, which was a half game ahead of Dallas in the standings. The Mavs handled their business against the

Spurs and Jazz (twice) to set up the high-stakes meetings with the Kings. Dallas routed the Kings by 36 in the first game, seizing control of the sixth spot, and then gave themselves a little cushion by grinding out a 107–103 win in the rematch a few nights later. Vlade Divac had a courtside seat for the latter game. He was the starting center on the best teams in franchise history, so Divac is still a legend in Sacramento despite his struggles during his stint as general manager. But Dončić holds a grudge for one particular personnel decision Divac made. After hitting a free throw with four seconds left that sealed the win, Dončić looked toward Divac and mockingly waved goodbye to him. "He shoulda drafted me," Dončić said as he came to the Dallas bench, pointing over his shoulder in Divac's direction. It's difficult to argue the point.

"We're just having fun out there," Dončić said postgame. "[Irving and I are] both happy. We're both doing some good things on the floor, and we have great teammates. I think this team is special."

Dallas's new lineup lost only once in the 17 games that quintet started together down the stretch of the regular season. Suddenly and stunningly, the Mavs morphed into an elite defensive team, allowing the fewest points per 100 possessions in the final 20 games of the season. They had the league's highest-scoring tandem, and the stars clearly enjoyed playing together.

"The chemistry is big," Dončić said after the Mavs rallied from a 22-point deficit for an April 7 overtime win over the Rockets. Irving and Dončić combined for 85 points in that game and engaged in an exhausted embrace in the final seconds before being surrounded by the rest of the team for a group hug. That scene epitomized the camaraderie that the Mavs had rapidly developed with a roster that had undergone a major renovation over the last year.

"That was kind of again, one of those 'in the moment' type things for us as brothers to embrace each other," Irving said postgame. "We know how hard we've worked and how much work it took to get to this point in the season."

The Mavs made an effort to recognize Dončić's work by launching a "Pravi MVP" campaign late in the season, using the Slovenian word for real. The slogan was seen on billboards in Dallas, Los Angeles, New York, and other cities. All his teammates and coaches wore T-shirts with PRAVI MVP across the chest before their April 10 game in Miami, when the Mavs won their 50th game of the season.

"He's mastered different nuances of the game and he's continuing to explore his abilities and his talents," Irving said. "And it's beautiful to be a part of. So, you know, the shirts mean a lot to us to represent him. But I think the most important thing he wants to do is win. And he's always put that first."

Dončić's work for the regular season was done after that night. He had clinched his first scoring title with 33.9 points per game and had also averaged 9.2 rebounds and 9.8 assists, a statistical combination never before accomplished in NBA history. The Mavs had essentially locked themselves into the West's fifth seed, so Dončić and Irving rested the final two games of the regular season, the rest of the rotation joining them for the finale.

For the third time in Dončić's six seasons, the Mavs would open the playoffs against the Clippers. So much had changed in the three years since the team's previous playoff meeting, when LA won in seven games. The Mavs had a new coach, a new general manager, even a new owner. Dončić was the only current Dallas starter who was on the Mavs' roster for that series. But Dončić needed only three words to sum up what he considered the biggest difference this time around:

"We have Kai."

CHAPTER 17

STANDING ON BUSINESS

Kawhi Leonard, the primary reason the Clippers had twice eliminated Dončić's Mavericks, sat out the final eight games of the regular season. He was dealing with inflammation in his right knee, which had undergone surgeries after injuries prematurely ended Leonard's previous two playoff runs. It had been three weeks since Leonard's last game action, and his status for the series opener—the entire series, actually—was in question.

Ninety minutes before Game 1, Clippers coach Tyronn Lue announced that Leonard wouldn't play that day. The Mavs caught a break. They failed miserably to take advantage. In fact, the Mavs never even took a lead that afternoon.

Dallas came out flat, looking like a team that had an 11-day layoff. The Clippers led by a dozen points after a quarter and by 26 at halftime. The Mavs only managed to score 30 points in the first two quarters, a total that Dončić had hit himself in a playoff half. They had their lowest-scoring quarter of the season in the second, when they had a grand total of 8 points on 2-of-21 shooting, managing to record twice as many turnovers as field goals made. Dallas rallied in the second half to make the 109–97 final score somewhat respectable, but the outcome was never in doubt.

"It really centered around the foundational point of talking about physicality and this being the playoffs," Irving said postgame. "A lot of guys aren't used to being here. A few young guys aren't used to being here, so they don't know what they can get away with and what the refs are going to call. I think this was a great first test for us."

Gafford had a dud, getting bullied by Clippers center Ivica Zubac en route to early foul trouble and finishing with 3 points and no rebounds in 14 minutes. Jones and Washington weren't much more impactful. It was Washington's first playoff game. Gafford's postseason experience consisted of one series, and Jones's 169 career playoff minutes were mostly in garbage time. "Relax," Kidd told his team on the day between games, believing that they came out tight.

Leonard returned for Game 2. So did the version of the Dallas defense that fueled the Mavs' late-season push from play-in territory to the West's fifth seed. This was a tough, physical game that Kidd compared to "'90s basketball at its best." Dončić, to the surprise of many, set the tone on the defensive end of the floor.

The Clippers game-planned to attack Dončić as much as possible, as many foes have done over his career. But he had proven all season that he could rise to the challenge. According to Synergy tracking, Dončić allowed only 0.76 points per possession as an isolation defender during the regular season, which ranked in the 83rd percentile in the league. The Mavs schemed to protect their superstar as much as possible, loading up with long-armed, active help defenders behind him, but Dončić took great pride in his drastic improvement as an individual defender. He didn't mind being a bullseye.

"I accept it," Dončić said that night. "It gets me going on the defensive end, too. That's fine. I think I played good defense today. I've just got to stay locked in."

According to ESPN Stats and Information, the Clippers shot only 2-of-17 from the floor when Dončić was the primary defender and missed all 11 shots that Dončić contested. After watching the film, Lue admitted that the Clippers became stagnant because they were so focused on hunting Dončić.

"It spreads to everybody else," Kleber said of Dončić's defensive intensity. "He's bringing the energy, and he's going to set the tone for us. And when he does stuff like that, it gives everybody juice."

Dončić's pride and competitiveness were on full display during one sequence of three defensive possessions midway through the fourth quarter. The Mavs were up six, having just taken the lead on a Dončić three over Leonard and a feed to Irving for a three after being doubled. The Clippers worked a pick and roll to get the isolation matchup they wanted: Leonard vs. Dončić. Leonard pounded the ball, taking 15 dribbles as he moved from the right wing to the elbow to the baseline without creating any separation, then settling for a tightly contested fadeaway that failed to draw iron. After Irving hit a floater to bump the lead to 8, it was Paul George's turn to go at Dončić, who again switched after his man set the high screen. But the Mavs sent help this time, doubling with Jones as George began to drive. George passed out of it, a hockey assist that led to Russell Westbrook's wide-open three from the opposite wing. Dončić responded by staring at the bench, waving his hands in front of his chest at first and then wildly over his head, telling the coaches that he didn't want help again. The Mavs bumped the lead back to eight after Dončić drove into the teeth of the defense and kicked the ball to Washington for an open corner three, and then the coaches granted his wish. The Clippers kept the same script: another high screen for George to get Dončić to switch. Dončić stayed in front of the nine-time All-Star as George danced with the dribble, maintained his balance after taking a forearm to the chest, and got a good contest as George settled for a step-back three from the top of the arc. As Kleber grabbed the rebound, Dončić took a step toward

Kidd to make sure his coach could hear his demand loud and clear: "Don't fuckin' double!"

Part of the reason teams make Dončić work so hard defensively is to force him to fight fatigue as he carries such a heavy load offensively. He finished this game with 32 points and nine assists, but it wasn't a pretty performance. He was 11-of-26 from the floor, 5-of-14 from three-point range. Dončić did, however, finish strong. His three with 7:03 remaining gave the Mavs the lead for good. He hit another step-back, this one over Harden from a few feet farther back, for the dagger with 1:26 remaining. Once again, Dončić roared toward the crowd, glaring at fans as he strutted down the sideline and shouted during the ensuing time-out. Final score: Mavs 96, Clippers 93. Series even as it headed to Dallas.

Nine minutes into Game 3, the American Airlines Center crowd held its collective breath. Dončić fell to the floor after Westbrook clipped his heel, and stayed down as the action went the other way, resulting in a wide-open three for Norman Powell. Dončić spent the next possession away from the ball, limping and rubbing his right knee, which isn't necessarily unusual for him. But Dončić checked out when a whistle stopped play, hobbling to the sideline and doubling over to lean on the scorer's table before trudging into the tunnel. Dončić returned to the bench a couple of minutes later and checked back in for the final 12.5 seconds of the quarter, much to the fans' delight and relief. Crisis avoided—for now, at least.

Leonard's problems with his right knee again emerged as a major storyline. He looked creaky, lacking his typical explosiveness, and sat out 11 straight minutes during one stretch of the first half. He played only 25 minutes of the game and seemed to disrupt the rhythm of the Clippers' other stars more than he contributed.

"It just didn't respond the way we wanted after the first game," Leonard said of his problematic knee postgame. "But we're going to get it right. Time will tell. We're doing all the right things."

Irving scored 19 of his 21 points in the second half—including 8 points in a three-possession flurry to close the third quarter—as the Mavs cruised to a 101–90 win despite Dončić's off shooting night (7-of-25 from the floor, 3-of-14 on threes). What really stole the show in the Mavs' 101–90 win, though, were a pair of confrontations in the fourth quarter. Both involved Washington, earning him Dallas cult-hero status.

The first occurred with 10:24 remaining, when LA's Terance Mann took umbrage with Washington looking at the Clippers' bench after Powell was called for an illegal screen on the other side of the floor. "So I decided to look at it again," Washington said later. After Mann confronted him, Washington made the "standing on business" meme come to life, crossing his arms with his feet planted wide apart, glaring at the Clippers' bench from half-court. Dončić skipped across the court as referee James Capers got between Mann and Washington and stood by his teammate's side with a shit-eating grin. "I wanted to get my flicks right for after the game," Washington explained. Dončić was one of 174,365 people who tapped the like button on Washington's postgame Instagram post featuring a photo of the instantly iconic pose.

A few minutes later, a scoreless Westbrook seemed to release some frustration with a rough foul on Dončić, grabbing his right arm from behind and pulling hard enough for Dončić to spin around. After Dončić approached him with his palms up, Westbrook welcomed him with a forearm shove to the chest. Washington responded by pushing Westbrook in the back, setting off the typical NBA brouhaha: some shoving and a lot of standing. Westbrook was called for two technicals and ejected. Washington was tossed, too, picking up his second T of the quarter and earning a loud ovation as he ran off the floor. "Always got to protect 77 at all costs," Washington said.

Leonard was ruled out a couple of hours before Game 4. He didn't play again in the series.

Dončić's right knee presented a problem, too. He described it as "really stiff" after the Game 3 win and was listed as questionable for Game 4. He played but didn't move well, preventing Dončić from creating space like he usually does with the ball in his hands and making him an easy target defensively.

Like the series opener when Leonard sat out, the Mavs came out flat and the Clippers came out firing. LA led by 23 after a quarter, when George's 16 points matched the Mavs' team total. He had 26 by halftime, hitting seven threes, celebrating one over Washington by facing the courtside fans and mimicking the crossed-arms pose. James Harden, the third star the Clippers acquired early in the season (when he successfully forced a trade for the third time in four years), was also in a groove with 18 at the half.

Dallas trailed by 31 midway through the second quarter by the time Irving scored his first bucket. He carried the Mavs for the rest of the afternoon, catching fire as Dallas tightened up its defense and chipped away at the deficit. The Clippers still had a comfortable 17-point lead at the half, but the deficit was down to 4 by the end of the third quarter. LA stretched the lead back to double digits four minutes into the fourth, and then Irving unleashed another scoring flurry: five buckets in a six-minute span, each one seemingly more difficult than the last. With 2:15 remaining, he drove down the middle, was enveloped in midair by three defenders, and still managed to execute an acrobatic finish, giving the Mavs their first lead since the game's opening minutes.

That lead lasted all of 20 seconds, as George answered with an incredibly tough off-dribble side-step three from the right corner. Irving missed in traffic on the next trip. Harden capped his 33-point performance with a couple of dagger floaters. Irving's 40 points weren't enough to prevent the Clippers from evening the series.

"I just got to help him more," Dončić said after the 116–111 loss. "I feel like I'm letting him down, so I got to be there. I got to help him more. He's given everything that he has, and he's been amazing for us the whole series."

Dončić produced a 29-point triple-double while playing 45 minutes on his sore knee, but his performance fell short of his MVP-candidate standards. He was 10-of-24 from the floor and 1-of-9 from three-point range, reacting to his lone made three by throwing his hands up and staring toward the rafters as if to thank the basketball gods for their mercy. He hadn't been able to find his touch all series, shooting 38.6 percent from the floor and 26.5 percent from long range.

Dončić was also awful defensively. According to Second Spectrum data, he got blown by on 12 of the 15 drives he defended. The 80 percent blow-by percentage was tied for the highest given up by a player who has defended at least 10 drives in a playoff game over the past 10 postseasons. Harden got hot in the fourth quarter by successfully hunting Dončić, who acknowledged his knee was bothering him but said "it shouldn't be an excuse, man."

"He wants to play well and knowing he wants to make a bigger impact, even though he's almost averaging triple-double for the series, but we're always critical of him and I think he's always critical of himself," said Irving, who had averaged 28.8 points while shooting 51.3 percent from the floor and 48.5 percent from three-point range in the four games. "So there's a young kid in the playoffs going against a team that beat him twice, so there's a little bit of a mental fatigue there as well. But I think this is what makes the beauty of sports come together. We have another opportunity on Wednesday to be in LA and be better. So hopefully these next two days will be good to him—well, I know they'll be good to him—and we'll be ready for Wednesday's game."

Dončić didn't look ready after the morning shootaround before Game 5. He was coughing and sniffling, symptoms of a bug he'd been battling for several days. An MRI had revealed that his knee was sprained, and he acknowledged he would "probably not" be playing on it if this were the regular season.

"I'm fine. I'll be ready for this game," Dončić said. That statement wasn't convincing, but Dončić's performance that night definitely was. He bullied the Clippers in a 123–93 blowout, scoring 20 of his 35 points in the paint and dishing out 10 assists, most off of drives.

"We knew at some point Luka was going to have a Luka game," Lue said.

"I always speak on his resilience," Irving said, sounding like a proud big brother. "He's not feeling a hundred percent, but he's still going to go out there and play. For me as a teammate, I enjoy that. I enjoy being around somebody like that that's going to push themselves but also be smart and still make an impact on the game—and still empty his clips, as we like to say."

Lue and George emphasized the Clippers' recent comeback from a 3–2 deficit, beginning with a Game 6 win in Dallas. Perhaps it was an attempt to plant seeds of doubt in the Mavs' mind. Of course, Irving wasn't part of that series. And Irving had a 12–0 record in closeout opportunities.

Game 6 ended up being a celebration of Irving, although he was late to the party. He scored only one bucket in the first half. At one point in the second quarter, Irving sensed that Dončić was making a concerted effort to get him involved. Irving calmly assured his co-star that he'd find his groove within the flow of the game. "Never a doubt with Kai," Dončić said with a laugh after Irving scored 28 points in the second half as the Mavs cruised to a 114–101 win.

That matched the most points that Irving had ever scored in a playoff half. Fittingly, Irving landed the knockout punch on the Clippers. He dribbled between his legs a couple of times while sizing up Clippers forward P. J. Tucker, then darted to his right, crossed over to his left, and went back to his right again before launching a fadeaway three. He fell to the floor in front of the Mavs' bench and couldn't see the shot go in, boosting the Mavs' lead to 23 midway through the fourth quarter, but he heard and felt it, finding himself in the middle of a congratulatory mosh pit. "Just seeing my teammates' reactions, that was the best part of it," Irving said postgame. "We knew that was kind of like the dagger in the series."

Dončić determined that his usual "amazing" wasn't strong enough praise for Irving after that performance to end this series. "I would say unbelievable, so it's even more special," Dončić said after scoring 28 points on 9-of-26 shooting while adding seven rebounds and 13 assists. "But just to have the guy like that on your team, it's a pleasure. Just working with him, just playing with him, it's a pleasure no matter what. He's always positive energy, always."

Just like that, Irving was the last of the older-generation superstars left standing in the playoffs. The Mavs took care of the Clippers with their trio of thirtysomething stars. Stephen Curry's Golden State Warriors got bounced in the play-in. Kevin Durant's Phoenix Suns got swept by ascending superstar Anthony Edwards's Minnesota Timberwolves. LeBron James's Los Angeles Lakers were eliminated in five games by the defending-champion Denver Nuggets. The realization hit Irving as he went through his postgame routine.

"I've been waiting, waiting, waiting for this time of my career to be in my 30s, mastering the game mentally, physically, spiritually, emotionally, IQ wise, being through tons of battles, failing on the public stage," Irving said, sitting at his locker before heading to the interview room. "I've gone through my fair share of losses to be able to understand what it takes to win and also appreciate the times like this when you have a special team around you and guys that are selfless. You don't want to take it for granted, because as a competitor, especially in this business, it doesn't come around often."

With admiration in his voice, Irving noted the emergence of young stars in the West who had "no fear." He had one on his side in Dončić, still only 25. Edwards, 22, had arguably just been the most dominant player in the first round. And the Mavs were about to run into Oklahoma City's Shai Gilgeous-Alexander, another 25-year-old MVP finalist and the face of the youngest No. 1 seed in NBA history.

* * *

FOR DONČIĆ, MOVING ON TO FACE THE THUNDER MEANT A matchup against Lu Dort, a rugged defender who looked like a linebacker. As if playing on a sprained right knee wasn't tough enough, Dončić ranked Dort among the top three perimeter defenders in the league, praise he reiterated the morning of Game 1 after the shootaround at Oklahoma City's Paycom Center.

The Mavs continued their trend of stinking it up in the series opener, a 117–95 Thunder rout, falling to 0–5 in Game 1s under Kidd. Dončić was held to 19 points on 6-of-19 shooting with five turnovers, snapping his streak of 24 consecutive playoff games with at least 20 points. His poor three-point shooting had become a troubling trend, as his 1-of-8 outing dropped Dončić to 22.7 percent from long range in this postseason. That included 5-of-35 (14.3 percent) over the last four games, the worst four-game stretch with at least 30 attempts in NBA history.

"Who cares? We lost," Dončić said when asked about the factors involved in his off night. "Just gotta move on to the next one. I've gotta be better. We've gotta be better. We gotta focus. They're a great team, a great defensive team, so it's not going to be easy at all."

Game 2 got off to a rough start from Dončić, whose face smacked into the hardwood when he got tripped up from behind by Dort in the opening minute. Dončić made sure that he wasn't bleeding and that all his teeth were still in place, then shook it off, sinking a catch-and-shoot three seconds later. He cracked a relieved grin when the net splashed and nodded his head as he backpedaled on defense, an indication all was well. Dončić hit three more threes in the quarter, when he scored 16 points. So much for that shooting slump.

For most of the night, however, the Thunder did a good job limiting the Mavs' stars. Irving was held to 9 points, matching the second-lowest total of his playoff career. Dončić had more buckets in the first quarter than in the next three combined, finishing with 29 points, a good night but below his norm. But OKC's game plan required loading up against Dončić and Irving—and P. J. Washington punished them for it. Washington, a 32 percent three-point shooter during the regular season, shot 7-of-11 from long range during a 29-point performance.

When things got tight midway through the fourth quarter, Dončić took control. He bodied Dort, which doesn't happen often, before hitting a short pull-up off the glass to push the Mavs' lead to 7. On the next possession, Dončić ran another high pick and roll against Dort and pirouetted into a one-legged fadeaway he released just beyond the free throw line. The Thunder didn't threaten again.

Dončić seemed amused by the "Luka sucks!" chants he heard as the Mavs closed out the 119–110 win. He curled his lip and bobbed his head to the beat. As the buzzer sounded with the series evened, Dončić bid farewell to the crowd the Mavs had just guaranteed they'd see again for a Game 5. "See ya, fuckers!" he shouted.

Washington starred again in Game 3, leading the Mavs with 27 points in a 105–101 win, hitting five of 12 three-point attempts. Dončić and Irving evenly split 44 points, highlighted by a late lefty floater by the latter over All-Rookie rim protector Chet Holmgren that was the dagger. The Thunder would happily live with holding the league's highest-scoring duo to that total, but Washington was forcing Coach of the Year Mark Daigneault to reconsider his defensive strategy.

"P. J. Washington. Mmm, mmm, mmm," Gilgeous-Alexander said postgame, dragging out every syllable when mentioning the name of his college teammate at Kentucky. "He's hoopin'. We've got to turn that water off if we want to win this series, for sure."

Gilgeous-Alexander's blend of skill and poise was the story of Game 4, as the Thunder evened the series and reclaimed home-court advantage with a 100–96 win. He had 10 points and four assists in the fourth quarter to key OKC's rally from a 9-point deficit. "He was unbelievable," Dončić said. "He kept making shots, and maybe at some point we got to send double-teams. He's just too good."

Dončić wasn't nearly good enough, and Irving couldn't pick up his slack. They combined for only 27 points—seven fewer than Gilgeous-Alexander had by himself. Dončić had a triple-double (18 points, 12 rebounds, 10 assists), but he was 6-of-20 from the floor and committed seven turnovers. He also missed a free throw with 10.1 seconds remaining when sinking both would have tied the score, balling up his fist and bopping himself on the forehead while sitting away from teammates on the bench during the ensuing time-out.

After too many of his missed shots and turnovers, Dončić barked at refs, sometimes instead of running back on defense. Kidd didn't call him out publicly on this occasion, but Dončić was once again getting distracted by his frustration. On the day between games, when the Mavs made the short flight over the Red River to Oklahoma City, coaches and teammates privately pleaded with Dončić not to let it happen again in Game 5. Dončić agreed, vowing to play with a smile, not a scowl.

"No bitching," assistant coach God Shammgod reminded Dončić as he stepped onto the Paycom Center court. It didn't take long for Dončić to be tested. A little more than four minutes into the game, Dončić was dribbling on the left wing and felt like he got bumped by Oklahoma City's Jalen Williams. He flipped up a 21-foot shot, figuring he'd get a whistle and a pair of free throws, and fortunately made it—but no whistle. After the ball went through the net, Dončić raised his palms for a split second and shot a look down the sideline at referee Kevin Scott. But Dončić caught himself, shaking his head, grinning, and jogging back on defense. No bitching.

Dončić's description of his mindset that night: "Just focus on basketball. Remember the thing I love, the thing I love to do. Just play basketball."

Dončić succeeded in controlling his emotions and the game while leading the Mavs to a 104–92 win that put them on the brink of clinching a Western Conference–finals bid. He put together his best all-around performance so far in these playoffs with 31 points,

10 rebounds, and 11 assists. He was efficient, committing only three turnovers and shooting 12-of-22 from the floor, 5-of-11 from three-point range, and 2-of-3 from the line. Only three free throws? "I don't want to talk about it," Dončić said, smirking and shaking his head.

He had managed to go all night without complaining and didn't want to start during his postgame press conference. The few conversations that Dončić had with the officiating crew were brief and cordial, sometimes with his hand placed gently on the ref's back.

"I talked to them normal without complaining—nothing," Dončić said. "I think it was the whole game, nothing. So I just go out there and hoop. Have fun, have fun. It was the old Luka—a smile on my face."

The fact that the Mavs led for the final 43 minutes, 59 seconds made it easier to avoid bickering with the officials. But there's a chicken-and-egg element to that. Kidd and Irving, in particular, had rational conversations with Dončić about how important managing his emotions was to the Mavs' championship ambitions—even when his complaints are "warranted," as Irving said.

"He's very emotional, as we all are as competitors, but the bigger picture is what matters," Irving said. "I think he can learn from this tonight, as well as all of us, and just continue to affirm to himself that when he is just focused on his game and he's focused on doing the right things, then we flourish as a team."

Game 6 wasn't so smooth. Gilgeous-Alexander, surrounded by shooting threats after OKC pulled Josh Giddey from the starting lineup earlier in the series, shredded the Mavs for 21 points in the first half while the Thunder hit 10 threes, half of those coming from the corners. Dončić wasn't able to refrain from offering occasional commentary to the officiating crew, but he maintained his cool despite committing five turnovers in the half. Dallas was down 16 at halftime.

The momentum flipped soon after Lively checked in early in the third quarter. The Mavs employed him in sort of a one-man zone, tasking him with shutting down the paint and sprinting to the corner to contest threes. Suddenly, Oklahoma City couldn't score, enduring a drought of 4:36 without a bucket before Lively checked out to get some rest. During that span, Lively came up with a steal, blocked a Cason Wallace corner three, contested shots all over the floor, and dominated the glass, while Dallas sliced a 17-point deficit to 6.

Lively played every second of the fourth quarter. In a game that featured two of the three MVP finalists, a no-brainer Hall of Famer, and the Rookie of the Year runner-up, the 20-year-old rookie was the most impactful player on the floor. He had 8 points, six rebounds, and unlimited energy in the quarter as the Mavs pulled off the comeback to eliminate the Thunder. He finished with 12 points and 15 rebounds, joining Hall of Famers Magic Johnson and David Robinson on the list of players who had double-doubles with at least 15 rebounds in closeout wins as rookies. Lively's most impressive stat of the day: Dallas outscored Oklahoma City by 26 points in his 30 minutes during the 117–116 win.

"It's insane, man, and he's doing this while being a rookie," Dončić said. "He has some unbelievable potential, and I'm just glad that the Mavs drafted him."

Dončić recorded his third straight triple-double with a 29–10–10 line. Irving scored 22 points to improve his closeout game record to 14–0. But the difference in this game, much like most of the series, was the Mavs' role players rising to the occasion. Lively was far from alone in that regard. Derrick Jones Jr. followed up his 19-point Game 5 by scoring 22 on 13 field goal attempts, all while doing his best to guard Gilgeous-Alexander. Washington didn't score until the fourth quarter, when he hit two clutch threes and fittingly hit the free throws that decided the game after Gilgeous-Alexander fouled him on another three-point attempt with 2.5 seconds remaining.

The Thunder had succeeded in their mission of slowing down

Dončić and Irving. Dallas's star duo averaged 40.4 points per game in the series, a drop of more than 19 points from their regular-season norm. But the Mavs still won the series in six.

"He's one of the best players in the world, but sometimes we lose sight that it's not just built [around Dončić]," Kidd said. "One guy can't get you there. You need a team. Right now, he's got a team that he believes in."

THE MAVS ADVANCED TO MEET THE WINNER OF THE NEXT DAY'S Game 7 between the Timberwolves and Nuggets. Dallas had been fortunate to land on the other side of the bracket from Nikola Jokić's Nuggets, delaying a matchup with the defending champions until the West finals, as Denver blew a big lead to the San Antonio Spurs on the final day of the regular season to lose its grip on the top seed. But the Mavs were likely headed to the Mile High City, as Denver was the 4.5-point favorite in the Game 7 on its home court.

Some fans probably booked their flights as the Nuggets took a 20-point lead in the third quarter against the Timberwolves. But Minnesota pulled off the miracle, storming back for a 98–90 win, making the Nuggets the first team in NBA history to blow that big of a lead at home in a Game 7. Jokić was out of the way. Instead, the Mavs would have to go through ascending superstar Anthony Edwards's Timberwolves to get to the NBA Finals.

"It's going to be fun," Edwards said of the matchup with the Mavs during his interview with TNT's *Inside the NBA* after clinching his first trip to the conference finals. "My matchup's gonna be Kyrie, so that's gonna be fun. We're gonna see what I can do with him."

Irving's ears perked up when he heard that while watching on his couch. "He said it right then and there, and I think the whole world was looking like, 'OK, better know what you're talking about,'" Irving said. "And I respect that. That no-fear mentality that he has is why I love him as a competitor and why I love him as a person. But when we're on that court, I know he's going to give his all and I'm going to give him my all."

Edwards wasn't ready for Irving. The eight-time All-Star came out in attack mode, scoring 24 points in the first half, 18 of those in the paint. Irving dazzled with his skill, repeatedly beating Edwards and other Wolves off the dribble before crafty finishes in traffic. The eight-time All-Star also outworked his 22-year-old foe. One of his layups came after he sprinted past a gassed Edwards to catch a 70-foot dime from Dončić seconds after a Wolves basket. But despite Irving's scoring explosion, the Mavs trailed by 3 at the half. "We probably would've [been] down 20 if he wouldn't have scored so many points," Dončić said. "So I appreciate him keeping us in the game."

Dončić came through as the closer, kidding that he "switched roles" with his co-star. He scored 15 of his 33 in the fourth quarter, capped by an off-dribble mid-range dagger over All-Defensive forward Jaden McDaniels with 49 seconds remaining. Dončić also had a couple of steals in the final two minutes, one of which might have been the best defensive play of his career. Dončić got caught in a two-on-one situation when veteran point guard Mike Conley Jr. penetrated against a rotating defense. Dončić took a bluff step toward Conley as if he would contest his floater, then recovered to get his right hand on the lob pass intended for 7-foot-1 center Rudy Gobert, preventing a dunk that would have tied the score.

The Mavs happily found themselves in unfamiliar territory after the 108–105 win at the Target Center: owners of a 1–0 series lead for the first time in Kidd's tenure.

The Mavs won that series opener because they continued their season-long trend of excelling in clutch situations, which happened to be the Wolves' most glaring weakness. They fell down by as many as 18 points in Game 2, but the Mavs managed to rally to give themselves a chance to pull off a sweep of the road trip. Dallas trailed by 2 when Edwards—smothered by Lively after the rookie center had to switch onto the All-Star guard on the perimeter—committed a turnover by tossing the ball out of bounds with 12 seconds remaining. The Mavs, and more specifically Dončić, had 12.8 seconds to work. "The play was to get Luka the ball and let Luka do what he does in those moments," Kidd said.

Dončić took the inbounds pass a few steps over the half-court line and waited for Lively to come set the screen. The Wolves switched, a pleasant surprise for the Mavs, leaving Gobert on an island against Dončić almost 40 feet from the basket. Gobert had just won his fourth Defensive Player of the Year award primarily because of his prowess in the paint, but contrary to popular perception, the big man ranked among the elite as an isolation defender as well. Minnesota coach Chris Finch was willing to take his chances with that matchup. That was fine with the Mavs, who spaced the floor to make it impossible to double-team without leaving someone wide open. "It was just time to get ready for the magic to happen," Irving said after the game.

Dončić took a few dribbles to move from the half-court logo toward the top of the three-point arc. He then crossed over right to left, getting Gobert to shift his hips a bit too much, as the big man was determined to make sure Dončić couldn't get off his signature step-back three. Dončić dribbled back between his legs and accelerated, threatening a drive. Gobert bit; Dončić slammed on the brakes and hit reverse. Dončić backpedaled to the *right*—not his preferred direction to the left, as he'd done on every other step-back during the playoffs—to create enough space to launch the three. Gobert managed to get what he considered a decent contest "for a regular NBA player. For Luka, it wasn't good enough."

After the ball swished through the net with three seconds left, Dončić glared at Gobert. For whatever reason, Dončić was among the many NBA players who had shown contempt for the Frenchman over the years. In this moment, that scorn flowed again.

"You motherfuckerrrrrrr!!!!" Dončić shouted. "You can't fuckin' guard me!!!!"

The Mavs still had to survive the final few seconds—Naz Reid's buzzer-beater from the right wing rimmed out, only the second of nine three-point attempts the Sixth Man of the Year missed that night. Dončić, who later said he "almost passed out" while the shot was in the air, punched the air as the win was secured. Then he stomped several steps to deliver one last message to a courtside fan who had been his verbal sparring partner all game: "Yeah! Go home, bitch!"

Minutes later, as Dončić met with the media in the cramped visitors' interview room, he jokingly denied cursing at Gobert, even though his lips were easy to read on a TNT replay. He pretended to be perplexed by the question and then shrugged. "I didn't say that. I was speaking Slovenian," Dončić said with a smirk.

Gobert, who had his back turned at the time, claimed that he couldn't hear Dončić shouting at him. However, he wasn't surprised that Dončić would say such a thing. "He says that every game," Gobert said while walking toward a Target Center exit, "so nothing new."

There was a same-ol'-story feel to Game 3, too. Once again, it was a tight game with five minutes to go. Just like the two games in Minnesota, that meant trouble for the Timberwolves.

Irving and Dončić took turns tormenting the Wolves' top-ranked defense as Minnesota's offense dried up in the final five minutes. Irving's lefty finish in the lane after penetrating against Edwards tied the score with 4:35 remaining and started a 14–3 Mavs closing run. Dončić and Irving accounted for all but 1 point—Daniel Gafford's free throw after an and-one alley-oop from Dončić. That was the dagger bucket off a brilliantly executed pick and roll, with Dončić patiently driving into the paint, forcing Gobert to commit to him and then flipping a left-handed lob over the bewildered big man's head.

The Wolves held a lead in the final five minutes of all three games in the series and were still in jeopardy of being swept. That had never happened in the era when play-by-play information is available, which started in 1997–98. Dončić declared after the 116–107 win that Irving, who had 14 of his 33 points in the fourth quarter, was "born for these situations." Irving concurred, adding that Dončić was, too. "Down the stretch, that's where we make our money, man," Irving said.

Dončić also scored 33 in the win, the third occasion in this playoff run that both of the Mavs' stars scored at least 30, something no other guard tandem had done during a single postseason in the past five decades. TNT color commentator Stan Van Gundy, who has 13 seasons of experience as an NBA head coach, was so impressed that he declared on the air that Dončić and Irving formed "the most talented backcourt in the history of the NBA." Kidd caught wind of it.

"There's a debate out there: Is this the best backcourt in NBA history?" Kidd said, perhaps to jab at critics who had doubted whether the co-stars could succeed together. "It's kind of cool."

It was also, as Irving pointed out, premature. He said that discussion "doesn't mean anything if we don't win a ring together." But Irving then indicated that a title was a matter of when, not if. "Our time will come." For now, they were one win away from the Finals.

THAT WIN WOULDN'T COME IN GAME 4. THE TIMBERWOLVES had the type of performance that's typical of a proud team determined to avoid a sweep, pulling out a 105–100 win to send the series back to Minnesota. A defensive strategy change also played a role in disrupting the rhythm of the Mavs' stars: Edwards was the primary defender on Dončić, and the longer, leaner McDaniels took the Irving assignment.

For the first time in his career, Irving's team failed to finish a series when it had a clinching opportunity. His 14-game winning streak in potential closeout games, the longest by any player in such situations, was over. "It's a new space," Irving said. "So now we just got to deal with this one, deal with this loss and get ready for Minnesota and enjoy that crowd there, man, because it's going to be hostile."

Nobody enjoys a hostile crowd more than Dončić, who often mentions that no NBA arena's atmosphere compares to some of the craziness he's experienced in places such as Türkiye, Serbia, and Greece. Sure, he would have loved to sweep the Timberwolves to punch the Mavs' ticket to his first Finals. But Dončić derives a certain menacing comfort from being the enemy of an entire crowd.

That's why Dončić frequently looks for a mouthy fan to use as motivation. He didn't need to search far in Game 5. Dončić eagerly reengaged the same courtside fan he'd coarsely bid farewell to following his clutch heroics a few games earlier. It quickly became a one-sided conversation. "You know that gets me going," Dončić said. "Everybody knows that by now."

Dončić scored on the Mavs' first possession, when Gobert goaltended on his short turnaround jumper, and then the show really started. On the next trip, Dončić rattled in a catch-and-shoot jumper from about 30 feet out on the left wing—right in front of his favorite courtside fan, and Dončić gave him a few words as he backpedaled on defense. A couple of possessions later, Dončić came off a screen set just past the half-court line and launched a step-back from the same spot. As the ball swished through the net, Edwards's shoulders slumped in disbelief that he couldn't afford to go under a screen set so far away from the hoop. Dončić waved sarcastically to the seats as he jogged to the other end of the floor. He scored again 39 seconds later, hitting a step-back just above the free throw line, and shooting another glance at the guy. After only 153 seconds, Dončić had scored 10 points and reduced a rowdy Target Center crowd to nervous murmuring.

Dončić's onslaught was only beginning. He had another scoring flurry later in the quarter, when reserve forward Kyle Anderson took a turn trying to contain him. Dallas ran a high pick and roll for Dončić on three straight half-court possessions, and he scored on each of them. On the first, as Anderson trailed him over the screen and Gobert hedged, Dončić snaked to a spot near the right elbow, created space by stepping back, and knocked down an uncontested 19-footer. Anderson went under the screen the next time, and Dončić let it fly from the half-court logo. When it went in, Dončić strutted sideways down the court so he could stare down his courtside target and talk some trash. Then Dončić caught Anderson leaning and rejected the screen, spinning to his right and accelerating into a pull-up three as Gobert retreated toward the paint. He jogged a few steps over the half-court line and unleashed a roar toward the silenced crowd. In less than 10 minutes, Dončić had scored 20 points and demoralized an entire arena.

"It's a good feeling, man. I can't lie," Dončić said. It felt a lot like his Game 7 humiliation of the Suns in Phoenix a couple of years earlier. Except this one was expected.

"Man, I was enjoying it," Irving said. "You're just watching a special performance take place.... When Luka starts off a game like that, we're a tough team to beat."

Dončić outscored the Wolves by himself in the first quarter as the Mavs jumped to a 16-point lead, and then headed to the trainer's room for treatment on his knee. It was Irving's turn to put on a show in the second quarter, scoring 15 points on 5-of-5 shooting. Dončić and Irving combined for 44 points in the half, four more than the Timberwolves. Dallas was up 29, the largest halftime lead ever by a team with a chance to clinch a Finals appearance. The only larger halftime lead in Mavs playoff history: 30 in Phoenix, when Dončić had matched the Suns' score by himself.

The game, and the series, was essentially over. While the suspense was gone, Dončić did provide some entertainment for the TNT crowd that stuck around through halftime. After Dončić muscled in an and-one floater to bump the lead to 36, a middle-aged fan in a second-row baseline seat decided to taunt him, rubbing his eyes to mimic a crying baby.

"Yeah? Who's crying, motherfucker?" Dončić retorted. Snoop Dogg, sitting courtside right in front of the ill-timed heckler, cracked up. Millions of people on their couches probably had the same reaction, as the quip was picked up by TNT's microphones and broadcast live.

Dončić and the Mavs shifted into celebration mode after he drove and dumped the ball off to Lively for one final dunk with 3:02 remaining. The Wolves called time-out to wave a white flag, and both teams subbed out their starters. Dončić and Irving—both of whom finished with 36 points to become the first pair of teammates to each score at least 35 in a conference finals game since Kobe Bryant and Shaquille O'Neal—bear-hugged in front of the bench before watching the last few minutes of the 124–103 win.

They had crushed any doubts about their compatibility as a duo. And six years after drafting Dončić, the Mavs had finally answered the question about whether they could build a contender around him, eliminating three 50-plus-win teams during their path to the Finals. The franchise pulled off a remarkable turnaround in the span of the year. The postgame presentation of the Oscar Robertson Trophy, awarded to the Western Conference champions—with Patrick Dumont front and center and Cuban off to the side—provided an opportunity to bask in the glory of the accomplishment. They had earned the right to face the Boston Celtics, who had by far the best record in the league before cruising through the East playoffs.

"It was a very hard road, very hard," Dončić said minutes later with the Magic Johnson Award trophy, given to the series MVP, on the table in front of him. "But we're not done. We have four more."

After wrapping up his media duties, Dončić met up with his dad, who had endured several hours of delays at Dallas's Love Field to get to Minneapolis just in time for tip-off. They stood outside the entrance of the visitors' locker room and chatted as Dončić held the MVP trophy in his right hand and a can of Fulton Lonely Blonde in his left. He sipped on the ale from a Minnesota brewery until Michael Finley smoothly grabbed the beer out of Dončić's hand en route to dapping up Saša. The job wasn't finished yet.

CHAPTER 18

THE QUEST CONTINUES

THE WEEK OFF BEFORE THE FINALS BEGAN ALLOWED DONČIĆ TO get much-needed rest and treatment on his sprained right knee, sore left ankle, and other accumulated aches and pains. It gave Kidd and the Mavs' coaching staff time to devise a game plan to combat the Celtics, who had the statistical profile of an all-time elite team, winning 64 games with the fifth-largest point differential in NBA history before a 12–2 run through the East bracket. And it provided space for Irving to psychologically prepare himself to return to Boston as public enemy No. 1.

Irving's No. 11 was once expected to hang in the TD Garden rafters, alongside the retired numbers of 24 Celtics greats and the franchise's 17 (and counting) championship banners. That anticipation was alluded to in a Nike commercial released in the fall of 2018, early into Irving's second season with the Celtics. It featured Irving playing one-on-one against his father, Drederick, on the famed TD Garden parquet floor. The elder Irving starred at Boston University, which retired his number, before giving up his pro career to raise Kyrie and his sister as a single parent after their mother passed away.

"He's the reason I wear No. 11," Irving narrated at the end of the ad. "I want to be the reason no one else will."

Less than eight months later, after Irving's pending free agency loomed over a disappointing Celtics season, he chose to leave Boston for Brooklyn. He'd been reviled by the Celtics' passionate fanbase ever since. Privately, he had been struggling with the grief of his maternal grandmother's death, but publicly, the fans perceived him as a brooding diva who refused to embrace the responsibilities of being a mentor for Boston's pair of rising stars, Jayson Tatum and Jaylen Brown.

No. 11 in Celtics green now belonged to reserve guard Payton Pritchard.

Irving's return to Boston would be perhaps the Finals' most prominent storyline. His first full season with the Mavs had given him a redemptive arc. After the off-court chaos in Brooklyn further tarnished his reputation, Irving had emerged as the Mavs' emotional leader and an appreciated role model for the team's younger players, including Dončić. Irving—who alternatively goes by Chief Hélà, the Lakota name given to him by the Standing Rock Sioux tribe when he reconnected with his mother's Native American roots in 2018—spoke frequently and freely about his "spiritual journey" and the sense of peace he finally felt in Dallas. A few days before the Finals began, Irving didn't mind reflecting on his brief, rocky stint in Boston.

"I know sometimes in sports, it's literally about the end goal and result and what you accomplish, and that's one thing," Irving said after a practice at the Mavs' facility. "But we're still human at the end of the day. I wasn't my best self during that time. When I look back on it, I just see it as a time where I learned how to let go of things and learned how to talk through my emotions."

Irving had faced the Celtics in the playoffs twice since leaving

Boston: in the 2021 first round, when the Nets eliminated Boston in five games, and in the 2022 first round, when they got swept. Those experiences didn't soothe any hard feelings.

"Fuck you, Kyrie!" chants welcomed him back during the 2021 series. After he scored 39 points in a Game 4 win to put Boston on the brink of elimination, Irving celebrated by deliberately stomping his left foot on Lucky the Leprechaun's eye in the TD Garden floor's half-court logo—a sacrilegious act to some Celtics fans and former players. One fan fired a water bottle at Irving as he walked off the floor, missing his head by inches. The man exited the arena in handcuffs.

Irving twice flashed his middle finger at Celtics fans during the 2022 series opener. That earned him a $50,000 fine from the league office. A few years later, days before playing in front of that crowd again, Irving expressed regret. He vowed to handle the hostility with poise this time around.

"I will say last time in Boston, I don't think that was the best— not this regular season, but when we played in the playoffs and everyone saw me flip off the birds and kind of lose my shit a little bit—that wasn't a great reflection of who I am and how I like to compete on a high level," Irving said. "It wasn't a great reflection on my end towards the next generation on what it means to control your emotions in that type of environment, no matter what people are yelling at you. I'm built for these moments, to be able to handle circumstances like that, and I've been able to grow since then."

THERE WAS ALSO A RATHER INTERESTING REUNION STORYLINE with one of the Celtics' key players, too. Kristaps Porziņģis, the Mavs' first swing (and miss) at a co-star for Dončić, had proven to be a phenomenal fit in Boston. He'd been traded to the Celtics the previous summer after a productive, out-of-the-spotlight 16-month stint in Washington. Much to the surprise of several current and former members of the Mavs' front office and coaching staff, Porziņģis had developed into one of the NBA's most efficient high-usage post-up threats and an elite rim protector—when he was on the floor.

Durability remained a problem for the 7-foot-3 Porziņģis. Injuries limited him to 57 games in the regular season, and in an unfortunately fitting twist, Porziņģis would be returning from an extended absence to face the Mavs in the Finals. He hadn't played since suffering a right calf strain in Game 4 of the first round, 38 days before the Finals opener. He didn't express certainty that he'd play in Game 1 against the Mavs until the day before the game. "I have to feel confident to go out there and leave it all on the floor and expect that I'm going to be healthy and completely fine," Porziņģis said.

Porziņģis's history with the Mavs, particularly his fizzled co-star partnership with Dončić, was a secondary storyline during media day, when reporters from around the world pepper players with questions for 10 to 15 minutes each the day before the Finals begin. When asked about the subject, Dončić didn't offer too much more than a shrug: "I don't know why it didn't work out. We were still both young. We tried to make it work, but it just didn't work. So moved on."

Porziņģis downplayed the notion that there was ever any drama during his Dallas tenure, especially regarding his relationship with Dončić. "It's always been good," Porziņģis claimed before lavishing his former teammate with praise, such as saying that Dončić is "one of the best players in the league, in the world." Porziņģis wasn't being completely honest, but he really didn't leave Dallas on bad terms with Dončić, and there was no benefit at this point to publicly discussing the passive-aggressive headbutting that had previously occurred between them.

"I know at that time there were some rumors there's like something in the locker room," Porziņģis said. "It was never like that. It's all just noise at the end."

How much could Porziņģis actually impact this series after such a long layoff? That was one of the biggest questions entering the Finals. When the starting lineups were announced 30 minutes before tip-off, it was revealed that Porziņģis would come off the bench, serving as a reserve for only the second time in his 474 games played in the NBA. He stayed in the back well after the rest of the players began warming up on the TD Garden court.

The arena jumbotrons showed Porziņģis as he made his way down the hallway toward the court, drawing a roar from the crowd. The fans erupted in a deafening frenzy when Porziņģis emerged from the tunnel and joined his teammates on the floor. Like the rest of the Celtics, Porziņģis wore a black T-shirt with "WALTON" across the chest in multicolored tie-dye print. They were honoring Bill Walton, the Hall of Famer who had passed away the previous week, an extraordinarily skilled 7-footer who battled injuries for most of his career. His last hurrah was helping the 1985–86 Celtics win a championship as a sixth man. There wasn't a better tribute to Walton than Porziņģis's Game 1 performance.

THE CELTICS LED BY 1 WHEN PORZIŅĢIS CHECKED IN TO THE game for the first time with 7:17 remaining in the first quarter. Less than five minutes later, Boston's lead had swelled to 10 and the Mavs needed to call a time-out to halt their momentum. The time-out came right after Porziņģis sank a jumper from just above the left elbow over Josh Green. Porziņģis had already scored 8 points and was picking on the Mavs from that spot on the court—an area he was discouraged from occupying during his Dallas tenure. Porziņģis's first points came on a pair of free throws after he caught the ball there and faced up against Dončić. He hit jumpers after doing the same thing against Jaden Hardy and Josh Green. When the Mavs put 7-foot Lively on him, Porziņģis drove past him and hung on the rim after throwing down a two-handed dunk, adding fuel to an already amped atmosphere.

It was full-blown delirium by the end of the quarter. The Celtics scored the final three buckets of the quarter, all on threes, including a 30-footer by Porziņģis. He swatted a couple of shots, snuffing an Irving pull-up jumper and rejecting Green's attempt to end a fast break with a poster dunk. The 11-point, three-rebound, two-block stint might have been the best seven-minute stretch of Porziņģis's career. It was damn sure the most meaningful. The Celtics led by 17 after the quarter, a lead that ballooned to as large as 29 points with Boston cruising to a 107–89 win.

"Tonight was an affirmation to myself that I'm pretty good, you know?" Porziņģis said after finishing with 20 points, six rebounds, and three blocks in 21 minutes off the bench. "Maybe I'm not perfect, but I'm pretty good and I can play like this. And I can definitely add to this team."

All night, the Celtics successfully dared the Dallas star duo to beat them with isolation basketball. Dončić scored 30, but he needed 26 shots to get it and only dished out one assist as the Mavs' offense was bogged down. Irving had a dreadful night, scoring 12 points on 6-of-19 shooting, his 31.6 percent field goal percentage the worst of his 14 career Finals games. He was primarily guarded by perennial All-Defensive selection Jrue Holiday, another major summer trade acquisition who had been the final piece to the Bucks' championship puzzle a few years before.

"It's a fun series," Irving said. "It was fun going into the game. It's still going to be fun. But there's going to be a level of chess that still has to be played."

Celtics fans booed Irving every time he touched the ball and cheered loudly every time he missed a shot. The crowd especially enjoyed Irving's brick off the side of the backboard on a corner three attempt in the first quarter and Porziņģis's rejection of his next shot. But Irving implied that the atmosphere made no impact on the outcome. "I thought it was going to be a little louder in here," Irving said, "but I'm expecting the same things going into Game 2."

When Game 2 came a few nights later, Irving's line about the noise level was featured prominently on the TD Garden jumbotron, alongside his picture. Dončić was dealing with another lingering issue from the Game 1 loss. He was downgraded from probable to questionable on the early afternoon injury report, when a "thoracic contusion" was added to his listing along with the right knee sprain and left ankle soreness. In layman's terms, Dončić had a chest bruise. He wasn't certain when the injury occurred, but he believed it happened when he took a charge on Derrick White. He was sure that it hurt like hell—so much so that he took a pain-killing injection hours before tip-off, although that wasn't revealed until ESPN reported it a couple of days later. The shots became part of Dončić's routine for the rest of the series.

Aside from the occasional wince, Dončić made little indication that he was playing through pain, particularly as he scored 23 points in the first half to keep the Mavs in the game. He finished with 32 points, 11 assists, and 11 rebounds, his seventh triple-double of these playoffs, a feat only Wilt Chamberlain and Nikola Jokić had accomplished in a single postseason. But Dončić, who played 42 minutes and again was frequently targeted on defense, faded in the fourth quarter, when he was 1-of-6 from the floor and committed a couple of costly turnovers. Dončić blamed himself for the 105–98 loss, pointing to his poor free throw shooting (4-of-8) and eight turnovers as the primary problems that "cost us the game."

"I've got to do way better in those categories," Dončić said after joining LeBron James, Charles Barkley, and Jerry West as the only players to post 30-point triple-doubles in a Finals loss. "But at the end of the day, we've got to make shots to win the game."

The Celtics had a bad shooting game, going 10-of-39 from three-point range. The Mavs were worse (6-of-26). Dallas players other than Dončić made only two of their 17 attempts from long range as the Mavs were held to double digits again. Irving had another dud performance, finishing with 16 points on 7-of-18 shooting, fueling "Kyrie sucks!" chants. He averaged only 14 points on 35.1 percent shooting (0-of-8 on threes) in the two losses in Boston, which ran his personal losing streak against the Celtics to a dozen games. The underdog Mavs had no chance to win the series with Irving playing that poorly. Irving knew it, and he told Dončić as much after the Game 2 loss.

"It started with me just telling my hermano I got to play better for him, alongside him," Irving said. "In order for us to accomplish our goal, we both have to be playing well and we both have to be doing the little things, doing whatever it takes to win. Easy conversation. But it started with me reaching out, just letting him know it's my fault, taking accountability for not playing particularly well."

As the series shifted to Dallas, Irving also reminded everyone that he had been part of a Finals comeback from an 0–2 deficit before. "I know what it takes," he said following practice the day before Game 3, which was as close to a must-win for the Mavs as a non-elimination game could be. There had been 156 teams that had lost the first three games of a best-of-7 series in NBA history; not a single one had rallied to win the series.

The Mavs caught a break going into Game 3 due to more medical misfortune for Porziņģis. He had limped off with 4:40 remaining in the Celtics' Game 2 win but indicated it wasn't a concern postgame: "I don't think it's anything serious. We will look at it tomorrow and go from there, but all good. I'll be good." Consultations with numerous specialists proved Porziņģis wrong. On the practice day in Dallas, the Celtics announced that Porziņģis had been diagnosed with a rare injury in his lower left leg: a torn medial retinaculum allowing dislocation of the posterior tibialis tendon. He was officially considered day-to-day, but Porziņģis's status for the remainder of the Finals was suddenly in doubt.

Porziņģis's absence could potentially swing the series. The Celtics had outscored the Mavs by 25 in Porziņģis's 44 minutes in the first two games, and the teams had been even with him on the bench. And he was ruled out of Game 3 a couple of hours before tip-off.

"IF YOU DON'T BELIEVE IN WINNING THIS TITLE, YOU SHOULDN'T be here," a hype video narrated by three-time Super Bowl champion quarterback Patrick Mahomes proclaimed before the Mavs' starting lineup was announced. Mahomes, a Mavs fan since his childhood growing up in Texas, sat courtside. So did Dirk Nowitzki, sandwiched by Steve Nash and NFL all-time rushing leader Emmitt Smith. The atmosphere at the sold-out American Airlines Center was electric.

Dončić arrived ready for the stage, as did Irving, who scored on the game's first possession after receiving a pass from his co-star. Dončić came out aggressive, hitting a step-back three over Tatum in the opening minute. A couple of possessions later, he muscled Holiday on a drive that ended in a layup. The Mavs jumped to a 9–2 lead. As the Celtics called time-out, Dončić approached a referee to inquire about why he didn't get a whistle on Holiday for an and-one.

The Mavs had one more burst midway through the quarter. Dončić dazzled as Dallas stretched its lead to 13 with another 9–2 run. He scored twice on drives after successfully hunting a switch onto Tatum, a solid defender but overmatched by Dončić's blend of zigzag ballhandling ability and brute force. Then Dončić caught Brown being indecisive in conceding the switch and hit Lively rolling down the middle of the paint for a layup plus a foul on help defender Xavier Tillman Sr., who had replaced Porziņgis in the rotation but didn't provide nearly the same level of rim protection. Dončić had complete control of the game, already registering 9 points and three assists in about half a quarter.

After Tatum interrupted the party with a three, Dončić hunted him on another switch. But Tatum stayed in front of him this time, and Dončić settled for a tightly contested step-back that he airballed. Dončić got cross-matched in transition and whistled for a foul when Tatum attempted to drive baseline. Dončić disagreed with the call, arguing that Tatum illegally used his off arm to hook him. Dončić waved his right arm in that motion as he approached ref Kevin Scott, then alternated between making the hooking motion with his left arm and pointing to the replay on the jumbotron. Scott didn't make eye contact with Dončić or heed his demand to watch the replay.

"C'mon, man," Dončić said to Scott after the ball was inbounded. As Holiday dribbled in front of him, Dončić turned his head to Scott and made the hooking motion one more time. The Celtics called a play to attack Dončić, bringing Brown up to set a screen and force a switch. Dončić went through the motions on the possession and was fortunate that Brown missed a three. When Irving hit his first three of the series seconds later, a pull-up to bump the lead back to 13, Dončić turned to ref James Capers to plead his case about the call against him a minute earlier. Dončić had another brief, one-sided conversation with Scott before subbing out on a dead ball the next possession.

The Celtics sliced the Mavs' lead to 6 in the 71 seconds that Dončić rested. The deficit was down to 1 by the end of the quarter, which concluded with the Celtics scoring 5 unanswered points during an embarrassing 38-second stretch for Dončić. He felt a tap from Al Horford on his wrist after releasing an errant step-back three from the right wing and blatantly flopped to sell a call that he didn't get. While sitting on his butt, Dončić barked at Scott before jogging back late on defense. The five-on-four opportunity resulted in Sam Hauser, Dončić's man, making a wide-open three from the top of the arc. Dončić complained to Capers before receiving the inbounds pass and muttered a few more words at him while bringing the ball up the court. Dončić missed another step-back three over Tatum and flopped again, this one even more egregious with no contact on the play. Tatum leaked out, caught a long outlet pass from Derrick White, and dunked with one second remaining. As the quarter ended, Dončić appealed to Scott in front of the Mavs' bench, but the ref put his hand up and walked to the other side of the floor. In a matter of minutes, playing in the most important game of his life, Dončić had gone from dominant to distracted.

Dončić struggled in the second quarter, going 2-of-7 from the floor and loudly protesting the lack of a whistle after a few of his misses. But the Celtics couldn't take advantage due to their own offensive inefficiency (20 points on eight-of-twenty-two shooting in the quarter) and Irving's hot hand (11 points, including three more threes). The Mavs maintained a 1-point lead going into halftime.

A few minutes into the third quarter, Kidd called a time-out after defensive lapses by Dončić led to open threes on consecutive possessions. First, Dončić just stood there and watched with his arms down as Holiday walked into a clean three. Then, Dončić got caught way out of position for no reason, giving up an easy baseline drive to Brown that forced the Dallas defense to rotate and resulted in a good look that Tatum knocked down. These gaffes were inexcusable— not the result of athletic limitations, but of inattention and a lack of effort.

After the time-out, Dončić missed a floater in the paint over White. He released a bit of frustration by raking White across the forearm as the Celtics guard received an outlet pass seconds later. Dončić didn't dispute this call, his second foul of the night, looking at crew chief Marc Davis and raising his left arm, just in case there was any confusion about who committed it. The Celtics needed only nine seconds to score, as Tatum blew by Dončić and dished to a cutting Brown for the dunk after collapsing the Dallas defense.

Boston was in a groove now. The Celtics' lead swelled to 10 with 6:09 remaining in the quarter after another display of poor effort by Dončić gave Boston an easy basket. After Tim Hardaway Jr.'s wild runner got swatted by White, Dončić put his head down instead of sprinting back on defense. As Holiday pushed the ball up the floor,

Dončić realized he had made a mistake and pointed ahead toward Tatum, who was next to him when the Celtics retrieved the ball and about 20 feet ahead three seconds later. Holiday found Tatum for another dunk.

As the crowd murmured, Dončić regained his composure well enough to exploit a switch onto Tillman for a layup. As the ball went through the net, Dončić again shouted at Scott for not giving him an and-one. He got another layup on the Mavs' next possession after an offensive rebound by Lively but griped incessantly for the next few minutes. After missing a floater contested by Tillman with 3:50 remaining, Dončić just pointed at Scott in frustration before subbing out to get a couple minutes of rest. The Celtics' lead was back to 12 when Dončić returned. It was 15 at the end of the quarter, which was punctuated by some olé work by Dončić as the screen defender on a pick and roll that Brown rejected before driving uncontested down the middle for a tomahawk dunk.

The Mavs' meltdown continued in the first minute of the fourth quarter. Dončić was called for an offensive foul on the opening possession for using his off arm to hook Brown on a spin move off of a post-up. Dončić apparently saw the sick humor in that call going against him, laughing as he flipped the ball to Capers. A Brown corner three continued the barrage. After an empty possession by the Mavs, White hit a wide-open three when Dončić got lost in traffic. Boston led by 21 as Kidd called time-out.

The Mavs somehow managed to claw back into the game despite Dončić seemingly spending as much energy battling the officiating crew as he did the Celtics. He picked up his fourth foul with 9:24 remaining—10 seconds after backing down Payton Pritchard for his lone bucket of the quarter—by reaching in to try to poke the ball away from Pritchard. Dončić raised his hand to claim the foul, but he still peppered Scott with some commentary.

Kidd had voiced concerns over the years that Dončić's frequent complaining was counterproductive, costing him calls due to the human elements of officiating. That could have been the case when Tatum got away with a clear foul on a Dončić drive after the Mavs had pulled within 6 points midway through the quarter, riding Dončić's hip as he went up for the layup, sending him sprawling into a baseline seat on the other side of the basket. The Mavs were fortunate that the Celtics' ensuing transition opportunity ended with Horford traveling. Dončić hollered his objections about the no-call during the dead ball.

The Mavs did get a whistle on their next possession, sending Irving to the line after Holiday bumped him on a three-point shot. He made them all, cutting the deficit to 3, an 18-point difference in the span of only five minutes. At this point, the problems the Tatum/Brown Celtics had over the years closing out tough playoff series seemed to be popping up. Case in point: the 2022 Finals, when Boston had a 2–1 over Golden State but lost to the Warriors in six games. Imagine the weight the Celtics would feel if they blew a 21-point fourth-quarter lead, something that hadn't happened in the Finals in at least 50 years, if ever.

With 4:38 remaining, Dončić got called for his fifth foul after getting tangled up with Brown while defending him on a post-up, causing both players to tumble to the floor. Dončić sat up, staring at Scott and raising both arms in a shocked shrugging gesture. He cranked his right arm backward, once again indicating he thought the call should have been an offensive foul for a hook. After Scott ignored him, Dončić pivoted on his backside to protest to Davis before Washington helped him to his feet. His lobbying to Davis continued unsuccessfully. For some of the ensuing time-out, Dončić sat on the bench, complaining to teammates about a call that Kidd didn't consider worthy of challenging.

Twenty-six seconds later, Kidd had little choice but to use his challenge. After an Irving miss, Brown received the ball on the right side of the floor before Dallas had set its defense. He saw Dončić in front of him and accelerated, knowing that the Mavs' star couldn't afford to pick up a sixth foul. As Brown crossed over left to right, Dončić slid his feet in an attempt to draw a charge 25 feet from the basket, a shockingly unwise decision considering the circumstances. They collided, Dončić's bruised chest to Brown's side, and both players hit the hardwood again. Dončić was called for a blocking foul, and as the ABC broadcast cut to a close-up shot of him, Dončić turned his head to the Mavs' bench and yelled, "You better fuckin' challenge that call!"

"The replay has determined that Dončić has not established a legal guarding position in the path of Brown," Davis announced after the replay review. The call stood. Dončić had fouled out for only the third time in his career—and the first time in the playoffs. With the Mavs' championship hopes at stake, Dončić would be forced to watch the final 4:12.

After the Mavs got a stop, Irving hit a pull-up jumper from the right elbow to cut the Celtics' lead to a single point. The Mavs didn't have their MVP candidate available, but they still had momentum. Boston had scored on only one of its 13 possessions since building that 21-point lead. Tatum missed again…but Brown slipped in for a putback to end a 4:37 scoreless drought for the Celtics.

Dončić could only stand helplessly on the baseline and hope that Irving (35 points) could lead the completion of an epic comeback without him. It was a one-possession game again with 1:20 remaining after Lively finished back-to-back possessions with dunks. But Brown responded with a clutch pull-up jumper, one of the signature moments that helped him land the Finals MVP. The Celtics pulled away for a 106–99 win, all but assuring that Boston's duckboats would be used in another championship parade.

"We had a good chance," said Dončić, who finished with 27 points on 11-of-27 shooting, in the aftermath of the loss. "We were close. Just didn't get it. I wish I was out there."

In the heat of the moment, as far as Dončić was concerned, the refs robbed him of that opportunity. He knew ripping the officials would only earn him a hefty fine, but he just couldn't bite his tongue. He complained that they weren't allowed to play a physical style and then hesitated.

"I don't want to say nothing. You know, six fouls in the NBA Finals, basically I'm like this," Dončić said, raising his palms in a shrugging motion as he had so many times during the game. "C'mon, man. Be better than that."

A day later, Dončić accepted accountability for allowing his frustration to get the best of him. Again. He admitted his sixth foul "probably wasn't the smartest thing."

"I just really want to win," Dončić said. "Sometimes I don't show it the right way, but at the end of the day, I really want to win. I've got to do a better job showing it a different way."

There's no harsher glare in the NBA than the spotlight on a ringless superstar who fails spectacularly on the Finals stage, when the whole basketball world is watching. Nowitzki felt it in 2006, when the Mavs fell apart after building a 2–0 lead over the Heat. LeBron James felt it in 2011, when the Mavs got their revenge at the expense of his superteam Miami squad. Tatum felt it in 2022. Now, it was Dončić's turn.

Dončić made for an easy target because his flaws are as obvious as his brilliant talent. He was relentlessly ripped in the media for the 48 hours between Games 3 and 4 for his petulance, lack of poise, and poor defense. Kidd had patiently prodded Dončić to make strides in those areas during their three seasons together, and now he had regressed at the worst possible time.

But Kidd felt that some of the scrutiny on Dončić went too far, particularly from former players with prominent media platforms, and spent much of his availability before Game 4 making that point. He thought some of it crossed the line from fair criticism to "personal attacks," adding that some media members feel that they "got to say something crazy to get a new contract or likes or clicks." Kidd didn't want one rough night to overshadow what had been a phenomenal run by a 25-year-old who had led the league in post-season points, rebounds, assists, steals, and minutes despite dealing with a series of injuries. And he wanted to make sure that Dončić knew that he had his back.

"What I'm more disappointed in is that we are at the highest stage where we have one of the best players in the world playing the game the right way, but we want to criticize some of the things that he does not do well," Kidd said. "But when he does do them well, we are going to come back and want to talk to him, and then when he says, 'No, I'm going to pass,' then what happens, right? I think sometimes it's just unfair or unwarranted to say those things. No one in this room is perfect, right? So, like, give my man a break. Let him play the game. Because we are all here to watch him play, and so let's just enjoy it. He's 25 years old. He will be better. Hopefully, he's better tonight."

Dončić, who had vowed to focus on "fun" in Game 4, responded with one of the most dominant halves in recent Finals history. He scored 25, including 18 in the paint as Porziņģis watched from the bench again, and dished out four assists as the Mavs built a 26-point halftime lead. The Celtics didn't score against Dončić as the primary defender until the third quarter. He also forced four turnovers defensively. The game got so out of hand that the Celtics started preparing for Game 5 with 3:18 to go in the third quarter, when coach Joe Mazzulla called time-out to pull his starters with Boston trailing by 36. The Mavs followed suit a couple of minutes later. Dončić's final stats: 29 points, five rebounds, five assists, plus 30 in 33 minutes.

"I think what you're seeing is him just taking accountability as best he can at this point in his life," Irving said after the Mavs avoided a sweep and extended the series with the 122–84 win. "He's a young person, still trying to figure it out. I give him that grace. Also, we have to give him a little tough love where we let him know and reiterate you got to stay off those [referees] a little bit. I think it's just lessons being learned."

The previous day, Dončić had also been discussing how his first Finals would be a learning experience. Then he caught himself, noting that the Celtics still had to win another game with his oft-used line: "We're going to believe until the end." After the Mavs got on the board with the Game 4 blowout, Dončić declared that he had "big belief in this team that we can do it."

But Game 5 back in Boston didn't provide much suspense, aside from Porziņģis being cleared to play despite knowing that his injury would require surgery and would sideline him well into the next season. Holiday scored on the opening possession and the Celtics never relinquished the lead. The Mavs trailed by 10 at the end of the first quarter, 21 at halftime after Pritchard's second buzzer-beating half-court bomb of the series. Final score: Celtics 106, Mavs 88, an 18-point margin of victory to clinch Boston's record-setting 18th NBA championship.

Dončić walked into the interview room for the final time of the season sore, exhausted, and disappointed. The Slovenian national team was scheduled to play in an Olympic qualifying tournament in Greece two weeks later, a daunting turnaround considering Dončić's aches, pains, and injuries. He didn't want to discuss that, saying he was just trying to get healthier and had some decisions to make. He didn't want to discuss much at all, but he pepped up a bit when asked about the Mavs' long-term outlook.

"I feel great," Dončić said regarding the franchise's future. "We did some great moves. I would say we've been together for five months. I'm proud of every guy that stepped on the floor, all the coaches, all the people behind. Obviously, we didn't win Finals, but we did have a hell of a season and I'm proud of every one of them."

A COUPLE OF DAYS LATER, GM NICO HARRISON HELD HIS SEASON-ending media availability at the Mavs' practice facility. Despite the loss, the vibe was a stark contrast to his exit interview the previous year, when the Mavs were in crisis mode and the future felt ominous. The Mavs had proven they could build a legitimate contender around Dončić, easing that perceived pressure.

Harrison's job now was to figure out how the Mavs could take the next step—a significant one, judging by the Finals result—to win a title. He preached a patient approach, saying he expected the "top seven or eight" players in the Mavs' rotation to be back next season. He challenged them all to return "10 to 15 percent better in mind, body, and spirit." That included Dončić.

"We're not where we're at without Luka. I think that's important to point out," Harrison said. "And we also won't be able to get where we want to go without the best version of Luka. If you look at a guy who after Game 3 had the world on his neck—the scrutiny, which was crazy, the amount of scrutiny that he had to face—for him to focus in and do what he did in Game 4, I just think it shows the character of him. He's willing to fight through adversity, and I think he's going to continue to get better.... I think you're going to see the best version of him."

Harrison referred to re-signing Derrick Jones Jr., the veteran-minimum bargain who thrived as Dallas's primary defender and starting small forward, as "priority 1A and 1B." Unlike the previous year, Harrison planned to keep the roster mostly intact. "But we're always going to try to get better," he said. "That's just the nature of the job."

Harrison couldn't reveal his hand, but he had an ambitious upgrade plan in mind. The target: Klay Thompson, who had grown to feel unappreciated after a 13-year run as one of the Golden State Warriors' famed four-time-champion "Splash Brothers." Thompson was no longer the perennial All-Star he was in his twenties, before a torn ACL and ruptured Achilles tendon robbed him of two and a half seasons of his prime, but he was still an elite three-point shooter with championship experience. The Mavs could have used both in the Finals.

For all of the focus on Dončić's defensive deficiencies, the Mavs didn't lose the series on that end of the floor. The Mavs allowed 109.1 points per 100 possessions to the Celtics, a defensive rating that would have ranked second in the league during the regular season, and only 107.0 with Dončić on the floor. Dallas's biggest problem was its poor perimeter shooting (31.6 percent from three-point range), as the Mavs failed to hit triple digits in any of their four Finals losses. "We felt we were a Klay Thompson away," Harrison said later.

But it'd require some smooth maneuvering for the Mavs to make competitive offers to Thompson or Jones, much less both of them, under the NBA's complex salary-cap rules. The salaries on the Mavs' books put Dallas over the luxury-tax line entering next season. That meant the Mavs only had the smaller version of the mid-level exception—a roster slot with a starting salary of up to $5.2 million—and the veteran minimum available, unless they shed significant salary.

This sort of situation is why one of Harrison's first hires was Andrew Baker, a capologist with a law degree poached from the Nets' front office. Failures in the fine print, such as the language regarding the final season of Jalen Brunson's rookie contract, can cause franchise-changing problems in the NBA. A mastery of the minutiae in the collective bargaining agreement is a must in modern front offices, especially for franchises who need to find loopholes to maximize the roster around expensive superstars.

In this instance, the Mavs' summer plans started with moving Tim Hardaway Jr., who had negative trade value due to his $16.2 million the next season. Those hopes were shared by Hardaway, who was eager to find a new home in the final year of his contract after falling out of the Mavs' playoff rotation, ranking ninth on the roster in playoff minutes. The Mavs were determined to find a trade partner willing to take Hardaway without returning much salary to Dallas or demanding a first-round pick.

The Detroit Pistons, a rebuilding team with ample space under the salary cap, emerged as a partner. The deal was agreed to a few days before free agency opened. Hardaway and three second-round picks went to the Pistons. The Mavs received Quentin Grimes, a 25-year-old wing who had 90 career starts with the Knicks before being traded to Detroit. Grimes would get the chance to compete for a three-and-D role in Dallas. More importantly, he was due to make $4.3 million, meaning the Mavs saved more than $12 million in the deal, creating flexibility for their ambitious free agency double. Dallas now had use of the larger version of the mid-level exception, which was for a starting salary of up to $12.8 million. The Mavs also created a $16.2 million trade exception in the deal, a slot they could use to pursue Thompson in sign-and-trade scenarios.

The discussions with Jones were complicated by his decision to switch agents late in the process. When he didn't accept the Mavs' offer of $27 million over three years, Dallas pivoted to their top alternative target. Gritty former New Orleans forward Naji Marshall pounced on the same offer in the opening hours of July 30 free agency. The Pelicans couldn't come close to matching it because they were hard capped by the new collective bargaining agreement's apron rules, which were designed to make it more difficult to create and maintain so-called superteams. It was the same reason the Mavs were forced to be so firm in their negotiations with Jones, who got a three-year, $30 million deal from the Clippers.

Thompson had made the emotional decision that he would leave Golden State well in advance of free agency, having felt disrespected by slow extension discussions during the season and the Warriors prioritizing the potential sign-and-trade of Paul George in late June. Thompson had two primary options on the table for his next destination: LeBron's Lakers and Luka's Mavericks.

Irving, fresh off a Finals appearance with the Mavs a year after the Lakers opted against recruiting him, reached out to Thompson to convince him to choose Dallas. Dončić wasn't involved; the recruiting role might never be comfortable for Dončić, and he was half the globe away anyway, preparing for the Olympic qualifying tournament with Slovenia. This was one of the perks of having a happy Irving on the roster. He had strong relationships with players throughout the league, including Thompson, his 2011 draft classmate and teammate on two Team USA gold-medal squads. Irving didn't have to sell Thompson on how he could benefit from playing with a pair of star playmakers and vice versa. Irving instead emphasized to Thompson how he'd found a sense of family with the Mavs coming off his own difficult breakup with his prior team.

Thompson and his agent, Wasserman's Greg Lawrence, met with Harrison and Michael Finley over dinner at the Bottle Inn in Hermosa Beach, California. Thompson spent much of the meal asking Finley about his experience changing teams late in his career. Finley had been a franchise cornerstone in Dallas during the early years of Nowitzki's career before being released for financial reasons and earning a championship ring as a key role player for the San Antonio Spurs.

The Lakers offered Thompson more money than the Mavs, discussing a four-year, $80 million deal, which would have required LA to make salary-dump trades. Dallas offered $50 million over three years, quietly lining up a deal to send Josh Green to Charlotte to make the salary math work. Texas's lack of a state income tax could make up some of the difference. It probably didn't hurt the Mavs' cause that the man explaining those numbers, Thompson's longtime financial advisor, Joe McLean, was an AAU teammate of Kidd's while growing up in the Bay Area. But on the other hand, the personal ties were also in favor of the Lakers. Thompson's father, Mychal, won two championships with the Showtime Lakers and has been the color commentator on the team's radio broadcast for years.

Ultimately, Thompson's decision came down to his chances of winning another championship. For the last two seasons, his locker at the Chase Center featured a laminated clip from the *San Francisco Chronicle*—pictures of the 26 players in NBA history who've won at least five titles. Thompson desperately wanted to be part of that club. He decided that Dallas provided him the best opportunity, having envisioned how he could help the Mavs while watching them lose in the Finals.

"I mean, they were so close to winning the whole thing," Thompson said at the press conference introducing him alongside Marshall and Grimes. "And I think we can help get them over that hump."

It was quite a coup for the Mavs. Thompson wasn't the most impactful player to move in the 2024 free agency period, as the 76ers landed George on a four-year max contract, much to the elation of 2023 MVP Joel Embiid, who had been prominent in early-season speculation about the next superstar to request a trade. But a Mavs franchise known for aggressive strikeouts in free agency, albeit under different management, beat out the NBA's most glamorous franchise for a coveted player.

Just months after much of the conversation about the Mavs within the NBA centered around Dončić's potential departure to chase his title dreams—and rivals positioning themselves to benefit from Dallas's downfall—a future Hall of Famer with four championship rings arrived with hopes of becoming the final piece of the Mavs' championship puzzle. The franchise had overcome a pair of massive roster-building mistakes during Dončić's career: pushing their chips in early on Porziņģis, who proved to be a poor fit, and botching the Brunson negotiations, allowing an undervalued, homegrown co-star to leave for nothing in return. The trade for Irving started a sequence of transactions that allowed the Mavs to sell title ambitions. Thompson bought the belief.

As one rival executive noted, for all the pressure that comes along with it, having a talent of Dončić's magnitude provides a significant margin of error. The journey often wasn't smooth during Dončić's first six seasons in the NBA, and the quest for a title continues. But in a league that changes swiftly, the Mavs managed to earn the most treasured commodity: stability with a superstar.

"This is the franchise that drafted me, and they gave me the keys," Dončić said late in the season. "I'm just glad I'm here in Dallas."

ACKNOWLEDGMENTS

THE SEEDS OF THIS BOOK WERE PLANTED BY THE SUPPORT OF MY ESPN colleague Brian Windhorst, who was a *New York Times* best-selling author before he became famous for the "What's going on in Utah?" meme. He fielded a call inquiring about a potential Luka Dončić book and immediately recommended me, perhaps because he didn't want to hear my incessant whining on his *The Hoop Collective* podcast about claiming my turf. I'm immensely grateful for his referral and his invaluable advice about the process of approaching such a project.

This book also wouldn't have been possible without the backing of ESPN. Thank you in particular to Cristina Daglas, Jim Merritt, Adam Reisinger, and Regan Estes for your support and understanding of the demands on my time. Also to Daniel Greenberg at LGR Literary and Ian Dorset at Hachette for their efforts in the production of this book.

Iztok Franko, a Ljubljana-based Mavs scribe who I had previously only interacted with on social media, could not have been a better volunteer tour guide when I traveled to Slovenia to research the roots of Dončić's story. Franko graciously showed me around his beautiful home country and introduced me to the rich Slovenian basketball culture.

Last but not least, thank you to my wife, Maria Rincon Mac-Mahon, aka the IT Department, for her ruthless, constructive criticism and relentless enthusiasm regarding this project.

SOURCES

CHAPTER 1

Cuban, Mark. "Steve Nash, Part 1." *Blog Maverick*, July 3, 2004, https:// blogmaverick.com/2004/07/03/steve-nash-part-1/amp/.

McCallum, Jack. "Oscar Robertson: The NBA's Forgotten Trailblazer." *Sports Illustrated*, Dec. 22, 2020.

Abdul-Jabbar, Kareem. "Kareem Abdul-Jabbar: What the NBA Championship Means to Me." Jacobin.com, https://jacobin.com/2021/07/kareem-abdul-jabbar-nba-finals-1971-championship-bucks.

Bonk, Thomas. "A Banner Day for Lakers: Kareem Takes His Post: 4 Players Bucks Got in Trade Gone, But He's Still on Job." *Los Angeles Times*, June 16, 1975.

Abbott, Henry. "LeBron James' Decision: The Transcript." ESPN.com TrueHoop, July 8, 2010, https://www.espn.com/blog/truehoop/post/_/id/17853/lebron-james-decision-the-transcript.

Windhorst, Brian. "NBA's David Stern Fines Dan Gilbert $100,000 for Outburst, Criticizes LeBron James' TV 'Decision.'" cleveland.com, July 13, 2010, https://www.cleveland.com/cavs/2010/07/nba_commissioner _david_stern_f_1.html.

Urbina, Frank. "Reliving LeBron James' Decision (Day 1): Nets, Knicks Get First Meetings." Hoopshype.com, June 30, 2020, https://hoopshype .com/2020/06/30/lebron-james-the-decision-2010-free-agency-rumors -meetings-july-1/.

Windhorst, Brian. "Gilbert Lets Out His Frustration." ESPN.com, July 9, 2010, https://www.espn.com/nba/columns/story?page=lebron leavescavs-100709.

James, LeBron (as told to Jenkins, Lee). "LeBron: I'm Coming Back to Cleveland." Sports Illustrated.com, July 11, 2014, https://www.si.com /nba/2014/07/11/lebron-james-cleveland-cavaliers.

Durant, Kevin. "My Next Chapter." Theplayerstribune.com, July 4, 2016, https://www.theplayerstribune.com/articles/kevin-durant-nba-free -agency-announcement.

Sharp, Andrew. "The Ongoing Failure of the NBA's 'Supermax' Era." Sports Illustrated.com, March 19, 2019, https://www.si.com/nba/2019/03/19 /nba-supermax-contracts-failure-kevin-durant-klay-thompson-bradley -beal-kemba-walker.

Wojnarowski, Adrian. "Anthony Davis Has Told New Orleans Pelicans He Won't Re-sign." ESPN.com, January 28, 2019, https://www.espn .com/nba/story/_/id/25868546/anthony-davis-told-new-orleans-pelicans -re-sign.

MacMahon, Tim. "All-Star James Harden Says Houston Rockets Are 'Just Not Good Enough.'" ESPN.com, January 12, 2021, https://www.espn .com/nba/story/_/id/30702503/all-star-james-harden-says-houston -rockets-just-not-good-enough.

McMenamin, Dave. "Kyrie Irving, Kevin Durant Defend Trade Requests: Good for NBA." ESPN.com, February 18, 2023, https://www.espn .com/nba/story/_/id/35689534/kyrie-irving-kevin-durant-defend-trade -requests-good-nba.

CHAPTER 2

Schmitz, Mike. "There Has Never Been an NBA Draft Prospect Like Slovenia's Luka Doncic." ESPN.com, October 4, 2017, https://www.espn.com/nba /story/_/id/20668236/there-never-nba-draft-prospect-slovenia-luka-doncic.

Hein, David. "Slovenian Luka Doncic Already a Big Name At Just 16." Fiba.basketball, April 23, 2015, https://www.fiba.basketball/en/news /slovenian-luka-doncic-already-a-big-name-at-just-16.

Kimes, Mina. "Will Luka Doncic Be the Next Star NBA Player from Europe?" *ESPN The Magazine*, April 9, 2018.

Sáez-Bravo, Luis. "Felipe: Bienvenido Doncic." *El Mundo*, May 1, 2015.

Sáez-Bravo, Luis. "La (Dura) Vida Sin Rudy." *El Mundo*, December 2, 2015.

Sáez, Faustino. "El CSKA Arrolla a un Madrid Atontado." *El Pais*, January 8, 2016.

MacMahon, Tim. "The Rise of Luka Doncic Happened Faster than Anyone Predicted." ESPN.com, January 29, 2021, https://www.espn.com /nba/story/_/id/30796251/the-rise-luka-doncic-happened-faster-anyone -predicted.

Gordon, Patris. "The Unauthorised Biography of Luka Doncic." December 14, 2019.

Stroggylakis, Antonis. "Luka Doncic Makes History with New Career Highs." Eurohoops.net, December 4, 2016, https://www.eurohoops.net /en/featured/357838/doncic-makes-history/.

Sáez, Faustino. "Luka Doncic, la Gran Eclosion." *El Pais*, December 12, 2016.

Sáez-Bravo, Luis. "Doncic al Rescate." *El Mundo*, December 9, 2016.

"Doncic y el Salto a la NBA: 'Quizás No Sea Mi Último Año en el Madrid.'"
El Periodico de Catalunya, October. 12, 2017.

"Turkish Airlines EuroLeague MVP for October: Luka Doncic, Real
Madrid." Eurohoops.net, October 30, 2017, https://www.eurohoops
.net/en/euroleague/543647/turkish-airlines-euroleague-mvp-october
-luka-doncic-real-madrid/.

"Europa Corona al Joven Rey." *El Correo,* May 21, 2018.

Givony, Jonathan. "Top Draft Prospect Luka Doncic Shines at EuroLeague
Final Four." ESPN.com, May 18, 2018, https://www.espn.com/nba
/story/_/id/23540410/top-draft-prospect-luka-doncic-shines-real-madrid
-euroleague-final-four.

"Luka Doncic's Incredible Clutch Three-Pointer Against Baskonia."
Eurohoops.net, June 19, 2018, https://www.eurohoops.net/en/acb
/698053/luka-doncics-clutch-three-pointer-against-baskonia/.

Madrid, Alex. "Luka Doncic Broke into Tears after His Last Game in
Europe." Eurohoops.net, June 19, 2018, https://www.eurohoops.net/en
/acb/698033/luka-doncic-broke-into-tears-after-last-game-in-europe/.

CHAPTER 3

MacMahon, Tim; and Windhorst, Brian. "How the NBA's Bottom-Dwellers
Are Putting on a Tanking Clinic." ESPN.com, February 26, 2018, https://
www.espn.com/nba/story/_/id/22573750/how-nba-bottom-dwellers
-putting-tanking-clinic-nba.

"Mark Cuban, Dallas Mavericks Owner, Fined $600,000 for Tanking
Comments." ESPN.com, February 21, 2018, https://www.espn.com/nba
/story/_/id/22573750/how-nba-bottom-dwellers-putting-tanking
-clinic-nba.

MacMahon, Tim. "Dirk Nowitzki Disagrees with Mavs Owner Mark Cuban
on Tanking: 'You Don't Want Culture of Quitting.'" ESPN.com, February
27, 2018, https://www.espn.com/nba/story/_/id/22591534/dirk-nowitzki
-dallas-mavericks-opposes-owner-mark-cuban-notion-team-tank.

Stein, Marc. "Orlando Magic's Dwight Howard Will Not Give Up Option
at Season's End." ESPN.com, March 14, 2012, https://www.espn
.com/nba/story/_/id/7688201/orlando-magic-dwight-howard-not-give
-option-season-end.

Broussard, Chris. "Dwight Howard of Orlando Magic Tells Team He'll
Stay through 2012-13, Sources Say." ESPN.com, March 15, 2012, https://
www.espn.com/nba/story/_/id/7689569/dwight-howard-orlando-magic
-tells-team-stay-2012-13-sources-say.

"Sources—Dwight Howard-to-Los Angeles Lakers Four-Team Deal
Complete." ESPN.com, August 9, 2012, https://www.espn.com/nba

/story/_/id/8252042/sources-dwight-howard-los-angeles-lakers-four
-team-deal-complete.

Cuban, Mark. "Lets Talk Mavs #MFFL." Blog Maverick, August 3, 2013,
https://blogmaverick.com/2013/08/03/lets-talk-mavs-mffl/.

Wertheim, Jon; and Luther, Jessica. "Exclusive: Inside the Corrosive Workplace Culture of the Dallas Mavericks." SI.com, February 20, 2018,
https://www.si.com/nba/2018/02/21/dallas-mavericks-sexual-misconduct
-investigation-mark-cuban-response.

MacMahon, Tim. "Why Didn't the Mavs Draft the 'Greek Freak'?" ESPN
.com, December 3, 2014, https://www.espn.com/blog/dallas/mavericks
/post/_/id/4703905/why-didnt-the-mavs-draft-the-greek-freak.

Garcia IV, Bob. "Mark Cuban Admits He Made Final Call to Pass on Drafting Giannis Antetokounmpo." Clutchpoints.com, July 13, 2017, https://
clutchpoints.com/mark-cuban-admits-he-made-final-call-to-pass-on
-drafting-giannis-antetokounmpo.

MacMahon, Tim. "Rajon Rondo, Coach Rick Carlisle Have Timeout Shouting Match during Dallas Mavericks' Win." ESPN.com, February 25,
2015, https://www.espn.com/dallas/nba/story/_/id/12378645/rajon-rondo
-coach-rick-carlisle-shouting-match-dallas-mavericks-win.

MacMahon, Tim. "Dallas Mavericks Coach Rick Carlisle Says No Regrets
about Rajon Rondo's Tenure." ESPN.com, November 29, 2015, https://
www.espn.com/nba/story/_/id/14251858/dallas-mavericks-coach-rick
-carlisle-says-no-regrets-rajon-rondo-tenure.

Bondy, Stefan. "Fraschilla: I Know Dirk, and Top Prospect Doncic Is No
Nowitzki." *New York Daily News*, April 27, 2018.

Bordow, Scott. "Kokoskov's Hiring Offers Clues to the Suns' Plans." *The
Arizona Republic*. May 7, 2018.

Sefko, Eddie. "A 6-7 Steve Nash? Euro Could Be." *The Dallas Morning News*,
May 13, 2018.

Bordow, Scott. "Suns Top Pick? Fraschilla Makes a Case for Ayton." *The
Arizona Republic*, May 17, 2018.

Turner, Broderick. "Doncic Is Wild Card in NBA Draft; Slovenia's 'Wonder Boy' Has Some Teams Salivating over the 19-Year-Old Phenom." *Los
Angeles Times*, June 12, 2018.

"Atlanta GM Travis Schlenk." The Woj Pod, February 17, 2019, https://
www.espn.co.uk/radio/play/_/id/27064511.

MacMahon, Tim. "Luka Doncic of Dallas Mavericks Was Best Player in
NBA Draft, Mark Cuban Says." ESPN.com, July 7, 2018, https://www
.espn.com/nba/story/_/id/24024474/luka-doncic-dallas-mavericks
-was-best-player-nba-draft-mark-cuban-says.

Stroggylakis, Antonis. "Divac on Why Kings Didn't Pick Doncic: Bagley

Is a Better Player for Us." Eurohoops.net, July 22, 2018, https://www
.eurohoops.net/en/nba-news/699800/divac-on-why-kings-didnt-pick
-doncic-bagley-is-a-better-player-for-us/.

CHAPTER 4

Shelburne, Ramona; and MacMahon, Tim. "DeAndre Jordan's Round
Trip: How Clips Star Dissed Dallas for LA Return." ESPN.com, July
13, 2015, https://www.espn.com/nba/story/_/id/13247673/how-deandre
-jordan-almost-left-los-angeles-clippers.

Wilkerson, William. "Rick Carlisle after the Mavericks' Sixth-Straight
Lloss: 'We Have to Get Angry.'" *Fort Worth Star-Telegram*, November 2,
2018.

Sefko, Eddie. "Carlisle: Meeting Wasn't Heated." *The Dallas Morning News*,
November 5, 2018.

Wilson, Jeff. "DSJ Loses Part of a Tooth, then Helps Mavs Win with Key
Play in Final Seconds." *Fort Worth Star-Telegram*, December 2, 2018.

Townsend, Brad. "Halleluka! Doncic Delivers." *The Dallas Morning News*,
December 9, 2018.

Sefko, Eddie. "Young Stars Look Formidable as Duo." *The Dallas Morning
News*, December 29, 2018.

Wilson, Jeff. "Stomach Bug, Not Trade, Keeps Smith Away from Mavs
Practice, but He's Still on the Block." *Fort Worth Star-Telegram*, January
15, 2019.

Townsend, Brad. "Backcourt Break?" *The Dallas Morning News*, January 16,
2019.

Stevenson, Stefan. "Is Mavs Guard Dennis Smith Jr. Really Sick or Playing
Games?" *Fort Worth Star-Telegram*, January 16, 2019.

Townsend, Brad. "Smith's Departure Remains Likely." *The Dallas Morning
News*, January 24, 2019.

Townsend, Brad. "Garden Party." *The Dallas Morning News*, January 31, 2019.

CHAPTER 5

Wojnarowski, Adrian; and Marks, Bobby. "Joel Embiid's Extension Pro-
tects Philadelphia 76ers in Case of Contractually Specific Catastrophic
Injury." ESPN.com, October 10, 2017, https://www.espn.com/nba/story
/_/id/20985023/joel-embiid-extension-protects-philadelphia-76ers-case
-contractually-specific-catastrophic-injury.

Stein, Marc. "Knicks Say Goodbye to Porzingis and Prepare a Possible
Hello for Durant." *The New York Times*, January 31, 2019.

Townsend, Brad. "Blockbuster Deal Puts Team in 'Win Very Soon' Mode."
The Dallas Morning News, February 1, 2019.

Stevenson, Stefan. "What's Behind Mavericks' Trade Bonanza? It's All about Luka." *Fort Worth Star-Telegram*, February 7, 2019.

Townsend, Brad. "'Noise' Now and Later?" *The Dallas Morning News*, February 8, 2019.

Townsend, Brad. "How the Mavericks Pulled Off the Trade for Kristaps Porzingis, Who Didn't Have Dallas as a Preferred Destination." *The Dallas Morning News*, February 4, 2019.

Sherrington, Kevin. "20-Year Plan." *The Dallas Morning News*, February 5, 2019.

Stein, Marc. "Inside the Porzingis Deal, and How the Knicks Did Better than You Think." *The New York Times*, February 6, 2019.

Kasabian, Paul. "Kristaps Porzingis Posts Cryptic IG After Knicks Trade: 'Truth Will Come Out.'" Bleacher Report, January 31, 2019.

Berman, Marc. "Inside Toxic Kristaps Porzingis-Knicks Marriage that Made Trade Inevitable." *New York Post*, November 8, 2019.

CHAPTER 6

Hamilton, Moke. "Mavs Reportedly Back Out of the Jimmy Butler Sign-and-Trade Deal." *USA Today*, July 1, 2019, https://sixerswire.usatoday.com/2019/07/01/mavs-have-reportedly-backed-out-of-the-jimmy-butler-sign-and-trade/.

Rogers, Martin. "Opinion: Luka Doncic More Than Ready to Carry Dallas as Dirk Nowitzki Passes Baton." *USA Today*, February 14, 2019, https://www.usatoday.com/story/sports/columnist/martin-rogers/2019/02/14/dirk-nowitzki-luka-doncic-2019-nba-all-star-game/2863908002/.

Baby, Ben. "'It's Just Been Amazing, Being with Dirk': After Another Triple-Double, Luka Doncic Reflects on Rookie Year Playing with Nowitzki." *The Dallas Morning News*, April 10, 2019.

MacMahon, Tim. "Luka Doncic Isn't Your Average NBA Rookie, and He Knows It." ESPN.com, December 20, 2018.

MacMahon, Tim. "Luka Doncic and Rick Carlisle—The Dissolution of Their Relationship; What Comes Next for the Dallas Mavericks." ESPN.com, December 15, 2021.

Townsend, Brad. "With Key Pair in Place, Mavs Seek Right Additions." *The Dallas Morning News*, April 21, 2019.

CHAPTER 7

MacMahon, Tim. "How Rick Carlisle Learned to Stop Worrying and Love Luka Doncic." ESPN.com, November 20, 2019.

MacMahon, Tim. "A Different Kristaps Porzingis Is Leading the Mavericks Alongside Luka Doncic." ESPN.com, January 2, 2020.

Townsend, Brad. "LeBron James Says Mavs' Luka Doncic 'Just Plays the Game the Right Way.'" *The Dallas Morning News*, November 2, 2019.

Townsend, Brad. "Kristaps Porzingis Played His Best Game as a Maverick in Loss to Knicks. Now, a Tough NY Road Trip Lies Ahead." *The Dallas Morning News*, November 8, 2019.

Townsend, Brad. "'I Was Feeling Sad': Luka Doncic Explains Hasty Post-game Departure Following the Mavs' Loss to the Clippers." *The Dallas Morning News*, November 27, 2019.

Townsend, Brad. "As Luka Doncic's Dominance Continues in Mavs' Win vs. Pelicans, Mark Cuban Raves About 'Underappreciated' Kristaps Porzingis." *The Dallas Morning News*, December 3, 2019.

CHAPTER 8

Amaranthus, Bri. "The Mavs Are Having the Most Fun In Orlando." SI.com, July 13, 2020, https://www.si.com/nba/mavericks/news/the-mavs -are-having-the-most-fun-nba-orlando-bubble.

Sefko, Eddie. "It's a Bubble Life: One Last Look at Mavericks' Experience at Disney." Mavs.com, September 4, 2020, https://www.mavs.com /bubble-life/.

Townsend, Brad. "The Mavericks Are Now the Talk of the NBA Bubble. That's the Luka Doncic Effect at Work." *The Dallas Morning News*, August 9, 2020.

Townsend, Brad. "After Taking Game 2, Luka Doncic Says Mavs 'For Sure' Believe They Can Win Series Against Clippers." *The Dallas Morning News*, August 19, 2020.

MacMahon, Tim. "Luka Doncic Says Mavericks 'Can Fight' with Heavy Favorite Clippers." ESPN.com, August 20, 2020, https://www.espn.com /nba/story/_/id/29700845/luka-doncic-says-mavs-fight-heavy-favorite -clippers.

MacMahon, Tim. "Mavs' Luka Doncic to Have MRI after Leaving Game 3 with Sprained Ankle." ESPN.com, August 21, 2020, https://www.espn .com/nba/story/_/id/29714477/mavericks-luka-doncic-return-game-3 -spraining-ankle.

MacMahon, Tim. "Mavs' Kristaps Porzingis Ejected after Second Technical for 'Being an Escalator.'" ESPN.com, August 17, 2020, https://www .espn.com/nba/story/_/id/29684265/mavericks-kristaps-porzingis-ejected -clippers-game-second-technical.

MacMahon, Tim. "Mavericks' Luka Doncic Calls Historic Triple-Double, Game Winner 'Special.'" ESPN.com, August 23, 2020, https://www.espn .com/nba/story/_/id/29727368/mavericks-luka-doncic-calls-historic -triple-double-game-winner-special.

MacMahon, Tim. "Clippers' Marcus Morris Denies That Step on Luka Doncic's Sprained Ankle was Intentional." ESPN.com, August 26, 2020, https://www.espn.com/nba/story/_/id/29743106/clippers-marcus -morris-denies-step-luka-doncic-sprained-ankle-was-intentional.

Youngmisuk, Ohm; and MacMahon, Tim. "Marcus Morris Sr.'s Battle with Mavericks' Luka Doncic Ends with Ejection." ESPN.com, August 30, 2020, https://www.espn.com/nba/story/_/id/29774262/la-clippers -marcus-morris-ejected-flagrant-foul-dallas-mavericks-luka-dončić.

Buha, Jovan. "'It Was a Crazy Night': How the Balkan Boys Bonded in the NBA Bubble." The Athletic, September 11, 2020, https://theathletic .com/2058113/2020/09/11/it-was-a-crazy-night-how-the-balkan-boys -bonded-in-the-nba-bubble/.

Yousuf, Saad. "'Fly on the Wall': Meet Jason Chinnock, the Man Document- ing the Mavs' Bubble." The Athletic, July 21, 2020, https://theathletic .com/1941746/2020/07/21/fly-on-the-wall-meet-jason-chinnock-the -man-documenting-the-mavs-bubble/.

MacMahon, Tim. "Dallas Mavericks' Kristaps Porzingis Has Knee Sur- gery to Repair Lateral Meniscus Tear." ESPN.com, October 9, 2020, https://www.espn.com/nba/story/_/id/30080038/dallas-mavericks -kristaps-porzingis-knee-surgery-repair-lateral-meniscus-tear.

CHAPTER 9

Caplan, Callie. "Mark Cuban Explains Why Luka Doncic Didn't Start the Mavs' Season In 'As Good off Shape As He Wanted.'" The Dallas Morn- ing News, December 29, 2020, https://www.dallasnews.com/sports /mavericks/2020/12/29/mark-cuban-explains-why-luka-doncic-didnt-start -the-mavs-season-in-as-good-of-shape-as-he-wanted/.

Caplan, Callie. "Whether a Conditioning Issue or Not, Luka Doncic Knows This About His Slump: 'I've Got To Do Way Better.'" Decem- ber 31, 2020, https://www.dallasnews.com/sports/mavericks/2020/12/31 /whether-a-conditioning-issue-or-not-luka-doncic-knows-this-about -his-slump-ive-got-to-do-way-better/.

MacMahon, Tim. "Luka Doncic Upset After Dallas Mavericks Fail to Call Timeout Late in Loss to Milwaukee Bucks." ESPN.com, January 15, 2021, https://www.espn.com/nba/story/_/id/30720445/luka-doncic-upset-dallas -mavericks-fail-call-late-loss-milwaukee-bucks.

Townsend, Brad. "Luka Doncic Shows Displeasure with Lack of Late Timeout Call in Mavericks' Loss to Bucks." The Dallas Morning News, January 15, 2021, https://www.dallasnews.com/sports/mavericks /2021/01/16/behind-a-timeout-dispute-shorthanded-mavericks-fourth -quarter-rally-fizzles-in-final-seconds-of-loss-to-bucks/.

MacMahon, Tim. "Dallas Mavericks Star Luka Doncic on Triple-Double in Loss: I Was Being Selfish." ESPN.com, January 17, 2021, https://www.espn.com/nba/story/_/id/30731793/dallas-mavericks-star-luka-doncic-triple-double-loss-was-being-selfish.

MacMahon, Tim. "Dallas Mavericks' Luka Doncic Critical of Team's Effort after Loss to Utah Jazz." ESPN.com, January 30, 2021, https://www.espn.com/nba/story/_/id/30803729/dallas-mavericks-luka-doncic-critical-team-effort-loss-utah-jazz.

Fischer, Jake. "League Sources Say Mavericks Quietly Gauging Kristaps Porzingis' Trade Value." Bleacher Report, February 22, 2021, https://bleacherreport.com/articles/2933005-league-sources-say-mavericks-quietly-gauging-kristaps-porzingis-trade-value.

MacMahon, Tim. "Why Kristaps Porzingis is Key to Dallas Mavericks' Second-Half Hopes." ESPN.com, March 11, 2021, https://www.espn.com/nba/story/_/id/30972031/why-kristaps-porzingis-key-dallas-mavericks-second-half-hopes.

Dixon, Schuyler. "Kristaps Porzingis Shrugs Off Trade Talk after Latest Injury." The Associated Press, February 26, 2021.

Ibarrola, Kriel. "3 Social Cues Point to Luka Doncic, Kristaps Porzingis' Strained Relationship." Clutchpoints.com, April 18, 2021, https://clutchpoints.com/3-social-cues-that-point-to-luka-doncic-kristaps-porzingis-strained-relationship.

Caplan, Callie. "Despite 'Frustrated' Playoff Return, Kristaps Porzingis' Late Dunk and Good Health Boosted Mavs' Upset Win." *The Dallas Morning News,* May 22, 2021, https://www.dallasnews.com/sports/mavericks/2021/05/22/despite-frustrated-playoff-return-kristaps-porzingis-late-dunk-and-good-health-boosted-mavs-upset-win/.

MacMahon, Tim. "Dallas Mavericks' Luka Doncic Questionable for Sunday's Game 4 Against LA Clippers with Neck Strain." ESPN.com, May 29, 2021, https://www.espn.com/nba/story/_/id/31533640/dallas-mavericks-luka-doncic-questionable-sunday-game-4-la-clippers-neck-strain.

MacMahon, Tim. "Luka Doncic Makes Playoff History But Says He Has Proved 'Nothing Yet' as Dallas Mavericks Lose to LA Clippers," https://www.espn.com/nba/story/_/id/31580333/luka-doncic-makes-game-7-history-says-proved-yet-dallas-mavericks-lose-la-clippers.

MacMahon, Tim. "NBA Playoffs 2021—Luka Doncic's Superstar Ascent Has Created a Timetable for the Dallas Mavericks." ESPN.com, June 6, 2021, https://www.espn.com/nba/story/_/id/31579933/nba-playoffs-2021-luka-doncic-superstar-ascent-created-table-dallas-mavericks.

CHAPTER 10

Cato, Tim; and Amick, Sam. "Inside the Mavericks Front Office, Mark Cuban's Shadow GM Is Causing a Rift with Luka Doncic." *The Athletic*, June 14, 2021.

Stein, Marc. "Mavs Part Ways with Gersson Rosas." ESPN.com, October 29, 2013, https://www.espn.com/dallas/nba/story/_/id/9899190 /dallas-mavericks-general-manager-gersson-rosas-part-ways.

Wojnarowski, Adrian; and MacMahon, Tim. "Rick Carlisle Won't Return as Dallas Mavericks Coach after 13 Seasons." ESPN.com, June 17, 2021, https://www.espn.com/nba/story/_/id/31654042/rick-carlisle-says-return -dallas-mavericks-coach-13-seasons.

Townsend, Brad. "After Departure of Rick Carlisle and Donnie Nelson, Mavs Look More Like a Dumpster Fire Than a Bastion of Stability." *The Dallas Morning News*, June 17, 2021, https://www.dallasnews.com /sports/mavericks/2021/06/17/rick-carlisle-informs-mark-cuban-that -he-will-not-return-as-the-mavericks-coach/.

MacMahon, Tim. "Rick Carlisle Returning to Indiana Pacers as Coach, Backs Jason Kidd for Dallas Mavericks Job." ESPN.com, June 24, 2021, https://www.espn.com/nba/story/_/id/31700917/rick-carlisle -returning-indiana-pacers-second-stint-coach-sources-say.

"Ex-GM Sues Dallas Mavericks, Claims One of Mark Cuban's Executives Sexually Assaulted His Nephew." WFAA.com, March 17, 2022, https:// www.wfaa.com/article/news/local/ex-gm-donnie-nelson-sues-mavericks -claims-one-of-cubans-executives-sexually-assaulted-nephew-team -denies-allegation/287-bd1b9dfb-9cc1-4cee-af4e-b001cd7580a0.

"Donnie Lawsuit Court Documents: Donnie Nelson Lawsuit." Scribd.com, March 17, 2022.

Townsend, Brad. "Sources: Mavericks Dismissed Director of Player Personnel Tony Ronzone in Wake of Last Year's Sexual Assault Allegation." *The Dallas Morning News*, April 19, 2021, https://www .dallasnews.com/sports/mavericks/2021/04/19/sources-mavericks -dismissed-director-of-player-personnel-tony-ronzone-in-wake-of -last-years-sexual-assault-allegation/.

Helin, Kurt. "Mavericks Respond, Say Nelson Lawsuit Part of 'Lengthy Scheme to Extort' Organization." NBCSports.com, March 19, 2022, https://www.nbcsports.com/nba/news/mavericks-respond-say-nelson -lawsuit-part-of-lengthy-scheme-to-extort-organization.

Van Natta Jr., Don. "Dallas Mavericks, in Response to Lawsuit, Accuse Ex-GM Donnie Nelson of 'Scheme to Extort as Much as $100 Million.'" ESPN .com, March 18, 2022, https://www.espn.com/nba/story/_/id/33539178

/dallas-mavericks-response-lawsuit-accuse-ex-gm-donnie-nelson
-scheme-extort-much-100-million.

MacMahon, Tim. "Dallas Mavericks Duo of Luka Doncic and Kristaps Porzingis Has New Coach Jason Kidd Excited." ESPN.com, July 15, 2021, https://www.espn.com/nba/story/_/id/31823727/jason-kidd
-excited-potential-dallas-mavericks-luka-doncic-kristaps-porziŋ́gis.

Townsend, Brad. "Mavs Introduce Jason Kidd, Nico Harrison with High Expectations for 'Overnight' Improvement." *The Dallas Morning News,* July 15, 2021, https://www.dallasnews.com/sports/mavericks/2021/07/15
/watch-mavs-introduce-new-head-coach-jason-kidd-gm-nico-harrison/.

MacMahon, Tim. "Former Dallas Mavericks Executive Haralabos Voulgaris Compares Franchise's Dysfunction to 'High School Drama.'" ESPN.com, October 21, 2021, https://www.espn.com/nba/story/_/id
/32443902/former-dallas-mavericks-executive-haralabos-voulgaris
-compares-franchise-dysfunction-high-school-drama.

"Was a Former NBA Bettor Running the Mavs?" ESPN Daily, October 21, 2021, https://www.espn.com/radio/play/_/id/32443751.

Spears, Marc J. "Nico Harrison on the Mavs' General Manager Job, Life at Nike, Kobe Bryant, Luka Doncic and More." Andscape.com, January 5, 2022, https://andscape.com/features/nico-harrison-on-the-mavs
-general-manager-job-life-at-nike-kobe-bryant-luka-doncic-and-more/.

Sefko, Eddie. "Mavericks, Doncic Officially Sign Five-Year Supermax Extension." Mavs.com, August 10, 2021, https://www.mavs.com/doncic
-signs/.

CHAPTER 11

Reynolds, Tim. "Dominant Luka: Doncic, Slovenia Headed to Olympics." The Associated Press, July 4, 2021, https://apnews.com/article
/slovenia-europe-tokyo-olympic-games-020-tokyo-olympics-ad175513e
7f73321b51da67e5030c181.

"Sasa Doncic: 'For Luka's Talent, Success Will Be Being Among Top 3 in NBA.'" Eurohoops.net, March 29, 2017, https://www.eurohoops.net
/en//425501/sasa-doncic-lukas-talent-success-will-among-top-3-nba/.

Lopez, Selby. "Luka Doncic's Triple-Double Powers Slovenia Past Lithuania, Clinches Nation's First Olympic Berth." dallasnews.com, July 4, 2021, https://www.dallasnews.com/sports/mavericks/2021/07/26
/olympic-wonder-boy-luka-doncic-debuts-at-tokyo-games-with-slovenia
-on-record-setting-pace/.

Caplan, Callie. "Olympic 'Wonder Boy': Luka Doncic Debuts at Tokyo Games with Slovenia on Record-Setting Pace." *The Dallas Morning News,* July 26, 2021, https://www.dallasnews.com/sports/mavericks/2021/08/01

/undefeated-and-upset-minded-luka-doncic-slovenia-down-spain-in
-toughest-tokyo-olympics-matchup-yet/.

Caplan, Callie. "With the Mavericks? With Slovenia? Doesn't Matter—
Luka Doncic Thrives When It's Win or Go Home." *The Dallas Morning
News*, August 2, 2021, https://www.dallasnews.com/sports/mavericks
/2021/08/02/with-the-mavericks-with-slovenia-doesnt-matter-luka
-doncic-thrives-when-its-win-or-go-home/.

Caplan, Callie. "'He's the Present and He's Next': Luka Doncic Logs Historic Triple-Double in Olympic Semifinal Loss." *The Dallas Morning
News*, August 5, 2021, https://www.dallasnews.com/sports/mavericks
/2021/08/05/luka-doncic-slovenia-lose-in-olympic-semifinals-vs-france
-will-face-australia-for-bronze-medal/.

Caplan, Callie. "After Olympics Bronze Loss, Luka Doncic Predicts
'Legitimate' Championship Future for Slovenia." *The Dallas Morning
News*, August 7, 2021, https://www.dallasnews.com/sports/mavericks
/2021/08/07/luka-doncic-slovenia-lose-to-australia-in-olympic-bronze
-medal-game-to-end-cinderella-run-in-tokyo/.

CHAPTER 12

MacMahon, Tim. "Dallas Mavericks Coach Jason Kidd Says Star Luka
Doncic Needs to 'Rely on His Teammates' This Season." ESPN.com,
September 27, 2021, https://www.espn.com/nba/story/_/id/32293940
/dallas-mavericks-coach-jason-kidd-says-star-luka-doncic-needs-rely
-teammates-season.

Caplan, Callie. "Mavs Coach Jason Kidd on Kristaps Porzingis: 'I Think
He's Going to Be an All-Star This Year.'" *The Dallas Morning News*, October 9, 2021, https://www.dallasnews.com/sports/mavericks/2021/10/09
/mavs-coach-jason-kidd-on-kristaps-porzingis-i-think-hes-going-to
-be-an-all-star-this-year/.

Caplan, Callie. "Luka Doncic Talks Relationship with Kristaps Porzingis, Mavs' Championship Goals and MVP Predictions." *The Dallas
Morning News*, October 19, 2021, https://www.dallasnews.com/sports
/mavericks/2021/10/19/luka-doncic-talks-relationship-with-kristaps
-porzingis-mavs-championship-goals-and-mvp-predictions/.

MacMahon, Tim. "Dallas Mavericks Coach Jason Kidd Calls on Luka Doncic to Stop Lobbying for Calls During Play." ESPN.com, December 4,
2021, https://www.espn.com/nba/story/_/id/32782920/dallas-mavericks
-coach-jason-kidd-calls-luka-doncic-stop-lobbying-calls-play.

MacMahon, Tim. "Dallas Mavericks' Luka Doncic Admits Having Issue
with Weight, Conditioning." ESPN.com, December 7, 2021, https://

www.espn.com/nba/story/_/id/32818403/dallas-mavericks-luka-doncic -admits-having-issue-weight-conditioning.

Caplan, Callie. "TNT's Reggie Miller Says Jason Kidd Thanked Him for Calling Out Luka Doncic's Weight." *The Dallas Morning News,* May 17, 2022, https://www.dallasnews.com/sports/mavericks/2022/05/17 /tnts-reggie-miller-says-jason-kidd-thanked-him-for-calling-out-luka -doncics-weight/.

Townsend, Brad. "Luka Doncic's Dominance, Kristaps Porzingis' Exit Made Rick Carlisle's Mavs Reunion All Too Familiar." *The Dallas Morning News,* January 29, 2022, https://www.dallasnews.com/sports /mavericks/2022/01/29/luka-doncics-dominance-kristaps-porzingis -exit-made-rick-carlisles-mavs-reunion-all-too-familiar/.

MacMahon, Tim. "Dallas Mavericks Star Luka Doncic Scores Career-High 51 Points, Wishes Kristaps Porzingis Well after Win." ESPN.com, February 11, 2022, https://www.espn.com/nba/story/_/id/33264758/dallas-mavericks -star-luka-doncic-scores-career-high-51-points-wishes-kristaps -porzingis-well-win.

CHAPTER 13

Townsend, Brad. "Mark Cuban Saying More 'Disciplined' Luka Doncic Has Been 'Humbled' Is Hardly News to Mavs' Star." *The Dallas Morning News,* February 22, 2022, https://www.dallasnews.com/sports /mavericks/2022/02/22/mark-cubans-comment-that-more-disciplined -luka-doncic-has-been-humbled-is-hardly-news-to-doncic/.

MacMahon, Tim. "Dallas Mavericks Star Luka Doncic Says Singing to Self Key to Laying Off Referees." ESPN.com, March 18, 2022, https:// www.espn.com/nba/story/_/id/33542307/dallas-mavericks-star-luka -doncic-says-singing-self-key-laying-referees.

MacMahon, Tim. "Dallas Mavericks' Luka Doncic Gets 16th Technical Foul of Season, Faces 1-Game Ban." ESPN.com, April 8, 2022, https://www .espn.com/nba/story/_/id/33701715/dallas-mavericks-luka-doncic-gets -16th-technical-foul-season-faces-1-game-ban.

Wojnarowski, Adrian; and MacMahon, Tim. "Dallas Mavericks Star Luka Doncic Ruled Out for Game 3 vs. Utah Jazz." ESPN.com, April 21, 2022, https://www.espn.com/nba/story/_/id/33780046/dallas-mavericks -star-luka-doncic-ruled-game-3-vs-utah-jazz-sources-say.

MacMahon, Tim. "'Poetic Justice': Utah Jazz Stars Donovan Mitchell, Rudy Gobert Connect on Game-Winner to Even Series." ESPN.com, April 24, 2022, https://www.espn.co.uk/nba/story/_/id/33795631/utah-jazz -stars-donovan-mitchell-rudy-gobert-connect-game-winner-even-series.

MacMahon, Tim. "Jason Kidd Says Dallas Mavericks Need 'Someone to Join the Party' after Dropping Game 1 to Phoenix Suns Despite Luka Doncic's 45." ESPN.com, May 3, 2022, https://www.espn.com /nba/story/_/id/33847069/jason-kidd-says-dallas-mavericks-need-join -party-dropping-game-1-phoenix-suns-luka-doncic-45.

MacMahon, Tim. "Jason Kidd Says Mavericks Need Players besides Luka Doncic to Step Up with Dallas in 2–0 Hole against Phoenix Suns." ESPN.com, May 5, 2022, https://www.espn.com/nba/story/_/id /33859096/jason-kidd-says-mavericks-need-players-besides-luka-doncic -step-dallas-2-0-hole-phoenix-suns.

MacMahon, Tim. "Luka Doncic, Fueled by Phoenix Suns' Trash Talk, Leads Dallas Mavericks to First Elimination-Game Win of his Career." ESPN.com, May 13, 2022, https://www.espn.co.uk/nba/story/_/id /33908040/luka-doncic-fueled-phoenix-suns-trash-talk-leads-dallas -mavericks-first-elimination-game-win-career.

MacMahon, Tim. "Luka Doncic, Dallas Mavericks Author Dominant Game 7 Effort en Route to Eliminating Phoenix Suns." ESPN.com, May 15, 2022, https://www.espn.com/nba/story/_/id/33924730/luka-doncic -dallas-mavericks-author-dominant-game-7-effort-en-route-eliminating -phoenix-suns.

MacMahon, Tim. "'I'm Still Learning': Luka Doncic Reflective after Scoring 40 Points in Game 3 Loss to Warriors." ESPN.com, May 23, 2022, https://www.espn.com/nba/story/_/id/33968198/learning-mavs -luka-doncic-reflective-scoring-40-points-game-3-loss-warriors.

MacMahon, Tim. "As Playoff Run Ends, Luka Doncic Says Improving His Defense Can Take Dallas Mavericks 'to the Next Level,'" ESPN.com, May 27, 2022, https://www.espn.com/nba/story/_/id/33991255/as-playoff -run-ends-luka-doncic-says-improving-defense-take-dallas-mavericks -next-level.

CHAPTER 14

MacMahon, Tim. "NBA Playoffs 2022: Jalen Brunson's Star Turn for the Dallas Mavericks has Massive Free Agency Implications." ESPN.com, April 25, 2022, https://www.espn.com/nba/story/_/id /33801390/nba-playoffs-2022-jalen-brunson-star-turn-dallas-mavericks -massive-free-agency-implications.

Begley, Ian. "Knicks Finalizing Rick Brunson Hire as Assistant Coach." SportsNet New York, June 2, 2022, https://sny.tv/articles/knicks-rick -brunson-assistant-coach-hire.

Wojnarowski, Adrian; and MacMahon, Tim. "Sources: New York Knicks Trade Nerlens Noel, Alec Burks to Detroit Pistons, Clear Cap Space

for Jalen Brunson Pursuit." ESPN.com, June 28, 2022, https://www
.espn.com/nba/story/_/id/34163217/new-york-knicks-viewed-strong
-favorites-sign-dallas-mavericks-guard-jalen-brunson-free-agency
-sources-say.

"Jalen Brunson on His Knicks Free Agency Move, Time with the Mavericks and More." Dallasnews.com, July 23, 2022, https://www.dallasnews
.com/sports/mavericks/2022/07/23/jalen-brunson-on-his-knicks-free
-agency-move-time-with-the-mavericks-and-more/.

"Mark Cuban Says Mavericks are 'Going to Be Fine' without Jalen Brunson." Dallasnews.com, July 13, 2022, https://www.dallasnews.com
/sports/mavericks/2022/07/13/mark-cuban-says-mavericks-are-going-to
-be-fine-without-jalen-brunson/.

MacMahon, Tim. "Mark Cuban: Mavericks Didn't Get Shot at Re-Signing
Jalen Brunson." ESPN.com, April 5, 2023, https://www.espn.com/nba
/story/_/id/36084951/mark-cuban-mavericks-get-shot-re-signing-jalen
-brunson.

Rader, Doyle. "'It's Disrespectful'—Mark Cuban Doesn't Like the Latest
Luka Doncic Mural in Deep Ellum." Mavs Moneyball, January 16, 2023,
https://www.mavsmoneyball.com/2023/1/16/23556506/its-disrespectful
-mark-cuban-doesnt-like-luka-doncic-mural-deep-ellum.

Townsend, Brad. "Local Artist Paints Over Luka Doncic 'Please Send Help'
Mural, at Doncic's Request." *The Dallas Morning News*, January 17, 2023,
https://www.dallasnews.com/sports/mavericks/2023/01/17/local-artist
-paints-over-luka-doncic-please-send-help-mural-at-doncics-request/.

MacMahon, Tim. "Why Luka Doncic and Trae Young are Linked by More
Than a Draft Night Trade." ESPN.com, January 18, 2023, https://www
.espn.com/nba/story/_/id/35467777/why-luka-doncic-trae-young-linked
-more-draft-night-trade.

Haynes, Chris. "B/R Exclusive: Jalen Brunson Dishes on Dallas Exit, Defy-
ing Critics." Bleacher Report, March 24, 2023, https://bleacherreport
.com/articles/10069939-br-exclusive-jalen-brunson-dishes-on-dallas
-exit-defying-critics.

"Jalen Brunson Interview." All The Smoke Productions, February 21, 2024,
https://x.com/allthesmokeprod/status/1760375325395997167?s=46.

Wojnarowski, Adrian. "Sources: Kyrie Irving Asks Nets for Trade Ahead
of Deadline." ESPN.com, February 3, 2023, https://www.espn.com/nba
/story/_/id/35583014/source-kyrie-irving-asks-nets-trade-ahead
-deadline.

"Kyrie Irving Suspended at Least 5 Games by Nets; Apologizes." ESPN
.com, November 3, 2022, https://www.espn.com/nba/story/_/id/34942326
/nets-suspend-kyrie-irving-least-five-games-pay.

McMenamin, Dave. "LeBron James Disappointed by Losing Out on Kyrie Irving, But 'Focus Is Shifted.'" ESPN.com, February 6, 2023, https://www.espn.com/nba/story/_/id/35603129/lebron-james-disappointed-losing-kyrie-irving-focus-shifted.

MacMahon, Tim. "Mavericks Tout Title Shot with Luka Doncic, Kyrie Irving Pairing." ESPN.com, February 6, 2023, https://www.espn.com/nba/story/_/id/35604983/jason-kidd-says-kyrie-irving-gives-mavericks-shot-title.

CHAPTER 15

MacMahon, Tim. "Kyrie Irving Felt Lack of 'Transparency' by Nets' Front Office." ESPN.com, February 7, 2023, https://www.espn.com/nba/story/_/id/35610289/kyrie-irving-felt-lack-transparency-nets-front-office.

MacMahon, Tim. "Kyrie Irving Debuts for Mavs, Scores 24 in Win over Clippers." ESPN.com, February 9, 2023, https://www.espn.com/nba/story/_/id/35620374/kyrie-irving-debuts-mavs-scores-24-win-clippers.

MacMahon, Tim. "Luka Doncic Hypes Kyrie Irving Pairing, Remains Out Friday." ESPN.com, February 10, 2023, https://www.espn.com/nba/story/_/id/35631837/luka-doncic-hypes-kyrie-irving-pairing-debut-happen-friday.

MacMahon, Tim. "Luka Doncic Calls 1st Game with Kyrie Irving 'Really Fun.'" ESPN.com, February 12, 2023, https://www.espn.com/nba/story/_/id/35643401/mavs-luka-doncic-calls-1st-game-kyrie-irving-really-fun.

MacMahon, Tim. "Kyrie Irving Asks Media to Keep Focus on Present with Mavs." ESPN.com, February 13, 2023, https://www.espn.com/nba/story/_/id/35654739/kyrie-irving-asks-media-keep-focus-present-mavs.

MacMahon, Tim. "Jason Kidd on Blowing Huge Lead: Mavericks Have to 'Grow Up.'" ESPN.com, February 26, 2023, https://www.espn.com/nba/story/_/id/35743925/jason-kidd-blowing-huge-lead-mavericks-grow-up.

MacMahon, Tim. "Luka Doncic, Kyrie Irving Combine for 82 Points in Mavs' Win." ESPN.com, March 3, 2023, https://www.espn.com/nba/story?id=35772960&_slug_=luka-doncic-kyrie-irving-combine-82-points-mavs-win.

MacMahon, Tim. "Luka Doncic, Devin Booker Exchange Words as Suns Top Mavs." ESPN.com, March 5, 2023, https://www.espn.com/nba/story/_/id/35793037/kevin-durant-jumper-lifts-suns-mavs-sparks-fly-late.

MacMahon, Tim. "Mavs Booed as Jason Kidd Calls Out Effort; Luka Doncic Admits Frustrations." March 25, 2023, https://www.espn.com/nba/story?id=35940160&_slug_=mavs-booed-jason-kidd-calls-effort-luka-doncic-admits-frustrations.

MacMahon, Tim. "Luka Doncic Won't Be Shut Down if Mavs Can Still Make the Playoffs." ESPN.com, April 4, 2023, https://www.espn.com /nba/story?id=36069154&_slug_=luka-doncic-shut-mavs-make-playoffs.

MacMahon, Tim. "'A Step Back'? Mavs Opt to Sit Kyrie Irving and 4 Others, Miss Playoffs." ESPN.com, April 7, 2023, https://www.espn.com /nba/story/_/id/36105747/kyrie-irving-5-ruled-mavericks-change-course.

MacMahon, Tim. "The End of the Dallas Mavericks' Season Marks the Beginning for a Few Franchise-Altering Questions." ESPN.com, April 8, 2023, https://www.espn.com/nba/story/_/id/36111588/the -end-dallas-mavericks-season-marks-beginning-franchise-altering -questions.

MacMahon, Tim. "Luka Doncic on Commitment to Mavericks: 'I'm Happy Here.'" ESPN.com, April 9, 2023, https://www.espn.com/nba/story/_/id /36139376/happy-here.

MacMahon, Tim. "Mavericks GM Optimistic about Re-Signing Kyrie Irving." ESPN.com, April 11, 2023, https://www.espn.com/nba/story/_/id /36162390/mavericks-gm-optimistic-re-signing-kyrie-irving.

Caplan, Callie. "Mavericks' Kyrie Irving Calls Out Fans, Media for Free Agency Pressure: 'I Am in No Rush.'" *The Dallas Morning News,* May 24, 2023, https://www.dallasnews.com/sports/mavericks/2023/05/24 /mavericks-kyrie-irving-calls-out-fans-media-for-free-agency-pressure-i -am-in-no-rush/.

Shelburne, Ramona. "LeBron James, Kyrie Irving and the Choice That Haunts the Los Angeles Lakers." ESPN.com, January 17, 2024, https:// www.espn.com/nba/story/_/id/39326035/lebron-james-kyrie-irving -choice-haunts-los-angeles-lakers.

CHAPTER 18

Beck, Howard. "Klay Thompson's Motivation Stares at Him Literally From His Locker." *Sports Illustrated,* December 23, 2022, https://www.si.com /nba/2022/12/23/klay-thompson-warriors-26-faces-locker-motivation.

Wojnarowski, Adrian. "Sources: Klay Thompson to Join Mavericks on 3-year, $50M Deal." ESPN.com, July 1, 2024, https://www.espn.com/nba /story/_/id/40475185/klay-thompson-join-mavericks-3-year-50m-deal.

ABOUT THE AUTHOR

Tim MacMahon reports on the NBA for ESPN. A native of Dallas, he's followed the Mavs for decades and currently covers the team.